A History of
Medical Informatics

A History of
Medical Informatics

Edited by

Bruce I. Blum
The Johns Hopkins University

Karen Duncan
Health Information Systems

ACM Press
New York, New York

ADDISON-WESLEY PUBLISHING COMPANY

Reading, Massachusetts ▪ Menlo Park, California
New York ▪ Don Mills, Ontario ▪ Wokingham, England
Amsterdam ▪ Bonn ▪ Sydney ▪ Singapore
Tokyo ▪ Madrid ▪ San Juan

This book is in the **ACM Press History Series**

Many of the designations used by manufacturers and sellers to distinguish their products are claimed as trademarks. Where those designations appear in this book, and Addison-Wesley was aware of a trademark claim, the designations have been printed in initial caps or all caps.

Library of Congress Cataloging-in-Publication Data

A History of medical informatics / [edited by] Bruce I. Blum, Karen
    Duncan.
        p.   cm. — (ACM Press history series)
    Proceedings of the ACM Conference on the History of Medical
Informatics held at the National Library of Medicine, Bethesda,
Maryland, Nov. 5–6, 1987: sponsored by the Association for Computing
Machinery, Special Interest Group on Biomedical Computing.
    Includes bibliographical references.
    ISBN 0-201-50128-7
    1. Medical informatics—United States—History—Congresses.
I. Blum, Bruce, I.   II. Duncan, K. A. (Karen A.)   III. ACM Conference
on the History of Medical Informatics (1987 : National Library of
Medicine)   IV. Association for Computing Machinery.   Special
Interest Group on Biomedical Computing.   V. Series.
    [DNLM: 1. Medical Informatics—history—United States—congresses.
W 26.5 H673]
R858.A2H57   1990
610'.285—dc20
DNLM/DLC
for Library of Congresss   89-17960
                                                                              CIP

ABCDEFGHIJ–HA–943210

Dedication

Medical Informatics is a very young field, and it is sad to observe that two of its leaders have passed away between the time of the conference organization and the publication of this volume. We dedicate this book to their memory; clearly, their contributions are a permanent part of the history we record.

Peter L. Reichertz (1930–1987) died just before the conference proceedings went to press, and that document was dedicated to his memory. We noted at the time that, although the conference was limited to the history of medical informatics in the United States, there were few in the field who had not been influenced by his work.

Marsden "Scott" Blois (1919–1988) made significant contributions in the areas of research, education, and professional leadership. He brought a clarity of thought and expression to this field that will not be duplicated soon; his *Information and Medicine* has earned the reputation of a classic.

Series Foreword

As the computer approaches its first half-century and increasingly informs the structure and quality of modern life, its past becomes an ever more important part of our national and human heritage. ACM Press' History Series aims at the recovery, preservation, and interpretation of the historical record of computers and computing. In addition to proceedings of ACM conferences on the history of computing and of similar conferences sponsored by other organizations, the series encompasses autobiographies, memoirs, and biographies; general historical surveys and monographs on special topics; and bibliographies and guides to archives, collections, and other sources for historical research. In conjunction with the Anthology series, it will also include annotated collections of classic papers documenting the development of various areas of computing.

Through the History Series, the ACM means not only to honor the pioneeers whose achievements constitute the history of computing, but also to encourage collaboration between computer professionals and the growing number of professional historians who are seeking to discern the developmental patterns that link those achievements with each other and with wider technical and social contexts and thereby give them their historical meaning. As editor of the Series, I invite proposals and inquiries from both communties.

Michael S. Mahoney
Series Editor

Book Foreword

The *History of Medical Informatics* grows out of the latest of a series of gatherings that began so auspiciously with the Conference on the History of Programming Languages in 1978 and continued with *The History of Personal Workstations*, the first volume of the ACM History Series. As Adele Goldberg noted in the planning document for the conference series,

> ACM, as the premier scientific and technical society for information processing professionals, has the unique ability to bring together scientists, developers, and users to exchange information about specific areas of the computing field. Many areas have existed long enough to warrant a focused effort to bring together, likely for the first time, those pioneers whose vision and research have made major contributions to these areas. … The intent of the conferences is to promote a better understanding of the visions that led to some of the most compelling past research efforts, the impact of this work on the current state of the art, and the potential for impact on the future.

The conference recorded in this volume realized that Janus-like goal of viewing the past with an eye to the future. In lean prose, the main contributors describe the systems that brought the computer into the medical laboratory and into the hospital, not only to record information but to capture the experience of practitioners. The chapters are informative and thought-provoking, nicely balancing pride with modesty. They show where medical informatics came from and shed light on its current direction.

Not all the themes that emerge from the presentations and discussion were part of the original program, and some have importance for more than medicine. For example, several speakers discuss in passing the virtues and drawbacks of various strategies of funding, and plead for research support that is less targeted on the grounds that the really important developments can't be foreseen. The evidence, they argue, lies in the work described here.

Other such themes will occur to the reader, as will questions about motivation and changing purposes. What follows is the beginning of a chapter in the early development of computing, reflecting a variety of perspectives and storing up resources for future historians.

Michael S. Mahoney

Preface

This volume contains the proceedings of the ACM Conference on the History of Medical Informatics held at the National Library of Medicine, Bethesda, Maryland, on November 5 and 6, 1987. The origins of this conference can be traced back to the 1985 ACM Annual Conference, which brought the editors together in a somewhat roundabout way.

Naturally, the two editors had known each other for some time. Starting in 1984, however, one of us (Bruce Blum) had ceased to be active in medical informatics, and it was an unlikely event that brought him back into the fold. At that meeting, Adele Goldberg, who was then ACM President, told of a new series of conferences on the history of computing. The first to be organized was the History of Personal Workstations; she expected many others to follow and invited the attendees to consider additional topics.

For Bruce Blum it seemed like an interesting forum to explore the history of medical informatics. Although there are many organizations dedicated to the application of computers to medicine, it seemed especially important to have this conference sponsored by a computer-oriented society. To understand why, a brief review of Blum's philosophy is necessary.

Much of the science of computer science is based upon the formalism of mathematics and logic; modern programming languages are the obvious illustration. This science is domain independent. However, much of the progress in computer application (and science) is the result of experience in the application domains. As our volume of knowledge grows and the boundaries among the subdisciplines solidify, the science tends to become isolated from its application. To Blum, the examination of this interaction between science and application is an important field of study.

There always has been a strong synergistic relationship between medicine and computer technology. Clearly, medical applications have had to wait for the availability of the technology, but the experience with medical projects has led to major innovations in computer science. One need only look to the first volume in this series. Two of the early workstations were driven by biomedical needs. (The LINC and PRO-MIS are reported on from a different perspective in these proceedings.) Other obvious examples include the development of expert systems, early signal analysis and laboratory instrumentation, and interactive information systems as illustrated by the hospital information system.

Thus, it seemed appropriate to Blum that a conference on the history of medical informatics should be sponsored by ACM. In this way, the participants could examine both the computer science foundations of medical informatics and the impact that medical informatics has had on computer science. He hoped that the conference could lead to an exchange of ideas between the implementors of application tools and the developers of the tools that they use.

It is questionable, however, that this hope will be realized. The computer subdisciplines have matured to such a degree that the synergy between theory and practice is taken for granted. There is an enormous growth of information, and few can afford the luxury of undirected reading. With a large body of material competing for a limited amount of time, it is doubtful that this book will be read by many outside the field of medical informatics.

Fortunately, there were other conference objectives. The most important of these was to examine what we initially set out to do in medical informatics and review our accomplishments in the context of our current understandings. Had we achieved our initial intent? Were we still attempting to solve problems that had lost their relevance? How had the dynamics of intellectual growth changed our perceptions?

Providing answers to the above questions was a commendable goal, but it would be presumptuous to assume that much could be accomplished in a short, history-oriented conference. Nevertheless, these proceedings provide the raw materials that will enable each reader to begin a more comprehensive analysis.

These pages also satisfy another conference goal: collecting the personal recollections of those who participated in the early history of medical informatics. The papers are primarily historic documents. They also are of interest as descriptions of intellectual development. Few require a medical background to comprehend; all make for enjoyable reading. And so, if we conference organizers could meet our goals only partially, at least we acted as a catalyst in bringing this collection into being.

There was one objective that we were able to satisfy fully. We brought together the pioneers who shaped the field that we now call medical informatics, and we had a wonderful party. The pleasures of the social interaction were limited to about 100 attendees. Some of that excitement lingers in these proceedings. We hope that you can participate in it.

We have organized this book to parallel the conference. By way of introduction, we include a brief biography for each presenter. We tried to identify some of their most important contributions to medical informatics, but we found them too numerous to list. Therefore the biographies simply chronicle experience and honors. Besides, medical informatics is a young field, and most of the participants are not yet ready for a summing up. The papers describe some of the contributors' accomplishments and reference those of their colleagues. You will not need a scorecard to enjoy what they have to say.

This narrative has left out the middle part: all the hard work that went from Blum's daydreaming to the present volume. To tell how that came into being, we return to Denver in October 1985. Karen Duncan, the coeditor, was attending the conference as chair of the Special Interest Group on Biomedical Computing (SIGBIO). Upon hearing of Blum's idea, she suggested that SIGBIO act as the conference sponsor, and SIGBIO endorsed this recommendation. There still were administrative details to be resolved, but—in effect—the ACM Conference on the History of Medical Informatics was underway.

A second meeting was held in Washington, D.C., at the Symposium for Computer Application in Medical Care (SCAMC) in November 1986. The goal was to set up a program committee and establish a program. Independent of the initial planning effort, Adele Goldberg had received letters from Thelma Estrin and Bonnie Kaplan indicating an interest in a conference on the history of medical informatics, and they were invited to join the program committee. Other members were solicited. A replica of the cover sheet from the conference proceedings is on page xii. It lists the final program committee. Jack Smith, the Treasurer of SIGBIO, agreed to serve as Treasurer, and John Parascandola became the Local Arrangements Chair.

John's involvement in this project deserves some mention. In our planning for the conference, SIGBIO was the sponsor and there were two supporting organizations. Don Lindberg, the Director of the National Library of Medicine (NLM), was gracious in offering the use of the NLM facilities as well as assistance in managing the conference registration and recording the presentations. He also freed the time of John Parascandola, chief of the History Section, to work with us. John was our professional historian, and he worked long hours attending to all those nonprofessional tasks that must be dealt with to produce a successful conference.

The second supporting organization was the Applied Physics Laboratory (APL) of The Johns Hopkins University. As a result of actions taken by Carl Bostrom, the director of APL, and Ted Poehler, the director of the Research Center, APL provided technical support, reproduction services and postage for the conference organization and publicity. Obviously, the financial commitment of SIGBIO and the substantial support provided by NLM and APL were essential to the undertaking and success of this conference.

Again, to return to the story line. The schedule for the conference was set, and the next activity was to establish the program. There was a meeting held at NLM attended by Thelma Estrin, Judith Prewitt, Ed Hammond, Helly Orthner, and Bruce Blum. A program was laid out, and this was later reviewed with Morris Collen and—via telephone— Homer Warner. Group dynamics worked, and the program was better than what any individual would have proposed.

The biggest problem we had in establishing this program was in the narrowing of the scope of the topic. We agreed at the program committee meeting held at SCAMC that the conference would concentrate on the history of informatics in the United States between 1950 and 1975. We also decided that the emphasis would be on clinical (as opposed to research or educational) applications. At the NLM program committee meeting we laid out a conference structure and proceeded to identify presenters who would provide insight into the specified topics. About 100 persons were identified; only 28 could be invited. The selection was difficult, but the outcome was commendable.

The rest, as they say, is history. Proceedings were prepared for distribution at the conference, and many of the authors revised their papers for this volume. Transcripts of the discussion also have been included. The original two-day program is reproduced on page xiii (Figure 3), and Figure 1 is a group photograph taken after the first session. We have organized this book into sections corresponding to the conference sessions. Each section has a brief editorial introduction intended to give a little of the flavor of the session. This is followed by a photograph and short biography of each presenter. Finally, there are the papers and transcripts of the session discussions.

There are many people who must be thanked for what they have done to bring the conference and this book into being. The names in Figures 2 and 3 list the principal contributors to the conference's success. Naturally, there were many others, and we wish to identify them here: Joe Mingioli and his staff at NLM who recorded the conference and the banquet address; Guy Hudgins of Ebon Research who supported NLM in conference registration and on-site support; Vince Sigillito of APL who ensured a supportive environment for the conference chair; Candy Zulick and Jane Scott of APL who provided secretarial assistance and managed a complex correspondence; the several groups at APL who prepared the final artwork and manuscripts, reproduced everything from stationery to fliers, and managed the mailings;

FIGURE 1
Group picture of con-
ference attendees

Karen Uchacz of APL who transcribed the audio tapes; the APL audiovisual group who are assisting in the (as yet unfinished) editing of the
video tapes; Adele Goldberg who, as President of ACM, made the organization of this conference very easy; Mike Mahoney who, as series
editor, reviewed the draft manuscript and made some very helpful suggestions; Pegotty Cooper, Donna Baglio, Janet Benton, Nhora Cortes-
Comerer, Sarah Hallet, and others of the ACM staff who helped with
the conference and this publication; and Jennifer Ballentine and the
staff of Ocean View who converted our manuscripts to this attractive
book.

At a personal level, we each would like to conclude with an individual statement. Bruce Blum already has acknowledged the help of
those colleagues and associates who made his idea into a reality. However, he has not yet mentioned Harriet. She provides the balance in his
life that allows him to take on foolish responsibilities cheerfully and
without apprehension. Thank you. Karen Duncan wishes to thank
George, who encourages and supports her in her pursuit of rainbows.

Bruce I. Blum
Laurel, Maryland

Karen Duncan
Los Altos, California

PROGRAM ORGANIZERS

Bruce Blum
Applied Physics Laboratory
Conference Chair

Program Committee

William Aspray, PhD
Charles Babbage Institute

Robert L. Chartrand, PhD
Library of Congress

Morris Collen, MD
Kaiser-Permanente Medical Group

Karen Duncan, PhD
Health Information Systems

Thelma Estrin, PhD
University of California, Los Angeles

W. E. Hammond, PhD
Duke Medical Center

Bonnie Kaplan, PhD
University of Cincinnati

Lois F. Lunin
Herner Company

Helmuth F. Orthner, PhD
George Washington University

Judith M. S. Prewitt, PhD
Medimatics, Inc.

Homer Warner, MD, PhD
University of Utah

John Parascandola, PhD
National Library of Medicine
Local Arrangements Chair

Jack Smith, MD, PhD
Ohio State University
Treasurer

Sponsored by
ACM Special Interest Group on
Biomedical Computing (SIGBIO)

Supporting Organizations
National Library of Medicine
Applied Physics Laboratory

Cooperating Organizations
American College of Medical Informatics
American Association for the Advancement of Science
Charles Babbage Institute for the History of Information Processing

FIGURE 3

Original two-day
program from the
*ACM Conference on
the History of
Medical Informatics:
Conference*

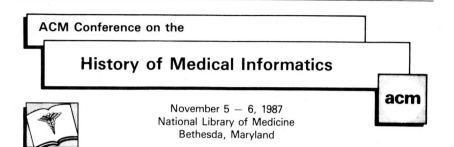

ACM Conference on the

History of Medical Informatics

November 5 — 6, 1987
National Library of Medicine
Bethesda, Maryland

acm

CONFERENCE PROGRAM

8:50 - 9:00	Welcome
9:00 - 10:30	Keynote Addresses Donald A. B. Lindberg, M.D. Joshua Lederberg, Ph.D.

9:00 - 10:30 Clinical Data Processing
Cesar A. Caceres, M.D.
Thomas L. Lincoln, M.D.
Hubert V. Pipberger, M.D. (Discussant)

11:00 - 12:30 Planting the Seeds - A Panel
Wilfred J. Dixon, Ph.D.
Robert S. Ledley, D.D.S.
Harold Schoolman, M.D.
Eugene A. Stead, M.D.
Bruce D. Waxman, Ph.D.
William S. Yamamoto, M.D. (Moderator)

11:00 - 12:30 Health Care Information Systems
Morris F. Collen, M.D.
Charles D. Flagle, Dr. Eng.
Carlos Vallbona, M.D. (Discussant)

Lunch   Lunch

1:30 - 3:00 Computing Systems
G. Octo Barnett, M.D.
Wesley A. Clark, Ph.D.
Charles E. Molnar, Sc.D.
Thelma Estrin, Ph.D. (Discussant)

1:30 - 3:00 Patient Management Systems
Homer Warner, Ph.D., M.D.
Melville H. Hodge
William E. Hammond, Ph.D. (Discussant)

3:30 - 5:00 Signal and Image Processing
Gwilym S. Lodwick, M.D.
Jerome R. Cox, Jr., D.Sc.
Judith M. S. Prewitt, Ph.D. (Discussant)

3:30 - 5:00 Clinical Decision Making
Lee B. Lusted, M.D.
Jack D. Myers, M.D.
Casimir A. Kulikowski, Ph.D. (Discussant)

Banquet   Lawrence L. Weed, M.D.

The banquet will be held at the Holiday Inn, 8120 Wisconsin Avenue. There will be a reception from 6:30 to 7:30.

Exhibits and demonstrations of various NLM projcts and services will be on display in the Lobby of the Lister Hill Center during coffee breaks and the lunch period on both days of the conference. The Learning Center will also be open to visitors during those times.

Sponsored by
**ACM Special Interest Group on
Biomedical Computing (SIGBIO)**

Supporting Organizations
**National Library of Medicine
Applied Physics Laboratory**

Contents

Medical Informatics in the United States, 1950–1975

Bruce I. Blum

Applied Physics Laboratory, The Johns Hopkins University, Laurel, Maryland

Because I was one of the conference organizers, I was asked to begin this collection with an introductory overview. This is a difficult task for me. I am not an historian, nor did I participate in the early history of medical informatics. In fact, when I first entered the field in 1976, each of the participants was an acknowledged leader. I held them in awe then, and I still do. However, now I am fortunate enough to consider them friends and colleagues as well.

The task of a historian is to take our knowledge of the past—individual strings of facts—and weave them into a fabric that displays order and provides meaning. Of course, one cannot capture all of the past; neither can one comprehend all of the present. Just as science abstracts physical reality to provide useful models, history is selective and directed. It is subject to the biases of both the author and reader.

In what follows, I begin with a personal perspective that offers a software engineer's introduction to medical informatics. I have not bothered to do any research on this subject. I rely on my memory and reference very few facts. Therefore, it is difficult to tell where my tapestry binds the historical threads and where it is simple invention. Of course, the validity of this introduction is not important; what matters is what the reader takes from the following chapters. My observations serve only to present a framework for those unfamiliar with the field.

Medical informatics covers a variety of applications, and I have found it useful to organize the field according to the objects that are processed and the tools that are used. For this purpose three classes of object are identified.

Data	The individual items made available to the analyst
Information	A set of data with some interpretation or value added
Knowledge	A set of rules, formulas, or heuristics used to create information from data and information

TABLE 1
Scope of medical computing

	1950s	1960s	1970	1980s
Data applications	Research	Prototype	Mature	Refined
Information applications	Concepts	Research	Prototype	Mature
Knowledge applications	Concepts	Concepts	Research	Prototype

Table 1 shows the progress in medical computing for each category of application. Within a category, research begins only after the supporting technology is mature enough to support it beyond the conceptual level. After the underlying assumptions are established, prototypes are used to provide operational feedback. Finally, some of the prototypes mature, and new, complementary applications are disseminated.

It can be seen in this table that, during the period 1950–1975, the history of medical informatics could be characterized as the operational success of the data-oriented applications, e.g., signal and image processing; the operational demonstration of information-oriented applications, e.g., patient management systems; and the conceptual demonstration of knowledge-oriented applications, e.g., artificial intelligence in medical decision making.

When I entered the field in 1976, my background was in information systems. Like many software engineers, I had a solid understanding of my technology and superficial knowledge about the domain in which it would be applied. After implementing systems for military and space applications, I had developed skills in exposing user needs and designing systems to satisfy them. Thus, when my supervisors at the Applied Physics Laboratory (APL) needed a programmer to lead a small collaborative demonstration project at the School of Medicine, I was selected.

The project was a success (by 1976 standards), and I was asked to stay on full-time at the Medical School. In 1984 I decided to return to APL for research in software engineering. Thus, I was not really active in medical informatics for very long. Still, it was an important period of consolidation. Dick Johns, the director of the Department of Biomedical Engineering, was very supportive; he allowed me to spend considerable time working on problems in medical informatics that were not related to my immediate tasks. Consequently, I was privileged to participate in an exciting transition whose roots are the subject of this history.

What were the 1976 standards by which my project was a success? Simply that the program worked and the sponsors liked it. I had been accustomed to building systems when the need was obvious. But in medical informatics, the needs were uncertain. Clearly, when one can formalize a problem it is not difficult to write a program and produce the prescribed solution. In the medical domain, however, the goals are to improve patient care, community health, provider education, etc. Unless the resulting program contributes to those goals, it should not be considered a success. (Fortunately, experience suggests that the program will not be used unless it is perceived to be useful.)

As I later found out, 1975 was a watershed year in the history of medical informatics. Prior to that time, the half-life of a computer application was equal to the publication cycle. That is, half the papers about computer applications reported on systems that were no longer operational. Some of this had to do with the cost of equipment. (For example, the Johns Hopkins Oncology Center's first computer, delivered in 1976, cost a quarter-of-a-million dollars and did not have much more capacity than the personal computer with which I write this chapter.) Nevertheless, most of the early project failures stemmed from the immaturity of the field and uncertainty about the operational constraints.

Much of the work described in this volume involved the demonstration of computer technology. There was a new tool, and Lusted, Schoolman, Stead, Warner, Waxman, Yamamoto, and others helped define and establish an environment in which to test how that tool could be employed. In narrow domains—such as those that I characterize as data oriented—the utility of the tool was clear, and it was used to support targeted investigations. As the Molnar and Clark paper points out, this was both the motivation for the LINC and the reason for its success. There was a concern for technology only to the extent that it enabled a solution to a domain problem. As the technology became more mature and easier to use, it became less and less an object of interest.

This transition is clear in the contrast between Estrin's review of the early concern for equipment resources and the papers by Cox and Lodwick that focus on the application of these resources. Estrin concludes her paper with an examination of why the Data Processing Laboratory (DPL) of the Brain Research Institute (BRI), despite its numerous successes and "firsts," ceased to function in 1979. A grant proposal, she begins, was approved but not funded.

> The computer research study section [that would have reviewed the proposal] had been disbanded, and our reviewers were primarily neuroscientists who did not understand microcomputers. The grant application refusal, coupled with the emergence of neurobiology as a central factor requiring BRI space, caused us to give up our DPL housing. But perhaps most important was the lack of recruitment of mathematically or computer-oriented neuroscientists by the BRI. After most of our strong supporters had moved or retired, BRI did recruit first rate neuroscientists; however, their interest in computer research was minimal.

Today, the field is called biomedical engineering, the computer is but one of many useful electronic devices, and most papers present their findings without any descriptions of equipment or programs.

Information-oriented applications in the mid-1970s were a different matter. In 1966 Jydstrup and Gross performed an analysis of three hospitals in Rochester, New York, and reported that about a quarter of the hospital costs were for information handling. Obviously, computers could help manage the process, but it was not clear how. Even if the equipment costs were disregarded, it still had to be determined what medical data should be collected, how they should be organized, and who should pay for it. For example, what should the medical record contain? Estrin's closing remarks include a picture of a physician's notes together with the Norbert Wiener comment that a "society can only be understood through a study of the messages and communication facilities which belong to it" (see page 156). That physician's messages offered no clues as to how automation could help.

One of the most important contributions to medical informatics, made in the late 1960s, had nothing to do with automation. Weed proposed a new form and flow for the medical record. The goal of this problem-oriented medical record was to interject the same discipline into patient care and training that one used in research. In time this record was converted into an automated form, and the resulting Problem-Oriented Medical Information System (PROMIS) advanced the state of the art in both hospital information systems and personal workstations. Yet, the automation of the problem-oriented medical record by itself was not sufficient. Indeed, as Stead observes, our solutions to the patient medical history requirement are still incomplete.

From the perspective of the mid-1970s, however, using the computer to present medical information was a very advanced concept. Quite a few of the papers describe the problems encountered with making such systems work. Subsequent successes with clinical information systems have made us less sensitive to the problems that these early developers encountered. There were few operational models to follow, much of the work was conducted in a research setting, and the user perceptions were naive. We have become so accustomed to computers in this age of the personal computer, that it is hard to remember how distant and imposing the computer seemed to its users at that time. Barnett's paper reminds us of the difficulty in determining how to apply a new technology in a medical setting concurrent with the development of new tools for that technology.

Before the mid-1970s, when the presenters were making the contributions they report on here, the equipment constrained the researchers' ability to realize their objectives and thereby get the necessary feedback to refine their concepts. Unlike those working in data-oriented applications, these investigators worked with fuzzy computational goals. Information is data organized for a use, and it was not clear what those uses should be. Would the users respond to the new data presentations? What effect would an information system have on an institution's operations and effectiveness? These were just some of the questions to be resolved; and Barnett, Weed, Caceres, Lincoln, Pipberger, Collen, Flagle, Hodge, Warner, and Hammond provided some of the answers. Caceres and Pipberger analyzed ECG data and found effective ways to report them; Lincoln showed how to automate a clinical laboratory; Collen provided great leadership in the field as he developed information system tools and an automated multiphasic health testing (AMHT) system; Flagle uncovered methods to evaluate the impact of the new technology; and Barnett, Weed, Hodge, Warner, and Hammond helped bring COSTAR, PROMIS, TMIS, HELP, and TMR into being.

Thus, in 1977, by which time I had the audacity to have already presented three papers on computers and medicine, a discipline of medical informatics was beginning to mature. Papers now were starting to report on five-year evaluations of information-oriented systems. Henley and Wiederhold had surveyed the automated ambulatory medical record systems (such as Barnett's COSTAR and Hammond's GEMISCH/TMR), and Orthner and Wist had organized the Symposium for Computer Applications in Medical Care (SCAMC). Although SCAMC certainly was not the first of the meetings devoted to the application of computers to medicine, it soon grew to be the dominant meeting in the U.S. It provided a national forum for sharing information, advancing the state of practice, and building a research base. It was at SCAMC (and the earlier meetings sponsored by Levy and Williams in Illinois) that I first learned of the work of others. These exchanges were central to my professional growth and competence.

Much of the difficult pioneering work was complete by the time that I emerged on the scene. A baseline for medical information systems had been established. In the decade that I was involved with medical informatics, the advances were quite remarkable. Lowered equipment costs increased awareness and demand. The expensive prototypes of the 1970s were refined into the effective systems of the 1980s. The SCAMC conferences broadened the community of users, developers, and researchers. We accepted what computers could do and explored new ways in which they could be applied. In 1966, when Jydstrup and Gross conducted their study, computers were perceived to be a labor-saving, cost-reduction mechanism. By the early 1970s, as Hodge was battling the press in the El Camino installation, the hospital information system was recognized to have both a care-management and a cost-control function.

Today, automated ECG analysis, computer-supported clinical laboratories, and hospital information systems are accepted as essential tools. Yet, as many of the contributors to this history observe, most implementations perform only a fraction of what has been demonstrated for a decade or more. Hammond put it as follows:

> As I scanned through old papers and reports in preparation for these remarks, I became depressed in the "sameness" of those proposals and descriptions with what is happening today. Then I realized there are major differences—today's systems work and are affordable.

Of course, today's systems do more than just work. They have shown us how to manage our information. As a result, there is a concern for a more thorough exploitation of the information. We now are experimenting with medical knowledge.

Clearly, some of the earliest work with computers was related to medical decision making. The seminal *Science* paper by Ledley and Lusted, as demonstrated by the citation analysis included in the Lusted paper, spawned many research projects. But to the computer science community, perhaps the most referenced work is that on Shortliffe's MYCIN, which was documented in book form in 1976. The revolution in our understanding of the role of knowledge in computing, popularized by the expert system and lucidly described in Lederberg's paper, has led us to think of this change in terms of the technology used. That is, we contrast static control and statistical algorithms with the dynamic application of heuristics and AI paradigms. But I think that this misses the point.

The evolution that I see is not one of implementation dogma; rather, it is one of the recognition and characterization of knowledge. For well-understood domains, and many examples are given in the following papers, formulas and statistical inference are the best knowledge representations. For other tasks, heuristics and cognitive models provide the greatest power. In both cases, we recognize Feigenbaum's "Knowledge IS Power." Moreover, that knowledge is cumulative.

In 1975, as the period of this history comes to a close, knowledge-oriented applications are still in the research stage. Warner with HELP (and slightly later McDonald with RMRS) showed how medical knowledge can be applied to patient data; concurrently, Myers with INTERNIST, Kulikowski with CASNET, and Shortliffe with MYCIN demonstrated how medical knowledge can be structured to solve patient-oriented problems. I see this trend in medical informatics (and for that matter computer application in general) as a movement from learning about the tool to an understanding of how that tool enriches our understanding of the domain. Medical informatics began as a tool-driven discipline; the intent was to solve problems that were constrained by the limits of manual processing. By the mid-1970s, however, experience with the tools matured, and the focus began to shift toward the essential medical problems, i.e., to the core knowledge.

I believe that this trend is visible in the material in this volume; I sense that it will be much clearer when the next period of this history is reviewed.

This completes my very personal view of the history of medical informatics. The flow followed the rubric presented in Table 1; it also echoes the structure of the conference. The organization of the sessions is obvious from the table of contents. Of course, some of the speakers' assignments were arbitrary. Most presenters were eminently qualified to share their experiences in several sessions, and there was never a requirement that their papers be rigidly guided by the session title. Thus, the table of contents suggests an order that the papers only casually observe.

In the remainder of this introduction I examine some general issues in the context of what the various authors tell us. The intent of what follows is to suggest some common themes among the papers. A secondary goal, which is perhaps more important, is to expose a framework for examining our current research.

Lindberg closed his keynote address question period with, "I hope this day ends with the firm conclusion that we need more theory and science behind our work. We also need academic departments to develop the field." What is this work and field? In a discussion of the term medical informatics, Warner concluded, "We are defining what we do [as we are talking about it]."

Is this a criticism? How well defined must our field be? A comment from Lederberg, made during the panel discussion, provides insight.

> One of the things that really squelches a real creativity is the demand put to an investigator that he know what he is doing before he gets support. Very creative people don't know what they are doing when they are first browsing around the field and trying to get their bearings in it. We ourselves are the enemy when we are impaneled to try to critique other people's proposals.
>
> There is a vast difference between exploratory and exploitative research. The latter, which is what most people do most of the time, is a foundation for your inquiry, and you do have to know what you are doing. But the real discoveries come when you don't know what you are looking for, when there is no way to anticipate the unknown.

Clearly, for exploitative research, a body of knowledge must be learned so that new work can build on what has been learned already. This is Kuhn's "science as puzzle solving" within the accepted paradigm. In medical informatics there is a large body of accepted learning that should be structured, added to, and taught. This is the field that Lindberg and Warner refer to. Although this may seem obvious, it is being recognized as a need only recently. For example, consider Shortliffe's student's comment of the early 1980s.

> Medical system implementors don't read (presumably because they "know" what they want). An enormous duplication of effort, both good and bad takes place. Bibliographies are typically incomplete, and fundamental issues are almost always overlooked. When reading is done, it is done incestuously. {1}

As one reads the papers that follow, one is struck by the enormous interaction among the investigators. How they shared and learned from each other. How they applied the technology to the problems in their specialties. This is the history of exploratory research, of a shift in perceptions and goals. By the 1980s the tools were mature. In fact, they were so powerful that many users were seduced into believing that the wheel that they were inventing was independent of experience with other wheels—hence the student's observation and Lindberg's conclusion.

We are accustomed to thinking of medical informatics as being a tool-driven discipline. Computers and medicine. Obviously, some of the conference participants became involved in this field because there was a specific problem that they felt computers could solve. But that was not the general rule. For many the association with computers began accidentally. As Barnett put it, "Much of what is accomplished in life as in science seems in large part to be dominated by luck, by the accident of being in the right place at the right time, with the right resources, the right funding, the right opportunities."

Several of the authors introduce their history with an observation regarding the limitations of human performance, which provided an incentive for their work. Lodwick notes, "The frequency of human error in diagnostic decision making generally, and in the interpretation of x-ray images specifically, is astonishingly high (est. 20% detection, 10% to 50% diagnosis). This high rate of error is largely unsuspected." Pipberger offers a similar justification for his work, "The diagnostic performance of experienced electrocardiographers was usually between 50% and 60%."

Other speakers examined the amount of information required in medicine and how it was learned and managed. Stead commented,

> In 1928 at the time that I entered medical school there were only two considerations given. One was that you make a good grade in organic chemistry, and the second was that you could borrow money. The reason for the organic chemistry requirement was that most medical education was memory-based and in those days there was relatively little theory in organic chemistry; it was nearly all straight memory.

But a reliance on memory does not imply a good education. Weed's address summarizes what we know of human cognition and considers how well this mode of teaching works. Myers concluded his oral presentation as follows:

We still find most medical schools teaching mainly by the technique of information transfer and lectures. How successful is a faculty going to be in transferring a million-and-a-half facts, individual items of information, to its students? I think the answer is obvious, and I certainly think that it's necessary that we change our mode of education from information transfer to problem solving techniques as many have expounded.

Some speakers were introduced to medical informatics from an interest in the technology. To Clark, it was an application area. For Molnar and Cox there was a concern with both the computer and the application. Warner was a cardiologist who was first introduced to electronics when the Ford Foundation made some money available for something other than existing patient care activities. The result was an analog device, experiments, results, an NIH grant, success, the recognition of new problems, and interactions with new investigators.

Other people had a background in engineering that helped direct their careers. Lusted was an engineer during World War II and chose to go to medical school after the war. His background in engineering and an interest in computing made him a prime candidate to play a key role on the NIH Advisory Committee on Computers in Research (ACCR). Ledley's career took a major turn during the Korean conflict. His interest was physics, his family desire was dentistry, and his first military dentistry assignment was at the National Bureau of Standards where the Standard Eastern Automatic Computer (SEAC) was. As a result of this lucky accident, he "began to really 'find myself'."

Several of the authors were appointed to positions that resulted in their lifelong commitment to medical informatics. In Collen's case, when the executive director of Kaiser Permanente decided that "it was time to begin to use computers in the practice of medicine," Collen became the choice in part because of his undergraduate degree in electrical engineering. Barnett was chosen to play a similar role by the general director of the Massachusetts General Hospital (MGH) because "there was no one else they could identify who was interested in academic medicine and who had any experience in working with computers."

Of course, not everyone began with an interest in computing. Lodwick detoured through pathologic anatomy on his way to clinical radiology and, in the process, focused on modeling bone tumors using the clinical and radiographic data in a large registry. Weed's initial concerns were the content and use of the medical record in the management of patient care; the automation of the record came much later. Dixon and Flagle used the computer as a tool to support their research; their work did not involve direct patient interaction.

Estrin entered the field in an interesting way. After receiving her PhD in electrical engineering, she observes, "I had trouble obtaining traditional employment as an electrical engineer because my commitment was not taken seriously; a common attitude towards women's careers in the fifties." A friend helped her locate a position in the Neurological Institute in New York City where she collaborated with physicians on EEG and EMG studies. As a resident of Princeton, she also participated in the social and intellectual life of the Institute of Advanced Study, which led to a friendship with the von Neumanns and later to an appointment as a computer engineer in the Weizmann Institute of Science in Israel. With this background, she was well qualified to join the Brain Research Institute at UCLA in 1960.

The Brain Research Institute (BRI) also played a role in introducing Yamamoto to the field. As a medical student, he read Wiener's *Cybernetics*, and it "struck a very important cord in my mind." (The book also had a profound effect on Molnar's career choice.) In time, Yamamoto turned to physiology, where he focused on the respiratory system. At a meeting in the BRI around 1960, he was giving a talk on how the brain functions. Waxman was in the audience, discussions followed, and in 1963 Yamamoto was invited to join the NIH ACCR.

Finally, a few of the participants came to medical informatics after other careers. Lederberg was a Nobel laureate, recognized for his contributions in bacterial genetics, before he began his work on DENDRAL. He was familiar with computers, knew Feigenbaum, Minsky, and McCarthy, and had an interest in exploring the use of computers in this kind of application. Myers, after retiring as chairman of the Department of Medicine, also began a new research career. He chose to explore how computers could be used in medical diagnosis. In both cases, their contributions drew on a rich background that helped to guide their research.

Although this catalog is incomplete, it serves to illustrate that there was a great deal of random chance that brought together the leaders of this new field. Barnett called it luck, but the result was really a selection process. It may have been luck and timing that determined which individuals would contribute to medical informatics, but their successes depended on the insight, intelligence, and hard work of each person. That was not a function of luck.

Among Barnett's lucky accidents were those of resources, funding, and opportunities. These were the seeds referred to in the panel title: the institutional and financial support for experimentation and development. Collen called the period from the early 1960s to about 1975 the "golden years." Never again would there be such "a tremendous outpouring of funds for medical informatics." Waxman, a principal source for funding, commented.

> When I joined the NIH I was under the impression that NIH was really serious and wanted to spend a lot of money trying to find out what could be done with computers. In fact, they weren't that motivated at all. They wanted to spend a few hundred thousands of dollars just to maintain an

impression. We were fortunate not to have realized that was the game plan because we wound up spending 50 to 60 million dollars over five years.

Evidence that money was spent productively is contained in many of the papers that follow.

Of course, eventually most of the seed money was expended, and the developments had to be accepted on their own merits. In a purely scientific discipline, the developments would be ideas and concepts that would be adopted or rejected on the basis of consistency and utility. With computer applications in medicine, however, the output included both concept demonstrations and engineered products. The latter were expected to "do something useful." But this was a period of expensive equipment; it was unrealistic to expect that the first prototypes would realize all of their cost-saving potential. The fact that the computers did save money helped at MGH and El Camino. The fact that the money saved might be societal rather than organizational hurt the AMHT effort.

Following Collen's talk, there was a discussion of how some development paths were able to ensure their success by responding to the needs of their users. Lincoln observed,

> Toffler has made the cogent remark that successful technologies have to make either a buck or a big bang, and we have only the first option in health care. Our technologies have to pay for themselves.

This is not really true. In 1979 Allan Cormack and Godfrey Hounsfield shared a Nobel Prize for their contributions to computerized axial tomography—the former for his mathematical models, the latter for his engineering of an effective product. Clearly, the revolution in diagnostic imagery that followed qualifies as a "big bang." Nevertheless, Lincoln's point is well taken. Much of the effort in medical informatics has been directed toward the engineering of solutions to the information management problems associated with medical education and care.

Many of the presenters focused on their activities in the development of information systems that could manage the patient's data in a more rational way. Today, in part as a result of their efforts, there are well-accepted models of what the medical record should contain. It now is clear that this information should integrate inpatient and outpatient care and be insensitive to the patient's geographic moves. Although there are few exemplar systems that illustrate how the medical record should be managed, the 15- to 20-year-old examples in the Barnett and Collen papers remain effective prototypes. Our major advancement is that, in Hammond's words, "today's systems work and are affordable."

This process of making concepts work is the engineering dimension of medical informatics. It can be viewed as the exploitation of the computer as a medical tool. Clearly, in the case of information management, the tool has enabled us to carry out tasks that we could not perform in the days before computers. Lindberg's description of the pre-automated laboratory reminds us of the number of tests that the older laboratories could manage. Without this automation we could not order tests based on the clinical need; we would be constrained by the laboratory's throughput. The same computers enable the management of resources, the communication of data, and the processing of algorithms. Indeed, a modern health care delivery system would collapse under the weight of its administrative burden without the support of computers.

There is also a scientific dimension to medical informatics. We see it in the new understandings that evolve as problems are solved and perceptions change. For example, see how Weed's assessment of the problem changes as his initial information management goals are realized.

> …we undertook the development of the PROMIS computerized system to support the human memory and to help in the coordination of the many providers working on a single patient. And the PROMIS system soon revealed that when you solve the memory problem of the human mind, you uncover a processing limitation that is even worse than the memory limitation. That is to say, with 55,000 displays of medical details instantly available at the doctor's fingertips, he could be overwhelmed by the task of integrating the relevant details from the unique patient with the relevant details now so instantly available to him on a computer screen. We came face to face with the realities and complexities in decision making that had been hidden under terms such as "clinical judgement" and "intuition" and "experience."

If medical informatics is to be the catalyst for a shift in the health care delivery paradigm (which naturally includes medical training), it will do so by addressing this second level of concern. Here the technology—in both computer systems and the representation of medical knowledge—is immature. Our tools are primitive; we have limited insight regarding how they may be used. Contrast this with the data- and information-oriented applications. Molnar said that Clark's "idea of a computer was something that cost 10 dollars and could be painted on any convenient flat surface." This vision is coming true. Hodge, in discussing Technicon's plans for the 1990s, stated that they don't consider equipment costs. "They are going to be so cheap that we won't care." Thus, computer technology is no longer an impediment to achieving the engineering goals; success only requires that the developers build on earlier applications. In fact, readers of the following chapters may find it interesting to find that they are only reimplementing older (and perhaps clumsier) systems.

The roots of the future of medical informatics also are to be found throughout this book. I have chosen to present it in the form of knowledge-oriented applications. Others have stated it differently. Schoolman, for example, quotes the First Stead Committee Report, which declares the goal of "educational methods which render obsolete the current system of libraries, textbooks, medical school curricula, and total dependence on memory and pattern recognition in clinical decision making and problem solving." Caceres describes a microcomputer-based system in his office in which medical assistants and computer tools make the first decisions; when the physician sees the patient, this material is available for his review. Kulikowski notes that the period under review closes with a transition from decision prototypes for specific diseases to a more general knowledge-based approach.

In each case there is a desire to formalize knowledge so that it can be applied more effectively and with less effort. We see this trend in the ECG analysis, the computer support to diagnostic radiology, the application of statistical and decision-analysis techniques, the use of alerts in the HIS, the PC-based tools such as QMR and the Knowledge-Coupler, and the use of inferential expert systems. Each of these contributions addresses some aspect of what we know about medicine and health care delivery. Every application frees the humans—providers and patients—to do those things for which they are better suited than machines are. Every unit of knowledge represents a potential addition to some larger, holistic view.

It may be argued that this introduction is biased and that it twists the history of 1950 to 1975 to conform with the author's understanding. I don't dispute this. But the period of study was very rich and exciting. It began with experiments in the use of a tool, and it shifted to the solution of medical problems as that tool improved. Today, medical informatics centers around two concerns: the identification of problem solutions for which our technology is inadequate, and the engineering of solutions to well-understood problems using mature technology, i.e., research and development. The major change since 1975 has been that our recognition of the problem has been tempered by experience with the tool. Applying what we have learned—development—has become a reality.

The important part of this book now follows. I hope that you find as much enjoyment in reading it as the authors did in bringing it to you.

Reference

1. E.H. Shortliffe, The science of biomedical computing. J.C. Pages, *et al.*, eds., *Meeting the Challenge: Medical Informatics and Medical Education*, Amsterdam: North-Holland Publishing Co., 1983.

A History of
Medical Informatics

THE KEYNOTE ADDRESSES

The conference began with some introductory and administrative remarks from the conference chair. The goal was to thank all those who had made the conference possible, to explain where the various meals would be served, and to fill time until the audience had assembled. Because this was the first opportunity that many of the attendees had to visit with each other in a long time, achieving the last objective proved to be a difficult assignment. There were two keynote addresses; each was followed by a brief question period.

Donald A.B. Lindberg, MD provided a sense of what life was like before and during the early days of computing. He drew on his fascinating collection of slides to illustrate the transition from analog clinical laboratory devices to modern expert systems such as AI/RHEUM. For example, his first slide showed the interior of the Whirlwind computer. It contained a telephone; the machine was very large, and this was the only way to coordinate operations and maintenance. Although the paper in this collection does not include those illustrations, it does convey the content of the address.

Joshua Lederberg, PhD presented a rich personal history as well as some observations about artificial intelligence (AI) and knowledge. He traced the conceptual threads that lead to his work on the DENDRAL Project at Stanford. Interestingly, he chose a problem that was best suited for the technology that they were experimenting with. Their success is a milestone in the history of computer application. The paper in this volume is an expansion of that included in the conference proceedings. Appended to it is a 1965 Stanford Artificial Intelligence Report that, as Dr. Lederberg put it, "is an excellent snapshot of the status of AI research as seen in 1965."

SPEAKERS

Donald A.B. Lindberg In Praise of Computing
Joshua Lederberg How DENDRAL Was Conceived and Born

Donald A.B. Lindberg, MD is director, National Library of Medicine. He received an AB degree from Amherst College in 1954 and an MD degree from Columbia University in 1958. Prior to joining NLM in 1984, he was affiliated with the University of Missouri, Columbia where his responsibilities included professor and chairman, Department of Information Science, School of Library and Information Science (1969–1971), director, Information Science Group, School of Medicine (1971–1984), and professor of Pathology, School of Medicine (1969–1984). He has written or coedited four books, was the chief editor of four proceedings, is on the editorial board of three journals, and is the managing editor of the Springer-Verlag Lecture Notes in Medical Informatics series. His honors include Distinguished Practitioner in Medicine (NAPM, 1983) and the Silver Core Award (IFIP, 1986).

Joshua Lederberg, PhD is president of The Rockefeller University (since 1978). He received his BA degree from Columbia College in 1944, entered medical school, and then took a leave of absence to do research with Dr. Edward L. Tatum at Yale University. While at Yale, where he received his PhD in 1947, he discovered the mechanism of genetic recombination in bacteria. From 1947 to 1959 he was professor of genetics at the University of Wisconsin. In 1958, at the age of 33, Dr. Lederberg was corecipient of the Nobel Prize in Physiology or Medicine for his work in bacterial genetics. He joined the faculty of Stanford University School of Medicine in 1959 and served as chairman of the Department of Genetics until coming to The Rockefeller University in 1978. While at Stanford he also held the titles of professor of biology and professor of computer science. He has received numerous awards, has worked on many government advisory committees, and serves on the boards of a variety of institutions.

3

In Praise of Computing

Donald A.B. Lindberg, MD
National Library of Medicine, Bethesda

I shall describe briefly some early work in applying computing systems to clinical laboratory, diagnosis, and medical records problems. If we compare the early work with what can be done now, we shall see many examples of enormous improvements in speed and power of computing techniques. A particularly striking difference in comparing 1960 with 1987 is the very much more widespread use of computing devices now and the shift in the pattern of scientific and business work to depend on automated information systems for support of ordinary professional functions. In other words, computing systems really work now, and lots of people really use them.

Let me first establish this contrast and share with you the pleasure this day brings to all of us in taking pride in these accomplishments. We should do this first, because I shall end by drawing attention to some desirable changes that have not occurred over the 25 years. The organizer of this conference, Bruce Blum, urged us to include personal remembrances, so I shall do so.

My own interest in computing arose grudgingly from two requirements, one scientific and one professional. I was working under NIH support on an infectious disease problem when I moved from Columbia Presbyterian to the University of Missouri in 1960, taking my NIH grant with me. This in itself may add an element of nostalgia, since most institutions no longer permit residents to hold grants and NIH can barely fund one-third of the applications from senior faculty nowadays. In any event, my interest turned to a systematic investigation of the (then and now) poor correlation between *in vitro* and *in vivo* antibiotic sensitivity of bacteria that infect lung and blood. I did not believe (and still do not believe) that 24-hour disc-diffusion growth inhibition was a reasonable measure of the bacteria's susceptibility to antibiotic killing or growth inhibition. I reasoned that the battle between bacteria and pulmonary macrophages was probably over in 20 minutes to an hour. Hence I wanted to study bacteria growing in liquid media, with and without antibiotics. To do this I, along with a sophomore undergraduate physics student, built a machine {1}.

The observations the machine permitted gave a great deal of insight into this problem, although never the ultimate secret {2}. Never-

4

theless we were able to prescribe therapy based on these experiments that unquestioningly cured patients with subacute bacterial endocarditis and other infectious diseases on whom others had given up. In any event, computers were necessary to process and organize the output data, and to model the processes of bacterial growth. The progression of steps we took in developing our data processing was rather pitiable in modern terms. First we learned how to wire nixie tubes to display the numbers that represented optical measurements of light-scatter (hence bacterial growth) in the hundred or so test tubes that cycled past the light source. In the next version of the machine we took these signals to a Victor adding machine printer. We pasted up the tapes in rows, then read down the resulting columns to sum growth over an individual tube. Next we output the whole run to paper tape which we read into a Burroughs 205 computer. This was the beginning of wisdom, but the Burroughs was not a nice computer, and paper tape was awkward. Our next step was to redesign the machine to output to a card punch so that we could process on the "modern" IBM 1620 computer. In both cases, the computers resided in "open shop" mode in the basement of the university mathematics department. The Computer Center director was a half-time job held by an assistant professor of mathematics who was never given tenure. We usually processed at midnight, because there would be no one to object if we vacuumed out the detritus from the tape reader.

All this was quite good fun with one exception: namely, I was simultaneously supposed to be directing and supervising clinical chemistry, clinical microbiology, and a section of the sophomore path class and doing frozen sections. The biggest practical problem was getting correct reports out of the clinical laboratories and to the clinics and wards. The blackest day I can remember was when I was called to deal with the potential problem that Clinical Chemistry might not get out any of today's reports before they reached quitting time. Even blacker was the discovery that they also hadn't reported the previous day's Auto-Analyzer runs.

My personal love was Microbiology. This was a well-run laboratory that always got the work out. Unfortunately the report slips—which pathologists in those days personally signed—usually contained a great and imaginative assortment of spellings of the bacteriological names. This may not have actually impeded patient care, since the clinical house staff receiving them also did not spell with much precision. It did, however, allow the professor of Microbiology to hold me and the Pathology Department up to ridicule and contumely. This academic paragon did not, of course, know that the Record Room had at all times hundreds of lab reports on which the patient names did not even match the patient unit numbers. These were not permitted to be placed in the charts, and hence were lost forever. Misspelling was only one of our problems.

I made a number of managerial changes to put a temporary "fix" on the reporting problem. The next morning was the brightest day I can remember; it suddenly occurred to me that the computing system I was using for the antibiotic sensitivity experiments could be used to solve my clinical laboratory problem as well. After all, I reasoned, computer programs always spelled things the same way day after day, and the tabulating printer certainly was faster than the folks running the laboratory typewriters. In addition, I could establish limits, so that at least some of the ridiculous errors could never again be reported out and truly life-threatening findings could be identified for telephone reporting. Once one yielded to this line of thinking, it immediately became obvious that the product of the clinical labs (with the exception of the Blood Bank) was purely information: hundreds of thousands of items per year. Tables outside the programs could contain editing and limits values, pointers to other medical record elements, pricing and quality control data, etc.

That day was my moment "on the road to Damascus." I had been seriously troubled by my divided loyalties between pushing ahead in the research laboratory, while simultaneously knowing the clinical laboratory needed attention. I would then spend futile hours correcting spelling and dilutions in the clinical labs while feeling neglectful of the research. That day I realized computers were the answer to the common problem in both settings: namely, information control. From that moment forward I have been professionally happy, and committed to working out the best uses of automated information systems.

The first electronic laboratory reporting system at Missouri (and I believe the first anywhere) was—as you can easily imagine—a kludge too {3, 4}. We could not do much better, since we did not even have a computer in the Medical School. I arranged a system of prepunched cards, in which each card contained a line of the ultimate lab report. These were arranged in a kind of pigeon roost from which the lab secretaries composed the messages. Using punch cards on the wards on which to write the clinical order to accompany the specimen worked out well, and various envelopes kept things together during the specimen processing. Incidentally, I was astounded a few years later to see that Warner Slack at the University of Wisconsin had devised an almost identical pigeon roost to hold the cards that provided the basis for his patient history system.

Getting our laboratory results printed on the wards was a problem, since there were no teleprocessing systems even if we had owned a computer. We solved this by converting the cards to paper tape, and using the paper tape to drive circuit codes into what Teletype Corporation called a "Stunt Box." This in turn activated the print circuits to teletype Model 28 printers which we installed in linen closets at the ward and clinic locations. The whole business was slow—and incredibly noisy—but it worked. We summarized the decks of cards—at midnight as usual—in the IBM 1620. This reduced each report to an individual punched card with massive use of "over punches" into the x and y fields. Most of the resultant cards had so many illegal codes that they looked like lace doilies. An easy by-product of all this was a billing punched card for each transaction. These were interpreted and sent to the Business Office. I took considerable glee in knowing that no one in the Business Office, nor in their auditors (Price, Waterhouse) had the slightest idea what to do with punched cards. Actually they read them and entered the numbers into posting machines.

The only downside effect of the new lab system was a deal I made to finance the operation. Since we were printing directly to the patient locations, I discharged 20 pretty coeds who had been employed to deliver lab reports. That was the first but not the last time I heard colleagues say I was "destroying life as we knew it."

This old digital laboratory reporting system did of course get replaced. We brought in an IBM 1410 for the Medical School and implemented what amounted to a fast turnaround batch system using punched card input and output. The memory on the 1410 was 40,000 characters; our languages were Autocoder, FORTRAN, and COBOL.

In this system the input was written to a patient record as well as a batch print file. Consequently patient unit numbers really had to be correct. We added Modulus Eleven self-check digits to all patient numbers, persuaded the Record Room to rearrange the filing system, and persuaded the hospital administrator that all his Addressograph-Multigraph plate-stamping equipment really needed replacing in any case. Self-check digits were also used for lab reports and specimen numbers. I imagine Missouri was first here too. I have never been able to understand how American hospitals got along without self-check digits, since European hospitals use them with an even better algorithm.

The 1410 system was implemented in the laboratories with a new kind of input terminal: what became the IBM 1092 Densely Coded Matrix. This was a joint development between IBM and the University of Missouri. Its original purpose was to enter size, shape, color, and cutting instructions for the garment trade in New York, but it seemed to me ideal for lab reporting. One used plastic overlays to redefine the key designations and microswitches to detect unique notches on the individual overlays.

The matrix keyboard got me my NIH automation grant. We had a terrific proposal to use the 1410 to do complete lab automation integrated into hospital patient record keeping. The obvious missing piece was some kind of device to input the data. Since the new IBM matrix device—indeed the whole 1050 system—was unpatented and unannounced, I could not include these descriptions in the grant proposal. I knew this would draw a site visit. At that time Melvin Belli had just pulled off his trial scene trick of leaving the leg-shaped package wrapped in butcher paper on the courtroom desk. I took a leaf from his book and draped the sheet metal prototype of our reporting device with an Operating Room sheet at the head of the Dean's Conference Room. Essentially we were daring the site visitors to ask us to breach our confidentiality agreement. It worked. They stared, but they never asked. And they approved the grant request.

The 1410 system worked quite well but was replaced in time by a true on-line system once the 360/50 became available. The latter got to be a rather extensive system, including a lot of quality control, cost analysis, interpretation, etc. {5}. I know some of those programs ran for fully 20 years.

In the course of this work the University of Missouri formed the Medical Computer Program, and I became its first director beginning in 1962. The commitment of the school to make a serious investigation of computers was made by the dean, Vernon Wilson. He encouraged us to test the question, "Could computers contribute something to teaching, practice, and research in medicine?," and he did this with much encouragement, advice, and support. He was a really fine academic leader. I saw the task to be to create an institutionally based information utility, to establish a multidisciplinary group including medical, engineering, and mathematical skills, and to support and encourage creative ventures in the professional services of the school and the hospital. Gwil Lodwick in Radiology at Missouri was certainly at the head of this list. It also included computer groups in Pathology, Dietary, the Dean's Office, and subsequently Surgery, then Medicine and Pediatrics. I still believe central information groups should be institutionally based, preferably as academic departments of their own; certainly not as service units within other departments.

Incidentally computer science has not been mentioned so far because there was none. I remember vividly some years hence getting a telephone call from the vice president for Academic Affairs at the University. He asked, "Is there such a thing as computer science? Someone wants to make a new department." Our group had spent a lot of time convincing the personnel people to believe in job descriptions and career ladders for computer programmers, system analysts, system programmers, technical writers, etc., so this was not so much of a leap of faith for us as for the Graduate School.

Other events must be mentioned briefly. Use at Missouri of the AMA Current Medical Terminology (CMT) tapes in the Consider system was really fun. We used sets of symptoms and findings from patient cases as search arguments against the AMA structured text that constituted fairly regularized disease definitions. This produced a differential diagnosis: at least diagnoses to "consider" {6}. The latter were of course ranked according to disease prevalence at the University of Missouri Medical Center as reflected in its discharge diagnosis file. These searches were first done in batch mode. It was clear, however, that teaching of students and residents would be greatly enhanced if we could go on-line. We did this using the IBM 1410 at a time when IBM had not yet produced even its first cathode-ray tube terminal. Our display was a Control Data Corporation CRT kludged onto the 1301 RAMAC disk controller. To his credit, the IBM field engineer showed us how to hook it up so the controller thought it had a second RAMAC unit. This CMT work has been subsequently extended by Scott Blois and his Reconsider collaborators, who have added many improvements in software services. To our mutual regret, AMA has not made comparable improvements to the data base itself.

I should mention, however, that even the early version of CMT (later called CMIT) contained literature references. These were part of the tape record, even though they were not part of the printed books. This impressed on me the tremendous power of the formal scientific literature, as well as the great scope of even the central core of medical knowledge. We frequently demonstrated the system with half-a-dozen excellent clinicians present, in addition to students and residents. I'm certain there never was a time when the differential diagnoses Consider produced did not far exceed the range of thinking and knowledge of the observers. Our simple reasoning that "you can't diagnose something you don't consider" was compelling then and remains so today.

The Regional Medical Program must be mentioned. To me, this was a wonderful development by the Federal Government. It turned out to be short-lived, but during this period we had the privilege of testing the Caceres PHS system for EKG interpretation {7}. Luther Terry was PHS surgeon general at the time. He called to initiate the demonstration and trial. This was the first time the Caceres system had been used "in real life" outside the Federal labs. Now that I am a "Fed," I can understand better why this was so. We tested it statewide in 22 different kinds of settings. We found it to be the most appealing and understandable of all the RMP-proffered aids to medical care. I should also note that in addition to Dr. Caceres, Hubert Pipberger from the Veterans Administration was most generous in giving me help and advice in this RMP project. I won't describe the Caceres system in detail. The bottom line scientifically is that it worked extremely well. In general practice settings, 90% of the tracings were normal; 70% from a group of three cardiologists were normal; and 50% from tertiary-care hospitals were normal. Fortunately "normal wave form" was a highly reliable statement, as were many of the 150 interpretations. The statements concerning complex arrhythmias were hampered by the relatively short length of tracing then being studied. The bottom line from the point of view of health services research was that the system, with its costly data acquisition carts, transmission, and processing charges was relatively expensive for a rural area like central Missouri but an instant economic success in cities like St. Louis and San Francisco {8}.

A turning point for me professionally came in 1971 after about 10 years of directing the Medical Computer Program. We had by then fully operational information systems in clinical laboratory, radiology, dietary, business office, and an institutional integrated file that combined all these medical data with discharge diagnoses, surgical operating room records, surgical pathology and cytology diagnoses, and EKG interpretations. The clinical literature system was laggard. We had established an SDI (Selective Dessemination of Information) system for scientific journal articles and were prepared to leave the rest to NLM! I realized at the time that the future of the field and my own desires lay in research and teaching, not with hospital service systems. The Computer Program had grown from five persons and $98,000 per year in 1962 to 125 people and over $4 million in 1970. Consequently we recruited Dr. Peter Reichertz to become director of the Computer Program, and I formed the Information Science Group. The latter has ever since been dedicated to efforts to train the cadre of scientists and health professionals that are needed to build the theoretical and scientific basis for future advances in this field.

This brings me to closing on the topic, what has *not* happened in 25 years? Briefly, we have *not* seen the creation of the body of theory and principles that should underlie our efforts. That we use better, faster computers and more pleasant display devices is simply due to our coupling with the aerospace and business technology evolution. More importantly, medical informatics has remained reasonably well coupled with advances in understanding of basic biomedical fields. This is a struggle: how to keep current in a technical area and in clinical medicine simultaneously. We can already see that the cutting edge research in molecular biology/biotechnology is seriously challenging even the best people in medical informatics to make room once again for brand-new ideas. Biotechnology is especially challenging because at the moment it benefits so much from mathematical computation at a time when medical informatics has halfway convinced itself it needs only symbolic reasoning.

The real value of a day of retrospection such as this one must surely be to see more clearly how to progress. The day is just starting, so we must not draw hasty conclusions. Yet I'll bet we will see and hear lots of reasons today to invest in individual creative investigators; that we will see many examples of the need for an atmosphere of interdisciplinary research on topics of fundamental importance; and that we will end the day wanting scope and support for building the formal academic basis for medical informatics.

References

1. Lindberg, D.A.B. and Reese, G. Automatic measurement and computer processing of bacterial growth data. *Proc Biomed Sci Instrumentation Symposium*, Los Angeles, California, June 14–17, 1963. New York: Plenum Press, pp. 11–20.

2. Lindberg, D.A.B. and Stewart, G.T. Exercises in the logistics of chemotherapy. *Antimicrobial Agents and Chemother* 1965; 168–176.

3. Lindberg, D.A.B. Electronic processing and transmission of clinical laboratory data. *Missouri Med* 62:296–302, 1965.

4. Lindberg, D.A.B. *The Computer and Medical Care*. Springfield, Illinois: Thomas, 1968.

5. Lindberg, D.A.B. Collection, evaluation, and transmission of hospital laboratory data. *Meth Information Med* 6:97–107, 1967.

6. Lindberg, D.A.B., Rowland, L.R., Buck, C.R., *et al.* CONSIDER: a computer program for medical instruction. *Proc Ninth IBM Med Symposium*, White Plains, New York, 1968. IBM.

7. Lindberg, D.A.B. and Amlinger, P.R. Automated analysis of the electrocardiogram. *Missouri Med* 65:742–745, 1968.

8. Lindberg, D.A.B. *The Growth of Medical Information Systems in the United States*. Lexington, Massachusetts: D.C. Heath and Company, Lexington Books, 1979.

Participants' Discussion

Thomas Lincoln	It seems to me that the Autochemists® did go into some use. For example, in the early 1970s it was used in the British private health services as a screening device, and it produced at least executive physical results. Would you comment on this?
Donald Lindberg	I actually have a photo of the Autochemist® at Kaiser-Permanente, but I thought conceivably somebody else would show it. There's no question it worked. The questions are what do you do with those 40 channels of information and what conceptual model lies behind your wanting them? And if there is a model, why did the Swedes and the British have a totally different set of so-called screening tests than we had in the U.S.? I just couldn't find any principles or any sense to it. I loved the technology. Nobody likes all those stainless steel pistons any better than I do, but we took a pass on it—we didn't put that in.
William E. Hammond	How far ahead did you know where you were going over this period that you described to us? How much of it was event-driven by things that happened and how much of it was a pathway that you knew you were heading for over that period of time?
Donald Lindberg	Well, I was always motivated toward discovery in biomedicine. That's why I was in a university rather than out running a clinical laboratory; that part of it was very definitely programmed. I think everyone in the field overestimates their own capability and underestimates the difficulties. That's part of it. We thought, we will quickly rap out the laboratory and then we will take on the clinical record, and when we have those two together we'll have a super teaching program and we can revise medical education and then … what?

But you know, everyone's like that. I remember the time Jordan Baruch showed me at the beginning of that MGH BBN program that they had a FASTRAN drum. As I remember it, the drum was 10 or 11 feet long and sat there humming nicely. I asked him what they were going to do with it, and he said, "We're going to computerize Mass General Hospital on this end of it, and then we'll do the other 12 hospi- |

12

tals in Boston." When I told that to Octo [Barnett], he said, "You should have been there the morning when all the oil leaked out of it."

I guess everybody responds to opportunities, and to me the most important opportunities are the intellectual working circumstances. The ideal is the place where you can actually have a multidisciplinary collaboration and a proper exchange of ideas. That's one of the reasons I love NIH. This kind of circumstance has enhanced all of the good work in our field. The lack of a harmonious collaborative environment has held back good people in bad places. I think that's a strong pattern we see. If I were going to politicize, I would say that I hope this day ends with the firm conclusion that we need more theory and science behind our work. We also need academic departments to develop the field.

How DENDRAL Was Conceived and Born

Joshua Lederberg, PhD
Rockefeller University, New York

This will be a somewhat personal history of how I came to work with Ed Feigenbaum on DENDRAL, an exemplar of expert systems and of modeling problem-solving behavior. My recollections are based on a modest effort of historiography, but not a definitive survey of and search for all relevant documents. On the other hand, my recollections will give more of the flow of ideas and events as they happened than is customary in published papers in scientific journals—accounts so dry that Medawar lugubriously called them fraudulent {43} (compare Merton & Zuckerman {44, 45, 61}). These authors point out that the standard scientific publication is narrow-mindedly devoted to the context of justification. The DENDRAL effort (along with much of medical informatics) is dedicated to discovery: Should we use a different standard for its history?

This is a first effort at historical research and informed consensus on the origins of DENDRAL; and we all understand the limitations of a personal account—especially about what others were thinking at a given moment. Built into the phenomenon of history, as soon as enough time has passed to enable some detached judgment, the evidence becomes frail, and we become vulnerable to the myths we create. Understanding all of these limitations, I will no longer qualify every remark: It should be implicit that each is "to the best of my recollection" or "as best as can be inferred from the fragmentary documentary record."

I will assume you are generally familiar with DENDRAL and will concentrate mainly on material not found in the published papers, especially as there is a comprehensive synopsis of its postnatal productions {41}. My story will focus on the period up to the recognition that what we were working on was a knowledge-based system (ca. 1971).

Because computer science is not my primary profession, my relationship to it has been more episodic; and I can more readily isolate how I came to take some part in it, at Stanford from 1962 to 1978, mainly in very close collaboration with Ed Feigenbaum, Bruce Buchanan, and a host of others. My central scientific commitments have been to molecular genetics, starting in 1945 when I was a 20-year-old medical student {38}. At Columbia and then at Yale, I worked on the

1. 1937–1943. Leibniz dream; Logic & Axiomatic Method: Studies in Columbia College

2. 1941, 1953, 1962. Computer hardware: Desultory exposures

3. 1947 ff. Information-theoretic formulations in genetics

4. 1953 ff. Introspections about the history of bacterial genetics

5. 1960. Instrumentation development for Mars exploration: NASA

6. 1955, 1959, 1961, 1963. Meet Minsky, Djerassi, McCarthy, Feigenbaum

   (In every biographic-historic account in science, one seeks an interplay of personality, ideas, institutional setting, and other externalities.)

FIGURE 1
Conceptual and experiential threads leading to the DENDRAL project

---

genetics of bacteria, a specialty which converged with the function of DNA as genetic information. My first academic appointment was at the University of Wisconsin from 1947 to 1958; then I went to Stanford in 1959 to take part in the reconstruction of its School of Medicine (formerly in San Francisco) at the Palo Alto campus. My intended role was to found a new Department of Genetics; I had no plan to be working with computers. Fate dictated otherwise: I met Ed Feigenbaum in 1963. Then, promptly after he moved from Berkeley to the Stanford faculty in early 1965, we initiated the collaboration that became the DENDRAL project.

These were hardly random events: I go back a few years to pick up the relevant premonitory strands, which I identify in Figure 1. It provides a roadmap for the narrative that follows.

(1) Starting in grade school, I had fantasies that echo Leibniz' dream (see {13}) of a "universal calculus" for the "alphabet of human thought," that all of knowledge might be so systematized that every fact could be tagged with a code. Compare Mortimer Adler's Propaedia {1}.

New York City in the late 1930s offered wonderful encouragement to self-improvement through education, in my own case at Stuyvesant High School and at the New York Public Library. There I was fascinated with the Dewey Decimal System, which was so helpful in locating the books. If I could but memorize that, it would be proxy for mastery of all the knowledge it classified. In those days, taxonomy dominated biological teaching too. (I will not detain you now with the perils of misplaced confidence in low-dimensional, or insight-free knowledge. They need to be remembered when we try to extract "knowledge" from an expert, measure how much we have, and so forth.)

Although I was committed from a very early age to a career in experimental biology, while in college I was eager to have some understanding of the epistemological roots of science, and I enrolled in several courses in logic and scientific method. At Columbia, I was fortunate to have some personal exposure to members of the philosophy department: Ernest Nagel, Justus Buchler, and James Gutmann. With their help, I read George Boole and Whitehead & Russell {58}, and tried to follow J.H. Woodger in his Axiomatic Method in Biology {59}— an effort to express what was then known of genetics and embryology in the formalisms of relational calculus. Our factual knowledge was sparse enough; but apart from that, I wondered if we really understood our assertions when they were expressed in the jargon of empirical biochemistry. Axiomatic reformulations of biology are only just now returning to the scene {3, 54, 57, 47}. They make the intellectual demand of coping both with the formal logic and the molecular biology.

That background gives some flavor of the retrospection about method that has entered my thought sometimes during, often after, my experimental research projects. That would precondition me to look to AI as a way of expressing my philosophy of scientific method, a perspective eloquently stated by Lindley Darden {66}.

(2) My first encounter with a "computer" was in 1941, in a lab for high school students sponsored by IBM {23}. My own instrument was a microscope, but one of my fellows was making innovative improvements on a punch card sorter/tabulator. It was an impressive manifestation of an electro-mechanical automaton, one that could certainly calculate more reliably than I could. It looked like fun. After the war, there was some publicity about the electronic machines, which I read at the level of *Scientific American* or *Science* magazines. But my own next step was the IBM 602A, on which I practiced in Fred Gruenberger's course at Wisconsin, in 1953, in order to get some concept of programming, albeit on a plugboard! One could do statistics on this machine, as did some of my colleagues in applied genetics, but I had no comparable excuse to play with it.

(3) That postwar period also saw the elaboration of information-theoretic formulations of genetics. We were starting to say that genes encoded the information needed to specify protein structure {14, 51}. This style of thought and expression became more explicit in the period after 1953 {25} with the recognition of the implications of the Watson-Crick molecular structure of DNA {22}. It would be backward for anyone in my field to ignore this way of looking at the biological world. Then, Marvin Minsky came to see me at Wisconsin in 1955 at the behest of some mutual friend to discuss automata. I am sure I had already heard of some of his own work.

(4) My own laboratory research was a very mixed bag of theoretical formulation and empirical encounter. I had been extraordinarily lucky on several occasions—but I didn't want to be a hostage to chance: Should there not be a more systematic strategy of problem formulation? And if one could do that, problem-solving might be a throwaway. Serious questions about the rational direction of science were invoked around an examination of why genetic recombination in bacteria had not been explored 40 years earlier {24, 60}.

(5) Starting with the observation of Sputnik, and a conversation with J.B.S. Haldane in Calcutta in November 1957 {67}, I had set out to assure that fundamental biological science was properly represented in the programs of space research that were just emerging. I had met Haldane on a date that was both a lunar eclipse and the 40th anniversary of the Soviet October Revolution (almost precisely 30 years ago). He taunted me with the prospect that we might see a red star (a thermonuclear explosion) on the moon during the eclipse. At best, that was a striking metaphor for the danger that scientific interests would be totally submerged by the international military and propaganda competition. They have never gained first priority; they might have been totally excluded. My own efforts were merely advisory and critical until 1960, after NASA had organized a Life Sciences Research Office and asked me to establish an instrumentation laboratory at Stanford. With Elliott Levinthal's able technical direction of the lab, we became actively involved in the conceptual design of approaches to test for life on Mars, at such time as there might be a mission. I know most of my colleagues thought that would be well into the 21st century, as we were a decade short of the lunar landings. But the possibility of finding another branch of evolution was of such compelling scientific interest, the stake was worth odds I knew were very long.

Both the internal activities of the Instrumentation Research Laboratory (IRL) and design discussions with the engineering managers of spaceflight missions (principally at Cal Tech's JPL) brought us into intimate conversation with technology of automation, process control, communications, and computer management. Furthermore, mass spectrometry soon emerged as a technology of choice for chemical analysis. It has enormous sensitivity, selectivity, and independence of prior bias as to the molecular species expected {33}. As we shall see, it also offered some special opportunities and challenges in computation.

In 1961, I was also invited to serve on a President's Advisory Committee (PSAC) panel on the management of scientific information. Our report {50} gives modest support to the implications of computer technology, along with "reproducing and microphotographing equipment" for information storage and retrieval. However, I had become acquainted with Eugene Garfield, the inventor of Current Contents, and had helped him set up a trial run of the Science Citation Index in the field of genetics {36, 19}. That experience (with its overtones of the classification of knowledge for purposes of retrieval) was an early success in the use of computers in support of scientific research.

By now, I concluded that I would have to learn much more about computers, at a hands-on level. The opportunity was engendered by the evangelistic efforts of Al Bowker and George Forsythe to establish an intellectual and technical base for, and broaden interest in, computers throughout the Stanford campus. In company with the development of a new division, then department, of Computer Science, and of a campus-wide computer center, elementary programming courses were organized. I enrolled in the BALGOL (Burroughs Algol) course given by Bob Oakford, over the summer of 1962. This had much of the flavor of a course in English for fresh immigrants, the class having a very broad distribution of age and of academic status, specialty, and sophistication.

I quickly succumbed to the hacker syndrome (and have suffered episodic relapses over the last 25 years). This was reinforced by the relentless rectitude of the machine in rejecting my errors—always so obvious in retrospect. "Next time, next time I will master the #@!!** system!" Well, I did shortly become reasonably proficient (eventually, in a range from assembly to higher level languages) mostly out of determination not to be made a fool. In those days, we had a B220—which would match a fairly feeble PC today—as the first campus machine. Its operating system would accept decks of punched cards in serial batch mode, with output either from the printer or new punched cards. The usual turn-around time was about 12 hours. If you got to the computer room around midnight, you might get another pass by 2 A.M. The democracy and night owl ambience of the batch system was a social mixer for several enthusiasts from wide-ranging disciplines. (I particularly recall Tony Hearn, who was starting his symbolic algebra system, REDUCE, on the IBM 7090). The impedance of a one-pass per day turnaround certainly did filter out all but the most enthusiastic. You also spent a lot of energy trying to simulate the machine in your own thought, in contrast to the casual, experimental mode—"Let's see if this works"—of today's interactive systems. This mode has unquestioned advantages; but it may weaken programming as a teaching discipline for logical rigor (except insofar as pure, unremitting failure teaches mainly discouragement).

Our first applications included some that are pertinent to medical informatics, but not to DENDRAL, in areas of genetic epidemiology {6}, including a contract to produce the child-spacing report on the 1960 census. Bob Tucker was instrumental in sustaining our effectiveness and sanity through that experience. When we discovered that "children" of some mothers were delivered at 3-month intervals, I again learned the familiar GIGO lesson, and a healthy skepticism for mass data repositories. Massive numbers do not take the place of quality controls on individual data entries. Some other inquiries, e.g., of inter-correlations of season of birth and birth weight with postnatal out-comes, taught us the difficulties of removing all the confounding factors. The usual "socioeconomic status indicators" do not begin to exhaust the vagaries of stratification of human behavior.

1962 also marked the recruitment of John McCarthy to Stanford. We met around the computer room, and soon discovered we had a common friend in Marvin Minsky. I had read Marvin's article on steps toward artificial intelligence in the January 1961, special issue on com-puters of the *Proceedings of the Institute of Radio Engineers* {46}, the first issue I received as a newly enrolled member (having joined at the urg-ing of Lloyd Berkner, chair of the Space Science Board). That article and McCarthy's intellect and excitement gave me a sense of tangibility of the possibility of engaging in AI research. When he showed me his new DEC PDP-1 and its interactive CRT displays (namely, Spacewar) I reached the conviction that "computers were going to change the whole style of scientific investigation." This was not going to happen with card-deck data entry.

We soon conspired in various projects to try to enhance the inter-face of computers with medical science. The most ambitious of these was an effort to attract Marvin Minsky to join the faculty of Stanford Medical School, but unhappily for us he decided to stay at MIT. We also began to talk about bringing interactive computing, via time-shar-ing, to Stanford, along the lines of Project MAC, which John had helped to design at MIT. These discussions ultimately led to ACME and SUMEX, the first community-access time-shared systems at Stanford, as we discovered that the NIH was able to fund research resources for health research through its Biotechnology Resources Branch. McCarthy's PDP-1 also led us to emulate it as a laboratory interface computer, and our IRL signed on as one of the test sites for the new LINC (laboratory instrumentation computer) whose development NIH was sponsoring. Lee Hundley and Nick Veizades provided the indis-pensable hardware engineering expertise to enable us to master this marvelous new machine. The LINC was, of course, the forerunner of the DEC PDP-8, and in turn, of the PC revolution.

Meanwhile, the IRL was getting more actively involved in mass spectrometry. Carl Djerassi had come to the chemistry department in late 1959, and we had developed a close personal and professional as-sociation around his academic research as well as his continued re-search direction of the Syntex Corporation. (Upon the company's relocation from Mexico City to new laboratories at Stanford Industrial Park in 1961, he asked me to advise on its establishment of the Syntex Institute of Molecular Biology.) He was an accomplished mass spectrometrist, and of course I leaned very heavily on him for the elaboration of this technology for space applications. Conversely, he knew nothing about computers, and I was eager to find helpful applications in the zone of our common interest. The IRL began to work on using the LINC to manage the formidable data management problems of real-time gas-chromatography mass-spectrometry {52}. One central problem was the efficient translation of mass numbers to molecular formulas.

As I reexamine that arithmetic play, it reveals some premonitions of the later work. So I will expand on it beyond the intrinsic worth of the solutions {29}. The mass spectrometer is an instrument that converts molecules of a sample material into ions that are accelerated and measured one by one. Further, by a combination of magnetic and electrostatic fields, each ion can be sorted by its mass number. For the initial discussion, we will consider only the molecular ion, ignoring further processes of fragmentation. At low resolution, we take atomic masses as integers (H = 1; C = 12; N = 14; O = 16; etc.). If we find a mass number of 14, this might be composed of H(14), C + H(2), or N. H(14) is a monstrosity: We have valence rules (H $\approx$ 1; C $\approx$ 4; N $\approx$ 3; O $\approx$ 2) that limit how many atoms can be bonded to a given atom. The ambiguity already seen at m = 14 is of course greatly multiplied in real cases, like m = 3675, a number which reflects the bounds of current instrumentation. Our first problem is to calculate all the compositional isomers consistent with a given mass number. At this level, it is a knapsack, or change-making problem: finding all the ways coins of different denomination can be combined to add up to a given sum. In nonnegative integers, this is a diophantine equation. Namely, we seek all the solutions (i.e., compositions in h, c, n, o) of:

$$h + 12c + 14n + 16o + \ldots = m.$$

The brute force approach is a set of nested iterations,

```
for (h = 1; h <= Z ; h++);
    for (n = 1; n <= Z ; n++) ... m' = h + 14n + ...
```

and test the m' sums for a match to m. One simplification is to augment m, $m'' = m + k == 0$ mod 12. We then eliminate c and find solutions in h, n, o that satisfy $(h + k) + 14n + 16o == 0$ mod 12. I would be interested to learn of deeper analytic approaches to the problem. For on-line computation, one thinks of constraining Z, at least by the mass still unassigned in each loop, to reasonable bounds. It transpired that the valence considerations also set constraints on possible values of h; and other tricks allowed still further pruning of the tree generated by the nest, greatly shortening the computation.

Prior aides to mass spectrometrists had been published tables (embracing 570 pages in print) that reported the compositions sorted by m, from about 1 to 500, with n and o no greater than 6 {4}. A full set of tables for m up to 1000 would take about 10,000 pages of fine print.

In reality, the masses of individual nuclides are not integers (subject to the so-called nuclide packing fraction), and we have

H = 1.0078252
C = 12.0 (by definition)
N = 14.003074
O = 15.994915

With a high resolution mass spectrometer, a given ion might be reported as 718.374 ± .006. Hundreds of compositions would match 718 in integers. One should use the fractional mass (.374) as equally important information in limiting the search. We no longer have an equation in integers, owing to the instrumental error. Nevertheless, various arithmetic tricks were devised that took account of valence rules, plausibility of composition, the negative and positive packing fractions of O and N, and the abnormal proportional discrepancy of H, to keep the search down to a manageable scope.

For paper and pencil work (in 1964) this was embodied in a handbook of some 50 pages, in which one could quickly look up the "mass defect" of numbers classified by residues modulo 12 {26}. Even that small book was later {35} obsoleted by an algorithm that depended on a one-page table with just 72 nonzero entries, and a few arithmetic steps easily done on a 4-function hand calculator. This algorithm has served well in the data system built for a GC-MS (gas-chromatograph/mass-spectrometer) designed around a MAT-711 MS {62} and the LINC computer. It has evidently been independently rediscovered in China {63}. By now, however, most machines are coupled with data processors that are oblivious to such economies. (And mass spectrometrists no longer give much thought to the arithmetic of this problem.)

The main point is self-evident: Contextual information could be incorporated early into the combinatorics and reduce a blind generate-and-test search by very large factors.

We turn now to the larger frame of chemical analysis. Molecular ions are important targets for mass spectrometry; in the ideal case they can give unambiguous compositional formulas. Of course, they tell nothing of the topological connectivity of the constituent atoms. To illustrate with a trivial case, C(2) H(6) O has a mass of 46.041866 but this does not distinguish methyl ether (CH3-O-CH3) from ethanol (CH3-CH2-OH), a medically significant matter! Within the mass spectrometer, however, the molecular ion also breaks up into a set of fragments (according to reasonably well-understood rules). The spectrum is the array of these fragments, revealed by their mass numbers. It is often an absolutely distinctive fingerprint, diagnostic of a specific structural isomer (as the molecular ion mass number is of the composition).

The elementary problem of inferring composition from molecular mass now well-solved, could we take the next step: model the chemist's inferential procedure in finding the structure from the spectrum?

How to represent organic molecular structures in graphs, and then their dissection into subgraph fragments, as occurs in the mass spectrometer, became my task for 1963 to 1964. Emile Zuckerkandl, an associate of Linus Pauling, also visited my lab during this interval. We started some of the first statistical studies on amino acid sequences of proteins, looking for hints of nonrandom regularities within sequences, and unsuspected evolutionary relationships among different ones. This is a substantial industry today {40}; there were not enough published data in 1963 to offer more than a few tantalizing hints.

(6) All this was then the ideological context of my meeting Ed Feigenbaum on April 6, 1963. This was a Saturday meeting that Karl Pribram had organized at the Center for Advanced Studies in Behavioral Sciences on computer models of thought. John McCarthy, Ken Colby, and several others were also present. I told Ed how I was groping for ways to represent chemical structures; he was already on the lookout for problem areas in science to which to bring his background on mechanized problem-solving. We stayed in good contact; I have a signed copy of *Computers and Thought* dated 1/17/64 {15}.

During 1964, I completed the preliminary graph-theoretical work on representation of organic molecular structures {30, 32, 28}. That had entailed going back to the elementary graph theory of the 19th century for canonical forms of tree structures {21}. Fortunately, George Polya had done some important work on generating functions in 1936 {49} and was most generous in his advice about that older literature. When it came to cyclic graphs, I had a particularly entertaining time, almost at the level of recreational mathematics {31, 34}.

For a century after the conception of organic molecules as ensembles of connected atoms subject to structural isomerism (Berzelius, 1831 {48}, Crum, Brown, Butlerov, and Kekule in the 1860s {20}), no more than desultory attention was given to the formal mathematics of their representation as graphs, to the potentialities of a connection between Hamilton circuits, convex polytopes, and organic molecules {53}. It is hard to account for such an egregious lapse, one possibly another candidate for the label of a "postmature discovery" {60}. The topology was perhaps too elementary to engage the interest of serious mathematicians—but there are still intractable problems in the enumeration of cyclic graphs (after automorphisms!). Related issues, like the notorious map-coloring problem, illustrate the still primitive state of analytical

FIGURE 2

Mappings of cyclic chemical structures onto trivalent graphs—convex polyhedra from {28}

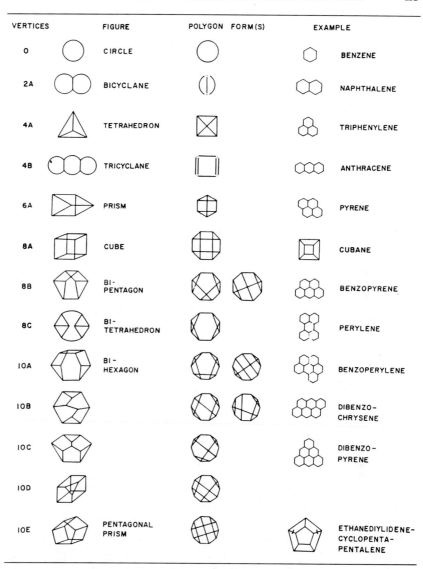

VERTICES	FIGURE		POLYGON FORM(S)	EXAMPLE	
0	○	CIRCLE	○		BENZENE
2A	◯◯	BICYCLANE	(|)		NAPHTHALENE
4A	△	TETRAHEDRON	⊠		TRIPHENYLENE
4B	◯◯◯	TRICYCLANE	‖□		ANTHRACENE
6A		PRISM			PYRENE
8A		CUBE			CUBANE
8B		BI-PENTAGON			BENZOPYRENE
8C		BI-TETRAHEDRON			PERYLENE
10A		BI-HEXAGON			BENZOPERYLENE
10B					DIBENZO-CHRYSENE
10C					DIBENZO-PYRENE
10D					
10E		PENTAGONAL PRISM			ETHANEDIYLIDENE-CYCLOPENTA-PENTALENE

approaches to the taxonomy of graphs. Cayley {12} made a stab (a fallacious one) at the enumeration of the hydrocarbons; this was improved on by Henze and Blair in the 1930s {5}. In the mid-1960s, Balaban and his colleagues in Romania began their extensive investigations independently of the work at Stanford {2}.

Chemistry has then developed a taxonomy of its own structures that has no coherent mathematical theme. It is full of colorful but trivial names that give no structural information: A few eccentricities like "windowpane" for four fused rectangles are a partial exception. A formidable burden in learning chemistry is the enormous amount of rote memorization that is entailed in associating names like butane, cholestane, cytosine, melezitose, xanthopterin—there are tens of thousands of these—with graphic representations. One may think of these as the passwords for admission to the secret society; they do deter many a student, and they may also impair a critical analytical perspective about organic chemistry. These pictures also have formal names, but the nomenclature that gives the rules for their translation occupies a thick book, mostly the idiosyncratic cases. DENDRAL-64 is a set of reports to NASA {30, 32, 28} that outlines an approach to formal representation of chemical graph structures, and a generator of all possible ones. Acyclic structures (trees) were readily tractable. Cyclic ones can be dealt with, mainly with the help of a few tricks that rely on an empirical enumeration of the underlying vertex graphs—this is feasible within the bounds of practical chemistry—which is analytically unsatisfying. It helped to learn about Hamilton Circuits of graphs (paths that touch each node just once) {27}, since the enumeration of these, and the elimination of automorphisms are greatly simplified.

When it came to the implementation of DENDRAL for (typical) organic molecules with imbedded rings, Harold Brown, Larry Hjelmeland, and Larry Masinter provided the group-theoretic general mathematical solutions to these perplexities {10, 8, 7}. A few molecules have been constructed precisely because they defy some constraints of topological simplicity—e.g., topological planarity, namely their connection graphs cannot be drawn on the plane without bonds crossing; as exceptions they make history and can be dealt with as such {31, 55}.

The DENDRAL generator was then designed so that only one canonical form of a possible automorphic proliferation is issued, greatly pruning the space of candidate graphs. This was the essential prerequisite for an AI program that could manage the generator and confront it with information derived from the mass spectrum. But I had no idea how one would go about translating these structural concepts into a computer program, nor whether this would be computationally feasible with available hardware. Even more telling, I had only secondhand access to the field of AI and barely knew how to relate these conjectures to the systematic approaches that were emerging {15}. It was fortunate indeed that Ed Feigenbaum came to Stanford just at this time. We promptly got together again and organized the collaboration that became the DENDRAL project.

Ed now deserves equal time in presenting his personal prehistory. Some of his oral history has appeared in McCorduck's book {42}. In addition, I have a few of his own words, excerpted from an electronic message:

Date: Thu 8 Mar 84 00:22:01 PST

From: Edward Feigenbaum <FEIGENBAUM@SUMEX-AIM. ARPA>

To: lederberg@SUMEX-AIM. ARPA

Subject: our history {*referring to some private notes*}

Josh, all of what you have written accords with my memory of things we discussed in 1965 as we quickly got to know each other better.

Your mention of mass spectral analysis as a problem domain in which we should work came as an answer to a question I posed you. I had decided that I wanted to work on constructing models of EMPIRICAL INDUCTION IN SCIENCE, within the methodology that I had learned from Newell and Simon, i.e., work on a concrete task domain, not in the abstract. So I needed a concrete task domain. You said you knew of one that contained the essence of the empirical induction problem, that you had been working on it for a while, you even had a computational algorithm underlying it (which immediately made me think: aha, legal move generator as in chess-playing programs). ALL of this conversation (embryonic research planning) took place AFTER I arrived at Stanford Jan 1, 1965, but I remember that I would not have sought you out for advice on the aforementioned puzzlement had I not met you earlier [April 1963] and learned of your interest in machine models of thinking. Recall: there were very very few people to talk to about machine models of thinking at Stanford in early 1965.

We didn't just "bump into each other" as in "lucky accident." You weren't at the [April 63] meeting by "lucky accident." I didn't decide to work with you on the mass spec analysis problem because it was of general intellectual stimulation. You had a definite interest in AI and I had a definite interest in hypothesis-formation/theory-formation. (Incidentally, do you remember how we went round and round on whether to deign to call what DENDRAL did "theory formation?" We decided on "hypothesis formation" to distinguish the case of one spectrum being explained by one (or a few) structures. We reserved the use of the term "theory formation" for a later date, for a more general approach, and decided to use it in describing Meta-DENDRAL (many spectra --> rule set).

P.S. Some things do appear to be "lucky accidents." It would appear to be a genuinely lucky accident that I chose to go to college at Carnegie Tech (an accident of Westinghouse scholarships and my family's financial condition), and a lucky accident that I met Herb Simon through Jim March, and that Herb paid attention to me, and that the Logic Theory program was invented while I was still a Carnegie Tech undergrad and that I was taking a seminar from Herb at the time of its invention. One level deeper: I was an ACTIVE RECEPTOR SITE re the idea of a computer. I had never even heard of an electronic digital computer before Herb handed me an IBM 701 manual, but... I had been entranced by mechanical calculator machines in high school and before. My father was an office manager/accountant and owned a giant, heavy Monroe or Marchant calculator. I became an expert on its use. I even remember dragging it with me miles on the bus to Weehawken High School, heavy as it was, just to show off my skill with this marvelous technology that no other kid in the high school knew anything about. So when Herb gave me that manual, he was projecting me five or six orders of magnitude into a territory I was already fascinated with. It was also very fortunate that my introduction to the electronic computer was via the computer as general symbol manipulator (Herb never mentioned that it was anything BUT that) and that my introduction to programming was via IPL 1 and 2. (I might add that such a sophisticated early view, given to me by Herb and Al Newell, has taken away most of the awe from later developments; everything else has seemed to be "merely" extensions of the great inventions and discoveries of the 1956–1959 period.)

END OF MESSAGE

It is now spring 1965, and our project is concretely launched. We began to think of and label it "Heuristic DENDRAL" to mark it as a refinement of the "DENDRAL Algorithm" for generating all the feasible structures. Ed and Richard Watson circulated a bulletin {16}, "An initial problem statement for a machine induction research project," to graduate students in computer science; but it was to take a few years of slow accretion to organize a cadre of collaborators. One of our first, research associate Georgia Sutherland, did a fabulous job on the formidable task of converting the concepts of DENDRAL-64 into a LISP program, interleaving its production with that of a baby: an early prototype of telecommuting. Her first report was issued February 1967 {56}: We finally had a working program with which we could all experiment with heuristics and other measures to bring its performance to practically useful levels. The choice of LISP was originally mandated by the good match of its data structures to trees, to the sparse connection tables of chemical structures. But the memory and bit crunching requirements were of course monumental—it's a wonder we got as far as we did with the hardware of the time. I used to remark, in arguments with ideologues, that in the last analysis it was the programming environment of INTERLISP that was its key advantage.

We were fortunate to have continued support from NASA and from DARPA to continue these explorations. We had quickly found that the campus IBM 7090 had too little memory to support our LISP programs; and we were eager to move to more interactive systems for program development. In 1966, our DARPA sponsorship gave us access to the Q-32 time-sharing system at System Development Corporation (Santa Monica) with a 100-baud teletype interface. My first experience with remote, time-shared hacking was a happy vision of future improvements. Then, John McCarthy acquired a DEC PDP-6, and we approached something closer to the modern era. Bruce Buchanan joined our group, and we had great benefit from his philosophical perspective, patience, insight, and administrative acumen, not to mention a lot of hard work in implementation of the software. We gained more and more collaborators, including the explicit involvement of Carl Djerassi and his associates as founts of authentic chemical expertise {64}. As our reports began to appear in refereed chemistry journals, we eventually bolstered our confidence that we were contributing to the scientific domain, as well as to system building—a point about which some of my colleagues had been skeptical. Broader access to these computer applications became possible with the help of the NIH-supported computer resources: ACME, a general time-sharing system for the Stanford Medical School, and SUMEX-AIM, a national resource to support research in artificial intelligence in medicine {11}. The history of SUMEX would take us into many lessons about the social organization of cooperative intelligence. However, as this account is now moving into a time of documented history and numerous publications {41}, I omit many details. Largely owing to the contributions of Carl Djerassi and his colleagues in natural products chemistry, the program was crammed with chemical information. It was becoming an effective assistant in the analysis of spectra and other analytical information. Buchanan recoded DENDRAL's knowledge of mass spectrometry, originally embodied in a collection of LISP procedures, into a table of explicit rules separated from the internal operations of the system. This redesign to facilitate augmenting, validating, and editing the informational (i.e., rule) base was a paradigm shift later to become the standard for expert systems. Balky resistance of the program to input of new ideas remained the limiting factor in its elaboration. At every weekly group meeting, a dozen new ideas would come up: But we knew that each one would take weeks to implement in tested software code, just to test it. Natural intelligence still enjoys a flexibility of hierarchical planning yet to be achieved in machine emulations {17}.

Throughout this time, we would ask ourselves the nagging question: Was the growing pragmatic success of DENDRAL in solving chemical problems teaching us anything about artificial intelligence? Had we simply crafted a special case, accumulating a hefty store of chemical knowledge from several experts? We did see the need for— and Bruce Buchanan made a stab at—a self-learning system, whereby Meta-DENDRAL could induce its own rules (as the chemist does) by introspecting about concrete data inputs of mass-spectral fragmentation of molecules of known structure. This showed real promise {10}, but was impeded by the insufficiency of computer horsepower needed when DENDRAL itself had to be invoked repetitively to test every new rule candidate induced.

We never got a grip on one idea that I hope to return to someday. DENDRAL is remarkably neatly structured (as implied by its name) as a generator of trees of candidate structures {39}. These can easily number in the billions or more, in practical cases. The efficiency of the program depends on the pruning of impossible or implausible cases, as early as possible; preferably large branches at a fell swoop. The order of application of the shears can have a large effect. To give a stupidly trivial example, if N (nitrogen) is absent, we don't generate molecules that may contain N, then retrospectively eliminate each of those twigs. We gave some forethought towards optimizing the sequence of shears; but we know this will be case-specific, sometimes in ways we have difficulty predicting. We should build in recurrent introspection about the shearing sequence, make that a specific planning objective, and experiment with it from time to time. These considerations (I called it Theta-DENDRAL for reasons not recalled) would have broad generalizability to rule-based systems: The sequence of invocation of rules is often totally inaccessible to the user, and rarely if ever (as far as I know) is it dynamically regulated.

We did do some work on the interesting trade-offs between storing memory of all partially completed branches versus regenerating them as needed. Finally, we had many discussions of the desirability of learning to read expertise from the world's published books, to bypass the oral tradition. The ultimate fantasy was to attach a high-order DENDRAL directly to a mass spectrometer, learning directly from Nature.

I wish I had the documentation, but I have an image of a conversation when I was pressing Ed about the limitations of DENDRAL as general intelligence: He responded with the illumination that I may paraphrase: "That's exactly the point! Knowledge, not tricks or metaphysical insight, is what makes the program effective—and that itself is an insight of general import." That is why I remark, we were trying to invent AI, and in the process discovered an expert system. This shift of paradigm, "that Knowledge IS Power" was explicated in our 1971 paper {17} and has been the banner of the knowledge-based system movement within AI research from that moment. (Compare Alan Newell's comments {65}.)

Shortly thereafter, Bruce Buchanan and Ted Shortliffe initiated the MYCIN project {9}. As Alan Newell remarked in his preface to {9}, MYCIN had no pretensions to deep theoretical structure of chemistry, none to outdoing the experts, but only to conveying that expertise as advisory to the general practitioner in optimizing the prescription of antibiotics. Their coding of MYCIN gave a fresh start to the design of rule-based systems that could be readily transported to other applications.

The published documentation after this time is quite rich, and I will refer to that for further historical development. Time now for the numerous morals of the story.

Most problematical is the public utility of private autobiography. But biography remains very popular, albeit the main lesson may be the very idiosyncrasy of personal history and character. Worse than no history would be a false conception of it, that it has rigorous rules. As my tale shows, chance does play an enormous role in bringing together people, ideas, situation in a productive way. Were we lucky? Who knows what the alternatives might have been?

One lesson of personality should be brought out, especially when the media enjoy characterizing the scientific enterprise as rapacious competition and selfishness. The fraternity that came out of the DEN-DRAL effort was a high in my life experience, matching the gratifications of scientific excitement and (perhaps belated) recognition. One is not always so lucky in one's colleagues; but we should not glamorize and confuse the pathology as the standard.

The project also dramatized the values of electronic communication in project management. Although we certainly met informally from time to time, most of our serious communication (be it a few yards down the hall) was by electronic mail. In this way, innumerable proposals and drafts could be posted on common bulletin boards and subjected to consensual review, often through scores of cycles of reiteration. Distance was no consideration, courtesy of the ARPANET, and communication could be sustained during momentary travel; collaboration continued when participants moved. (Of course, the manuscript for this chapter has been shared between Rockefeller and Stanford.) Such draft texts, program modules and outputs needed critical scrutiny of a kind that is only possible when one has a copy of the file to work on from one's own terminal. I went so far as to characterize this mode of communication "The New Literacy," and I meant it {37}. Databases should not be thought of as static, final repositories but as bulletin boards, subjected to dynamic critical attention by the entire knowledgeable community.

Stanford University, in the 1960s, was a fortunate place to be for the pursuit of scientific innovation, and equally for a highly interdisciplinary program. Computer science, medical science, and chemistry were all in a surge of rapid expansion and new opportunity. If there were no specific facilitations for these kinds of interactions, nor were there rigid impediments. There were potential problems of disciplinary homes for the degrees sought by graduate students; but in the event we never found any students who looked for a degree in what might have been a difficult hybrid of say genetics, chemistry, and informatics. The graduates in the project were able to justify themselves by the standards of the major department. The *laissez-faire* philosophy of the institution worked admirably, so long as we were able to secure funding. While we had the usual share of crises, we should look back in awe at the forbearance of the three agencies, NASA, DARPA, and NIH, who did make significant risk investments in a novel venture. Needless to say, all of the senior professors were also staking their credibility in the process. There is no guarantee that untenured faculty would have been able to feel so secure.

The greatest hurdle in efforts to replicate the experience would be to find experts willing and positioned to be able to forego continued immediate productivity in their own fields, for the sake of longer term ends in system building. Students and fellows may be intimidated by the demands of working across disciplines, and some were concerned that there would be a limited market in say artificial intelligence in molecular biology. Their prudence may be pragmatically justified. The process of knowledge extraction is unbelievably arduous: As always, 90% of the effort must go into debugging and validation. The process can give the expert an opportunity for critical self-reflection about the foundations of the scientific domain. Some of the return on investment of DENDRAL was in its motivating a fresh study of the conceptual structure of organic chemistry, apart from its actual application in computer programs. This is to be commended in problem choice in other areas of application, scientific or otherwise.

The choice of organic chemistry and mass spectrometry as an object domain was a matter of careful reflection. It was rich in experimental data, and in a conceptual framework of mechanism that lent itself to model construction on the computer; I had no taste for purely statistical correlations. I might have preferred molecular genetics as more germane, and closer to my own experience. But in 1965 I did not feel it had ripened sufficiently to allow a secure theoretical framework for the necessary deductive tests of candidate hypotheses. (By 1975 it had, and this perception was the root of the follow-on MOLGEN project {18}.) In his 1961 review, Minsky had been rather critical of generate-and-test paradigms: "for any problem worthy of the name, the search through all possibilities will be too inefficient for practical use." He had chess playing in mind with 10^{120} possible move paths. It is true that equally intractable problems, like protein folding, are known in chemistry and other natural sciences. These are also difficult for human intelligence. The heuristics we have evolved biologically tend instead to relate to real world faculties like speech and image recognition. Nevertheless, solution spaces of 10^6 to 10^{12} candidates are both interesting and feasible challenges to computation, and many are of scientific or technological consequence. Our particular problem in chemical analysis is one of exhaustive elimination, to find ALL solutions that match the spectral data set. Further measures may then be needed for a final disambiguation. Theorem-proving is a reasonably good analogy. Our chemical heuristics are second order: to find efficient ways of rigorously pruning the search tree, though it can be helpful to find a single approximate solution from the most plausible genera of chemical structures (e.g., rings limited to 5 or 6 nodes) and examine ways in which it can be altered and give the successfully matching spectrum. Whatever heuristics are used, no search branches can be discarded without the rationale being transparent to the chemist. Unlike chess or image understanding, chemistry does have an intrinsic mathematical structure that permits its move generator to heed the constraints of the data, so that efficiency is more readily achievable. And we have criteria, both for a formally correct candidate (a graph in canonical form), and to know when it is a solution, i.e., the test generates a spectrum that matches the data. We played against Nature. In chess (and in war), you have to play against another "expert."

Other areas of natural science deserve a fresh reconnaissance to inspire a reexamination of their conceptual structure. Biology, in particular, will soon suffocate in the sheer bulk of knowledge about DNA and protein structures, and the complex interactions of the causal chains they initiate, unless new epistemological machinery can be invented. Our education of physicians and scientists must also place more stress on the skills needed to acquire new knowledge as needed than on rote memorization that will promptly be obsolete {68}.

Finally, I would remark that I have never viewed research on artificial intelligence as having much bearing on how the human brain functions: There are too many differences in architecture and in levels of complexity, connectivity, and programmability. Nor do I see how neurobiology has contributed very much to AI. At the highest level of problem-solving routines, expert systems do of course exploit human experience. Lindley Darden's discussion of "the history of science as compiled hindsight" {66} eloquently captures my own perspectives. My interest in AI has little to do with my background as a biologist, a great deal with curiosity about complex systems that follow rules of their own, and which have great potentialities in preserving the fruits of human labor, of sharing hard-won traditions with the entire community. In that sense, the knowledge-based system on the computer is above all a remarkable social device, the ultimate form of publication.

Acknowledgment

It is impossible to give fair and sufficient credit to the many graduate students, collaborators, and programmers who made this effort possible. Where possible, they have been named in {41} and its bibliography. We are also indebted to the agency sponsors, primarily in DARPA, NIH, and NASA whose financial support made the work possible. They often made us work hard on our proposals to justify that support; but it clearly was a gamble that demanded a gift of confidence of unusual measure. The author would also like to acknowledge the National Academy of Sciences for permission to reprint material from Topological mapping of organic moelcules, by J. Lederberg, *Proceedings of the National Academy of Sciences*, vol 53, pp. 134–139, 1965.

Bibliography

In addition to the references tabulated, the following archival sources would be instrumental for further historical research:

The Stanford University Computer Science Department: A.I. Lab Reports (microfiches available from Scientific DataLink, Comtex Sci. Corp.) Most of these are indexed in {41}.

Annual reports to NIH on the DENDRAL and SUMEX projects. Archived at Stanford and Rockefeller Universities.

Annual reports to NASA on the S.U., Department of Genetics Instrumentation Research Laboratory. Archived as above, and inventoried by the U.S. NTIS.

Peer critiques, NIH study sections and councils. Available, in principle, from NIH under the FoI Act. This should be a rich resource in tracing contemporary reactions.

Buchanan, Feigenbaum, Lederberg, notes, correspondence, and electronic mail files. To be archived, as above.

References

1. Adler, M.J. Propaedia (outline of knowledge). *Encyclopedia Britannica*, 15 ed. Chicago, 1985.

2. Balaban, A.T. (ed.). *Chemical Applications of Graph Theory*. New York: Academic Press, 1976.

3. Balzer, W. and Dawe, C.M. Structure and comparison of genetic theories: (I) Classical genetics. *Brit. J. Phil. Sci.* 37, 1 (Mar.), 55–69, 1986.

4. Beynon, J.H. and Williams, A.E. *Mass and Abundance Tables for Use in Mass Spectrometry*. New York: Elsevier, 1963.

5. Blair, C.M. and Henze, H.R. The number of structurally isomeric alcohols of the methanol series. *J. Amer. Chem.* 53, 3042–3046, 1931.

6. Bodmer, W.F. and Lederberg, J. Census data for studies of genetic demography. *Proc. III Int. Congress of Human Genetics*, Baltimore: Johns Hopkins Press, 1967, pp. 459–471.

7. Brown, H. and Masinter, L.M. Algorithm for the construction of the graphs of organic molecules. *Discrete Mathematics* 8:227–244, 1974.

8. Brown, H., Hjelmeland, L., and Masinter, L.M. Constructive graph labelling using double cosets. *Discrete Mathematics* 7:1–30, 1974.

9. Buchanan, B.G. and Shortliffe, E.H. *Rule-based Expert Systems*. Reading, Mass.: Addison-Wesley, 1984.

10. Buchanan, B.G., Smith, D.H., White, W.C., Gritter, R., Feigenbaum, E.A., Lederberg, J., and Djerassi, C. Applications of artificial intelligence for chemical inference, XXII. Automatic rule formation in mass spectrometry by means of the meta-DENDRAL program. *J. Am. Chem. Soc.* 98:6168–6178, 1976.

11. Carhart, R.E., Johnson, S.M., Smith, D.H., Buchanan, B.G., Dromey, R.G., and Lederberg, J. Networking and a collaborative research community: A case study using the DENDRAL programs. In Peter Lykos, (ed.) *Computer Networking and Chemistry*, ACS Symposium Series, No. 19. Washington: American Chemical Society, 1975.

12. Cayley, A. On the mathematical theory of isomers. *Phil. Mag.* 47, 444–446, 1874.

13. Cohen, M.R. and Nagel, E. *An Introduction to Logic and Scientific Method*. New York: Harcourt, Brace and Company, 1934.

14. Ephrussi, B., Leopold, U., Watson, J.D., and Weigle, J.J. Terminology in bacterial genetics. *Nature* 171: 701, 1953.

15. Feigenbaum, E.A. and Feldman, J., (eds.). *Computers and Thought*. New York: McGraw-Hill, 1963.

16. Feigenbaum, E.A. and Watson, R. An initial problem statement for a machine induction research project. Stanford AI Memo # 40, 1965.

17. Feigenbaum, E.A., Buchanan, B.G., and Lederberg, J. On generality and problem solving: A case using the DENDRAL program. *Machine Intelligence* 6, Meltzer, B. and Michie, D., (eds.). Edinburgh: Edinburgh University Press, 1971, pp. 165–190.

18. Friedland, P. and Kedes, L. Discovering the secrets of DNA. *Comm. ACM* 28:1164–1186, 1985.

19. Garfield, E. *Citation Indexing—Its Theory and Application in Science, Technology, and Humanities*. Philadelphia: ISI Press, 1979, p. 274.

20. Gould, R.F., (ed.). *Kekule Centennial. Advances in Chemistry Series 61*. Washington: American Chemical Society, 1966.

21. Jordan, C. Sur les assemblages de lignes. J. fuer die reine und angewandte. *Math.* 70,185 (1869).

22. Judson, H.F. *The Eighth Day of Creation: Makers of the Revolution in Biology*. New York: Simon & Schuster, 1979.

23. Kinney, H. The year of the gifted children. *Think* (IBM) 45:12–17, 1979.

24. Lederberg, J. Genetics and microbiology. *Symposium on Perspectives and Horizons in Microbiology*. Rutgers: Rutgers Univ. Press, 1955, pp. 24–39.

25. Lederberg, J. A view of genetics. Les Prix Nobel, 1958, pp. 170–189.

26. Lederberg, J. *Computation of Molecular Formulas for Mass Spectrometry*. San Francisco: Holden-Day, Inc, 1964.

27. Lederberg, J. Hamilton circuits of convex trivalent polyhedra (up to 18 vertices). *Am. Math Monthly* 74, 522–527, 1965.

28. Lederberg, J. Systematics of organic molecules, graph topology and Hamilton circuits. A general outline of the DENDRAL system. NASA CR-68899. STAR No. N66–14075, 1965.

29. Lederberg, J. Online computation of molecular formulas from mass number. NASA CR-95977; Accession # x68–18613, 1966.

30. Lederberg, J. DENDRAL-64. A system for computer construction, enumeration & notation of organic molecules as tree structures and cyclic graphs. Part I. Notational algorithm for tree structures. NASA CR-57029. STAR No. N65–13158, 1964.

31. Lederberg, J. Topological mapping of organic molecules. *Proc. Nat. Acad. Sci.* U.S. 53, 134–139, 1965.

32. Lederberg, J. DENDRAL-64. Part II. Topology of cyclic graphs. NASA CR-68898. STAR No. N66–14074, 1965.

33. Lederberg, J. Signs of Life: Criterion system of exobiology. *Nature* 207, 9–13, 1965.

34. Lederberg, J. Topology of molecules. *The Mathematical Sciences* (COSRIMS). Cambridge: MIT Press, 1969, pp. 37–51.

35. Lederberg, J. Rapid calculation of molecular formulas from mass values. *J. Chem. Ed.* 49, 613, 1972.

36. Lederberg, J. Foreword to *Essays of an Information Scientist* by E. Garfield. Philadelphia: ISI Press, 1977, pp. xi-xi.

37. Lederberg, J. Digital communications and the conduct of science: The new literacy. *Proc. of the IEEE* 1978, 66(11):1314–1319.

38. Lederberg, J. Forty years of genetic recombination in bacteria. A fortieth anniversary reminiscence. *Nature* 327:627–628, 1986.

39. Lederberg, J., Sutherland, G.L., Buchanan, B.G., Feigenbaum, E.A., Robertson, A.V., Duffield, A.M., and Djerassi, C. Applications of

artificial intelligence for chemical inference, I. The number of possible organic compounds. Acyclic structures containing C, H, O, and N. *J. Am. Chem. Soc.* 91:2973–2976, 1969.

40. Lewin, R. National networks for molecular biologists. *Science* 223, 1379–1380, 1984.

41. Lindsay, R.K., Buchanan, B.G., Feigenbaum, E.A., and Lederberg, J. *Applications of Artificial Intelligence for Organic Chemistry: The DENDRAL Project.* New York: McGraw-Hill Book Co, 1980.

42. McCorduck, P. *Machines Who Think.* San Francisco: W.H. Freeman and Company, 1979.

43. Medawar, P.B. Is the scientific paper fraudulent? *Saturday Rev.* (1 Aug.), pp. 42–43, 1964.

44. Merton, R.K. *Social Theory and Social Structure.* New York: Free Press, 1968, pp. 4–7.

45. Merton, R.K. The sociology of science: An episodic memoir. Merton, R. K and Gaston, J., (eds.). *The Sociology of Science in Europe.* Carbondale, Illinois: Southern Illinois University Press, 1977, see esp. pp. 119–120.

46. Minsky, M. Steps toward artificial intelligence. *Proc. Inst. Radio Eng.* 49:8–30, 1961.

47. *Models for Biomedical Research.* Washington, D.C.: National Academy Press, 1985, p. 180.

48. Partington, J.R. *A History of Chemistry*, Vol. IV. London: Macmillan & Co. Ltd., 1964.

49. Polya, G. Kombinatorische Anzahlbestimmungen fur Gruppen, Graphen und Chemische Verbindungen. *Acta Math.* 68, 145–254, 1938.

50. Pres. Sci. Adv. Comm. Science, Government, and Information. Panel on Scientific Information Report. (A. Weinberg, chmn.) Washington: USGPO, 1963.

51. Quastler, H., (ed.). *Essays on the Use of Information Theory in Biology.* Urbana: University of Illinois Press, 1953, p. 273.

52. Reynolds, W.E., Bacon, V.A., Bridges, J.C., Coburn, T.C., Lederberg, J., Levinthal, E.C., Steed, E., and Tucker, R.B. A computer operated mass spectrometer system. *Analytical Chem.* 42, 1122–1129.

53. Rouvray, D.H. Graph theory in chemistry. *RIC Reviews* 4:173–195, 1971.

54. Savageau, M.A. *Biochemical Systems Analysis. A Study of Function and Design in Molecular Biology.* Reading, Mass.: Addison-Wesley, 1976, p. 379.

55. Simmons, H.E. and Maggio, J.E. Synthesis of the first topologically nonplanar molecule. *Tetrahedron Letters* 22, 287–290, 1981.

56. Sutherland, G. DENDRAL—a computer program for generating and filtering chemical structures. Stanford Artificial Intelligence Memo # 49, 1967.

57. Thomas, R., (ed.). *Lecture Notes in Biomathematics. Kinetic Logic: A Boolean Approach to the Analysis of Complex Regulatory Systems.* Berlin and New York: Springer-Verlag, 1979.

58. Whitehead, A.N. and Russell, B. *Principia Mathematica,* 3 vols, 2nd ed. London: Cambridge at the University Press, 1950.

59. Woodger, J.H. *The Axiomatic Method in Biology.* London: Cambridge at the University Press, 1937.

60. Zuckerman, H.A. and Lederberg, J. Forty years of genetic recombination in bacteria. Postmature scientific discovery? *Nature* 327:629–631, 1986.

61. Zuckerman, H.A. and Merton, R.K. Patterns of evaluation in science. Institutionalization, structure and functions of the referee system. *Minerva* 9:66–100, 1971.

ADDITIONAL REFERENCES

62. Rindfleisch, T.C., Smith, D.H., Yeager, W.J., Achenbach, M.W., and Wegmann, A. Mass spectrometer data acquisition and processing systems. *Biomedical Applications of Mass Spectrometry, First Supplementary Volume,* Waller, G.R. and Dermer, O.C., (eds.). New York: John Wiley and Sons, Inc., 1980, Chapter 3, pp. 55–77.

63. Huang, Z. and Wu, W. MDAL: A novel algorithm for the computation of empirical formulas in high-resolution mass spectrometry. *Biomedical Env. Mass. Spec.* 13:187–191, 1986.

64. Djerassi, C. Organic chemistry: A view through steroid glasses. *Modern Organic Chemistry: Scientific and Historic Perspectives,* Seeman, J.I., (ed.). Washington: American Chemical Society, 1988.

65. Newell, A. Intellectual issues in the history of artificial intelligence. *The Study of Information: Interdisciplinary Messages.* Machlup, F. and Mansfield, U. New York: Wiley Interscience, 1983, pp. 187–227.

66. Darden, L. Viewing the history of science as compiled hindsight. *AI Magazine* 8(Summer): 33–41, 1987.

67. Lederberg,J. Sputnik 1957–1987. *The Scientist* Oct. 5, 1987.

68. Lederberg, J. *Computers in Science, Communication and Education, AAMC Symp. on Medical Informatics,* held March 7, 1985, pp. 62–70. *Medical Education in Information Age.* Washington: AAMC, 1986.

Appendix

This memo is an excellent snapshot of the status of AI research as seen in 1965, and therefore is appended in its entirety.

STANFORD ARTIFICIAL INTELLIGENCE PROJECT   April 5, 1965
Memo No. 30

AN INITIAL PROBLEM STATEMENT FOR A
MACHINE INDUCTION RESEARCH PROJECT

by E.A. Feigenbaum and R.W. Watson

Abstract: A brief description is given of a research project presently getting under way. This project will study induction by machine using organic chemistry as a task area. Topics for graduate student research related to the problem listed.

The research reported here was supported in part by the Advanced Research Projects Agency of the Office of the Secretary of Defense (SD-183).

We are engaged, in conjunction with Professor Lederberg of the medical school, in a research project which offers possibilities for graduate research, both well defined problems suitable for C.S. 239 projects and not so well defined problems suitable for PhD thesis topics. In this memorandum we will define the problem briefly and then outline some suggested projects. If you are interested in any of the projects or topics suggested, or have a topic to suggest related to this project see either of us for further details.

The long-range goal of this research is to attempt to come to grips with the problem of induction by machine. That is, how does one build a machine (write a program) which can interact through a suitable interface with its environment and build and improve models of the environment.

The specific task area chosen in which to attack this problem is organic chemistry and in particular, the determination of the structure of organic molecules from mass spectrograph data. The problem presently facing a chemist is roughly the following:

1. A quantity of an organic molecule is supplied to a mass spectrometer.

2. The molecules are bombarded with electrons which break up the molecules into ionized subparts.

3. The mass spectrometer outputs a spectrum (i.e., a distribution of the masses of the subparts).

4. The largest mass in the distribution which occurs in any quantity above a given noise level is that of the parent molecule.

5. By trying various combinations of atoms the chemist finds molecular compositions which have a mass equal to that determined in 4. If the resolution of the mass spectrometer is fine enough the determination of a unique composition is possible.

6. Once the chemical composition, or possible compositions, of the molecule is determined, the chemist uses various heuristics in conjunction with the mass spectrum to determine the structure of the molecule.

The computer science problem is to automate the above process. At the present time we see the project as progressing in the following stages.

Stage O—Display of Chemical Structures

Professor Lederberg has developed a linear notation for organic molecular structures. Further, he has devised an algorithm which, given a chemical composition as an input, will produce as an output all topologically unique organic structures corresponding to this composition. The system is called "DENDRAL" and exists as an Algol program for the B-5000 written by Larry Tessler.

At the present time many of the structures are not chemically meaningful. Therefore, our first task will be to develop a system which will interact with a chemist and the DENDRAL system and determine rules for chemically meaningful structures. These rules will be automatically incorporated into a "filter" for the DENDRAL system.

Presently a program for the PDP-1 exists which accepts a linear DENDRAL string and displays a chemical graph on the Philco scope. The problem then of Stage O is to improve this program and to develop the software for tying it in with Larry Tessler's program through the disc and which will allow us to use LISP on the 7090 from the Philco scopes.

Stage 1—Chemist at the Philco Keyboard

During Stage 1 we will develop the programming techniques which will allow a dialogue to take place between the chemist and the system for growing the filter on the DENDRAL output. This system will involve the display of a graph and the chemist's determination of whether or not it is chemically meaningful. The system must then question the chemist to find out what rules the chemist is using for his determinations and accept his answers in a suitable language. In general, the chemist will not be explicitly conscious of the rules he is using, and the machine will serve the important function of helping to bring these rules to a precise awareness.

The end result of Stage 1 is that we will have an improved DENDRAL system and have learned some important and useful computing techniques. An improved DENDRAL system and associated display should also be of value to those interested in the problems of information retrieval associated with the chemical sciences.

Stage 2—Mass Spectrograph Analysis

In Stage 2 a chemist and a machine interact in real time through the medium of a scope, scope keyboard, typewriter, and possibly light pen or tablet. If the machine were used strictly for performing clerical and algorithmic processes, the following dialogue would result.

1. The machine would be supplied with the mass spectrum and would display on the scope face a histogram and the chemical composition(s) of the molecule.

2. The chemist using his experience and peripheral information would then input a linear description of a trial structure which would then be displayed on the scope as a chemical graph, or the DENDRAL system would be invoked to systematically display chemical graphs which correspond to the given composition.

3. The chemist, using his knowledge of likely places for breaks to occur in the above structure when under electron bombardment, would indicate such a break on the graph. The machine would then compute the mass of the subparts and indicate whether or not such a mass exists in the histogram. Or, the chemist would indicate a mass number in the histogram and the machine would indicate whether or not a subgraph exists which has this mass and if it does exist indicate which subgraph it is.

4. The chemist may also want to move various subgraphs from one place to another and then proceed as above. The machine will then compute the linear canonical form of these new graphs and possibly change the display to a canonical form. Further, the DENDRAL system may be invoked to systematically change a given subgraph.

5. The chemist eventually finds a structure which he hypothesizes as capable of yielding the mass spectrum.

What we want is for the machine to be used not only for clerical work, but more importantly to learn from the chemist's behavior and therefore take over much of the analysis on its own. To this end we visualize the following variation of the above dialogue.

Initially the machine would input the correct structures corresponding to different chemical compositions. The chemist would then proceed to present an example analysis of this structure in conjunction with its mass spectrum; finally concluding with the known result that the structure could have yielded the given mass spectrum. During this process the machine will probe the chemist for the rules leading to his behavior. The machine will incorporate these rules in a data structure, which will allow the machine to perform a similar analysis.

The machine will then be given a chemical structure corresponding to a given mass spectrum and will be asked to proceed on a step by step analysis of its own. The machine will report its "reasoning" to the chemist as it proceeds. When the machine makes an incorrect step the chemist will interrupt, and a dialogue will take place until the machine can make the correct step.

Finally, when the machine can correctly analyze structures known to correspond to given mass spectrums, the system will be given a composition and the DENDRAL generator will be invoked to systematically present for analysis possible structures. Then a dialogue of the following type will take place: The machine will proceed with an analysis as far as it is able and then the chemist will take over. As the chemist manipulates the graph with machine aid, the machine queries the chemist for the rules governing his behavior and a dialogue takes place.

Eventually the chemist reaches a hypothesis that the given structure could or could not yield the given mass spectrum. The machine then proceeds to analyze the structure on its own to see if it would reach the same hypothesis. If not, a further dialogue takes place until the machine can reach the hypothesis of the chemist.

When the machine seems adequate at this task we proceed to Stage 3.

Stage 3—Good Initial Guesses as to Chemical Structure

In Stage 2 the man and machine proceeded systematically through the structures produced by DENDRAL. Clearly for any large structures the number of isomers of a given chemical composition could run into the millions. Therefore, the chemist must make a good initial guess as to a possible structure and only rely on the DENDRAL generator to modify subgraphs. Again the chemist and system interact, with the machine querying the chemist to determine the rules for proposing initial structures. The procedures to be followed will be similar to those of the previous stage.

Stage 4—Refinement of the System

When Stage 3 is completed the system will be a good mass spectrum analyzer. However, the data structures produced during this stage will be complicated, duplicated, and in general unlikely to be optimal. Therefore, the program, and associated data structures which result from Stage 3, will be carefully analyzed to determine how to write an efficient, compact system and to determine which sections contain general chemical knowledge and which contain knowledge of a specialized character, useful mainly for mass-spectrograph analysis. The final efficient program which results will form the software for some experiments to be undertaken by a suggested Mars probe and the efficient program minus the specialized structures will form the basis for a system to be applied to some other chemical tasks such as the synthesis of organic molecules.

The following problems suggest themselves as possible research projects.

1. **Display problems**: In order that the display of the chemical graphs be as useful as possible to the chemist, it should display the graphs in a form as close as possible to that to which the chemist is trained. This task is difficult to do automatically with our present experience. Therefore, one possible approach at this time is to develop a system which automatically displays a graph close to that desired by the chemist and then allows the chemist to manipulate substructures by simple rotations and bond-length adjustments. Another possibility is to allow the chemist to "draw" the graph from the keyboard or with a light pen when it is available.

   Because of the size limitations of the scope face, it will not be possible to display large molecular structures in their entirety. Therefore, it would be useful to have a "window" mechanism which will allow the chemist to study subsections.

   Other features are needed which will allow one to save displays, display more than one graph at a time, and perform text editing on the linear input. It would also be useful to allow the chemist to build an initial structure and to later make insertions and deletions as well as move a given substructure to another point on the graph.

As the work on the display proceeds, feedback from chemists will indicate other useful refinements to the display system.

2. Various programs need to be written which will allow us to use the facilities of the 7090 from the Philco keyboard.

3. **Problems relating to DENDRAL**: DENDRAL is a system for canonical representation of chemical structures. However, the chemist is usually not trained in this system and would probably find it easier to input a noncanonical linear string. Therefore, it would be of value to have a routine which would convert this string to a canonical one.

Other more abstract problems relating to the DENDRAL generator are supplied by Professor Lederberg in Appendix A.

4. **Mass spectrograph analysis problems**: The chemist will want to have a histogram displayed or some display containing equivalent information. The chemist will further want to indicate a given mass number and have the system determine whether or not there is a subgraph with the indicated mass. The work on this problem will lead to abstract on the searching and comparison of list structures.

It will also be of use to the chemist to be able to indicate a given bond as a likely place for a break to have occurred when under electron bombardment and have the system determine if the masses of the subparts are in the distribution. The chemist will also want to be able to invoke the DENDRAL generator to systematically mark and change subgraphs.

5. **The DENDRAL filter growing problem**: As mentioned before, the DENDRAL generator will generate all topologically unique structures regardless of whether or not they are chemically meaningful. The problem here is to grow, on-line, a filter which will only allow chemically meaningful structures to be displayed. To solve this problem, techniques need to be developed so that the chemist can be questioned for his rules of chemical meaningfulness and so that his responses can be dynamically incorporated in a changing data structure. Because the chemist will not always give correct rules, methods must be introduced to guard against the possibility of incorrect rules permanently entering the system. Persons interested in natural language and the computer or formal languages may be interested in this phase of the work.

6. **Advanced mass spectrograph analysis problems**: Related to the problem above will be the development of techniques which allow the rules supplied by the chemist for analyzing structures to be directly introduced into an internal machine structure. This

structure will allow the system to perform the same functions as the chemist and report to the chemist the important stages of its analysis. The detailed problems in this area will only become clear as we proceed.

It would seem to us that the problems related to the display are the most suitable for M.S. projects as they are quite well defined. The more challenging problems related to the DENDRAL system and filter and Stage 2 would seem to be of the greatest interest to those contemplating doctoral research.

References

Lederberg, J. DENDRAL-64: A system for computer construction, enumeration and notation of organic molecules as free structures and cyclic graphs. *Interim Report to the National Aeronautics and Space Administration*, December 15, 1964. (Available from either author of this memo).

Lederberg, J. Topological mapping of organic molecules. *Proc. Nat. Acad. Sci.* 53:134–139, 1965. (Available from either author of this memo).

Appendix A

A number of problems in combinatorial graph theory, abstract groups, symmetry, and related subjects have arisen. Some of these would contribute to the elegance and efficiency of the DENDRAL system. Other questions are more abstract and have been suggested by the chemical graphs.

a. Enumeration of cyclic trivalent graphs. This includes the polyhedra. Grace (a former Stanford mathematics graduate student) has done a possibly vulnerable enumeration up to the 18th order.

b. Efficient test for isomorphism and reduction to canonical forms.

c. Programming to anticipate symmetries and avoid retrospective elimination of isomorphs.

d. What is the least polyhedron lacking a Hamilton circuit? Now known $20 < n < 46$.

e. Generalization of the Hamilton circuit (in the sense of mapping a graph on to segments of a circle) to mappings on higher order figures. In DENDRAL-64 the treatment of non-Hamiltonian cyclic graphs* remains somewhat messy.

f. Heuristic approaches to finding a Hamilton circuit of a graph.

g. Enumeration of graphs with some 4-valent vertices. In DENDRAL-64 this is also somewhat messy, being treated by the collapse of 4-node circuits into 4-valent nodes.

*e.g.:

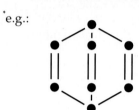

Participants' Discussion

Alfred Weissberg	What was the problem with the graphical automorphisms? Was it in determining the uniqueness of the multiple answers with some of the representations?
Joshua Lederberg	Well, the automorphisms were problems we tackled at the very beginning and we found algorithms to do it. It was very necessary; that was part of the conceptual structure from the very beginning. In order to do that in a manageable way we had to do a series of mappings of the actual structures. If you've got 30 carbon atoms arranged in every possible way, you've got a rather large combinatorial problem trying to look through all of them. The valence of carbon is limited to four, and that's why it is a fairly sparse matrix and you don't use matrix algebra for dealing with it. There's some illustration of that in the figure in my paper. It is one of the early pictorial products.

We found that you could do a series of mappings. You can map any linear chain of atoms onto an edge and then just put a number onto that edge to indicate how long it was. You then have condensed polytopes that you could then map onto what we call vertex graphs; that is, these are graphs with just single edges between tri- and quadrivalent nodes. Each edge might be labeled with the number of bivalent nodes on them and then you have the task of finding the canonical forms of those.

The trick for establishing canonical forms that we found most effective was to reduce the vertex graphs to Hamilton circuits. That raises the question: Are there trivalent planar graphs that don't have a Hamilton circuit? We investigated that problem and we found that, within the domain of complexity that we could deal with anyhow—vertex graphs up to about 26 or so, and that's enormously complex—they all did have Hamilton circuits. So we did find expedients that enabled us to solve the automorphism problem. Once you are down to the Hamilton circuit work level it is fairly easy to crack that problem.

Lindley Darden	I'm very interested in your desire to automate strategies with theory. I wonder if you care to speculate about the new epistemological machinery that you mentioned here. What might that be like?

Joshua Lederberg   Well, I'm not sure the one relates to the other at this stage, in terms of theory formation. In DENDRAL we answered this at a first-order level, and I don't think there's a huge difference between the way in which DENDRAL solves its problem and the way that I do when I face the data. I do adduce a variety of potential candidates; how I arrive at which are the most plausible ones is a murky question. In part it's what I learned yesterday, what I read about before, or various kinds of patterns unconsciously derived that may guide that surge. But since I know I can't trust my own intuition in order to deal systematically with this kind of problem, I eventually have to generate all possible solutions even in my own dealing with it. It makes this a rather special kind of a problem in a way.

When you are doing a face recognition you're satisfied if the pattern presented to you results in a name that you remember as connected with that face. You're not required to get the list of all individuals ever born who might match the same criteria. But, it's perfectly plain too that there are very efficient ways of truncating the searches. We very rapidly go to different levels of abstraction, developing rules about the rules, in ways that we simply haven't implemented very well in our computer programs.

As far as the machinery that's involved, we discover new rules on the spot just by introspection, and we use them in the way we refine the data. Sometimes we remember them, and sometimes we don't. We discover rules about those rules and we jump up and down in that hierarchy probably six or eight steps in our own combinatorial games when we are trying to think about solutions to a problem. We don't do it as systematically as the computer does; we don't have rules of formal correctness for sentences—and we can get into trouble that way—but we manage. That flexibility makes up for the rigor in some measure in our human experience.

I don't know what machinery we're going to have to develop for dealing with the problems of development. It may be useful to go through some of the numbers. There are three billion nucleotides, give or take one significant figure, in the human genome. There are people who want to map it from beginning to end. I think that would be a very particular datum about a particular piece of DNA. Then the interesting questions only begin to emerge at that point. We're guessing that only about one percent of that is informationally active, although that's still burdened by various uncertainties. So we end up believing that there are about 100,000 significant gene products that we're going to have to take care of—there are 100,000 transcriptionally active segments in the human genome. Many of them will be proteins; some of them will be other pieces of DNA; some of them may be God knows what at this stage—we shouldn't keep a closed mind about that. Each of those products is a formidable research enterprise in itself. Several lifetimes have gone into the elucidation of hemoglobin, which is just one of them. There are new ones being discovered all the time. Out of the 100,000 that we have good reason to believe are there, we can guess the identity today of about a thousand, maybe a couple of thousand, but this is moving very, very quickly.

I used to try and keep track of all the ones that actually had been structurally encoded, and it's hard to right now. A few hundred of them have been isolated and dealt with as material entities in the lab. A score of them have had intense examination and have required several lifetimes of work each in order to get at what they are. So just to find out what the units are is an agenda for biological research through the next century.

That would not require any great epistemological innovation. You solve the problem there by closing your thinking so as to exclude everything but the one gene product that you are interested in; you find out everything you can about that. But in development you now have to imagine that each of these products is regulating every other one of them—some of them more intensely than others, and some of them at a trivial level. To try to imagine how you are going to model development when you have those possibilities of mutual interaction in the rates of production of each of those products modifying every other developmental pathway is going to be—that is a daunting problem! I don't know the epistemological apparatus needed to deal with it. So we have at several levels just handling the data at that level and understanding what it is that's reliable, how you translate sequences into shape and then into function, and what these elements interact with. But trying to get a more formal model of a system as nonlinear as this and with so many constituents is going to take new approaches.

PLANTING THE SEEDS—A PANEL

Following the two keynote addresses, there was a panel entitled "Planting the Seeds." The six presenters were seated at a table. They were Bruce D. Waxman, PhD, Robert S. Ledley, DDS, Eugene A. Stead, MD, Harold Schoolman, MD, Wilfred J. Dixon, PhD, and William S. Yamamoto, MD. Dr. Yamamoto, as moderator, began the discussion. Each panelist then made a short presentation.

The program committee chose the theme of "planting the seeds" to recognize the contributions that each panelist had made to medical informatics. To provide a focus for the discussion, an emphasis was placed on the question of "how we got to where we are." Following the short presentations, there was a discussion among the panelists and the audience.

This was the first session of the conference to involve a relatively large number of people, and both the presentations and discussion reflected some of the excitement of a reunion. Unfortunately, not all of this spontaneity can be captured in a transcript. Nevertheless, the editors have attempted to record the content of the panel accurately and to preserve some of its good humor.

Prior to the conference, the panelists were invited to prepare longer personal statements reporting on their reminiscences and achievements. Four did so, and their papers are included in this section. Drs. Dixon and Ledley prepared (and later revised) more complete papers; Drs. Yamamoto and Waxman wrote short personal essays. Each augments the panel discussion. These papers follow the panel transcript.

SPEAKERS

William S. Yamamoto
Wilfred J. Dixon
Robert S. Ledley
Bruce D. Waxman
Harold Schoolman
Eugene A. Stead, Jr.

William S. Yamamoto, MD is professor and chairman, Department of Computer Medicine, George Washington University (since 1983). He received an AB degree from Park College in 1945 and an MD degree from the University of Pennsylvania in 1949. He joined the faculty of the University of Pennsylvania in 1950 and moved to George Washington University to become professor and chairman, Department of Clinical Engineering (1971–1983). He is on the editorial board of three journals including the *IEEE Transactions on Biomedical Engineering* and *Computers in Biomedical Research*.

Wilfred J. Dixon, PhD is president, BMDP Statistical Software, Inc. Until his retirement in 1986, he also was professor of Biomathematics (since 1967), Biostatistics (since 1955), and Psychiatry (since 1973), University of California, Los Angeles. He received a BA degree from Oregon State College in 1938, an MA degree from the University of Wisconsin in 1939, and a PhD degree from Princeton in 1944. He has held offices in the Institute of Mathematical Statistics, the American Statistical Association and Biometric Society, and the International Statistical Institute. He is associate editor of *Biometrics* and *Annals of Mathematical Statistics*.

Robert S. Ledley, DDS is director of Medical Computing and Biophysics Division (since 1975); professor, Department of Radiology (since 1974); and professor, Department of Physiology and Biophysics (since 1970), Georgetown University Medical Center. He received a DDS degree from New York University in 1948 and an MA degree from Columbia University in 1949. He has written, edited, or coauthored eight books and has been awarded numerous patents. He is the editor-in-chief of four journals including *Computers in Biology and Medicine*.

Bruce D. Waxman, PhD is the acting chief of the Development Integration Division, Research and Engineering Directorate, Defense Mapping Agency. He received a BA degree from the University of Pennsylvania in 1952, an MA degree from the University of Connecticut in 1955, and a PhD degree from the University of Chicago in 1973. He was the executive secretary, Advisory Committee on Computers in Research, NIH (1961–1965); the chief of the Special Research Resources Branch, NIH (1965–1968); director, Health Care Technology Division, NCHSR (1968–1973); and a senior research scientist at NCHSR until 1983.

Harold Schoolman, MD is deputy director for Research and Education, National Library of Medicine (since 1977) and clinical professor, Georgetown University (since 1970). He received the MD degree from the University of Illinois in 1950. He joined the faculty of the Cook County Graduate School of Medicine in 1954 and became affiliated with the Veterans Administration Hospital—Hines, Illinois, in 1962. He moved to Washington to become director, Education Service, Central Office, Veterans Administration in 1967 and joined the National Library of Medicine in 1971. His honors include the NIH Director's Award (1983).

Eugene A. Stead, Jr., MD is Florence McAlister Professor Emeritus of Medicine, Duke University (since 1967). He received the BS and MD degrees from Emory University in 1928 and 1932. After faculty appointments at Harvard, he became a professor of medicine (1942–1946) and dean (1945–1946) of the Emory University School of Medicine. In 1947 he joined Duke University as Florence McAlister Professor of Medicine and chairman, Department of Medicine. He has been an officer in several professional organizations and an editor of three journals. His numerous awards include the Distinguished Teacher Award, ACP (1969), Abraham Flexner Award for Distinguished Service to Medical Education, AAMC (1970), and the Kober Medal, AAP (1980).

Planting the Seeds: Panel Transcript

William Yamamoto The commission of this panel is announced in the program as "Planting the Seeds," which is a particularly apt title. I have had the privilege of knowing every member of the panel here and of course many of you in the room. In the context of discussing how we got where we are from where we were, and that is what this panel will try to do, each of us will speak briefly to the issue of planting the seeds from different perspectives. We also will leave a large portion of the time for the various medical informatics generations represented in this room to have a free discourse about where the skeletons are or if there are any. We want to know what curious happenstances may have affected you, also. But first we'll have an informal discussion among the panelists internally about various aspects of the development of the field which is now striving to achieve a certain self-identification in a specific way under the rubric of Medical Informatics.

Although one can't completely avoid being autobiographical, I will try to minimize this aspect of my history as it relates to the planting of seeds. For me, 1945 was a curious year, because it marked the end of major events worldwide. I arrived in Philadelphia to go to a school of medicine, and one of the first things I did accidentally while trying to find the medical school was to wander into the school of engineering. I turned down the hall in the wrong way, entered a room where there was an armed guard, and was promptly ushered out. I later discovered that was the room where the ENIAC computer had been packaged to be shipped to Aberdeen. So that was the curious long row of black light- and meter-covered panels that I saw to the left of me. I suppose I've unwittingly been in violation of national security for 43 years now.

However, I really didn't become interested in computing until 1948 when I was a medical student waiting for the delivery of a baby in OB/GYN. I started reading Norbert Wiener's book *Cybernetics* which then introduced me to a whole bunch of equations that to this day I must confess I really do not fully understand, because I'm basically a physician. I've never been well trained in mathematics. Like the poet in the "Song of Bernadette," it's one of those things for which I yearn but I really would never understand.

51

Anyway, the book by Norbert Wiener struck a very important chord in my mind. As a medical student I had long been convinced that I didn't understand what I knew was being taught to me. I've been in pursuit for quite a few years now, to try to understand what it means when you say you understand something. Since my professional career has been as a teacher in the school of medicine, I have spent all these years trying to explain. You cannot explain that which you do not understand, and those are two verbs which we cannot really define. Medical informatics, particularly in its recent incarnations that deal with things like expert systems and artificial intelligence, focuses more and more on this issue. Because of this quest, it has been my privilege to watch the seeding of many ideas in many sites and to see those seeds take expression fruitfully.

My own peregrinations led me into physiology where I focused on an object system, respiration. I am still working on the problem of how to explain why you breathe harder when you run, and I don't have the answer yet. I probably shan't, but I'll still be looking. That took me to UCLA around 1960 on several trips. On one of those trips to the Brain Research Institute I was having a discussion on how the brain functions, or how we thought it did. My talk was on Sunday morning, and apparently Bruce Waxman was somewhere in the audience. The preceding day had been somewhat acrimonious so, having had the privilege to go to a small private sectarian college in Missouri, I was familiar with scriptures, which I had the temerity to quote.

I have never had the chance to ask Bruce whether it was my quotations of scriptures or whatever else I said that day, but in consequence I was invited by him in 1963 to join a committee of the NIH called the Advisory Committee on Computers in Research (ACCR). The purpose of the committee was to stimulate the use of computing in biomedical science. Eventually that committee became the first study section of NIH. Its mission was plainly planting seeds, namely dollars, and recognizing the activities of individuals in medical institutions across the country active in bringing this new technology—computation—onto the biomedical scene. So for planting the seeds, the principal farmer was NIH.

You cannot understand the whole change in our society unless you understand the role of the ACCR and its successors. Machines were primitive and expensive, and they could only be sustained as facility installations. It took people of unusual vision, with ability and drive, to develop activities using this new machinery in whatever field was appropriate. So as you move across this panel you will find to my right Will Dixon, who is probably the premier representative of the evolution of mathematical and statistical computing; Hack Schoolman, who represents the National Library of Medicine as well as many other areas; Gene Stead in the broad areas of clinical medicine as well as notions of the effective use of medical knowledge; Bob Ledley, who is best described as an eclectic, but especially in imaging and logic; and finally Bruce Waxman, who is the living representation of the role of the government. Coming back to my end of the table, I suppose my role is gadfly.

I have had the privilege of watching some of the great leaders in this field play the role of farmers or toilers. When I first joined the ACCR at Bruce's invitation, Lee Lusted, Scottie Pratt, Homer Warner, and many of you in the room were already engaged in this activity, and it was my privilege to be basically a spectator. That was a privilege that to this day I cherish. There were others on the committee who are not in this room like Max Woodbury, Norman Shapiro, Allen Newell, and Alan Perlis, many of whom have gone back into the primary computer science areas. One must mention Helen Gee and Carol Newton, but the short list in my mind's eye grows as I contemplate the times.

The ACCR in my opinion was an unusual mixture of totally free, imaginative, brilliant intellect. They were all intellectual risk takers and the discourses that I passed around the table were of a kind that seem to have vanished from most places today. I don't think that the seeds would have been planted as well had we been a different group or been at a different time. I don't know what was the governing factor. Everybody in his own parochial way was excited, but each in a very catholic way was happy to support the interests and developments of others wherever they appeared in the country. We are still planting seeds, perhaps more reluctantly today because of the nature and the demands of money, but seed planting continues.

As this panel reviews the seed-planting activities of two to three decades ago, we in some sense are reaping part of the harvest. We also are happy to see that seed planting is still going on, even though in a much diminished way. The story of the impact of computation on human society has not yet been written out in full. I don't think it will ever be written out fully, any more than the impact of printing on the human adventure of thought will be written to completion.

Wilfrid Dixon   It was during the 20 years from 1959 to 1979 that I directed the Health Sciences Computing Facility at UCLA. This major computing resource was funded by the NIH Division of Research Resources to provide statistical and computer support for medical research. From the perspective of the present it is hard to remember how tentatively the now-ubiquitous computer was used 25 years ago. Hence it is difficult to convey the excitement we felt in being part of a revolutionary change in the way research is conducted. In the early sixties computer access was limited almost exclusively to the computer expert, and there were very few of them in the biological sciences. Furthermore, most scientific computing resources were designed for physical scientists, and they lacked the hardware—especially storage—and applications software—especially statistics—to support biology. Even where assistance was provided, the consultants rarely spoke the language of the biologist. This facility was then established to remedy these deficiencies, and it provided the focus for a large number of innovative and important studies.

The mission of the facility included participation in substantive research, and research and development in the statistical and mathematical methods and advanced computer systems needed to support it. Because the underlying theory available to biologists was often less extensive than in the physical sciences, the need for graphical representations, interactive methods, and effective data handling was greater. Finally, being less comfortable with the technical aspects of computing, our research community required specialized assistance in using the tools. Conversely, since our research was concerned with the methods required to meet special and continually changing needs rather than satisfying a predefined set of externally derived specifications, our training, consultation, software distribution, and computer service activities were an essential part of the total experiment. They provided the criteria for measuring the success of previous phases of the project and the basis for determining the future directions.

At the time the facility was established I'd already begun the effort to develop package programs, which was then a novel concept for statistics. This effort continued at the Center and evolved into the BMDP (BioMeDical Package) statistical programs now widely used. Other notable achievements of the Center include the development of early time-sharing systems, innovative work in graphics, and collaboration and support for a number of significant biological research projects.

When the computer was introduced into the biological environment, it put the techniques of the statistician to a severe test—a test that often found them wanting. The problem was not how to look at a small set of data optimally but how to look at a large set of data reasonably. Missing data and bad data are a fact of life in biology, a fact largely ignored by traditional statistics. The promise of the computer was exciting but the reality was often far from satisfactory. Our basic goal was to develop techniques suitable for a computer and accessible to the biologist who is neither a statistician nor a computer expert.

We not only developed the software to support this effort but also provided the computing resource and the consultants to enable scientists to use the new tools. Our statisticians worked as an integral part of the research team; in turn they fed the practical needs of the research projects back into our software development, making it responsive to the real needs of medical research. The programs were not only widely used but also widely copied. Indeed, the Statistical Package for the Social Sciences (SPSS) began as a direct copy of our statistical algorithms with modifications to the control language used to specify the analysis.

I won't give the details of a number of the other projects, but they included graphics and various modeling procedures, how to use a computer which was large for that time—the IBM 360/91—and developing graphics terminals to go along with such an elaborate system. We were also involved in a number of collaborative research projects. About 2000 investigators had accounts at the Center over the years it existed. We worked very closely with major projects such as genetic linkage, schizophrenia, heart disease, tissue typing, and so on.

In summary, support of the type we provided is no longer necessary. Anyone can get access to a computer and use it effectively. While there continues to be room for improvement in research methods and software, good tools are widely available. However, much of the progress made in medical research in the sixties and seventies would not have been possible without support of such centers as the one we have at UCLA which attracted unique groups of scientists to work together to make the computer's promise a reality. Many of the projects begun with the support of the Center developed into major studies with considerable impact in the scientific community. We were fortunate to have been participants in an exciting and rapidly developing enterprise and fortunate in our association with our scientific collaborators, our own staff, and leaders in the Division of Research Resources and the Computer and Biomathematical Sciences Study Section.

In terms of history it might be interesting to note that every year for the those 20 years we produced an annual report which would run to 500 pages. Those interested in following a variety of the other projects, perhaps up to 100 or 200 of them, could follow their progress over a period of 10 or 15 years by studying these annual reports; they were very extensive.

Harold Schoolman   When I was asked to represent the National Library of Medicine's institutional memory in its involvement in the history of medical informatics I set down an outline in which I was fully prepared to show you pictures of John Shaw Billings, of the *Index Medicus*, of the first Hollerith card sorter, and of GRACE, the machine that did the first photocomposition for the publication of *Index Medicus* in 1964. Then I got a letter from Bill saying he didn't want any of that; he only wanted me to take five minutes to identify a few issues.

In order to present those issues to you I need to do a little bit of historical background. In 1967 the United States Congress, recognizing the increasing importance of emerging communications and computer technology in information management, established by a joint resolution the Lister Hill Center for Biomedical Communications as a division of the National Library of Medicine. The Library, in attempting to get advice from the academic community on how the Lister Hill Center should pursue its charges, engaged the Association of American Medical Colleges (AAMC) to create a series of symposium meetings to provide us with advice. Following this, the AAMC created a committee to study the problem explicitly. The committee, which was chaired by Gene Stead, published a report in 1971 that has become known as "The First Stead Committee Report."[1] I don't know why it is known as The First Stead Committee Report because Gene had been on and chaired so many committees before that it was probably the 50th or 60th.

The opening page of that report, under the heading of the Essence of the Report, reads as follows:

> The Lister Hill Center for Biomedical Communications should have as its eventual goal the development of educational methods which will render obsolete the current system of libraries, textbooks, medical school curricula, and total dependence on memory and pattern recognition in clinical decision making and problem solving. These major changes will come only with the development of new sources and new types of manpower ready to devise new approaches to the problems of medical education and the delivery of health care. Their long term objective will not be limited to improving existing systems, but will include devising newer systems using a different mix of men and machines than now familiar. This revolution will require a faculty who have mastered communications technology and who are eager to sail in as yet uncharted educational waters.

At that time I think all the members of the academic community who understood that paragraph were on Gene Stead's committee, because there was within the academic institution itself not only no place in which this activity could be undertaken, but there wasn't even any recognition that this activity belonged within the medical school. It is interesting to note that the AAMC in the last two years has published several reports, including the GPEP Report The Physician of the 21st Century and another report[2] on the role of information in medical education.

Let me just quote briefly a paragraph from that later report which says that:

> ...the Association believes that the knowledge explosion which is occurring in medicine and the basic biomedical sciences, coupled with the physician's responsibility for lifelong learning dictates that medical students and practitioners learn to use new strategies for managing the information and knowledge available to them for the treatment of patients. It

---

[1] In Education Technology for Medicine, a special issue of the Journal of Medical Education, Vol. 46, #7, part 2, July 1971.

[2] Medical Education in The Information Age, Proceedings of the Symposium on Medical Informatics, Association of American Medical Colleges, January 1986.

is necessary for our medical schools to change the process of education to de-emphasize the acquisition of knowledge and emphasize information organizing and problem solving. Medical information science, computers and new understanding about the processes of clinical decision making can be powerful factors in education and information management and analysis.

So clearly, over a 17-year period there has been a considerable change in the environment, at least as it is manifested by a number of people who are now willing to accept the advice of "The First Stead Committee Report."

In 1971 we were confronted with how to implement "The First Stead Committee Report." There were three fundamental issues with which we were concerned. The first was the training of the manpower. After considerable discussion it was agreed that the initial training effort should be designed not so much to train people in medical informatics as a career (because there was no career opportunity for them if you indeed got them trained), but rather to train administrators and senior faculty in the medical schools in order to enhance the environment and receptivity. Hopefully one day we would be able to create within the medical school the recognition and establishment of medical informatics as an acceptable and accepted departmental discipline.

About five years ago we decided that the environment had improved sufficiently so that we could shift to a more classical research and career training in medical informatics *per se*. When we first started the training we had as many as ten training programs. That constituted almost every institution in which it was possible to mount a training program at the time. Subsequently, through a series of financial restrictions, the number of training programs was reduced. When we made a new offering for a new training program in 1983, there were more than 20 applications of which 17 were approved. We now have eight funded programs, and we will fund more if money becomes available. So clearly the number of institutions capable of mounting a training program has increased.

However, the second objective of creating a recognized discipline within which there might be a potential career in the academic community, one cannot be quite as enthusiastic about. After many, many years there is now at least one department of medical informatics, several divisions of medical informatics in other departments, and one institute that is a combination of engineering, computer, and medical sciences. But there is also a great demand and even a great argument among the academic community as to how this now somewhat more recognized discipline is to be incorporated into medical school. The Association of Vice-Presidents for Health has advocated the development of an office within the Office of Vice-President; others have argued for the development of departments or for other means. The argument has at least shifted from "why should we do it" to "how should we do it," and that I consider to be a considerable improvement.

So the second issue, which is unresolved as yet, was how to establish medical informatics as a recognized discipline with career opportunities. We attempted to support that activity by creating New Investigator Awards and Research Career Development Awards in that field. We have advocated and testified before Congress for more than six years now for the development of centers of excellence in the field of medical informatics, a mechanism that is well known at NIH and has been successfully pursued in many other disciplines. Unfortunately only two senior officials of medical schools, presidents or vice-presidents for health, have ever testified in support of the centers of excellence. We have suffered from the lack of a vocal constituency, but I think we are beginning to see a change in that. The change is being brought about partially in the manner I've described through the academic community's recognition of the increasing importance of information management in all aspects of medicine. But it is also being brought about by the revolution in biology to which Dr. Lederberg referred to earlier this morning, in which the information management aspects of that problem are probably as great if not greater than the biological aspects of that problem. And so we are being forced, reluctantly or not, into the development of a much broader and more effective constituency that will help promote the so far unresolved issue of a true discipline of medical informatics recognized by the academic community.

The third issue with which we were concerned is the reorganization of thinking in medical education and in medical practice to, as the Stead Committee recommended, at least alter the balance of medical education between building a knowledge base and learning clinical decision making. The greater part, if not the total curriculum of medical education, was designed to build a knowledge base. George Miller once wrote that the acquisition of problem-solving skills was never taught in any medical school; it was assumed to be acquired like a contagion by exposure to clinicians who exercise what was thought to be good problem-solving judgement. That's still the mechanism by means of which people learn problem-solving skills, but hopefully that too is changing. The appropriate relationship between man and machine is the challenge that is probably the least touched on and where the least progress has been made in the medical curriculum and in medical practice. Perhaps that is the continuum that will take us into the future.

Eugene Stead   My role in life has been a practicing doctor, a medical educator, and a some-time cardiovascular research investigator. The thing that moved me most toward an interest in computerization was in the practice of medicine. In 1928 at the time I entered medical school there were only two considerations given. One was that you make a good grade in organic chemistry and the second was that you could borrow money for tuition. The reason for the organic chemistry requirement was that most medical education was memory based, and in those days there was relatively little theory in organic chemistry; it was nearly all straight memory. I happen to have a good memory and I happened to make an "A" in organic chemistry, so clearly I was a candidate for medical school. The second question was "...Son, can you borrow the money to pay your tuition?" I don't know that that's changed any yet. The Atlanta Rotary Club put up the money, and I went to medical school.

It's perfectly clear that in the practice of medicine you operate in two spheres. One sphere contains the things you do every day. You clearly know the material, you don't need to look up anything in a book or consult a reference. But that always touches on a second sphere, the things that you haven't thought about in quite a long time. Anyone practicing medicine sensibly has to have at his command easy access to those facts he may once have been exposed to but has forgotten. It seemed obvious even in the days when we wrote our report for the Lister Hill Center many, many years ago that medical education would eventually move toward open book examinations. That is, one would examine a student in the same way that he would actually use the material in practice. It became clear that if one were going to do that, then it would be nice to have information collected and stored in ways which would make it more easily accessible than having to make many trips to the library.

I was extraordinarily fortunate during most of my career. I had 90 medical students, all of whom were in the library for some portion of each day, and all of them were telling me what I didn't know each day. I spent a certain amount of time in the library so I could return a little information back to them. It was a great system, but obviously not one that was going to survive if we could come up with a better system. In the days in which we wrote the plan for the Lister Hill Center, the initial emphasis was placed on audiovisual education. A number of us on the committee decided we would broaden the mandate to give equal importance to the question of computerization and to producing an educated faculty to carry this out. One of the things I did in that time was to examine the audiovisual production factories which had been established in various medical schools over the last 15 years. The thing that impressed me most was that they were nearly all entrepreneurial. They were never institutional efforts and when the entrepreneur left, no matter how good the material, it gradually faded from sight. Ten years later you could no longer find the material in the medical school that had once been so proud of it.

I began to look too at certain computer activities, particularly around Duke University Medical Center, and it was clear they were going to have the same characteristics. Somebody would have the idea, the energy, and the money. Somebody would set up the shop and then leave, and the activity tended to disappear. So my primary activity in the computer world has been to establish at Duke what I would call institutionalization of the programs, to put them and their faculty in the same relationship to the university as a professor of anatomy, biochemistry, or physiology. I wanted to have the positions there that we could get out and try to fill with the best persons possible. Fortunately in the practice of medicine this turned out not to be too difficult an assignment, because once you begin to get computerization established in a reasonable framework in the department—and we did this initially in cardiovascular medicine—you then begin to generate a whole series of things that the staff suddenly discovers after a period of four or five years that they can't live without. And once they discover that they can't live without it, you simply begin to charge for what you have been doing for free. Before long you've got a reasonably secure base and a reasonable amount of money.

The question of getting informatics into the medical school curriculum turned out to be a somewhat more knotty problem. Duke allows one year of student activity in a variety of areas—one can go into a basic science laboratory, or one can go into the Institute of History for instance. But the one thing that they wouldn't give credit for was anything in the area of informatics. It's taken a long time to get the basic science faculty to appreciate that there were other disciplines that were equally as important in medicine as the traditional tools of physiology, biochemistry, and anatomy. Within the last year that's beginning to occur. Duke now has recognized that the third-year experience can be other then the traditional sciences of the medical school, and medical informatics now is a third-year track through the medical school. It's these kinds of endeavors that I've played with in the computer world, but I'm practically a virgin; I really never have touched a computer.

I'll leave you with just one word about the practice of medicine in the future. More and more it's going to concern itself with taking effective care of people with chronic illness. Elevated cholesterol is a classical example. If a physician determines that you have high cholesterol, and he decides he ought to do something about it, that's a lifelong commitment. But he has no way in his present record system to take care of you. He has not arranged his system so he knows where you are, knows when you are supposed to be tested, and what the tests were like; he has no way of knowing if you move from Durham to Seattle, but he needs to know, because if he enters into this kind of contract, he must move along with you.

If we're going to do anything of this kind in preventive medicine it's going to require an entirely different record system in the doctor's office then anything we've had before. The medical community is slowly beginning to appreciate the fact that not only are computers going to be introduced into the research activity, but in the end, if any physician wants to know what he is doing for anybody, he's got to change the medical records system for his office into a new way of doing business.

Robert Ledley[3]   In planting the seeds I think some of the seeds are money, which is key of course, and I see on the panel individuals who administered the first grants in this area. But a lot of the seeds must be the knowledge, which is the thing that the money is to propel, and developing the knowledge was my goal. I got into medical informatics from the point of view of computer engineering, although actually my background was very mixed. In the 1950s I started out using the first computer, the SEAC, which was the first high-speed digital computer with an electronic memory rather than a plugboard memory. Actually I think it was the first one in the world. The computer fascinated me because I thought that this was the way of getting into computer applications in medicine. It seemed that this was the panacea. Well, it was a panacea but not as tremendous as I had thought. It didn't work out as fast as I thought it would; it didn't solve all the problems immediately.

Around 1959 I met Dr. Lee Lusted, and we worked out what we called the "reasoning foundations of medical diagnosis," which apparently stimulated a tremendous amount of work in these areas and has been called the seminal paper in starting a lot of this work. It's very hard to believe, looking back, but there's no way I could have visualized at that time how influential that paper would turn out to be.

Later in the early 1960s I got into imaging, and the first thing we built was a film scanner. I think it had a lot of influence on the development of imaging methods; after all in medical school the more well-known heavy users of computers are the radiologists, the people in the imaging departments. It was just a film scanner, and in those days there weren't any interfaces. One had to wire the scanner directly into the computer. It was a lot of engineering fun, but in the meantime we had developed the method of syntax pattern recognition.

Eventually we applied our methods to chromosome analysis. By the end of the 1960s we had pretty much completed that project and were able to do automatic chromosome analysis with banding as it

---

[3] The following is an extract from Dr. Ledley's oral remarks. It is included in this section to provide some flavor of his presentation. A more complete paper with illustrations is included at the end of this section.

existed in those days. Of course the banding, the chromosome analysis, and the genetics just continued developing. It didn't wait for us.

We put out a little book on different applications of imaging in such fields as eye grounds, chest X ray, microscopic blood work, lung alveola sizes, electron micrographs, and huge number of other areas. In the sixties we established a journal, *Computers in Biology and Medicine*, that is still going. Obviously this kind of work is accelerating rather than decreasing.

One of the things we did, which I think also had a tremendous influence, was to develop the first whole body CT scanner in 1973 called the ACTA Scanner (for Automatic Computerized Transverse Axial Scanner). It had a lot of firsts on it. For instance it had the first digital memory for medical TV display. The first image we made on this ACTA Scanner was kind of interesting. It was a bowl of water in which we put a skull—the skull I used when I took anatomy when I was at school—and inside the skull was a navel orange. You could see the orange part and the pithy white part of the peel. We thought that was pretty good at the time, and it was good for an X ray to distinguish among these objects. So we went on with that and had a little victory celebration.

We were under tremendous pressure from the physicians at Georgetown University Hospital because they wanted the machine to be usable for patients right away. We built it in the hospital room and, a couple of days after we got our first picture, they were working on patients on the spot. Of course the field has barrelled along so fast since then that this very machine can be seen now at the Smithsonian Institution in their medical science exhibit. Well of course we wrote it up, and you can see some of the old pictures that we made in those days in our 1974 *Science* article. We used color so you could see the different densities with much more accuracy.

Of course having had the first whole body CT scanner we were able to do a lot of "first" applications such as radiation treatment planning with CT, which is now a big field. Three-dimensional images, which we first did, now is also a big field, and so on. All of these things have taken off as fields in their own right.

After that image processing became even more intensive. I went into whole-picture processing and invented and patented the first whole-image processor. It eventually was sold as the DeAnza 5000, which a number of you who are in the field know about. We had four memories in this particular one. Again, a tremendous number of applications in medicine which are used now came from these beginnings. We use the same whole-picture processor in a digital subtraction angiography unit.

Finally, let me mention one more thing that we have done in our laboratory. This is the Protein Identification Resource (PIR), which is the worldwide primary source of protein sequence data. Originally Dr. Margaret Dayhoff was principal scientist, and at the present time Dr. Winona Barker is principal scientist. The PIR is available to all who wish to telephone our computer. We also distribute the tapes to other organizations who then redistribute them throughout the world. These groups help with the distribution of the PIR and help with the collection of the information, and we at PIR make sure that the quality of the information is correct and accurate, which is absolutely essential if our PIR databank is to be productive and really influential as the unique world source databank of protein sequencing.

Back in the early 1960s I wrote a book on the use of computers in biology and medicine. In that book there are many, many applications in areas in which we were just getting started or hadn't even been started at that point. It's interesting to look at it today and see that almost all of the things in there either are whole fields of their own or coming along rapidly. So it's hard to say things change.

I have what I call a circle of knowledge. When I first started out what I felt I knew was inside the circle, and what I didn't know was everything outside the circle. But the most important thing was the circumference of the circle, which is what I knew about what I didn't know, because that's the most important. As I learned more and more, the most important thing was that I learned more and more about what I really didn't know about. Because when you are outside the circle, the things you don't know, you don't even know that you don't know (Figure 1). Unfortunately as time goes on and you get to the mature stage, you realize you don't necessarily learn more but you sure know a lot more about what you don't know.

Bruce Waxman   I'm struck by the enormous sense of accomplishment that is represented here in this room. Over the last several months, as I've thought about this meeting, I've had an opportunity to wonder whether we really had done anything over the last 25 to 30 years. At any particular point in time in the early or mid-1960s, especially if you were with the government, you might have wondered if anything useful was happening, given all the money spent.

At times progress seemed so small and insignificant and yet, looking back over the years it's just incredible what we've accomplished. The work that Will Dixon just talked about virtually revolutionized the practice of statistics in this country, and it was a biomedical activity that started it. The magnificent work of Hubert Pipberger and Caesar Caceres has become commonplace. You can't go to a hospital today and have your EKG taken without benefiting from their early work. The clinical chemistry activities that Don Lindberg discussed have also become ubiquitous. The hospital information systems that Octo Barnett and Mel Hodge worked on are taken for granted. The imaging work

FIGURE 1
Circles of knowledge

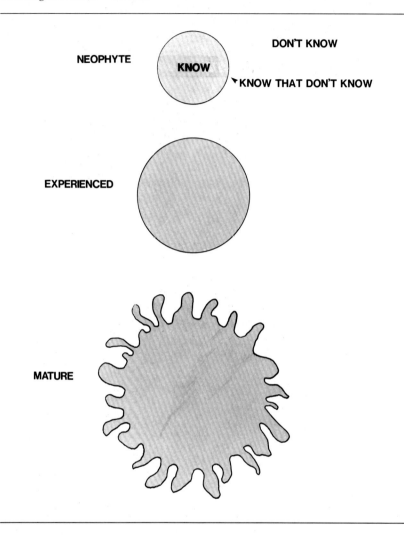

that Bob Ledley pioneered is beginning to produce absolutely marvelous developments, especially in recent years. Perhaps Jerry Cox will talk about some of that later. Although the work was done for biomedical purposes, Clark and Molnar's LINC machine virtually revolutionized the computer industry. Larry Weed's work has also had an enormous impact.

Looking back over all this time, it's a tremendous compendium of accomplishments! And yet, at each point in time, I can't help but remember how disappointed I was that nothing seemed to be happening, which is the sort of parochial view that one has if progress is viewed over too short a time span. Sometimes I've played the game of "What would have happened if?" What would have happened, for instance, if I had not been so incredibly naive in 1960? For example, when I joined the NIH, I was under the impression that NIH was really serious and wanted to spend a lot of money to find out what could be done with computers. In fact, they weren't that motivated at all. They wanted to spend a few hundred thousands of dollars just to maintain an impression. We were fortunate enough not to have realized that was the game plan, and we wound up spending 50 or 60 million dollars over five years.

Again I've wondered, if I'd been successful in discouraging Bill Raub from supporting work in AI, what would have happened? But I wasn't. Bill went ahead and supported that work, and it's had an interesting influence on things since. We will need even longer to judge this one.

It's very, very satisfying to look back over all this time and see how many of these things were successful.

Participants' Discussion

William Yamamoto Bruce, when you switched to the National Center for Health Services Research, that was a dramatic change in the orientation in which you were planting seeds. You were instrumental in getting me to leave Penn and go to George Washington University as a consequence. You switched your interest to the application of computers in public sector medicine: management information, access, costs, quality, and other things that are current shibboleths. Before that your main stress had been science. You had influence on the dramatic change in the direction in which public computer policy and interest went. I don't know what was going through your mind when you made that switch other than you had got a very interesting proposition, I would guess from Paul Sanazzaro and others.

Bruce Waxman This happened as I recall about 1966 or 1967. I think that move was motivated largely because I had felt frustration in the inability of computing to show any fundamental impact in basic research. I thought perhaps its role might be more in applied aspects of medicine. I went over there because the interests were more in medicine *per se* than in biology. That was what was motivating me.

William Yamamoto I'd like everyone in the room to have a chance to either reminisce or clarify—to rewrite the history of things.

Helmuth Orthner Your presentations clearly show that the experiments and projects that were conducted lead to success only after a number of years. That is, you cannot just fund a project for three years and then stop. These projects take five to ten years, and only then you find the payoff. The NIH funding cycle is typically three years. Maybe in certain research projects it's five years, but it's very difficult to establish something longer. What are your comments on this?

Harold Schoolman From the Library's point of view, we are very sympathetic to this, and we have maintained funding of a number of projects for considerably longer. NIH in general is moving to extended funding periods with established investigators—at least for five years and then, with the recommendation of the committee, for an even longer period. I think there is a general appreciation of the fact that you bring up. The means by which it can be successfully implemented, I think resides much more in the education of the academic and administrative community. But in general, independent of the type of research being done, for administrative reasons there is an increase in sympathy for longer funding activity.

William Yamamoto   Look at the history of funding for research in all directions. There are notable long-term projects which NIH did foster. For example, statistical research at UCLA went well over 12 years. It seemed to me as a "perpetual" study section member that the AIM-SUMEX project was an immortal project for funding. When I sat on the DRR Council some years ago there was another program called General Clinical Research Centers in which institutions with incredibly low priorities were being funded for 10, 12, and 14 years. Biomedical Engineering laboratories like Dr. Cox's laboratory in St. Louis and another at Case Western Reserve in Cleveland have merited and earned long-term historical support. As is proper however, they had to resubmit and be re-reviewed periodically, so they were able to carry out long-term projects. The few I mention are just a small selection of a longer list of programs supported for a time.

You cannot develop hospital information systems unless you also have long term funding, but sources are mixed. In the U.S., examples were the activities of corporations like the National Data Corporation and the succession of Lockheed and Technicon in the El Camino project. Small parts of federal funding played a role in the El Camino project, mostly in the evaluation. The National Data project, which came up and disappeared, was not at all government sponsored.

The program that Dr. Morris Collen has conducted for a number of years—I remember site-visiting that back around 1963 or 1964—received a substantial period of support but was largely self-sustained. I recall the funding history of the PROMIS system. I was sitting in a car on a railway bridge with Bruce Waxman and I said to him, "When 20% of your portfolio is in one project, I think that you are in trouble."

We also spent a substantial amount of time trying to replicate the LDS MEDLAB system for a period of about three or four years at five sites in the United States. We discovered that kind of project fails if you can't replicate Homer Warner. The ability to sustain a coordinated activity of many individuals in an institutional setting depends, it seems, on reproducing the idiosyncratic abilities of the principle investigator. Today many of those things which were integrated in the old MEDLAB system have been piecemealed out. So the migration of science or scientific products in the United States is not just a function of long-term support, but it is also a function of how society views what tasks are appropriate for public support as opposed to corporate support or the talent of individuals.

Now, the present violin string I harp on concerns the distinction between big science and little science as it relates to the intellectual problems in medical informatics. There are many problems that need small support but for long periods of time. For instance, I have three unfinished manuscripts on my desk, and they will probably still be unfinished several years from now. They are problems I had begun working on perhaps 15 to 20 years ago. One time I asked for continued funding on a National Library Medicine grant in which I proposed to have a computer program explain another program. We had been investigating certain database theories in a previous grant, and I discovered that I didn't know what I was talking about. So I wrote a renewal proposal that said, "I don't know what I am talking about, but this is what I think I need to do." Very appropriately the review panel said to me, "Well, when you know what you want to ask, then come back to us."

There is also a scale of science dealing with the nascent levels of ideas where you don't need either long-term or large-scale funding but the university culture demands that faculty have grant support. The lead sentence in one of the papers I would like to write reads as follows: I wish to prove that "my heart leaps when I behold a rainbow in the sky" is a computation. The rest of the paper does not require long-term financial support as far as I can see. I don't know if I'll ever finish that paper, but I have a pretty good idea of how the first three pages will go. Thus I describe small computer science that needs not many dollars but long support. So information science funding is a spectrum. Whether it impacts the whole industry or whether it's going to create a new discipline, we cannot predict. Dollars and time are not necessarily trade-offs but separate characteristics to consider in research support.

All we can have as seed planters, whether we are intellectual seed planters or financial seed planters or organizational seed planters, is the confidence that society has enough talent buried in it to continue a momentum from the initiative of individuals. The difference perhaps between European efforts and ours may be that the European nations are somewhat smaller than ours and have a smaller gene pool from which to draw.

Jochen Moehr   I am in Canada now, but my experience is based on work done in Germany. From the perspective of a European, one gets the impression that the points alluded to by the previous discussants are important. However, medical informatics could have taken different routes.

In Germany—and I think it is recognized by everybody here—Peter Reichertz has had a very important goal-setting function. One of his merits was to concentrate very early on education in medical informatics. In the U.S., programs were mostly at the graduate and post-graduate level, established in the early seventies, while in Germany, medical informaticians were educated starting at the undergraduate level. This emphasis in Germany provided for a broad basis of the field.

Another important difference in the development in Europe is that the research done there was not determined by fundable projects as much as being carried on by institutions that had patient care obligations and service functions. A few institutions in the United States were doing this type of research also, such as Massachusetts General Hospital [in Boston] and Latter Day Saints Hospital [in Salt Lake City].

Both developments may have contributed to the fact that less of the leading edge of technology advancement was achieved in Europe, but greater success with more comprehensive approaches was realized, achievements in hospital information systems, for instance. In this country the whole administrative side of medical informatics is not very well represented in medical informatics research. On the other hand, the achievements in fields like expert systems are outstanding. These examples show that the course of history was determined by certain factors and that the result we see on this continent is but one of several alternatives.

William Yamamoto   In Germany they have institutes, starting with the Kaiser Wilhelm and the Max Planck Institutes, that have the characteristic of being able to foster long-term research along certain directions. I do not know to what extent their short-term research funding parallels ours, but it seems to me looking at NIH in particular, and to a lesser extent NSF funding in the United States, that the philosophy is expressed in the occasional epithet: If you give enough typewriters to enough monkeys you'll eventually get a sonnet.

I think that the philosophy of spreading or broadcasting support for science—which is an historic notion I think if you look back in the early activities at NIH—is a sound one. It means that you have to sacrifice somewhat the length of time for which things are supported in the interest of finding those foci from which originality arises.

Harold Schoolman   I agree with you philosophically, but I think that Dr. Orthner's point is correct that the nature of work in many aspects of informatics is such that the most productive of people take six, seven, or eight years to "complete" a project, and that the funding mechanisms of most funding institutions are not geared for single funding commitments of that length. It is something that you suffer with. The only consolation I can offer is that many such institutions confronted with problems of that length had been successful in maintaining funding for the required length of time even though it meant repetitive applications. The difference between repetitive application and the noncompeting renewal, I'm not sure is an issue of sufficient importance to worry about. Much more critical in my mind would be the establishment of centers of excellence that create for that institution the core foundation and the core support on a long-term, continuing basis that will assure that at least the basic resources are available.

Morris Collen   I would like to try to tie together some of the important contributions of the three major streams of funding that occurred through what I call the golden years—that dozen years from the 1960s to the middle of the seventies. The tremendous contribution that NIH made through its Division of Research Resources to support computers for biomedical research has already been mentioned. The centers that were established and exist to this day are UCLA, one of the first, and then the University of Utah, Washington University, Johns Hopkins, Tulane, Stanford, and the Northeast group. All these were supported by NIH in the 1960s. When the ACRC came along, it supported all the computer applications in biomedical research.

Later on in the 1960s, as was mentioned very briefly, Paul Sanazzaro became the first director of the National Center for Health Services Research. He established the Health Care Systems Study Section which, in parallel with the ACRC, would review grants for computer applications in health care. Some of the same people would move between the two—the names have all been mentioned—reviewing scientific research studies for the Advisory Committee on Computers in Research and practical computing applications for the National Center's Health Care Systems Study Section.

The third funding stream was the Regional Medical Program, which funded computer applications under the Heart, Cancer, and Stroke Act of 1965. By the end of the sixties and early seventies, millions of dollars were being poured through these three streams and computers began to spread all through the hospitals in this country.

Around 1974 our country had economic problems, and President Nixon started cutting down on research support, which resulted in the NCHSR&D closing down the original nine health services research centers. A new director, Dr. Rosenthal, came into the National Center, and soon more research centers were started, including Lindberg's at the University of Missouri, Columbia. After 1975 we have never had such a tremendous outpouring of funds for medical informatics as we had in those golden years.

Gwilym Lodwick   I have shared Bruce Waxman's disappointment in the progress that has occurred when one works with computing. On the other hand, as a radiologist I was one of the first to use the computer in radiology, and there weren't very many people around who really understood what I was up to. It has taken a great deal of time. New generations have appeared in the interval. Now radiologists are used to computing. They are used to CRT displays, and they are used to turning the knobs to get better images. They're really very cognizant of the role of computers in medical practice and radiology. Now, some of the tools that were developed in the early sixties will be put to work. So there is that long turnaround when you are practicing and working in a medical group. You don't expect to turn around the medical world overnight.

Bruce Waxman   Jerry Cox has a Lucasfilms production that shows what one is able to accomplish in radiology. About a year-and-a-half ago I saw the people at Lucasfilms produce a demonstration on a rather extraordinary computer called PIXAR that they had designed. They had in fact taken CT scan data and reconstructed a three-dimensional, almost holographic image. They were able to rotate it in three dimensions so that you could not only see the entire bone structure but also the outline of the skin and fatty tissue. I thought then that if you really wanted to do something interesting, you could use CAD/CAM capability to model the kind of prosthesis that I have in my leg and essentially fit the prosthesis to the CT image rather than do it the clumsy way the orthopods do this sort of thing now. Its just a remarkable advance in terms of what we're able to do.

Jerry Cox   I didn't bring the tape Bruce referred to because I thought this was a nostalgia conference, and that tape is not nostalgia. In fact that reminds me of the quip that "nostalgia ain't what it used to be," but I think this conference is a lot of fun so I don't believe that. That tape, in any case, is available from SIGGRAPH, a Special Interest Group of the Association for Computing Machinery. It's one of the SIGGRAPH review tapes.[4] It's two hours of really spectacular graphics and image processing. We are doing wrist joint visualization, but actually I think it's Johns Hopkins that's doing the hip replacement visualization.

Joshua Lederberg   I'd like to respond to and generalize a little bit from what Harold Schoolman was saying about strategies of research support. What we've heard already—and it applies to many other fields as well—shows the imperatives of pluralism as opposed to overcentralized decisions about the direction of scientific opportunity. The wisest people sitting around the table can make very big mistakes. I think the opportunity to go to different agencies, as has been the case, is very impor-

---

[4] See "Visualization in Scientific Computing," a special issue of *Computer Graphics*, Vol 21, #6, Nov. 1987. This report is accompanied by two hours of videotape published as issues 28 and 29 of the *SIGGRAPH Video Review*. To request price information and order copies, contact ACM Order Department, P.O. Box 64145, Baltimore, MD 21264, (301) 528–4261.

tant in the development of our field, and it was absolutely instrumental in being able to get started. For our overall national system of research support, maintaining that pluralism is a very important principle. The increased term of grants is equally so. People simply cannot do creative work if they have to come back to the well and justify where they are on a two- and three-year time scale. You spend all of your time writing the grant applications.

I do not agree with Dr. Yamamoto in his congratulations to the Study Section for turning him down. One of the things that really squelches a real creativity is the demand put to an investigator that he know what he is doing before he gets support. Very creative people don't know what they are doing when they are first browsing around the field and trying to get their bearings in it. We ourselves are the enemy when we are impaneled to try to critique other peoples' proposals.

There is a vast difference between exploratory and exploitative research. The latter, which is what most people do most of the time, is a foundation for your inquiry and you do have to know what you are doing. But the real discoveries come when you don't know what you are looking for, when there is no way to anticipate the unknown.

Finally, none of these things can happen without the shelter of institutions. I doubt the grant system can be radically reformed. Anything the government does must be hemmed in with so many rules for accountability that the other fount of pluralism is the institutions where the research is actually done. What doesn't succeed in one place can succeed in another, provided the institutions maintain their viability. When every last bit of flexibility is taken away from you, for example the relentless pressures on indirect cost recovery, there is just nothing left to be able to provide that flexibility.

I'd like to remark on how long it takes to do something useful. I would date the DNA revolution from 1944 when Avery discovered that it was DNA that was responsible for genetic transformation in the pneumococcus. Until about 1980 I could make a rather quizzical self-examination and ask the question, "Up to this moment has anybody's life been saved from knowledge we would not have had if we didn't know the structure of DNA?" And up until 1980 the answer essentially was "No." It took at least 35 years to get the actuality of practical applications precisely because this was such a revolutionary discovery. The building of the infrastructure and the framework in which to make good uses of it extended for a very long time. I used to be somewhat self-critical about what was going on in technology transfer and so forth, asking why things didn't happen sooner. I now realize these things could not have been accelerated. There was such an enormous knowledge structure that had to be built to make it effective, that it would have taken almost all that time even under ideal circumstances.

That notion has to be understood more realistically in the areas we are talking about.

Finally, we've had a marvelous colloquy here that provides data about the history of our field. I think it's wonderful that it's being recorded and that we can get further commentary. Morris Collen has asked us to deposit our published papers at the National Library of Medicine. My view is that's sort of carrying coals to Newcastle. Most of those papers that are in the published literature are there in the journals. As Lindley Darden and others have emphasized, it's the unpublished material that has to be preserved. I hope we will have a little group come out of this meeting that will talk more seriously about exactly what needs to be done in order to be sure that a rapidly vanishing history is somehow properly captured.

Planting the Seeds

William S. Yamamoto, MD
George Washington University, Washington, D.C.

I started thinking about computing in 1948 when I first became intrigued by the book *Cybernetics* by Norbert Wiener, and problems of respiration in exercise. The combination of problems was too complicated to deal with symbolically, and I wanted a physical representation of the mathematics involved. Such considerations found me firmly embedded in computing by the mid-fifties. By happenstance, I found myself giving a presentation at UCLA on a Sunday morning to a group at the Brain Research Institute. Apparently because of my interest in neural computing, or perhaps because I had the temerity to cite scriptures on a Sunday morning in a scientific session, Dr. Bruce Waxman invited me in 1963 to join the ACCR, which was an *ad hoc* committee to promote medical use of computers in research.

It was for me a most marvelous committee and my first opportunity to deal publicly with the great figures of that day in computing. Many are here and on the panel, including Dr. Waxman, himself. I would characterize myself as a passive observer in most of my life, and thus I had the privilege of being on the committee with Drs. Lusted, Pratt, Warner, and Dixon of the medical area; and the informative and amusing discourse they had with the likes of Norman Shapiro, Max Woodbury, Allen Newell, Joseph Weizenbaum, and Allen Perlis. The ACCR had as its mission the planting of the seed literally to develop the NIH portfolio in computer research in medical institutions. Our concern included physical facilities, machines, methods, ideas, the laboratories wherever computer use was possible. You must realize, also, that, even in the business and administrative sectors, computers in the early sixties were more in the stance of promise than production.

Planting the seed was a marvelously exciting activity. Machines changed. The LINC was promulgated, and transistorization and integrated circuits appeared. Early on computer research seemed enormously expensive. Also it was fraught with both difficulty and unexpected consequences. As a scientific panel, ACCR reviewed grant proposals and also engaged in lengthy discussions about what was or was not feasible. Everybody was an enthusiast of a type which today is called a "hacker." I can still recall being on an airplane, I don't remember where, but it was undoubtedly to or from a site visit with Homer

74

Warner. He, in addition to all the materials that a site visitor usually has to carry around, was carrying around some printouts and program consequences of early work that he was doing on pediatric cardiology diagnosis. We spent much of our flight time looking at printouts. Everyone had a very parochial interest. Mine were signal processing and mathematical representation. Becoming a member of ACCR to serve my government, as it were, was an exciting adventure, a privilege that has changed me in a manner from which I have not recovered. Most of the people on that panel and study sections over the years seed every section that meets for this symposium on medical informatics. Computing now brings us together to review this history. Interest in computation has brought together one of the most exciting adventures in modern science and philosophy—the reification of ideas.

I would like to make only one contemporaneous comment about this experience. When it began, it was largely concerned with simple problems in representation, numerical computation, the acquisition and disposition of biological signals, in the use of statistics as the basis for inference, and the several forms of management information. I don't know to what extent these areas are now enclosed in the rubric "medical informatics." I have the unfortunate feeling that that rubric and its practitioners tend to focus too heavily on what is now regarded as knowledge engineering or symbolic data processing, and have grown away from things which charmed others of us around this conference site. De-emphasized by our times are physical or biological signals, the operation of the health care enterprise, and its information systems for a reportorial, fiscal, and managerial point of view. We have become preoccupied with what we call ourselves and what constitutes an orthodoxy. In those early days, I must say, every idea was new. Impossible ideas were the most amusing: Everybody was at the same primordial state. Planting seed, I think, in many ways is more exciting than harvesting the fruit. Although we should not claim that today we are harvesting a great deal of fruit, the trees are sturdy saplings and there is much yet to come. Unhappily, I don't think we shall ever be able to relive those early days when Dr. Waxman, in particular, actually used to effervesce with the idea of giving away our dear Uncle Sam's money to someone who wanted to compute in the medical sector.

Health Sciences Computing Facility, University of California, Los Angeles, 1959–1979

Wilfrid J. Dixon, PhD and Patricia M. Britt
BMDP Statistical Software, Los Angeles

Introduction

From 1959 to 1979, Will Dixon directed the Health Sciences Computing Facility (HSCF) at UCLA. This major computing resource was funded by the NIH Division of Research Resources to provide statistical and computer support for medical research. From the perspective of the present, it is hard to remember how tentatively the now ubiquitous computer was used 25 years ago. Hence, it is difficult to convey the excitement we felt in being part of a revolutionary change in the way research is conducted. But in the early 1960s, computer access was limited almost exclusively to the computer expert, and there were very few of them in the biological sciences. Furthermore, most scientific computing resources were designed for the physical scientist, and lacked the hardware (especially storage) and applications software (especially statistics) to support biology. Even where assistance was provided, the consultants rarely spoke the language of the biologist. HSCF was established to remedy these deficiencies, and it provided the focus for a large number of innovative and important studies.

The mission of the facility included participation in substantive research, and research and development in the statistical and mathematical methods and advanced computer systems needed to support it. Because the underlying theory available to biologists was often less extensive than in the physical sciences, their need was greater for graphical representations, interactive methods, and effective data handling. Finally, being less comfortable with the technical aspects of computing, our research community required specialized assistance in using these tools.

Conversely, since our research was concerned with the methods required to meet special and continually changing needs, rather than with satisfying a predefined set of externally derived specifications, our training, consultation, software distribution, and computer service activities were an essential part of the total experiment, providing the criteria for measuring the success of previous phases of the project and the basis for determining future directions.

At the time HSCF was established, Will had already begun an effort to develop "package programs" (then a novel concept) for statistics. This effort continued at the center and evolved into the BMDP Statistical Programs, now widely used. Other notable achievements of HSCF included advances in statistical methodology, the development of an early timesharing system, innovative work in graphics, and collaboration and support for a number of significant biological research projects.

Research Strategy

From the inception of the project, we were convinced that effective tools for adapting the computer to the needs of the biologist could be developed only in the context of real research studies. Given the excitement generated by computer access and the regional focus of the facility, we were able to choose our collaborative projects from a very broad range of studies, so we deliberately selected projects that presented severe challenges to our existing methodologies. For example, early in the project, we worked closely with Dr. Phillip May on his schizophrenia study, which put particularly heavy demands on file systems and on data screening and missing value handling. Similarly, our association with the Brain Research Institute spurred development of a time series program based on the fast Fourier transformation algorithm, as well as graphics and computer-to-computer communication, while our collaboration with the City of Hope resulted in further file handling software.

Given constant interaction among projects, advances in one area led to advances in others. The stages of an evolutionary cycle of statistical development typically proceeded as follows:

- Support for projects in need of statistical analysis
- Design of further experiments from the findings of these analyses
- Adaptation of available statistical techniques to the needs of the designed experiments
- Development of computer-based extensions to the existing statistical techniques
- Research in new statistical techniques made feasible by new computing power
- Development of mathematical bases for these techniques
- Development of the mathematics required for computer implementation of the new techniques.

This kind of cycle was also typical of the evolution of supporting research in other areas except that the interactions became more complex as new dimensions were added. Real achievements in one area required supporting advances in other dimensions. As solutions to specific problems were found and developed into effective tools, they became part of the input to the next projects. Thus, our fundamentally practical approach to the problem grounding each development in the needs of an initially independent study, permitted us to develop a coherent and interrelated set of tools and methodologies.

To facilitate this kind of interaction among the various aspects of the project, we adopted the following guidelines:

☐ Project personnel were encouraged to participate in a variety of investigations. The involvement varied from assistance with using the computer or advice on appropriate analytic methods, to collaborative research. The gain to the facility was insight at a variety of levels into what problems required solution, the approaches that were considered, and the difficulties anticipated or encountered.

☐ Software packages that would be of general use were identified and the necessary research and development was carried out. As tools were developed, they were prepared for export through terminal access and, in the case of the statistical software, through distribution on tape to a worldwide community of users.

☐ Project personnel were encouraged to engage in research in their areas of special interest. Most of the resulting studies furthered the research objectives of the project, since, by virtue of the climate created, staff members were most interested in the application of computer technology to biomedical research.

Statistical Software

When the computer was introduced into the biological environment, it put the techniques of the statistician to a severe test—a test that often found them wanting. The problem was not how to look at a small set of data optimally, but how to look at a large set of data reasonably. Missing data and bad data are a fact of life in biology—a fact largely ignored by traditional statistics. The promise of the computer was exciting, but the reality was often far from satisfactory.

Our basic goal was to develop techniques suitable for a computer and accessible to the biologist who was neither a statistician nor a computer expert. We not only developed the software to support this effort, but also provided the computing resource and the consultants to enable scientists to use the new tools. Our statisticians worked as an integral part of the research team. In turn, they fed the practical needs of the research projects back into our software development, making it responsive to the real needs of medical research. The programs were not only widely used, but also widely copied. Indeed, SPSS began as a direct copy of our statistical algorithms, with modifications to the control language used to specify the analysis.

Other Core Research Projects

HSCF research topics included statistical techniques, methodology for clinical trials, mathematical models, systems for data storage and retrieval, graphics, and interactive use of the computer. The selection of specific project objectives resulted from our perception of the general needs of the investigators, our experience in trying to meet them, and the interaction of our core research with the collaborative projects in which we were involved.

For the time, the HSCF computing resources were powerful and flexible, providing interactive computing on an IBM 360/91, one of the "super computers" of its day. We wrote a timesharing operating system to make it possible to support a number of interactive terminals. Developing one's own operating system seems an extraordinary activity for a resource dedicated to the support of medical research, but, given what was available at the time, it was a very necessary accomplishment. Similarly software was developed for managing files for developing interactive data input templates; and for a database management system.

HSCF was also involved in early research in graphics. We developed a convenient graphics language and a number of exploratory applications in statistics and modeling. Promising work included techniques for rotational examination of objects (including multi-dimensional visualization of data points), identification of subgroups defined by given variables, stratification, multiple plots, etc. Although our results were encouraging, the cost of adequate graphics hardware was great at the time, and the techniques did not seem to be comfortable for most investigators. We first used an IBM 2250 graphics terminal and later an IMLACO terminal but eventually decided that the project, while exciting, was not cost effective. From the present perspective, it is clear that it was simply too far ahead of its time. Old films of our work look both promising and timely today.

Collaborative Research Projects

From the outset HSCF had a regional orientation. In 1961, there were 30 non-UCLA institutions whose biomedical researchers obtained computing support at BSCF, all but one of them located in a west-coast state.

FIGURE 1

FOR RELEASE: FROM: Al Hicks
                                        UCLA Public Information Office
Sunday, July 21, 1963   BR 2-8911, Ext. 2342

More than 100 medical research projects at UCLA are currently receiving computer support at the University's new Health Sciences Computing Facility--the nation's largest data processing center for medical research. Dr. Wilfrid J. Dixon, right, is director of the new facility, which consists of powerful IBM 7094 and 1410 data processing systems. Here he discusses current projects with Dr. Sherman M. Mellinkoff, left, dean of the UCLA School of Medicine, and Dr. Foster Sherwood, center, UCLA vice-chancellor. The new $3,300,000 computing center was made possible by a grant from the National Institutes of Health.

# # #

By 1964 the distribution was much broader including the American Red Cross, Harvard, Rutgers, Tulane, the University of Arkansas, the Mayo Clinic, and Yale. About a quarter of the facility's time was devoted to such usage.

The first teleprocessing unit, an IBM 1013 data transmission terminal at Pacific State Hospital in Pomona, California, was operating in 1964. By 1967 there were 10 remote batch stations. Interactive and graphics terminals were added beginning in 1968. By the mid-1970s a large fraction of computer usage, both remote and local, was via terminal.

HSCF was deeply involved in many projects somewhat less involved in some, and served as a utility for a great number of others. The attached table lists a few projects featured in the 1974 Annual Report (chosen from hundreds supported that year), and gives some sense of the breadth of our activities. Approximately 2000 investigators had accounts at the center, and support was provided to medical research not only at UCLA but also at a number of other institutions, including several VA hospitals, Cedars-Sinai Hospital, City of Hope, University of Southern California, Los Angeles County Hospital, and the Salk Institute. Almost all of the University of California campuses had projects supported at HSCF.

Among the important studies with which we were closely involved were

- Tissue typing studies led by Dr. Paul Terasaki. These studies deal with serotyping for transplantation and have contributed key insights in immunology. One of our statisticians was (and continues to be) a key member of this research team, and the project made important contributions to the development of our analytic procedures.

- Genetic linkage studies directed by Drs. M. Anne Spence and Kenneth Lange. These studies led to the development of genetic counseling tools, and continue to make significant contributions to basic understanding of genetics.

- Research on schizophrenia, led by Dr. Phillip May. This project established the superior effectiveness of tranquilizers over shock and psychotherapy in dealing with schizophrenia. This was a long term study, and a large number of variables were observed. As a result, it taxed our data handling and analytic resources. Its needs drove many of our software developments and further accelerated development of statistical methods.

Early studies of the effects of diet on heart disease with Drs. Seymour Dayton and Lee Pearce. This study was the first to suggest an increase in cancer mortality with heavy use of polyunsaturated fats.

Summary

Support of the type we provided is no longer necessary. Anyone can get access to a computer and use it effectively, and, while there continues to be room for improvement in research methods and software, good tools are widely available. However, much of the progress made in medical research in the sixties and seventies would not have been possible without the support of such centers as HSCF, which attracted unique groups of scientists to work together to make the computer's promise a reality. Many of the projects begun with the support of HSCF developed into major studies with considerable impact on the scientific community. We were fortunate to have been participants in an exciting and rapidly developing enterprise—and fortunate in our association with our scientific collaborators, our own staff, and leaders in the Division of Research Resources and the Computer and Biomathematical Sciences Study Section.

Collaborative Projects Featured in 1974 Annual Report

Department	Subject
Surgery	Analysis of results and complications in total hip replacement
	Models of factors affecting adequacy of coronary blood flow
	Body fluids
Biochemistry	Analysis of steady state enzyme kinetics using interactive graphics
Brain Research Institute	Information retrieval
	Analysis and modeling of EEG correlates of neurobehaviorial processes
	Computer networks
	EEG findings in dyslexics
	EEG studies of hemispheric specialization
Kaiser Foundation	Outreach medical services
L.A. County	Alcohol project
	Evaluation of drug abuse programs
	Immunization surveillance
UC San Francisco	Carcinogenesis bioassay
Salk Institute	Radioimmunoassay and statistical analysis of assay data for certain neural substances
	Clinical investigations using somatostatin
Psychology	Interventions in families with adolescents at risk for schizophrenia
Anatomy	Sudden infant death

Collaborative Projects Featured in 1974 Annual Report

Department	Subject
Pharmacology	Chromatography/mass spectrometry in studies of clinical response in drug abuse
Medicine	Pediatric care
Sociology	Japanese/American study
Dentistry	Task analysis (delivery of dental care)
Public Health	Rural health and family planning (Ghana)
	Cervical cancer studies
Syntex Labs	Clinical trials
Calif. College of Medicine	Analysis of results of estrogen replacement therapy in postmenopausal women
Psychiatry	Analysis of patterns of language usage by mothers of autistic children
	Genetics
	Neurophysiology
	Computing resource
	Development of electrophysiological phenomena in autistic and normal children

Medical Informatics: A Personal View of Sowing the Seeds

Robert S. Ledley, DDS
Georgetown University Medical Center, Washington, D.C.

Introduction

I am writing this paper as a personal and rather chatty account of some of the circumstances that led to a number of the research accomplishments of my career. If I were asked which of these accomplishments I feel are most well known today, I would mention four in particular. The first I would call the "reasoning foundations of medical diagnosis," which is the title of the paper that appeared in *Science* that I wrote together with Dr. Lee B. Lusted in 1959 {1}. This paper has been called the "initiating" paper in medical informatics. The purpose of the paper was to outline methods by which a computer might assist the physician in making a medical diagnosis. In the article we proposed the use of many mathematical methods that today are included in the field of artificial intelligence. In that paper we used methods of Boolean algebra or symbolic logic to help identify the disease diagnosis, we included the application of Bayes's formula for cases in which the probability of a correct diagnosis has to be estimated, and we also included the use of mathematical value theories for selecting the treatment. The paper itself stimulated great interest, and what pleased me most was how much it stimulated other researchers to subsequently publish their views on a huge variety of methods and techniques for accomplishing computer aids to medical practice.

The second of my accomplishments which is generally known today is the development during 1973 of the first whole-body CT scanner, called the ACTA Scanner, which was put into routine clinical operation at Georgetown University Hospital in February of 1974 (Figure 1) {2}. The design of the ACTA Scanner laid the foundation for modern CT scanners and also for many of the fundamental aspects of magnetic resonance imaging. The ACTA Scanner first used the convolution algorithm for image reconstruction in computerized tomography, first used a digital image memory for driving a TV display which included color coding of the CT values, first incorporated a tilting gantry, and was first in many other innovations. The first ACTA Scanner built in my laboratories is now on permanent exhibit at the Smithsonian Institution's National Museum of American History in Washington, D.C.

FIGURE 1
Victory celebration
of staff who built the
ACTA Scanner

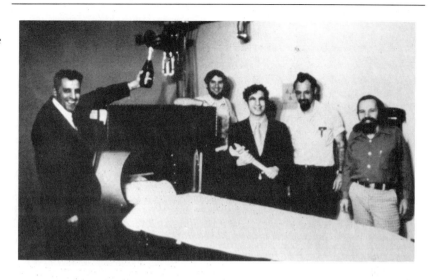

My third accomplishment was the early development in 1962 of computerized medical imaging and pattern recognition (Figure 2) {3}. Automatic computerized aids to chromosome analysis was the initial problem chosen, and along the way we developed a film scanner called FIDAC that interfaced to an IBM 7090 computer, we developed the method of syntax-directed pattern recognition, we developed the hardware and software for the interactive editing of chromosome images prior to the advent of modern digital image memories, and we developed a rapid television scanner for input to an IBM 360/44 computer, and many other innovations. Initially, I worked with Professor Frank H. Ruddle, and then with Dr. Herbert A. Lubs. We actively assisted in helping establish medical imaging research groups in England, in Canada, at the Lawrence Livermore Laboratories, and at the University of Florida, by constructing FIDAC instruments for them and giving them our software. We believe our research papers have stimulated many scientists to work in the computerized imaging field. In 1968 I established the scientific journal *Pattern Recognition*, which quickly became a standard source of articles in the general field, even up to the present time.

Finally, the Protein Identification Resource (PIR) (formerly the Atlas of Protein Sequence) is widely known as the world's primary, comprehensive knowledge-base for protein sequences {4}. Although I was the first principal investigator in 1962 of the NIH grant that led to the initial Atlas {5}, and I am presently principal investigator of the Protein Identification Resource {6}, the Atlas and the PIR were mainly

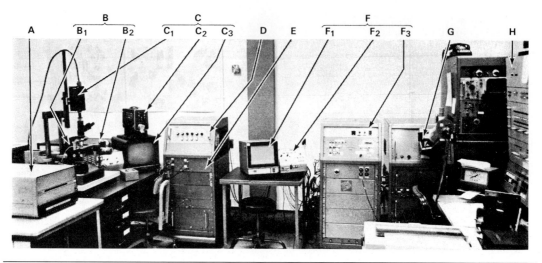

FIGURE 2

Picture of my biomedical pattern recognition laboratory as it existed in the early 1970s. Current equipment for automated chromosome analysis at National Biomedical Research Foundation. A: Hard copy picture printer; B: SPIDAC (Specimen Input to Digital Automatic Computer); B1: Leitz microscope; B2: motorized stage; C: VIDIAC (Vidicon Input for Automatic Computer); C1: Vidicon scanner; C2: control; C3: TV monitor; D: Silicon video memory system; E: Automatic stage control unit: F: MACDAC (Man-Machine Communication with Digital Automatic Computer); F1: display; F2: control console; F3; control unit; G: FIDAC (Film Input to Digital Automatic Computer); H: IBM 360/44 computer.

developed by my late colleague and associate Dr. Margaret O. Dayhoff (Figure 3) {7}. However, I list this as one of my important accomplishments, because I like to believe that my encouragement and occasional management of the PIR helps to ensure that it will continue to grow as a primary biomedical resource for scientists engaged in advancing biomedical science from a molecular genetic viewpoint.

On the other hand, if I was asked what other scientific accomplishments I have made in the past that in fact I wish were better known today, I would have a rather long list. The list would first include some of the books that I have authored, namely the handbook *Computers in Biology and Medicine* {8}, which was published in 1965 to assist biomedical researchers in using computers, the engineering text *Digital Computer and Control Engineering* {9}, published in 1960, which was the first textbook for engineers written about how to build a digital computer, and *Programming and Utilizing Digital Computers* {10}, published in 1962, which included what I believe is the first chapter written in a book on artificial intelligence, namely the chapter on "Programming to Achieve Intelligence."

FIGURE 3
Dr. Margaret
Dayhoff, who
worked with me
for 23 years

With respect to my continued work in medical diagnosis, I wish that some of my analytical results in symptom disease relationships and further analysis of Bayesian probabilities were more well known {11}. Actually, many of these results were based on my early work in the 1950s on computational methods on Boolean algebra {12} and the formulation of antecedence and consequence problems in Boolean algebra {13}. These methods were originally developed for use in the logical design of digital circuits {14} but were then applied to the medical problems {15} and also to operations research intelligence problems {16}. Although the logical circuit design methods are well known to engineers, they are, unfortunately, not associated with my name as originator but have blended into general engineering knowledge.

Of course, since we built the first whole-body CT scanner, we were able to write the first articles on three-dimensional reconstruction from sequential CT sections (Figure 4) {17}, on the determination of bone calcium concentration from CT scans {18}, on the use of CT scans for planning radiation therapy (Figure 5) {19}, and many more {20}. Again, although these results are now well known, unfortunately the fact that the first papers on such applications of CT were developed in my laboratories is not well known.

In medical imaging as well, I have a number of accomplishments which are well known but are not now associated with me. In particular, I initiated the field of syntax-directed pattern recognition {21}. In 1971, I developed and received a patent for the concept of the special-purpose image array processor which I called TEXAC (later sold as the

FIGURE 4
Early illustration
used to show the ob-
jective of extracting
an image of the ver-
tebrae from sequen-
tial CT scans

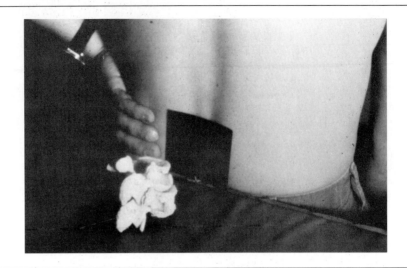

FIGURE 5
Illustration of one of
the first displays
from the ACTA
Scanner radiation
therapy planning
programs

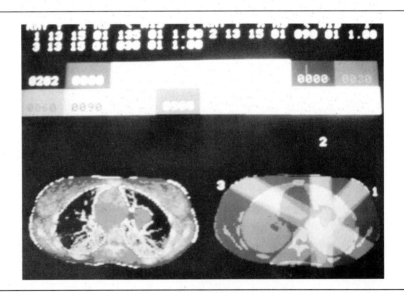

DeAnza IP5000) {22}. In medical imaging we developed the first methods for analyzing the three-dimensional structure of Golgi-stained neurons {23}, and we helped stimulate the medical imaging field by
publishing a dozen applications of computer analysis of medical images in such areas as automated chest X ray measurements, pap smear
analysis, differential white blood cell recognition and counting, automated lung alveolar section measurements, analysis of synapsis in electron micrographs, and many more {24}.

Finally, I have often wished that some of our other instrumentation developments were more well known, such as the CENOG (Computerized Electro Neuro-ophthalmograph) {25} which computerizes, quantitates, and integrates in a single instrument almost all ocular-motor and vestibular ocular-motor tests, the GUDFU (Georgetown University Digital Fluoroscopy Unit) {26}, which was one of the first digital subtraction angiography units that had capabilities still not incorporated in commercial units, and the AGA (Automated Genetic Analyzer) {27}, which uses a robot arm to automate the southern blot experiment for detecting genetic defects on a molecular level and promises to bring this capability into the hospital clinical laboratory. Also, more recently we have developed a modern, stand-alone automated chromosome analysis machine called the Metachrome {28}.

In addition, I should not forget that in 1965 we wrote the first computer programs for analyzing the optical system of the eye {29}, and that the first research accomplishment of my career was the development in 1952 of dental force analysis, which explains why human teeth have cusps and has important applications to the construction of complete dentures and other dental procedures {30}.

My Early Years

But getting back to the story of my career, my serious scientific education started in 1943 in the physics department at Columbia University where I went to college. In those days undergraduate physics included only two semesters of college physics, and undergraduate mathematics ended with three semesters of calculus; almost all other physics and math courses were given as graduate studies. Taking a few graduate physics courses convinced me I should take more math, which I did, but after taking many graduate math courses, I discovered that this math was not the mathematics of physics. So, after a stint in Columbia Engineering School, I went back to graduate physics. I was trying to "find myself," about 20 years ahead of the kids of the 1960s. But things only went from bad to worse when my parents convinced me that a career in physics was not feasible, because in those days (it's hard to believe this now) everyone knew that physicists were either independently wealthy gentlemen or starving dedicated scientists, and I was neither. The solution was to send me to dental school (there are a few dentists in my family) with the promise that I could continue my physics as a well-to-do dentist. So off to NYU Dental School I went, from 8:30 A.M. to 5:00 P.M. each day, after which I took the subway up to Columbia to take physics courses from 6:00 P.M. to 10:00 P.M. each evening. Thus, I was studying gross anatomy, histology, pathology, microbiology, physiology, etc. at the same time as atomic physics, nuclear physics, analytical dynamics, quantum mechanics, etc. I started out each morning carrying 12 sandwiches, and the bag was empty each evening. Professor Rabi would poke fun at me saying I was the only physics student he knew who could pull a tooth. I was working hard at "finding myself." After graduating from Dental School in 1948, I continued and practically exhausted all the graduate physics and math courses at Columbia by 1950, when I picked up a master's degree. But Columbia physics was truly exciting; I had such famous teachers as I.I. Rabi, E. Fermi, H.A. Bethe, W. Lamb, H. Yukawa, J.A. Wheeler, and others. I learned years later that they were all at Columbia because of the "Manhattan Project" (i.e., the atomic bomb project).

Suddenly, in 1950, because I was a dentist, I found myself in the Army. It seems that the North Koreans decided to go south, and I was given the choice of volunteering as a first lieutenant or being drafted as a private. As a first lieutenant I was sent to medical field service school, and after that, because I was a physicist, I was stationed at the National Bureau of Standards (NBS) in Washington, D.C. to work in the Dental Research Section there.

Computer Science

That was a stroke of good luck; I began to really "find myself." The day I arrived at NBS I found out about the SEAC (Standard Eastern Automatic Computer) (Figure 6) {31}, the world's first high-speed electronic digital computer in which the programs were stored digitally in the computer's memory. (The ENIAC had a plugboard-wired program; I believe that Wilks's computer in England began to operate two weeks after SEAC, and the UNIVAC was still not operational.) I had previously realized that although, conceptually, physics equations could be written to describe any biomedical phenomenon, such equations would be so complex that they could not feasibly be solved in closed form. Thus, the SEAC was my panacea, because the equations would become tractable to numerical methods of solutions. Or so I truly believed at the time. That was to be my field, application of computers to biomedical problems.

Unfortunately, the first problem was to learn about SEAC, and I enthusiastically took up the task. The engineers who designed SEAC were very friendly, and they unhesitatingly taught me all about the SEAC's engineering design. I carried out my first research project, applying SEAC to my dental force analysis. In 1953, I was out of the army, and I took a job in the computer division at NBS to continue learning about digital computers. They had just completed designing and building a second computer called DYSEAC, and were applying it to an experimental computerized air controller system using National Air-

FIGURE 6
The SEAC console in 1950 with my wife, who was one of the first programmers, at the controls

port radar. My job was to do the programming so that an operator using a joy stick cursor could interactively enable the computer to track all aircraft in the area. That was undoubtedly the first real-time, interactive graphics program that also incorporated time-sharing for multiple terminals. And it was written in hexadecimal machine code, because assembly languages and high level languages like FORTRAN had not yet been developed. Although the project was successful, the air controller system was not well written up in the scientific literature by the staff at NBS.

In studying the engineering of digital computers, I came across the problem of the systematic design of digital logic circuits, which was not well worked out at the time. To solve this problem I developed new mathematical computational methods in symbolic logic (or Boolean algebra). These methods were just as applicable to military intelligence problems as they were to digital logic design, and so in 1954 I wrote an article for the journal *Operations Research* on a "digital logic machine." Further developments of mine included the general formulation of Boolean algebraic computational problems in terms of solving for antecedences and consequences of given Boolean functions, the development of methods in multivalued Boolean logics, and in the application of Boolean matrices to solve Boolean equations. This area has subsequently become a mathematical field in its own right.

At that point a series of events occurred that finally brought me back to my original intention, computers applied to medicine. Eisenhower was president, Weeks was secretary of commerce, and Astin was director of NBS, when the Post Office Department asked NBS to evaluate a so-called battery additive (which I believe was Coca Cola) that was sent through the mails. NBS said the additive didn't work, Weeks said the NBS didn't understand the "play of the marketplace," Astin (who lived on Battery Lane) was put on the hot seat, and the budget of NBS was slashed, and Eisenhower couldn't care less. The computer division was the first to go. IBM hired the computer design group "en masse," and the rest of the engineers were dispersed around the country. I eventually was offered a job by George Shortly, a brilliant physicist who was editor of *Operations Research*, because he liked my paper on the digital logic machine. The job was at the Operations Research Office, a part of The Johns Hopkins University. There I continued my development in computational methods and logic. One day I met George Gamow; he introduced me to the DNA problem, made me a member of his amino acid tie club (there were about 20 members, and I think I was lysine), and encouraged me to apply some of my methods to that problem.

Next, in 1956 I took another operations research job at George Washington University (GWU), but within a few months the director of this group, Dr. Glen Camp, told the Navy Department that they should revitalize sailing ships, and so he lost his contract. But GWU was loyal to its employees, and to relocate me they arranged an interview with Professor Earnest Frank, chairman of the Electrical Engineering Department of the Engineering School. This was my second lucky stroke, because Earnest Frank had developed the theory of vector electrocardiology (at the same time and independently of Otto Schmidt), and therefore he welcomed with open arms an engineer who was interested in biology and medicine, and incidentally also was knowledgeable in the new, hot, engineering field of digital computer design. I immediately arranged one of the first digital computer engineering courses in the country in 1957, and that led to my writing of the first textbook for engineers on how to design a digital computer, namely *Digital Computer and Control Engineering*, published by McGraw-Hill in 1960.

Medical Informatics

My friends, knowing of my combined interest in engineering and biomedical research, introduced me to Dr. Lee Lusted, who at the time was at the NIH and was an engineer and a physician. Our common interests immediately became apparent and resulted in our work on the reasoning foundations of medical diagnosis. The idea of using computers to assist in medicine had, of course, been discussed from time to time by many people, but a specific idea of how to go about it had not been published. My attempts in the area were actually first made a few years earlier while I was at the NBS where I put together a deck of the McBee key sort cards (the cards with the holes around the margins) for diseases of the tongue. Each card was a disease, and the holes represented symptoms, and the symptoms related to the disease of the card were punched out to the card margin. Then, if needles were pushed through the edge holes of the deck of cards corresponding to a selection of symptoms, the cards that dropped would be only those corresponding to diseases having these symptoms. I even made a little device for facilitating the shaking and dropping of the cards, and as I carried this deck and my device around the halls of NBS, it didn't take the physicists more than a fraction of a second to say to me, "Oh, you're going to automate medical diagnosis, huh?" Of course, the cards did not truly carry out the logic that was required, and of course no probabilities were involved. But this work led Dr. Lusted and me to our first research accomplishment in medical informatics in 1959.

In our work we proposed the use of Boolean algebra or symbolic logic to eliminate disease possibilities based on the patient's symptom profile. We worked out methods for determining the most effective combination of medical tests for making the diagnosis, using the logical concepts of redundant and independent symptoms for the situation at hand. Where a number of disease diagnosis possibilities still occur, we proposed the use of conditional probabilities and Bayes's formula to determine the probability with which the patient may have the alternative diseases. Our theory demonstrates the importance of *not* considering symptoms as independent even if the assumption of independent symptoms simplifies the computations. The use of conditional probabilities in the diagnostic process leads naturally to the use of value theory in the choice of treatment. We proposed the use of transition probabilities (i.e., the probability that a change in the state of health of the patient will occur) in the choice of treatment, as well as the use of transition values in such a decision. We felt that our quantitative theoretical formulations help the analysis of the diagnosis-treatment problem and point to directions that should be taken in the collection of statistical data. Also our methods have direct application to the judicious evaluation between two or more possible new treatments, and so forth. Dr. Lusted and I wrote many papers on these concepts, and I also included these in my book, *Use of Computers in Biology and Medicine* {8}.

But I'm getting a little ahead of myself again. Back in 1957, and with the recommendation of Dr. Lusted, the National Academy of Sciences' National Research Council (NAS-NRC) asked me to do a survey of the potential of the use of computers in biology and medicine. This survey was supported by the Air Force and was to result not only in a survey {32} but also in a handbook to assist biomedical researchers in their use of computers.

The survey that I carried out for the NAS-NRC gave me the unique opportunity to talk with many biomedical researchers throughout the country about the potential of computer applications in biomedical research. These were incorporated in some detail in the handbook *Use of Computers in Biology and Medicine* {8}. However, the dean of the Engineering School at GWU at the time was unwilling to put significant resources into such applications of computers, and therefore I was unable to initiate my own research in this field. But at the NAS-NRC I was advised that I might start an independent, non-profit organization devoted exclusively to computers in biology and medicine, and indeed we did that. The NAS-NRC kindly gave us office space, loaned us office furniture and equipment, and the National Biomedical Research Foundation (NBRF) was established in June of 1960.

Medical Imaging

One of the first projects I initiated at NBRF was to build a film scanner and digitizer for inputting images into a digital computer. It consisted of focusing a flying spot from a CRT raster scan through the black and white image on the film, then detecting the transmitted light with a photomultiplier tube, and finally digitizing the electronic signal into four bits representing up to 16 gray-level values. The binary stream was interfaced directly into a computer. At first we adapted a 16 mm camera for the purpose, and later in 1963 a 35 mm reflex camera was used. The first system was built onto a laboratory cart, but later scanners consisted of two racks of electronic equipment. The scanner, called FIDAC, had a 2000×2000 pixel resolution, and inputted the gray-level data at the maximum rate of which the computer was capable. If unexposed film were used, the FIDAC could produce gray-level images. It must be realized that digital electronic technology in 1960 was not what it is today; all circuits had to be designed, built, and tested; there were no integrated circuit chips, and individual transistors were used. The computers of that time had no general interface boards; the FIDAC was wired directly into the computer.

And, of course, NBRF could not afford a computer, or even afford to purchase time on someone else's computer. But I had faith that if we built the scanner, someone would give us free time on their computer. And our white knight turned out to be a combination of IBM and Westinghouse. Looking back now, it was incredible that IBM paid for computer time on their 7090 computer at the Baltimore Westinghouse plant, and that Westinghouse let us wire our scanner directly into their computer while they were printing their payroll checks and calculating sensitive military data. Our first attempt at connecting the 7090 resulted in scrambled data, but IBM flew in a team of eight expert engineers to find that they had given us some connector pin numbers backwards. Eventually, and at no charge, IBM loaned us three top programmers who worked with us for several years, and the Goddard Space Flight Center gave us free computer time on their collection of IBM 7090 and later IBM 7094 computers. The imaging work was first supported by the Joseph P. Kennedy Jr. Foundation, and later by grants from NIH. Initially we worked on automated chromosome analysis together with Dr. Barbara Migeon of The Johns Hopkins University; later we cooperated with Professor Frank H. Ruddle of Yale University on the chromosome problem.

In 1964 I was invited by the Medical Research Council of England to a conference in Oxford, to discuss our imaging hardware and software developments. They purchased a FIDAC and our programs (Figure 7), and then later they hired Dr. Denis Rutovitz to head their automatic chromosome analysis group. The FIDAC was flown to England, and we crated its parts in wooden boxes carefully measured to fit through the cargo door of the aircraft. But at first the airline men could not get the boxes into the plane, and I remember standing in the middle of the Dulles Airport runway to show the men how to turn the boxes so they would fit through the door onto the plane.

I invented syntax-directed pattern recognition for recognizing objects such as chromosomes in any orientation, and the BUGSYS programming language to implement the syntax techniques. BUGSYS consists of a collection of conceptual pointers (bugs) that are programmed to move over the image to determine boundaries, areas, orientations, curvatures, etc. involved in the pattern-recognition and measurement process. Using these methods we developed programs to separate touching objects, separate overlapping chromosomes, etc. We were able to successfully classify chromosomes into the classical A-G groupings just in time for the advent of banding patterns. So we continued on and studied Giemsa banding profiles, and finally were able to discriminate individual chromosomes according to the Paris convention with 96% accuracy. We also applied our scanner and computer imaging methods to the first three-dimensional analysis of Golgi-stained neurons from sequential microtome sections of the neurons. We had an NIH grant awarded for this purpose, and obtained our neuron material from Dr. Van der Loos of The Johns Hopkins University and Dr. Alden Dudley of NIH.

In 1968 NBRF obtained a grant from the John A. Hartford Foundation for the down payment on an IBM 360/44 computer. We also applied for a grant from the NIH to support the computer, but for some reason the award was delayed. Meanwhile, with no signed sales agreement, our trusting friends at IBM actually delivered and installed the computer. Finally, the NIH grant was awarded, and, being the honest fellows we were, we signed a sales agreement and paid the quarter-of-

FIGURE 7
A FIDAC film
scanner

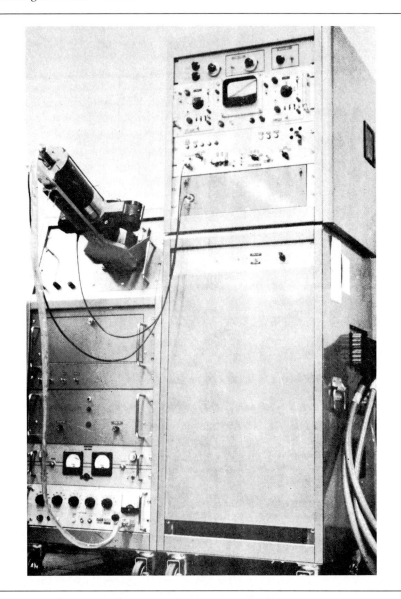

a-million dollars for the computer. The computer was well used. We designed and built an interactive graphics system for our pattern recognition laboratory in 1968, developed a computer-controlled microscope in 1969 (Figure 8), and by 1971 we had completed a high-speed vidicon scanner that could input into the computer a raster of 672×450 (or over 300,000) pixels in one-third of a second, a speed that was orders of magnitude faster than other scanners being developed at that time. At that time we were cooperating with Dr. Herbert Lubs, of Yale Univer-

FIGURE 8

Picture of the SPIDAC instrument showing the microscope, the motorized stage, and a portion of the manual control panel. Of course, the SPIDAC is also under computer control. The vidicon scanning camera appears above the microscope. A Xenon light and its power supply and filter arrangement are behind the microscope. The entire apparatus is shock mounted.

sity, and later also with Dr. Paul Ing of the University of Colorado, on the chromosome analysis.

By 1970 it became clear that the field of computers in medicine was well accepted by academic institutions. It was suggested by both George Washington University and Georgetown University that NBRF became an affiliate. Even though between 1968 and 1970 I was back as a part-time professor in the GWU Engineering School, I felt that having our laboratories in the midst of the Georgetown Medical Center would be more advantageous. Therefore, at the invitation of Dr. John Rose, dean of Georgetown University (GU) Medical School, NBRF affiliated with GU, moved into an area in the newly completed Preclinical Science Building, and I became a professor in the Physiology department of the Medical and Dental Schools. The space we occupied (and still occupy today) was designed to be a computer center. In the seventies architects always put them in the basement—and in our case, actually underground. There is a lawn above us, and we call our offices the "ivory dungeon." By late 1971 we had set up at Georgetown what was one of the most advanced computer image-processing laboratories ever assembled at that time, containing unique equipment developed by us. The graphics interface, called MACDAC, used the early Tektronix "write-through" storage scope, since digital display memories were not yet generally available. The vidicon scanner, called VIDIAC, used a scan-converter tube to temporarily store an image for later input to a computer at slower than TV scan rates, for computers at that time could not accept information that fast. The computer-controlled motorized microscope stage we developed, called SPIDAC, was very high speed and had a positional accuracy of one-and-a-quarter microns. We had developed a very high resolution drum scanner, and finally we had an improved FIDAC film scanner. All these interfaced directly into the IBM 360/44 computer.

Thus, by late 1971 we had used our imaging system to automatically recognize all chromosome spreads on a glass slide within one minute, and then to relocate them for operator review and interactive editing of touching and overlapping chromosomes, and then to perform a karyotype based on the Giemsa banding patterns of the chromosomes. In addition we applied the system to the analysis of many other biomedical images.

Although we were very successful in our work on medical image processing and had an approved NIH grant for our laboratories due to be renewed, disaster threatened in early 1973 when Nixon, who was president, impounded some of the NIH funding, and the grant was not paid. We also had another spate of bad luck. I had asked NIH for a contract to build a "stand-alone" computerized chromosome analysis instrument to be based on a smaller computer than our IBM 360/44, but the contract was given to Jet Propulsion Lab (JPL). The review committee made a site visit to JPL but not to NBRF, and deduced that JPL had a "better chance of developing a vidicon scanner" than NBRF, apparently not realizing that we at NBRF already had built a vidicon scanner and were already using it for chromosome analysis. But, as fate would have it, in retrospect, I have great difficulty complaining about the committee's decision.

In fact what I had thought was bad luck turned out to be another stroke of good luck, for it led directly to my development of the first whole-body CT scanner Administratively, we embarked on the development of the CT scanner, both to save Georgetown University some money and to help keep the NBRF bioengineering and imaging group alive. By February 1974 the CT scanner had been completed and both administrative goals fulfilled. Then, lo and behold, in May of 1974, NBRF received a check and the original grant award. It seems that someone went to court and unimpounded the NIH funds, and our previously approved grant was paid one year late. Thus if the grant had been paid in 1973, or if we had received the contract, we would never have developed the first whole-body CT scanner. And in the end we were awarded the grant anyway, and it turned out that in 1987, 14 years later, we built the Metachrome instrument, a sophisticated, stand-alone, automatic chromosome analysis instrument that includes the high-speed (within a few minutes) finding of chromosome spreads on a glass slide using present-day modern computer and electronic technology. But I am getting ahead of myself at this point.

The NIH grant that was finally awarded in 1974 was for medical imaging hardware and software. Based on our previous experience in image processing, the grant application proposed building a new and innovative type of image processor, which would consider whole pictures as "arguments," and process all the pixels in the argument pictures within the frame-grabbing time of a TV camera, namely within one-thirtieth of a second. Thus, for instance, if two pictures were to be added, pixel by pixel, then the value of each pixel of the resulting picture would be the sum of the values of the corresponding pixels in the argument pictures. Conditional operations were also included, where for example, a pixel in the resulting picture would be replaced only if the corresponding pixel in the first argument was greater than that in the second argument, etc. We called this whole-image array processor TEXAC, for Texture Analysis Computer. Its great value lies in the extreme speed with which the whole-image operations can be performed, and we have applied it to the chromosome analysis, muscle fiber analysis, platelet aggregation studies, tracking vacuoles in nerve fibers, etc. I received a patent in 1978.

The original electronic implementation proposed in the grant application involved sets of three image-converter tubes for each image memory, but by the time it was actually fabricated in 1976, digital memories became readily available. The contract NBRF gave DeAnza Systems to fabricate the TEXAC specified that our design was to be held confidential, but DeAnza, seeing a good thing, made it a product, namely the IP5000 and subsequent machines. By the time NBRF hired some lawyers, DeAnza was bought by Gould Inc., a very large electronic firm, and the U.S. government sided with Gould. It is ironic that recently, according to *The New York Times*, Gould Inc. has been accused of overcharging the U.S. government for image-processing equipment and has been prevented from bidding on government contracts.

In any event, I believe it is fair to say that the concept of whole picture image array processors, originated at NBRF, has had a great influence in the field of image processing, and, in fact, at an IEEE meeting in Washington, D.C. in 1977, a report on and demonstration of TEXAC was given the "best paper" award.

Computerized Tomography

As I mentioned above, we worked on CT because in early 1973 all our other bioengineering funding suddenly disappeared. Hearing about our problem, Dr. John Rose, dean of the Medical School, told me that Dr. Luessenhop, chief of Neurosurgery, was about to spend $500,000 for some type of scanner, and since we made "scanners" perhaps we could make it cheaper and save the university money and support our group as well. I checked with Dr. Luessenhop to find he was planning to purchase Hounsfield's computerized tomographic head scanner, announced by EMI, Ltd. The idea of computerized tomography was well known to me; in the 1960s, Kuhl at the University of Pennsylvania had constructed an instrument to perform computerized transverse axial tomography with signals emanating from the body injected with radioactive material; Tretiak had scanned X rays of a femur bone taken at different angles and reconstructed a cross-section in 1971; and in the early 1960s Cormack had completed an experiment demonstrating the accuracy of the reconstructed absorption coefficients. Thus, looking at the EMI brochure, I couldn't see why their proposed scanner required scanning through a water bath, which limited its use only to the upper part of the head. Also, the cross-sectional images shown in a book by Takahashi on *non*-computerized transverse axial tomography really made me feel that a whole-body computerized transverse axial tomograph could be feasibly developed. For if such reasonable, albeit fuzzy, cross-sections could be obtained without a computer, then the use of a computer, as shown by Cormack, should result in clear, sharp images. So I told the dean that I could develop a whole-body CT scanner, not just limited for use on the head, and for half the cost. The university said that NBRF should do the development, and if it worked, the university would pay for it. I called it the ACTA Scanner (for Automatic Computerized Transverse Axial Scanner). We started in June of 1973, and it was in routine clinical operation in February of 1974.

The development of the ACTA Scanner was perhaps the ultimate exercise in the cross-disciplinary approach, involving the design of mechanical equipment of considerable complexity, the handling of high voltage X ray equipment that was moving, the development of electro-optical mechanisms of a non-trivial nature, the sophisticated handling of real-time computer-input data, writing highly detailed and efficient numerical-analysis computer programs, and utilizing advanced display techniques. And these had to be coupled with a system design formulated for the medical needs of the physician, involving radiological methods, neurosurgical requirements, concepts in pathology, and anatomical knowledge. The vocabulary required for a detailed understanding of the practical medical needs and potentialities of such a system had to be understood by the engineer and translated into specific component design utilizing the current engineering "state of the art." Gross anatomy, mechanical design, oncology, theory of gears and cams, elements of radiology, electro-optical methods, radiation physics, digital computer engineering, pulmonary physiology, mathematical methods of Fourier analysis, osteology, assembly-language programming, and many more were all intimately involved in our cross-disciplinary development.

It was uncanny; almost all my scientific studies and much of my previous scientific experience, were required for the development. The diversity of my background now made sense; I sometimes felt as if I had somehow been guided for this purpose. I had taken a course in mechanical design during my short stint in Columbia University's Engineering School, which I needed to be able to design the mechanical gantry; from my study of gross anatomy I knew that the gantry should be tiltable to clearly see the spinal discs; I was familiar with ordinary x-ray tomography because when I was in the NBS Dental Research Section, they were perfecting the Panorex, an x-ray tomograph that imaged all the teeth on one film by rotating the x-ray tube around the patient's head; I had pioneered in computerized image processing and display; and I had taught courses in numerical analysis at the GWU Engineering School.

The first step in our work was to simulate the system on our own computer, an IBM 360/44. After considerable experimentation with various approaches, we chose the one that presented the results immediately after the mechanical scan was completed and that required no "water bag," so that any place on the whole body could be scanned. Thus, the diagnostician could see the results from the patient immediately, thereby being able to make another scan or give contrast me-

FIGURE 9
The balsa-wood
model of the ACTA
Scanner that I made
using a G.I. Joe doll
as the patient

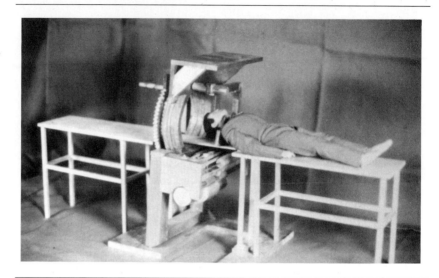

dium, etc. while the patient was still on the scanning bed. In general, the picture-reconstruction problem turned out to be primarily in numerical analysis and assembly-language programming. We chose as our algorithm a convolution and initially used the formulation of Ramachandran and Lakshminarayanan published in the *Proceedings of the U.S. Academy of Sciences* in 1971. (Many years later I found out that Hounsfield needed the water bath because he used the wrong algorithm; all modern CT scanners use the convolution algorithm as I originally did.) Then I made a balsa wood model of my concept to impress my staff with the fact that we were actually going to make this "far out" machine (Figure 9). In this way we could visualize the entire prototype scanner while its individual components were being designed.

I knew that a successful medical instrument must present the physician with immediate information in the form that can most easily be assimilated, and I emphasized the result-display aspect of the design. Towards this end, a color-coded key method was conceived so that the physician could obtain numerical results at a glance by observing colors on the picture corresponding to numerical ranges. The various anatomical structures, as distinguished by differing relative-absorption coefficients, are displayed as colors on a color TV screen. By looking at the screen, the physician can at once comprehend the anatomical pictorial pattern, as in studying ordinary x-ray plates, and gain numerical data as well by means of the color codes. The use of the TV display also has the advantage that the picture appears constantly (whereas in Hounsfield's head scanner, the picture was swept out only once every 10 seconds and a Polaroid time exposure had to be made). Since radiologists are remarkably adept at observing substantial detail in black-and-white X ray images, a black-and-white TV was also included. This high-resolution TV display, based on a digital image memory, was a "first" in medicine (and, in addition, presented four times the resolution of the Hounsfield machine).

The working environment and the attitudes of colleagues probably have as much to do with the success of such a project as does technical skill. There is no doubt that those of my medical colleagues who encouraged me the most may not have had the least idea of the extreme engineering sophistication required and the great difficulties that had to be overcome. The sustained and unrelenting encouragement we received was perhaps our greatest asset, for it enabled us to carry out a dedicated effort over a prolonged period of time. However, we cannot say that we did not have detractors. There were those who predicted doom, those who insisted the project required 10 times the financial effort and six times as long for the development, and those who tried to erode our enthusiasm. Of course, after we had been successful they said that the accomplishment was minimal, and anyone could have done it, and something far better is just about to be done by somebody else.

Our first scan was made of a navel orange placed inside a human skull, all of which was put into a plastic bowl filled with water (Figure 10). The skull was only half immersed in water, and the orange floated on the surface of the water inside the skull. The ACTA Scanner was making a vertical cross-section of the bowl, and we waited anxiously as the scanner completed its mechanical movement. We were excited to see the picture instantly flash onto the TV screen. There before our eyes the water, the skull, and the orange were all clearly delineated. Even the difference between the more dense outside orange layer of the peel could be distinguished from the inner, white, pulpy part of the peel, and the plastic of the thin bowl could be seen.

Murphy's law, that "if anything can go wrong, it will," was always at work. Take one of our first human patients for example. He was supposed to have a middle-fossa brain tumor. The ACTA Scanner showed a large edematous mass in the right frontal lobe and no ventricles. So the neurosurgeon said, "Don't feel so bad, it's only your first scan. Keep on plugging." But the next morning, after surgery, we got an excited phone call: "Guess what??? The patient had severe edema through the right frontal lobe!" Then there was our first case of enlarged ventricles. Posteriorly there were dense patches in the ventricles, and I couldn't figure out how that kind of noise could get in there. But after one glance the neuroradiologist said excitedly, "Look at those great choroid plexuses." So I went home to review neuroanatomy from my 25-year-old textbook.

FIGURE 10
First picture made with the ACTA of a cross-section of a bowl of water inside of which was placed a skull, and inside of the skull was placed a navel orange.

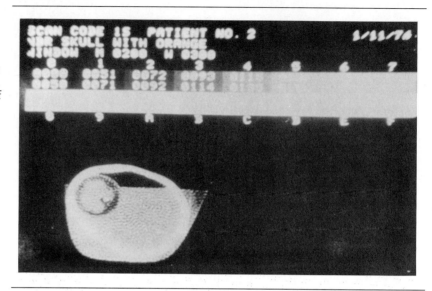

The most memorable of the earlier cases was the lung scan of an oleothorax. This condition is caused by the injection of oil into the lung of a tubercular patient (a treatment used about 50 years ago); the body forms a capsule around the oil. The ACTA scan of the patient showed the low density oil still in the patient's lung, floating on top of the more dense serous fluid, all of which was inside of an even more dense fibrous-tissue capsule. In addition, the heart cross-section showed the atrial chambers, filled with blood of the same density as the serous fluids of the oleothorax, and heart muscle of the same density as the fibrous tissue capsule. All on a living, breathing patient.

After the first series of successful ACTA scans, bottles of champagne suddenly materialized out of our neurosurgeon's desk drawer. The chairman of the Physiology Department and the dean of the Medical School, the medical director and the administrator of the hospital, the chancellor of the Medical Center, and all our friends showed up, and a picture of our group was taken as I held a gigantic wrench used to put the machine together. Amid the loud shouts of joy could be heard muted sighs of relief.

But in fact there was no letting up, and our sighs of relief only lasted a fleeting instant. All the X ray manufacturers visited Georgetown to see the ACTA, including GE, CGR, Picker, Phillips, Siemens, and Ohio Nuclear (later known as Technicare), to name a few. Even Hounsfield and EMI representatives visited me several times. We offered rights to the ACTA in return for long-term research support, but the medical X ray companies showed no interest; rather their interest seemed to be to examine the ACTA so they could return to their factories to *copy* It. The worst case was Ohio Nuclear: They came out with a close copy of the ACTA in late 1975. At the same time, chiefs of radiology departments from universities and hospitals around the country also came to visit, and a group of leading radiologists requested that we build each of them an ACTA Scanner. So, with the acquiescence of both the NBRF and GU, we started a for-profit business, called DISCO (Digital Information Science Corporation), and began to manufacture ACTA Scanners with the hope of either using the profits to support our research or selling DISCO in return for research support. In September 1975, Pfizer Inc. established Pfizer Medical Systems and took over the ACTA Scanner in return for close to 10 years of research support.

My Recent Years

My recent years have been mainly devoted to applying modern computer, electronic, and imaging methods to medical problems. There have been dramatic changes in computer hardware and software, and the computer revolution is still going on. Large-scale integrated circuits are becoming pervasive in electronic engineering, and the nature of electronic design is being rapidly transformed. The practice of medicine and surgery, in combination with the new technologies, is being transformed, and medical and surgical miracles are becoming commonplace.

Genetic engineering is already showing results, and scientists are seriously considering the sequencing of the entire human genome, but the functional result of a gene is the protein that results. The Protein Identification Resource (PIR), contains the world's main database of such protein sequences. In 1978 NBRF donated its IBM 360/44 to the University of the District of Columbia, and purchased a VAX 11/780. The VAX holds the protein sequence database and has been a great workhorse for the past 10 years. Scientists from all over the world can gain telephone access to the database. In addition NBRF provides magnetic tapes of the database. Any scientist working with what is believed to be a new protein should check with the PIR. In our own work evolutionary trees are developed from protein sequence alignments, and important relationships between proteins have been discovered. I believe that the directions for the future are with the PIR.

Usually the people involved in the inception of a new field can only barely envision its eventual impact on society and science. I recall the beginnings of the computer field in the early 1950s, in which I was fortunate to play a part. Few appreciated at the time the extent of the pervasiveness that the computer was destined for in modern society. Even in the early sixties, my work with the application of computers in medicine was considered "pioneering." Nevertheless, there is a certain delight, indeed thrill, in being part of that whole new development in science and technology. I certainly did not foresee at the time I wrote the "reasoning foundations" paper with Lee Lusted how large and important the field of medical informatics would become. The field of computerized tomography was imbued with this same excitement. It is heartening to see how pervasive CT is in medicine and to see the great influence my first whole-body CT scanner had on the industry. Even the magnetic resonance machines use features first incorporated in the ACTA Scanner. Now the future lies in genetic engineering, in working with the molecular basis of human disease; and computer technology and pattern recognition are intimately involved. I certainly am looking forward to witnessing the great new developments that undoubtedly lie ahead.

Acknowledgments

Over the years the NBRF staff did not change much, and there were many long-term engineers and scientists who made the research accomplishments possible. James B. Wilson, Louis S. Rotolo, and Margaret O. Dayhoff were with me the longest. Mr. Wilson and Mr. Rotolo are engineers and worked on the software and hardware of the imaging developments, the ACTA Scanner, the TEXAC, and other instrumentation. Dr. Dayhoff developed the *Atlas of Protein Sequences*. Mr. Thomas Golab was and still is chief electronics engineer and worked on all the image processing developments, and on the ACTA Scanner. Dr. Hon K. Huang, Mr. Menfai Shiu, and Dr. George C. Cheng developed software for image processing, and Dr. Huang and Mr. Shiu wrote programs for special applications of the ACTA Scanner. Mrs. Marilyn Belson and Dr. Rosalie Dunn carried out automated chromosome applications.

Drs. Winona Barker and Lois Hunt have been intimately associated with the *Atlas of Protein Sequences* and are the principal scientists of the PIR. Dr. Barker is co-principal investigator with me of the NIH research resources grant for the PIR.

Without the dedication and loyalty of these individuals and the work of a number of more transient associates, the research carried out by the Foundation could not have been accomplished.

References

1. Ledley, R.S. and Lusted, L.B. Reasoning foundation of medical diagnosis. *Science* 130(3366):9–21, 1959.

2. Ledley, R.S. and Luessenhop, A.J. Report on the initial use of the ACTA Scanner. Society of Neurological Surgeons, 1974. Ledley, R.S.,

Schellinger, D., and DiChiro, G. New transverse axial tomographic unit: introduction and initial results. *10th Symp. Neuroradiologictum,* Punta Del Este, Uruguay, 1974. Kiker, W.E. and Ledley, R.S. The ACTA Scanner. *Proc. SPIE,* 47:40–43, Kansas City, 1974. Ledley, R.S., DiChiro, G., Luessenhop, A.J., and Twigg, H.L. Computerized transaxial x-ray tomography of the human body. *Science* 186:207–212, 1974; reprinted in Sondak V, *et al. Computers and Medicine.* Dedham, 1979, pp. 155–160.

3. Rotolo, L.S., Wilson, J.B., Ginsberg, M.D., and Ledley, R.S. Digital computer picture processor, *Proc. 16th ACEMB,* 1963, pp. 14–15. Ledley, R.S., Ruddle, F., and Migeon, B. Computer analysis of chromosomes. *Proc. 16th ACEMB,* 1963. Ledley, R.S. High-speed automatic analysis of biomedical pictures. *Science* 146:216–223, 1964.

4. Orcutt, B.C., George, D.G., and Dayhoff, M.O. Protein and nucleic acid sequence database system. *Ann. Review Biophys. Bioeng.* 12:419–441, 1983. Barker, W.C., Hunt, L.T., Orcutt, B.C., George, D.G., Yeh, L.S., Chen, H.R., Blomquist, M.C., Johnson, G.C., and Seibel-Ross, E.I. Protein and nucleic acid sequence databases of the protein identification resource. *Genetic Maps 1984,* O'Brien, S.J., (ed.), 3, 522–553, Cold Spring Harbor Lab, 1984. Barker, W.C., Hunt, L.T., George, D.G., and Orcutt, B.C. A resource for protein identification. *The Role of Data in Scientific Progress,* Glaeser, P.S., (ed.). Elsevier Science Pub., 1985, pp. 127–133. Reprinted in *CODATA Bulletin* 56:28–34, Nov. 1984.

5. Dayhoff, M.O. and Ledley, R.S. The use of computers in protein biochemistry. *Digest 15th ACEMB,* 34, 1962. Dayhoff, M.O. and Ledley, R.S. Comprotein: A computer program to aid primary protein structure determination. *Proc. Fall Joint Computer Conf.,* 1962, pp. 262–274.

6. Barker, W.C., Hunt, L.T., George, D.G., and Ledley, R.S. The protein identification resource. *Federation Proc.* 44(6):1925, 1985 (Abstract).

7. Margaret Oakley Dayhoff, 1925–1983. *Bull. of Math. Biol.* 46(4): 467–472, 1984.

8. Ledley, R.S. *The Use of Computers in Biology and Medicine.* New York: McGraw-Hill, 1965.

9. Ledley, R.S. *Digital Computer and Control Engineering.* New York: McGraw-Hill, 1960.

10. Ledley, R.S. *Programming and Utilizing Digital Computers.* New York: McGraw-Hill, 1962.

11. Ledley, R.S. and Lusted, L.B. The use of electronic computers to aid in medical diagnosis. *Proc. IRE* 47(11):1970–1977, 1959. Ledley, R.S. and Lusted, L.B. The use of electronic computers in medical data processing. *IRE Trans. Med. Elect.* ME–7:31–47, 1960. Lusted, L.B. and Ledley, R.S. Mathematical models in medical diagnosis. *J. Med. Ed.* 35(3):214–222, 1960. Ledley, R.S. and Lusted, L.B. Computers in medi-

cal data processing. *Operations Res.* 8(3):299–310, 1960. Ledley, R.S. Using electronic computers in medical diagnosis. *IRE Trans. Med. Elect.* ME–7:274–280, 1960. Lusted, L.B. and Ledley, R.S. Medical applications of electronic computers. *Proc. 3rd Intl. Conf. Med. Electronics*, 1960, pp. 10–14. Ledley, R.S. and Lusted, L.B. The dynamic treatment-reevaluation cycle in medical diagnosis. *Digest 1961 Intl. Conf. Med. Elect.*, 1961. Ledley, R.S., Oestreich, A.E., and Lusted, L.B. Conditional probabilities in medical diagnosis. *Digest 15th ACEMB*, 2, 1962.

12. Ledley, R.S. Many-component propositional two-valued logic and general propositional constraints, National Bureau of Standards, 1954. Ledley, R.S. The absolute simplest form in digital circuit design, National Bureau of Standards, 1954. Ledley, R.S. A digitalization, systematization and formulation of the theory and methods of the propositional calculus, Nat. Bur. Stand., Report No. 3363, Feb. 1, 1954.

13. Ledley, R.S. Digital computational methods in symbolic logic, with examples in biochemistry. *Proc. Nat. Acad. Sci.* 4:498–511, 1955. Ledley, R.S. Boolean matrix equations in digital circuit design. *IRE Trans. Elect. Computers* EC–8:131–139, 1959.

14. Ledley, R.S. Boolean matrices applied to sequential circuit theory and threshold logics. *Switching Circuit Theory and Logical Design*. New York: AIEE, 1961, pp. 266–291.

15. Ledley, R.S. Digital computational methods in symbolic logic, with examples in biochemistry. *Proc. Nat. Acad. Sci.* 4:498–511, 1955.

16. Ledley, R.S. Mathematical foundations and computational methods for a digital logic machine. *J. Operations Res. Soc. Amer.* 2:249–274, 1954. Ledley, R.S. and Rotolo, L.S. A heuristic concept and automatic computer aid for operations simulation. *Naval Res. Logistics Quarterly* 9:231–244, 1962.

17. Huang, H.K. and Ledley, R.S. Three dimensional image reconstruction from in vivo consecutive transverse axial sections. *Comp. Biol. Med.* 5:165–170, 1975. Ledley, R.S. and Huang, H.K. Three-dimensional reconstruction of consecutive transverse axial images from the ACTA-Scanner. *Proc. ACEMB*, 1975.

18. Kiker, W.E., Hinz, T.W., and Ledley, R.S. Variation of ACTA Scanner numbers with the physical properties of the scanned material. *Med. Phys.* 3:42–44, 1976. Huang, H.K. and Ledley, R.S. Correlating the CT numbers of body constituents with their mass densities and calcium concentrations. *Proc. SPIE* 96, Palos Verdes Estates, CA, 1976, pp. 288–293. Huang, H.K., Wu, S.C., and Ledley, R.S. Evaluation of the mass density distribution of the human body in vivo—theoretical aspect. *Proc. 29th ACEMB*, 62, Boston, 1976. Bradley, J.G., Huang, H.K., Ledley, R.S., and Ray, R.D. Correlations between ACTA numbers of bone and

its calcium levels. *Proc. 29th ACEMB*, 108, Boston, 1976. Huang, H.K. and Rotolo, L.S. Evaluation of mass densities of body tissues and calcium concentrations of bone by computerized tomographic techniques. *Biophysical J.* 17:247a, 1977. Huang, H.K. and Wu, S.C. The evaluation of mass densities of the human body in vivo from CT scans. *Comp. in Biol. Med.* 6:337–343, 1976.

19. Ledley, R.S., Wu, S.C., and Granke, R.C. Isodose distributions of multiple beams radiation for body inhomogeneities: An application of the ACTA-Scanner in radiation therapy. Abstr. of paper given at 61st annual meeting of Radiological Soc. N. Am., 1975. Wu, S.C. and Ledley, R.S. Application of the ACTA-Scanner in the radiation (Co-60) therapy for body inhomogeneities. *Proc. 29th ACEMB*, 436, Boston, 1976. Ledley, R.S., Rotolo, L.S., and Joseloff, S.H. Application of CT scans in the radiation (Co-60) therapy for body inhomogeneities, *Biophysical J.* 17:246a, 1977. Scheer, A.C., Ledley, R.S., and Huang, H.K. Radiation therapy treatment planning with computerized tomography. *Biophysical. J.* 21:129a, 1978.

20. Hinz, T.W., Kiker, W.E., Bransford, C.L., and Ledley, R.S. Patient dose distributions during transverse axial scanning tomography. *Med. Phys.* 1:115, 1974. Huang, H.K. Experiment on the transverse axial scan of a specially designed phantom by using the ACTA-Scanner, NBR Report No. 741115-ACTA, 1974. DiChiro, G., Axelbaum, S.P., Schellinger, D., Twigg, H.L., and Ledley, R.S. Computerized axial tomography in syringomyelia. *New Eng. J. Med.* 292(l):13–16, 1975. Schellinger, D., DiChiro, G., Axelbaum, S.P., Twigg, H.L., and Ledley, R.S. Early clinical experience with the ACTA-Scanner. *Radiology* 114:257–261, 1975.

21. Ledley, R.S. and Wilson, J.B. Concept analysis by syntax processing. *Proc. Amer. Documentation Inst.* 1:1–8, 1964. Ledley, R.S., Rotolo, L.S., Golab, T.J., Jacobsen, J.D., Ginsberg, M.D., and Wilson, J.B. FIDAC: Film input to digital automatic computer and associated syntax directed pattern recognition programming system. *Optical and Electro-optical Information Processing Technology*. Cambridge: MIT Press, 1965, pp. 591–613.

22. Ledley, R.S., Kulkarni, Y.G., Rotolo, L.S., Golab, T.J., and Wilson, J.B. TEXAC: A special purpose picture processing texture analysis computer. *Proc. 15th IEEE Comp. Soc. Intl. Conf.*, Wash. D.C., 1977 (Prize paper), pp. 66–71.

23. Ledley, R.S., *et al.* Photomicrographic analysis of central nervous system (Progress Report). NBR Report No. 65081/04472, 1965. Ledley, R.S. Analysis of the dendrites of a neuron photographed in a single section. *Biophys. Soc. Abstr.*, p. 129, 1966. Belson, M., Dudley, A.W., and Ledley, R.S. Automatic computer measurements of neurons. *Pattern Recognition* 1:119–128, 1968.

24. Ledley, R.S. Practical problems in the use of computers in medical diagnosis. *Proc. of the IEEE* 57:1900–1918, 1969. Ledley, R.S. and Rotolo, L.S. Application of pattern recognition to biomedical problems. *Automatic Interpretation and Classification of Images*, Grasselli, A., (ed.). New York: Academic Press, 1969, pp. 323–362. Ledley, R.S. Use of computers in biomedical pattern recognition. *Advances in Computers*, Vol. 10, New York: Academic Press, 1970, pp. 217–252.

25. Ledley, R.S., Rotolo, L.S., and Kattah, J.C. Computerized electro-oculography (CEOG). *Proc. 31st ACEMB*, Atlanta, 1978, p. 100. Ledley, R.S., Rotolo, L.S., Kattah, J.C., and Duffy, R.A. Computerized electro-oculography (CEOG). *Proc. 3rd Ann. Symp. on Comp. Appl. in Med. Care*, Wash., D.C., 1979, pp. 598–602. Ledley, R.S. and Kattah, J.C. CENOG: computerized electro neuro-opthalmograph, *Georgetown Med. Bull.* 33(4), 10–19, May 1980. Ledley, R.S., Rotolo, L.S., and Buas, M. Computerized electro neuro-opthalmograph (CENOG). *ACM '80, Proc. Ann. Conf.*, Nashville, 1980, pp. 66–74.

26. Ledley, R.S. Digital difference radiology. MEDINFO 83, *Proc. 4th World Conf. on Medical Informatics*, Van Bemmel J.H., *et al.* (eds.). Elsevier Publ. Co., 1983, pp. 355–358. Ledley, R.S. Digital fluorographic method and system, US Patent #4,450,478, May 22, 1984.

27. GUMC introduces revolutionary automatic genetic analyzer. Georgetown Univ. Med. Center Report 9(3), [3], Winter 1984. Ledley, R.S., Gersten, D.M., Zapolski, E.J., Golab, T.J., and Rotolo, L.S. Automating the DNA hybridization. *MIDCON/85*, Chicago, Illinois, 1985.

28. Ledley, R.S. and Lubs, H.A. Metachrome instrument, frontiers of engineering and computing in health care. *Seventh Ann. Conf. IEEE/EMBS*, 1985, pp. 986–990. Buas, M., Golab, T.J., and Ledley, R.S. Automated chromosome analysis. *MEDINFO 86*.

29. Cheng, G.C. and Kwok, H.M. Automatic ray tracing of the optical system of the eye. *Proc. 18th ACEMB*, 1965, p. 46. Ledley, R.S., Cheng, G.C., and Ludlum, W.M. Computer ray tracing of the optical system of the schematic eye. *Nature* 211:930–932, 1966.

30. Ledley, R.S. The relation of occlusal surfaces to the stability of artificial dentures. *J. Amer. Dent. Assoc.* 48:508–526, 1954. Ledley, R.S. Mastication and denture stability. *J. Amer. Dent. Assoc.* 50:241–242, 1955. Ledley, R.S. A new method of determining the functional forces applied to prosthetic appliances. *J. Prosthetic Dent.* 5:546–562, 1955.

31. Computer development (SEAC and DYSEAC) at the National Bureau of Standards, Washington, D.C. NBS Circular 551, Jan. 25, 1955.

32. Ledley, R.S. The use of computers in biology and medicine, Nat. Acad. Sci., Nat. Res. Council, 1960. Ledley, R.S. and Lusted, L.B. Biomedical electronics. Potentialities and problems. *Science* 135(3499):198–201, 1962.

Planting the Seeds: Personal Observations

Bruce D. Waxman, PhD
Defense Mapping Agency, Washington, D.C.

Reminiscing over biomedical computing 25 years ago is much like recalling one's prenatal impressions! There is also a temptation to invent examples of inspiration *post facto,* testifying to one's gifts of insight. Nevertheless, a few early recollections have that childlike aura of remembrance, are not modest, and may be worth sharing.

One such was a quite accidental attendance at a Mathematics Society meeting at the Pennsylvania State University. The date, 1956, and the speaker, Dr. Grace Hopper. She told stories of the early days of computing for which she has become so famous. You have all probably heard them before. The recollection, however, is not so much of the specifics of these stories, but of being told of enormous power to process data and study relationships. The excitement remained dormant, residually stored in my subconscious, and then, in 1958 when consulting for Dr. Ruth Whitemore, a pediatric cardiologist at Yale, the Hopper experience emerged, full-blown. Ruth Whitemore was the only pediatric cardiologist in Connecticut at the time, and in great demand. Finding a mechanism for more broadly sharing her particular expertise was very tempting. It seemed feasible as a minimum to automate her skills at EKG interpretation. What was not known was that Bob Ledley and Lee Lusted had already suggested the potential for computer-aided diagnosis and Cesar Caceres had recently embarked on a program to automate the interpretation of EKGs. You are all aware that EKG interpretation techniques are now commonplace; almost any local hospital will have such capability neatly bundled in the EKG machine's microprocessor.

The preoccupation with automated medical diagnosis persists and has spawned a great deal of activity in AI. Incredibly, the initial and still very tentative work in medicine has been used as justification for a vast array of activities in military and intelligence applications. Clearly it is appealing, just as it was to imitate Ruth Whitemore's skills, to capture in a computer program the expertise fundamental to scarce and time-consuming tasks. What is objectionable and distracting, is labeling this form of computing "intelligent," with the implication that machines are capable of human cognition. I had no idea, in those early days when my office supported Lederberg's original work, that it

111

would take off quite the way it did. Unlike the current preoccupation with AI, what Caceres did in those early days was highly reductionist, dealing only with those empirical data that could be manipulated by straightforward mathematical/statistical techniques—undoubtedly why he was so successful. There was no mystique.

In 1960, Dr. James Shannon, then director of the National Institutes of Health, created an Advisory Committee on Computers in Research. The impetus was from the National Academy of Sciences, which had advised Shannon to explore the potentiality of computers in biomedicine. The members of that committee shared high enthusiasm for their mission and in the course of two years managed to spend over 50 million dollars on computer-related biomedical research. As Executive Secretary of that committee, under the leadership of Lee Lusted, I shared in the great excitement and opportunities of those times. No one, certainly not Dr. Shannon, had intended anything of that magnitude, and when the NIH hierarchy awoke to the reality of these expenditures, the committee was summarily chastised. By this time, however, the field of biomedical computing had been established and developed momentum of its own. Work prospered, undaunted by the bureaucracy. The research supported by the committee's recommendations is quite well chronicled in the four-volume series by Ralph Stacy and myself, *Computers in Biomedical Research* (Academic Press, 1965–1974).

A particularly rewarding sequel to this series of events relates to the sponsorship, by the aforementioned committee, of the LINC computer. Twenty years later, in a gala attended by everyone including the Secretary of Health and Human Services, the current director of NIH and just about everyone else that had anything to do with the development, the LINC was heralded as the undisputed progenitor of the minicomputer—a circumstance for which NIH can take great credit!

Later

By the mid-1960s enough had transpired for a few of us to become a bit philosophical. At least one recurrent theme, espoused by Bill Yamamoto, views strategic planning for research much like the process described by Asimov in his *Foundation* trilogy. The point of the Asimov/Yamamoto injunction is that those creative enough to do pioneering work are unlikely to find immediate acceptance for their ideas. There is too much inertia associated with conventional wisdom. Acknowledging this, members of the Second Foundation (an Asimov literary construction) consistently attempt to deliberately and unobtrusively "plant the seeds" of change in the present with the expectation that their effects will emerge later.

There are numerous instances of individuals and institutions that were either totally negative or skeptical about the use of computers in medicine and biomedical research. The processing and analysis of clinical laboratory data by computer was suspect early on because it was believed that it would lead to a totally unjustified use of such tests. Use of CT scanning was vigorously questioned because of its expense and the lack of clinical validation. There was concern that every hospital in the country would want one when presumably such instruments should only be located at so called "centers of excellence." Similar skepticism was associated with automated hospital information systems, patient monitoring, and various radiological systems. These technologies are now so much a part of the normal clinical regimen of diagnostic tools, so commonplace, as to cause bewilderment that they were once highly controversial.

It is not possible to look back without giving great credit to Larry Weed and his PROMIS system, which so revolutionized thinking about medical record systems and, more generally, the rational administration of medicine. For those of you who wonder what ever became of PROMIS, the National Cancer Institute's PDQ system, an absolutely elegant spin-off, provides encyclopedic information on all forms of cancer treatment.

Will Larry Weed ever forgive Octo Barnett for COSTAR? It is not problem oriented (except in a most limited form); it certainly does not have the conceptual elegance of PROMIS, and yet at this writing there must be 300 to 400 COSTAR systems around the world. While specific evaluations may not have been conducted elsewhere, in the California health clinic environments COSTAR was a major factor in mitigating the cost and rationalizing the delivery of medical care. At another level, data produced by several San Diego-based COSTAR systems provided the statistics needed for designing a highly revolutionary (and subsequently successful) plan for financing medical care for indigents.

More Recently

In 1979, when I wandered out to San Diego to install and supervise the dissemination of COSTAR, I renewed my acquaintance with Bob Livingston, with whom I had worked in 1964 at NIH. Bob invited me to spend some time in his laboratory when I wasn't busy peddling COSTAR. In his letter of invitation he said something about being glad to have my brains in his lab. Now, Bob's lab has all kinds of brains lying around in jars! Eventually I convinced myself that he wasn't being literal, and spent, on and off, a very happy three years thinking about brain mapping.

What Bob was most excited about then, and still is, might be called his "Colombian" view of biology. He understood long ago, in a very profound way, that the biological world is three-dimensional. It bothered him that most biological research, while occasionally giving lip service to the third dimension, rarely directed research in that direction. He kept saying again and again that the really important aspect of his brain research, and biological research in general, was to look at things in all their dimensionality. This very simple, and all too obvious proposition, has motivated him for many years. It seemed so appealingly obvious that I got myself rather entrapped in his intellectual web.

It's of considerable interest that within the last two years great progress has been made in three-dimensional imaging, not only with respect to the reconstruction of pixel data, but also in graphics technology where wholly realistic (and occasionally "more than realistic") models have been constructed. The application of these new computational capabilities to visualization research are quite remarkable. One of the more notable examples is the volumetric 3-D reconstruction of CT scans. It is likely that the next important contribution of computer science to biomedicine will be in this direction. In particular, 3-D mapping of the brain as well as molecular modeling will benefit the most. The clinical implications for this 3-D technology are very obvious and practical applications in clinical imaging are developing daily. The technological breakthrough here is the advent of parallel processors with huge memories, capable of up to gigaflop speeds and at prices, depending on size, as low as $80,000.

A Seed of Dissent

Having rummaged around in the past and a bit in the future, I find it hard to escape the impression that most of what has happened was serendipitous. I reluctantly subscribed to this imperative although it has always made me uncomfortable. In writing here, to a large extent, serendipity is being justified, since much of the neat stuff just described "happened by accident." It certainly wasn't planned by the NIH or the U.S. Public Health Service. However, is such a monolithic research strategy in national or human interest? It is disturbing to observe that despite a current annual NIH budget of $6 billion, we do not have a cure for cancer, AIDS, or any other significant chronic disease. Certainly there has been a general increase in our understanding of the biosystems that are involved, and yes, the survival rate for many forms of cancer have improved, but are we getting $6 billion worth? If this were just an idle question, for which there were no alternatives, it might not merit attention. However, specific, goal-directed research, on any reasonable scale, has never, outside of the pharmaceutical industry, been attempted in the biomedical community. Serendipity is only *one* of a large number of possible strategies, and yet it has become so ingrained in our research and bureaucratic culture that it is largely unchallenged. Somehow the idea that scientific and/or technical progress depends entirely on accidental development is counter intuitive!

Recently my professional activities in R&D have been associated with the Department of Defense. Despite the recurrent climate of criticism for the magnitude and management of defense programs and expenditures, many of which do not equal the NIH budget, much of the *modus operandi* is goal oriented. The experience has convinced me that there are other highly effective strategies than those employed in biomedicine. This turns out to be a very complex set of issues, not only at broad philosophical levels, but also in terms of the specific ways that government institutions manage R&D. The easy excuse for raising this controversial issue here is the invitation to discuss the Planting of Seeds!

COMPUTING SYSTEMS

The technical program began with a review of the hardware and software that provided the foundation for medical informatics. Thelma Estrin, PhD, was the discussant and served as the session moderator. The conference organizers left the structure of each session to the discussant, and in this case Dr. Estrin began with a personal introduction that provided a context for each speaker. Because her comments have been expanded in the enclosed paper, the transcript of these introductory remarks has not been included.

The first presentation was a joint discussion of the origins and history of the LINC. Charles E. Molnar, DSc and Wesley A. Clark, DSc alternated in their personal recollections. There were numerous slides, and they moved through them rapidly. We were told that the slides would melt if they lingered too long. A paper by Wesley Clark had been presented at the ACM Conference on the History of Personal Workstations, and a copy of it was included in the conference proceedings. (It has since been published in the *Personal Workstation* volume of this series.) In what follows, there is an edited transcript of their presentation at this conference. This paper, together with some of the illustrations from the talk, complements the earlier LINC reference.

The final speaker in this session was G. Octo Barnett, MD. At the request of the program committee, he focused on the early days of computer application and the demands that it placed on software development. One of the figures that he showed was a 1965 dialogue from a prototype remote computer system. It checked spelling, prompted the users, and offered rudimentary "help" assistance. Its 110-baud line and TTY interface suggested that 1965 was a time for visionary rather than practical applications. Within a half-decade, however, COSTAR began to turn that around. The section contains Dr. Barnett's prepared paper with some illustrations from his talk.

116

SPEAKERS

Charles E. Molnar and Wesley A. Clark   Development of the LINC

G. Octo Barnett   History of the Development of Medical Information
Systems at the Laboratory of Computer Science at
Massachusetts General Hospital

Thelma Estrin   The UCLA Brain Research Institute Data Processing
Laboratory

Charles E. Molnar, DSc is professor and director, Institute for Biomedical Computing, School of Medicine (since 1983) and director, Computer
System Laboratory (since 1972), Washington University. He also holds
the appointment of professor in the Departments of Computer Science,
Electrical Engineering, and Physiology. He received BS and MS degrees
from Rutgers University in 1956 and 1958 and a DSc from the Massachusetts Institute of Technology in 1966. In 1985 he was granted the
Javits Neuroscience Investigator Award in recognition of his contributions in the neurologic and communicative sciences.

Wesley A. Clark, DSc is a senior consultant to academic, governmental,
and industrial organizations (since 1972). He cofounded the consulting
group of Clark, Rockoff and Associates in 1984 and has acted as visiting
professor of Computer Design at Washington University since 1986. He
received an AB degree from the University of California, Berkeley in
1947 and a DSc (Hon) from Washington University in 1984. He joined
the MIT Whirlwind Computer Project in 1952. In 1964 he was appointed research professor of Computer Science at Washington University and later directed the Computer Systems Laboratory (1967–1972).
He received the ACM-IEEE Eckert-Mauchly Award for Computer Architecture and is a charter recipient of the Computer Pioneer Award of
the IEEE.

G. Octo Barnett, MD is professor of Medicine at the Harvard Medical School and also at the Harvard-MIT Division of Health Sciences and Technology, MIT (both since 1980). He has served as director, Laboratory of Computer Science, Massachusetts General Hospital since 1963. He received a BA degree from Vanderbilt University in 1952 and an MD degree from Harvard Medical School in 1956. He is on the editorial board of seven journals including *Computers in Biomedical Research, Computers in Biology and Medicine, Computer Methods and Programs in Biomedicine,* and *Methods of Information in Medicine.*

Thelma Estrin, PhD is assistant dean for Continuing Education, School of Engineering and Applied Science and director, Extension Division of Engineering and Science, UCLA. She received BS, MS, and PhD degrees from the University of Wisconsin in 1948, 1949, and 1951, respectively. In 1961 she became a major participant in launching the Data Processing Laboratory at the UCLA Brain Research Institute and served as director of the laboratory from 1970 to 1980. She served as president, IEEE Engineering in Medicine and Biology Society and was elected a fellow of the IEEE and AAAS in recognition of her contributions to the application of computers to biomedicine.

Development of the LINC[1]

Charles E. Molnar, DSc
School of Medicine, Washington University, St. Louis
Wesley A. Clark, DSc
Clark, Rockoff and Associates, New York

Charles Molnar Like Bill Yamamoto, I was provoked by Norbert Wiener's book *Cybernetics*, which I picked up around 1956 from a book sale table while on Varick Street in New York to buy electronic parts. The bright red cover caught my eye. I had never heard of the title word before, and the book was cheap, so.... The book had lots of stimulating ideas that confirmed my notion that there might be some relationship of electrical engineering ideas and methods to understanding the nervous system.

I was attracted to continue my graduate study at MIT in part because of the Wiener connection, but mostly as a result of an accidental meeting at Rutgers with visiting interviewers from the MIT Lincoln Laboratory. After a visit to Boston in the spring of 1957, I was offered a Staff Associate position by two groups at Lincoln Laboratory and chose between them by a coin flip. Since it was an important decision, I used a half-dollar. Immediately on moving to Massachusetts in July of 1957, I became involved with both Bill Papian's Advanced Development Group 63 of the Computer Division at Lincoln and with Walter Rosenblith's Communications Biophysics Group of the Research Laboratory of Electronics on the MIT campus in Cambridge.

There was already in progress an active collaboration between the two groups, involving Wes Clark, Belmont Farley, Larry Frischkopf, and Jack Gilmore, and I got involved immediately in their studies of the alpha rhythm of the EEG and its possible interpretation using neural net models. My immediate supervisor at Lincoln was Wes Clark, who frustrated me severely by refusing to tell me what to do. It took me all summer to get the message; I began painfully to acquire the habit of deciding for myself. During the next eight years I shuttled between the two groups (and also the Air Force Cambridge Research Laboratories) and developed a split professional personality that has persisted to this day.

At the time there was a great deal of interest at MIT in applying some of the ideas about stochastic processes and techniques in signal processing and control theory to experimental studies of the nervous

---

[1] The presentation at the conference was made alternately by Molnar and Clark. The final editing of the transcript was made by Charles Molnar.

system. Walter Rosenblith had a vision of a "thermodynamics" of nervous activity that would relate the macroscopic aspects of brain function to the "statistical mechanics" of individual neuron activity. This led to the need to study ensembles of neural signals, rather than "typical examples," which in turn created a need for collection and processing of large quantities of electrophysiological data recorded by gross electrodes. With the rapid development of microelectrode recording techniques, the need to analyze nerve spike discharge patterns as stochastic processes rapidly became apparent as well, creating even more challenging problems in data collection and analysis.

Some specialized devices had already been built for EEG analysis and also used for visual and auditory evoked response studies. Most memorable was a marvelous analog auto- and cross-correlator that repeatedly played back a section of tape recording of the signal of interest, and used analog (vacuum tube) multipliers and integrators. Bob Brown of the Communications Biophysics Group (somewhat anomalously abbreviated as CBL) was a designer and chief nursemaid. This unique device, with its rotating-drum delay device, was an electromechanical marvel that survived for years through a series of redesigns without losing its ability to arouse John Barlow's passionate embrace and spirited defense of it against later digital interlopers. There were also other specialized devices for signal analysis (ALMIDO—Amplitude and Latency Measuring Instrument with Digital Output), and for experiment control (GOBAK— Goldstein's Overexpensive Belt-driven Automatic Knobtwister).

The first digital machine to appear in CBL was the Average Response Computer, ARC-1. This was built at Lincoln using technology developed there for the TX-2. The ARC-1 served as an engineering demonstration that exercised TX-2 digital modules and contained an early experimental transistor-driven ferrite core memory. The ARC-1 was an almost immediate success. Once the air conditioner was tuned to accommodate it, the new core memory was debugged, and the diabolic consequences of a minor short circuit in a cable connector hood attached to the paper tape punch were eliminated. ARC-1 displayed averaged responses or nerve-spike histograms, while the data were being collected; this offered a qualitative change from the earlier procedure of next-day analysis of tape recorded data using the analog correlator or the TX-0. Another reason for the successful application of the ARC-1 was that it was clearly a laboratory tool and was therefore not inundated with other kinds of users eager to exploit a scarce and expensive resource. It just did what came natural, and one didn't need to feel guilty about letting it idle while attending to other aspects of an experiment.

A commercial instrument with similar features was soon developed and successfully promoted by Manfred Clynes. It was called the

FIGURE 1
William N. Papian, who was head of Lincoln Laboratory Group 63 in 1981 when LINC development began, and later was head of the Computer Research Laboratory at Washington University in St. Louis, where work on the LINC Evaluation Program was carried out after the summer of 1964.

CAT (Computer of Average Transients), and many laboratories soon acquired it or competing instruments that soon appeared in the marketplace.

Wesley Clark   At Lincoln Laboratory we had been working to push the state of the art in digital computers in general. The group was started in the pre-transistor era. By the time Charlie joined the group, things were beginning to move in the transistorized computer direction. By the way, when Charlie spoke of accidentally joining Group 63, it was an accident of fate that we're here at all. I think that if Charlie's coin had selected Herb Sherman's communications group at Lincoln, the LINC probably would not have been undertaken.

Figure 1 shows Bill Papian, who was at the time the LINC began the head of Group 63. Many of you will recognize this grand man. A month ago at the 35th Whirlwind reunion in Boston he looked just the same, except that he now has a white goatee of great distinction. Bill continued to provide organizational leadership as we moved from Lincoln Laboratory to the MIT campus and then to Washington University.

The tradition that we were carrying forward at Lincoln Laboratory had started with the Whirlwind computer at MIT and continued with the Memory Test Computer (MTC) and later the TX-0 and TX-2 computers at Lincoln. By the time Charlie came, the TX-0 was operating, and the TX-2 was underway but not completed. The tradition that was being carried forward was the use of computers, even very large ones, in an interactive way that we now recognize by the name *real time*. That is, the machine must be fast enough to do something useful before you forget what it is that you are trying to do. Of course, all machines are really used in this way, even when we don't think of it as real time, because somebody's got to care about the results. To be useful in the laboratory, machines need to interact with the user or the laboratory environment in a rapid and tightly coupled way.

A cartoon in a recent issue of the *Wall Street Journal* was captioned, "Time keeps everything from happening all at once." The only thing you had to worry about in traditional computer design was that steps should take place in a certain sequence. Computer science, which was just being formed as a discipline, would continue over its first two decades to ignore time itself as an important parameter. Generation after generation of computer science students were taught that time wasn't important; only sequence and "functionality" were important. How fast things worked overall was important, but interaction with users in real time was not. So, we had generation after generation of new machines in which interactive, real-time work was not possible.

The LINC design effort led to the "demonstration prototype," shown in Figure 2. The parts of the LINC of greatest interest to the user are the four console modules shown and the keyboard. The upper right-hand module is the LINC Tape unit, a small-scale version of a tape unit that had been developed by Tom Stockebrand for the TX-2. The TX-2 was a room-filling machine, and its tape system was to scale, with 15-inch reels driven by five-horsepower motors.

The display module on the top left has a pair of CRT display screens, one with short persistence and one with long. It seemed to be a good idea at the time; the two displays later became two logical channels on one display. The data terminal box, on the lower left, has a panel with various jacks and knobs; it was to provide easy connection to laboratory equipment and had control knobs. On the lower right, the control console contains switches and indicator lights, used both to operate the LINC and also to provide a beginner with a way to test his understanding by following machine operation step-by-step.

This machine was successfully demonstrated at a meeting of the National Academy of Sciences/National Research Council in Washing-

FIGURE 2
The console boxes and keyboard of the LINC demonstration prototype connect through an amplifier to electrodes held by Gail Andersen, secretary to the LINC group in 1963.

ton, D.C. in the spring of 1962, and then demonstrated in laboratories on the NIH campus in Bethesda. The first of these was Robert Livingston's Laboratory of Neurophysiology, where the LINC was used for the first time to average auditory evoked potentials from electrodes implanted in an awake and behaving cat. The LINC was then moved to the laboratory of Mones Berman, by which time fatigue of the demonstrators and the machine had set in and made the demonstrations less productive and less fun.

The photo in Figure 2 was taken shortly after the prototype had returned from Bethesda and after the entire project was moved from Lincoln Laboratory to a site in Cambridge near MIT under unusual circumstances. (I'm the only person that I know who has been fired from MIT for insubordination three times; this move to Cambridge was the second such occasion.)

Right after the Bethesda demonstrations, we began to plan machine design changes and space renovations needed to mount an evaluation program. You have already heard about the growing NIH interest in supporting work of this kind through the Committee on Computers in Medicine, and you will hear still more later from Lee Lusted. We were fortunate enough to have had Bill Papian as a member of that committee. Our work had been closely observed, and a search for funding to mount a program to evaluate the LINC—which is to say to get some kind of market base going—was undertaken by Bruce Waxman in a marvelous display of civil service at its best. He, among other things, very imaginatively dropped 25 dollars in a poker game to one potential funding source—a colleague of his within the government. But Bruce, I don't want to say any more about it than that.

We moved to Cambridge to mount a really unprecedented program. The LINC Evaluation Program was to bring together 14 pairs of biomedical researchers who had volunteered to take responsibility for learning how a machine of this kind could be used in a laboratory, including the tasks of building their own machine and keeping it alive throughout the two-year course of the program. The ultimate disposition of the machines would be determined only after the evaluation program was over, with productive machines to be left with their successful users. It was quite an imaginative idea. Charlie likes to say that it was I who thought up the idea for them to come and build their own machine. Charlie in fact had that idea. It was outrageous, but we did it; we pulled it off! We had only a few months to do it; it still seems amazing that we could have done it, but there will be more about that later.

Charlie Molnar We had less than a year from the time the decision was made to do the Evaluation Program until the first batch of users would arrive in Cambridge to assemble their machines. This gave us about 10 months, starting at Lincoln and then working in a new location, with a small core group, to redesign a very shaky prototype into a form that could be assembled and maintained by 14 groups of inexperienced users. Critical help was provided by colleagues drawn mostly from MIT and Lincoln Laboratory, but with significant additional support from Jerry Cox and Maynard Engebretson from Washington University. Beside the technical tasks, there were also the problems associated with soliciting proposals from potential users and selecting the best set. These were dealt with by our nationally representative LINC Evaluation Board.

There was not much time for fussing and fretting over decisions; I have often felt that if we had had six months longer to do the job, we would not have been able to do it at all. The short schedule made it possible to postpone everything else in our lives (almost: my wife Donna gave birth to our first son Steven in April 1963, and I did get to visit them in the hospital). The short schedule also made the apparent technical risks of design decisions smaller than the time risk of taking an extra day to decide. So we had to think hard, think fast, and think right.

Figure 3 shows the redesigned LINC, later called the "Classic LINC." The phrase may have been coined by Joe Hind, one of the

FIGURE 3
The "Classic LINC" as it had been assembled by George Gerstein late in 1964 in St. Louis. The portable oscilloscope was both a LINC display device and a maintenance tool.

FIGURE 4
The tape apparatus of the Classic LINC allowed copying of tapes through the use of two transports. Loading and unloading of tapes required the use of only two push buttons on the front panel.

Evaluators. The four console modules of the Classic LINC are shown individually in Figures 4–7. Superficially, they look much like the console modules of the demonstration prototype, but each of the modules had been completely redesigned. The tape unit (Figure 4) had been greatly simplified by replacing many relays with electronic switches, and using an utterly simple method of controlling tape motor action

FIGURE 5
Display of the Classic LINC, removed from its box for rack mounting. The numbered knobs allowed movement of cursors on the display and other functions now commonly controlled with a mouse.

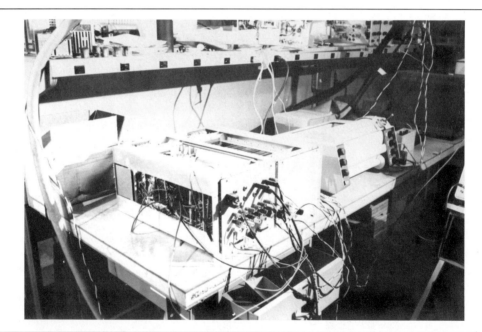

FIGURE 6
Classic LINC data terminal chassis, with a plug-in unit on the left side containing an interface to the plotter and other equipment

FIGURE 7
The Classic LINC control console, which allowed easy following of program steps using its switches and lights

(the two motors were connected in series across the power, and one or the other was short-circuited when motion was desired). The display (Figure 5) now had a single CRT in a standard Tektronix laboratory oscilloscope chassis. We designed specialized plug-in units that were equipped with user knobs, moved there from the data terminal box. The data terminal box (Figure 6) was redesigned so that it also held two plug-in units that could each contain special interfaces required by different experiments. The control console (Figure 7) appeared simple; this was the result of an enormous amount of careful design by Wes that made it a superb tool for learning about how the machine executed its instructions. Wes adhered religiously (some said fanatically) to his position that every important thing that went on in the machine had to be visible from the console.

The electronics cabinet (Figure 8) was modified to reflect our earlier experience as well. A rear view of the "fantail" shows the connectors for the many cables needed to connect it to the console modules. As before, it was treated as the "black sheep" in the family and put as distant from the console modules as the physical and electrical limits of cabling would allow. The power supply was put on the bottom of the cabinet, instead of the back door; now the cabinet wouldn't tip on soft carpets, or fall on you when the back door was opened. The tape elec-

FIGURE 8
The skeleton of the LINC electronics cabinet, with circuit cards, power supplies, and cover panels removed. Thirty-foot cables to the rest of the LINC came to the two rows of connectors on the lower right.

tronics were moved from the very bottom of the cabinet to eye level, where access and adjustments were easier. (The redesigned tape electronics had three screwdriver adjustments as compared with about 40 in the demonstration prototype, so this didn't really turn out to matter.)

It is a little hard to remember in this era of VLSI circuits and extensive CAD tools what it was like to design and build this machine. It used one kind of integrated circuit in a few critical places—a TO-5 can containing two transistors back-to-back so that their temperatures would match. Figure 9 shows a typical circuit board from the LINC, complete with discrete transistors, diodes, and resistors. The picture

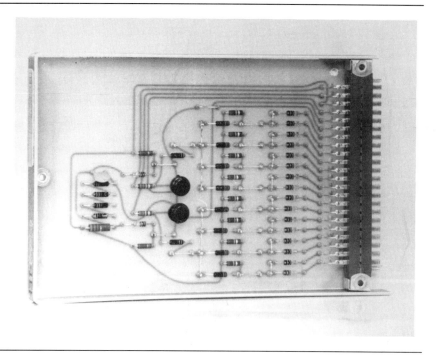

FIGURE 9

A typical circuit card from the LINC. Most were standard Digital Equipment Corporation System Modules; some were designed specially for the LINC and manufactured by others.

(Figure 10) of the back panel of the LINC illustrates just how many details there were in the design and fabrication of the LINC. The documentation for all of this, which was sold as a package to prospective LINC kit builders, contained several volumes with the size and texture of a telephone directory, as well as more than a hundred C-size drawings that had been made by hand with exquisite care. The integrity of the documentation, both during the design phase and during manufacturing, was kept under control only through the extraordinary discipline of Mishell Stucki. Anything that got past the "Mish Filter" could be trusted to be consistent and correct!

Wesley Clark   The console modules of the LINC could be taken out of their boxes and mounted in standard 19-inch racks along with other laboratory equipment. Figure 11 shows Charlie in his Air Force uniform, working with a rack-mounted LINC; during the LINC development he was on active military duty at the Air Force Cambridge Research Laboratories at Hanscom Field, and allowed to participate in the LINC program in order to build a LINC for the Air Force.

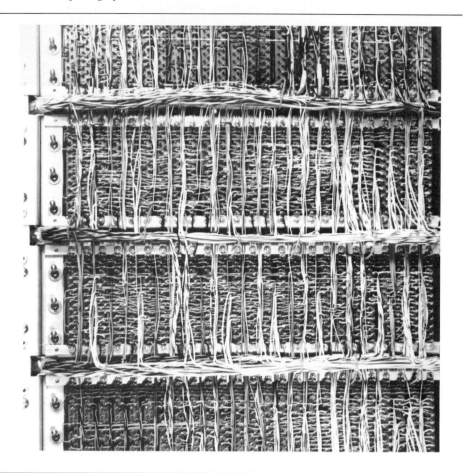

FIGURE 10

A close-up of a portion of the backpanel wiring of the LINC. Each wire had to be connected and soldered by hand; this was done for us by Flow Corporation in Cambridge. Users had to install circuit cards and cables as a later step.

We launched into the crash redesign effort in the spring of 1963, with the arrival of the first wave of scientists from seven groups scheduled for July, and the second wave for August. We had to work very hard and very fast. There was little choice; the users could not afford to come for a month during the academic year, and so commitments had been made for them to come to MIT in the summer of 1963, put their machines together, and learn enough computerology to give them the confidence needed to take their machines home to their own laboratories.

The photo in Figure 12 was taken during one of the several crises during the completion of the development and debugging of the redesigned LINC. Jerry Cox, on the right, is looking rather skeptically at

FIGURE 11
Charles Molnar using a rack of equipment that intermixed parts of the LINC demonstration prototype with other equipment. This modularity was retained in the Classic LINC design.

Severo Ornstein. Both of them are working out a debugging problem; this was probably during "the great memory-scare weekend."

Well, the users arrived right on schedule, but we were two weeks behind. We had to hold the fort while the parts for the first seven machines were completed and delivered. Figure 13 shows Irving Thomae lecturing on LINC memory operation. He, Mary Allen Wilkes, and Severo Ornstein lectured and taught while we resolved the final design and manufacturing details. Others helped as well; Figure 14 shows the late Tom Sandel, who was the chairman of the LINC Evaluation Board, explaining to Gerhardt Werner, then of Johns Hopkins, who was one of

FIGURE 12
Severo Ornstein
(left) and Jerry Cox
discussing a LINC
debugging problem.
Drawings of the
LINC are taped to
the wall on the left.

FIGURE 13
Lectures and discussions, here led by Irving Thomae,
occupied the LINC
Evaluation Participants while parts for
their LINCs were
being manufactured.

FIGURE 14
Tom Sandel and Gerhardt Werner; Tom was Chairman of the LINC Evaluation Board that oversaw
the program; Gerhardt had come to build a LINC.

the summer visitors. Mishell Stucki maintained the discipline needed to
keep the tedious wiring of back panels for seven machines going at
Flow Corporation even while many design changes were being made.

Finally, the wired frames arrived and were snatched from the elevator by their eager recipients; people began working on their machines even as the electronics cabinets were coming up to the fourth
floor on the slow freight elevator. Figure 15 shows impatient hands
lacing loose wires on a backpanel just moments after it arrived. Somehow, each of the groups succeeded in assembling its machine, with
only a few explosions and fires along the way. On the day that the first

FIGURE 15
The first LINC backpanels to arrive had been wired, but not yet laced together. Anxious users finished the job, using surgical ties to lace loose wire bundles together.

group of LINCs was turned on, the resulting electrical overload caused a fire in the basement and knocked out all of the power. This stopped work on the LINCs, but dart-playing continued by flashlight.

Once the machines were running, every one of the groups had to write a program for the LINC to demonstrate, for a problem from their own laboratory, that they knew what they were doing. And they all did! Everyone worked night and day, and by the time each month was over every one of the seven groups had written and run programs on its own LINC and packed it onto a moving van for its trip home. We got proud and excited phone calls from each of the groups as they unloaded and unpacked their machines and got them running in their own laboratories. None of the groups had any serious problems getting their machine reassembled and running; record time from arrival was about a half-hour.

Under the creative management and political savvy of Walter Rosenblith of MIT, an ambitious plan had been made for a center for

FIGURE 16
Wes Clark visiting Jerzey Rose (left) at the University of Wisconsin. Rose became one of the most zealous of LINC users. The LINC in the background was typical in its mixing of LINC parts with other laboratory equipment.

research and development of computer technology for the biomedical sciences. It was interdisciplinary, interinstitutional, and so forth. It was a very grand thing, and it was in fact funded by NIH. It was quite amazing that organization and funding went through so smoothly and so rapidly. I don't think that NIH has ever done anything like that since, nor should it. It was a little too much to handle, and that operation came apart shortly after the end of the two summer sessions in Cambridge. We were left in the doldrums while the group fragmented; for good reason many of us, and the responsibility for the continuation of the LINC program, ended up in St. Louis, with strong encouragement from Jerry Cox and Provost George Pake of Washington University.

Charles Molnar   The LINCs that were built during the two monthlong sessions in the summer of 1963, and other copies put together by additional users during the next year or two, dissolved in the laboratories around the country. In a typical installation, such as that in the Laboratory of Neurophysiology at the University of Wisconsin (Figure 16), it was hard to distinguish the LINC from other laboratory apparatus. The

University of Wisconsin, beginning with the LINC that had been put together in Cambridge by Joe Hind and Dan Geissler, acquired a number of additional LINCs over the years, and made major contributions to the development of programs for data collection and plotting. Harold Shipton, at Iowa, also built several LINCs for his group of users. Their LINCs, along with others, continued to operate for many years. The last Wisconsin LINC was retired in 1987; a LINC in Nelson Kiang's Laboratory in Massachusetts is reported to be still in service.

The primary objective of the LINC design had been to create a tool that would address issues of data collection and management and provide interactiveness with the user and the laboratory environment. It was surprising to see how rapidly the removal of these bottlenecks led to pressure to improve the arithmetic and computational capabilities of the LINC; this demand of LINC users was expressed at their second meeting, which was held in St. Louis in early 1965. As a result, several new instructions to enhance computation were added to the LINC, and effort devoted to writing arithmetic packages such as floating-point routines and Fourier transform programs. Other major support efforts in St. Louis during the next several years included continuing refinement of a sequence of LINC Assembly Programs, leading to LAP-6, which combined an effective screen editor, file-management system, and assembler into a compact and coherent package. The University of Wisconsin contributed important tools for plotting and data management, and many LINC users developed and offered more specialized programs.

Reflecting on the unique experience of the LINC, it is clear that there was some magic combination of ideas, technology, needs, and people that made it all work. Technologically, the LINC was no great shakes; certainly the most important component of its success was the clarity and logic of the conception that Wes had of what was needed and possible. Once the vision was presented, a great many people became believers and committed themselves without reservation to making it happen. The importance and the achievability of the goal were clear enough that making it happen was the most important thing for enough people for a long enough time.

Having a machine that was a personal tool was an important part of the magic. For a few of us brought up at Lincoln Laboratory, there had been the experience of "hands-on" use of the TX-0 and TX-2, if only for scheduled intervals of an hour or two several times a week. (Bill Papian once remarked that, as a consequence, my education in computing might well have been the most expensive ever.) The idea that such a computing style could be "affordable" was obviously compelling to the potential LINC users.

The technology in the LINC was not new, but its tight integration into a system, and the simplicity of the form that it took in the LINC, were critical to the reliability, maintainability, and usability of the LINC. The analog–digital and graphics subsystems, designed by Bill Simon, the power supply, done by Don Malpass, the simplified tape transport and memory, which I undertook, and the sophisticated tape control, done by Severo Ornstein all had to (and did) do their jobs efficiently and reliably. The LAP-1 operating system for the LINC, written by Mary Allen Wilkes, and its successors and variants made a major contribution to the accessibility of the LINC, as did the excellence of the concept and execution of the crucial introductory manual *Programming the LINC*, by Mary Allen and Wesley.

One consequence of the LINC style was that the LINC could enter the existing laboratory of an investigator without a need to create new organizations and new staffs to put the tool into use. Skills in applying the LINC to research problems were acquired directly by the investigator, his colleagues, and his students. The courage and determination of the initial participants in the LINC Evaluation Program played a crucial role in showing that it could be done. They were brave to commit their time and talent to this endeavor; they plunged headlong into it; they took the early steps in what became an exponential growth of laboratory computing.

The courage needed should not be underestimated. Not long before the LINC program began, Lincoln Laboratory offered the TX-0 to Walter Rosenblith's Communication Biophysics Group at MIT, which (after anguished discussion) turned it down because no one was sure enough about how to apply it to overcome intimidation by its cost, size, and uniqueness.

Certainly the reduced cost, complexity, and apparent size of the LINC helped its acceptance, as did the advertising of the program as an evaluation program with admitted risks. No doubt the fact that many groups, rather than one, would be taking the plunge together, also helped; the burden of success or failure could be shared, and the pool of ideas and skills broadened. Clearly the exertions and imagination of the early LINC users were as crucial an ingredient in the ultimate success of the LINC as were the clarity and firmness of our view of what was needed and could be done.

Acknowledgments

Development and early dissemination of the LINC was generously supported by the Division of Research Resources of NIH through grants and contracts to the MIT Center Development Office and later to Washington University and other groups that contributed to the further development and early use of the LINC.

Countless individuals made irreplaceable contributions to the development of the LINC and its early use. Many of these are identified in {3}.

Bibliography[2]

1. Clark, W.A. and Molnar, C.E. The LINC: A description of the laboratory instrument computer. *Annals of the New York Academy of Sciences*, 115, pp. 653–668; Whipple, H. (ed.). *Proceedings of a Conference on Computers in Biology and Medicine*, New York, May 27–29, 1963. Published July 31, 1964.

2. Clark, W.A. and Molnar, C.E. A description of the LINC. *Computers in Biomedical Research*, Vol 11, Stacy, R.W. and Waxman, B.D., (eds.). New York: Academic Press, 1965.

3. Clark, W.A. The LINC was early and small. Goldberg, A., (ed.). *A History of Personal Workstations*, New York: ACM Press and Reading, Mass: Addison-Wesley Publishing Co., 1988, pp. 347–394.

[2] Note: A complete set of references is given in {3}. {1} was the earliest report on the LINC, and described the demonstration prototype. {2} describes the Classic LINC, and {3} is a recent and more comprehensive historical account of the LINC development.

Participants' Discussion

Helmuth Orthner	How many LINCs were actually assembled? How much training did the investigators receive? These were neurophysiologists, I assume?
Wesley Clark	The number authorized under the formal program was 16. Twelve machines were to go out to various sites around the country and four more were to be retained by the core staff for continued work and improvements. But another half-dozen or so machines were built in the summer of 1963—a matter of opportunism and the completion of partially constructed instruments. Subsequently, about 50 of those so-called "Classic" machines were built. Then the LINC design became a LINC-8 some years later, which in turn became a PDP-12. I think there were about a thousand PDP-12s. That's a small number by today's standards, but there was no market yet. The participants had not much prior computer training and came from the disciplines of psychology, physiology, genetics, pharmacology, biophysics, and neurology.
Charles Molnar	I'd like to comment on a couple of things I heard from Wesley. One of the important things was that the biological scientist get into the use of the tool. The tool was done in such a way that he could genuinely feel he understood it and could manage it and bend it to his will. The thing we did not like to see was people calling themselves "biologists" or "computerniks." Wesley called this kind of thing "hardening of the categories." So avoiding hardening of the categories was one of the important principles and objectives. The other thing was that at some point in the past Wesley said—and we all thought he'd gone around the bend this time—that his idea of a computer was something that cost 10 dollars and could be painted on any convenient flat surface. We lost on that one too.
Lindley Darden	Is there a LINC still in existence that is being preserved as a museum object?

Wesley Clark   Yes, there are some machines still working 25 years later in various places—at least that was true 2 years ago. There is a LINC in one corner of the Computer Museum in Boston. It's not doing anything, but I think it was one of their first exhibits. It's been downgraded and pushed into a corner. There is also a working machine in Dallas: I was just using it in a law case that I was involved with down there in the first half of this year. It's destined to go to the Computer Museum as well.

History of the Development of Medical Information Systems at the Laboratory of Computer Science at Massachusetts General Hospital

G. Octo Barnett, MD

Harvard Medical School; Laboratory of Computer Science, Massachusetts General Hospital

The reconstruction of history is always a difficult task. The important decisions, the critical issues never seem to be adequately documented and cannot easily be recalled. It is difficult enough in affairs of national importance to try to establish "who knew what, and when did he know it?" In considering the history of the activities of the Laboratory of Computer Science at Massachusetts General Hospital, I have found it equally difficult to try to establish "what did we do, and why did we do it?"

I have little confidence in my judgment as to what were the important contributions of the Laboratory of Computer Science in the first decade of its existence, and even less confidence in my ability to recall and to interpret appropriately the contributions of a host of individuals who participated in the effort.

The only option seems to be to frame this presentation as a series of flashbacks consisting mostly of hazy memories of incidents and selected extracts from grant requests and progress reports. I do not pretend that these flashbacks constitute either a valid scientific quest or a valid historical review, and I fully appreciate that these memories are greatly colored by the events and the activities that have happened since that time.

Two observations, however, seem uniquely important. Claude Bernard wrote, "Art is I; Science is We." I cannot emphasize too strongly this statement in reflecting over the history of the Laboratory of Computer Science, which it has been my privilege to lead for almost 25 years. I have been enormously fortunate in having had the opportunity to work with a large number of enormously creative, imaginative, and effective colleagues who have played a major role in the contributions we have made in the past 20 years. No presentation would be complete and accurate without giving recognition to these individuals. I have often felt that my primary responsibility was to recruit good colleagues, and then try to provide the environment where they could be optimally productive.

There are too many people to name individually in this short presentation, but I will identify some of the key individuals in relation to specific projects. I know that I will fail to recognize many individuals who have made important contributions; this failure haunts me in my writing of an historical account of the Laboratory.

The second observation I would offer is that much of what is accomplished in life and in science seems in large part to be dominated by luck, by the accident of being in the right place at the right time, with the right resources, the right funding, the right opportunities. I believe this to be true in much of what we have accomplished at the Laboratory. I feel most fortunate that 30 years ago, due to a chance association of living with a group of MIT electrical engineering graduate students, I became acquainted with computer technology and became captivated by it as an idle recreation. I still live in fear that someday it will be discovered that I am getting paid for doing my hobby, and that I will have to get a real job.

Preparing this manuscript has been somewhat of a revelation and somewhat distressing. Technology has developed at a fantastic rate and yet progress in implementation has been laborious and slow. I found it interesting and somewhat entertaining to read two paragraphs I wrote in reviewing this field for the *New England Journal of Medicine* {1} almost 20 years ago:

> Early interest in bringing the revolution in computer technology to bear on medical practice was plagued with over enthusiasm, naiveté and unrealistic expectations. The use of computers would, it was held, allow rapid and accurate collection and retrieval of all clinical information, perform automatic diagnosis, collect, monitor, and analyze a variety of physiological signals, perform and interpret all laboratory tests immediately, and replace the telephone and the medical record by fulfilling their functions. In fact, however, attempts to apply computer technology to medicine have had only limited success, with numerous failures. The growing pains encountered in applying computer technology are not unique to medicine; the same types of experiences have been realized in all other areas of computer application. Indeed, one of the benefits of the computer revolution is that it stimulates and requires an intensity of thinking, a level of sophistication and a strictness of semantic behavior that are needed badly in the development of improved methods of delivering health care.
>
> The initial wave of optimism and enthusiasm generated by beguiling promises of an immediately available, total hospital computer system has passed. Now, efforts are directed toward the painful, slow evolutionary process of developing and implementing modules or building blocks for individual functions. There is now a keen appreciation of the wide gap separating a demonstration project, however impressive, and an operational service system in daily use. Stringent reliability requirements and the difficulties attendant when nontechnical personnel (with a high turnover rate) use a computer system on a round-the-clock basis have been two of the key limiting factors in HIS development. In addition, the very high initial costs often stagger hospital administrators; demonstration of

cost-benefit savings is difficult. If the experience of other industries is repeated in hospitals, the use of computers in hospitals will not reduce total medical care costs, but will lead to more effective use of the resources at hand and to improved patient care.

We are still in this painful, slow evolutionary process. We still face the reliability problems, the high initial costs. In reading these old articles I am impressed at how valid were our concerns 20 years ago and how many of the issues we confronted then are still valid. For example, let me share several paragraphs of an article published in 1969 {2}:

> In papers devoted to the problems of hospital information systems, there is often a strong feeling of déjà vu. For the past decade it has been repeatedly claimed that computers will be of enormous usefulness in patient care and in hospital practice. On innumerable occasions our old men have dreamed dreams and our young men have seen visions. Yet, when we critically examine what is actually being implemented in our hospitals, we are most impressed by the number of slow or halting starts, and the number of projects that have been abandoned or in which the objectives have been greatly watered down. The discrepancies between the visions and the realities are startling.
>
> What is the cause of this state of underachievement when the need is so great, and the technology supposedly so powerful? This is a significant problem which merits considerable analysis. It is our thesis that a considerable portion of the difficulty involves the recognition and solution of the "interface" problems.
>
> There are three important classes of interface problems: (1) the interface of the hospital with the development and implementation of a computer system; (2) the interface of the user with the computer terminals; and (3) the interface of the programmer with the computer system.
>
> When one reviews the developmental projects which have been undertaken, there are several recurring themes. First, the magnitude of the problem is usually grossly underestimated and there is almost always inadequate concern for defining objectives and for planning. Hospital and medical staffs have had little prior experience in innovation in the area of information processing, and in many situations, the critical decisions are made by individuals in isolated departments who do not possess a broad view of the needs of the hospital.
>
> Second, the computer industry has often displayed a considerable lack of understanding and of sophistication. On a number of occasions, the sales and promotional aspects of marketing hospital computer systems have been quite misleading and have led to false expectations.
>
> Third, the hospitals have rarely made the depth of commitment of both administrative and professional staff that is required to develop and implement a viable system. This commitment must be in terms of years, in order to provide the exposure and experience necessary to copy with the complexity of the problems.

Fortunately, the illusionary concept of a total hospital information system is now disappearing, and there is a wider acceptance of the need for an evolutionary, stepwise development over a period of years. Total systems suffer from limitations in terms of both definition and appropriate technology. We neither understand all the dimensions of the problem, nor do we have management structures or computer facilities that could support a total system. It now appears that the most logical course is the development of a series of modular systems, which will be interconnected and will evolve toward handling more and more of the information-processing aspects of patient care. It has been repeatedly demonstrated that the introduction of a radically new technology causes fundamental changes in the habit patterns and in the desires of the hospital staff. The objectives and procedures of the computer development must also evolve as we gain experience with computer systems in daily hospital operation.

My first flashback relates to my initial contact with the Hospital Computer Project contract held by MGH and a firm in Cambridge named Bolt Beranek and Newman (BBN). This contract, funded jointly by the National Institutes of Health and the American Hospital Association, began in 1962. The effort was directly related to the genius and imagination of one of the senior managers at BBN—Jordan Baruch. BBN was active in the early development of time-sharing computer systems, and had developed one of the first time-sharing systems on a PDP-1. Jordan had a vision of the useful impact that such a system would have on the information processing needs of a hospital, and persuaded the NIH to fund the effort. NIH insisted that there be a medical collaborator and MGH was drafted—with little knowledge or insight on the part of MGH as to what was involved. There is an ancient letter in the files from the MGH director to the NIH stating that MGH would be glad to participate with the understanding that there would be no cost to MGH—after 25 years and the expenditure of many millions of dollars, this request seems somewhat lacking in foresight.

The time-sharing technology developed by BBN was at the cutting edge of computer science at that time, and the use of time-sharing at MGH was one of the first demonstrations of the potential power of remote access to a real-time, on-line database. Jordan's early papers and reports are still fascinating in the range of the vision and the validity of many of the objectives. From the initial formulation, the system was conceived as being interactive and conversational in real time. The dialog was to have error-checking, to have on-line help, and to be branching in response to the particular set of entries given by the user. One of the most radical of the specifications was the plan to include "standing orders" in the computer so that it could automatically detect and respond to specific data entries or to specific values of the database. Jordan referred to this as "event-detection" or as an always active "demon" which continually monitored the database. This is the first plan of which I am aware to take advantage of the computer system to use preformulated rules and is a model of what are now used extensively as "criterion-rules" or "on-line quality assurance."

The second flashback memory relates to how I initially became involved in the MGH medical information system developments. BBN had demonstrated impressive progress in developing computer technology, but there was little progress in hospital applications, and little involvement of the medical or nursing staff. I believe that the NIH site visit committee strongly suggested to MGH that it should take a more active role in the planning and management of the Hospital Computer Project, and that MGH should provide professional leadership. Following this advice, John Knowles (who was then General Director of the MGH) and Bob Ebert (Chief of Medicine) consulted with members of the computer student section and with NIH staff. It is my impression that two of you here today—Homer Warner and Bruce Waxman—were instrumental in my being recruited in 1964. This recruitment was facilitated by the circumstance that there was no one else they could identify who was interested in academic medicine and who had any experience in working with computers. In several conversations with Knowles and Baruch, I became intrigued with their vision and with the potential to combine my hobby in computers with the practice of medicine. I am sure that none of us anticipated the problems we would encounter, the amount of time, effort and money that would be required, or the years of development that lay ahead.

My next flashback memory is of the first two years of the activities of the Laboratory of Computer Science from 1964–1966. Our initial efforts were focused on the development of an admission discharge census system, a laboratory reporting system, and a medications ordering system.

The computer system used in the initial time-sharing development was a PDP-1 computer with 16K of 18-bit words memory which supported five simultaneous users. This system was later upgraded to a PDP-1-D which had 48K of core memory and which was supposedly capable of supporting 64 simultaneous users.

There were no telephone line communication tariffs that could be used for data communication, but we were able to obtain a tariff for direct current telegraph communication that had been established for communication along railroad tracks. The telephone company was generous in not requiring us to lay the railroad track between BBN in Cambridge and MGH in order to justify providing the 10-character/second-DC communication. The terminals were standard Model 33 Teletypes which were placed on a few of the floors of MGH in 1964–1965.

All programs were written in assembler. Initially all programming was done only on the central console teletype. Program creation and debugging would take weeks to months, and changes to a running

FIGURE 1
A prototype demon-
stration

```
CALL    MED

    MEDICATION ORDER


3:47 PM 1/21/1965
1  TIME AND DATE    11:15AM 1/20/1965
2  DOCTOR    R GREENE            FIX    ←HOW    LAST,FIRST
2  DOCTOR    GREENE,R
3  PATIENT    101A    JACK,MARY MISS    35    F
4  ORDER
   4.1    RX,ELVIL,25MG,IM,4ID,I        Misspelled drug name,
...DO YOU MEAN...    ELAVIL              computer lists back drugs
                                         with similarly spelled names.

   Y
ELAVIL
ROUTE NOT LISTED ?    PO               Formulary does not list IM
RX,ELAVIL,25MG,PO,4ID,I                route.
   4.2

-THANK YOU-
```

program had to be strongly justified. One BBN report stated the criteria for revision to be: "What contribution will such revision make to the knowledge garnered by the project" and "Is a new principle involved?"

Using this PDP system located 10 miles distant from MGH, we were able to provide what for those days were very impressive demonstrations of how a computer might be useful in processing medical information. Figure 1 illustrates a simple dialog from that period. We were, however, never able to do more than limited demonstrations, and were therefore never able to test any of the programs in actual operation. The major problems were unreliability of the computer system, slow speed of communication, very limited functional capabilities, and user unfriendliness of the Teletype as an input instrument. In addition, because of the limitations of programming in assembler language, any debugging or enhancements of the programs required weeks to months to accomplish.

Probably of greatest importance, it became obvious that there was an incompatibility in philosophy between the goals of BBN and the goals of the Laboratory. This difference can be illustrated by quoting one of the early BBN reports which stated: "For now we shall ignore questions of priority, time, and cost. Let us work purely with definitions and ideas." In my judgment, these definitions and ideas, which had been formulated by BBN, were highly creative and had great promise. The hospital, however, marched to a different drummer in being more pragmatically oriented. The research project was rapidly losing credibility in that it could not meet the challenge of being used by regular hospital staff carrying out the normal daily tasks of patient care. Demonstration programs, however impressive, and promises for the future, however grandiose, could not substitute for the reality that all our computer programs could only function in the hothouse atmosphere of parallel operation for several days to several weeks and operated by our own research staff. There was no possibility for evaluating whether or not a hospital could be usefully served by such a system, and certainly no hope that we could persuade the hospital to spend its own money to implement such a system.

The next of these random flashbacks relates to the origin of MUMPS. At one of the first NIH project reviews, J.C. Shaw was one of the site visitors. Shaw is one of the early great pioneers of programming who worked at Rand Corporation with Newell and Simon. He had developed an interpretive language known as JOSS which he discussed over lunch at the site visit. One of the MIT students who was working with us on the project decided to implement the language on an MIT system over Christmas holidays. BBN management became fascinated with the language and over the next two years implemented a number of versions of the language under the names of Telecomp and Stringcomp. These languages provided algebraic programming support and had only primitive string handling functions and no file handling capability.

At about this time, Jordan Baruch persuaded General Electric to enter the business of time-sharing computer support for the hospital industry. This new GE subsidiary, known as Medinet, had very ambitious goals—to develop simultaneously time-sharing hardware, a new language, and a complete set of hospital information applications. The company never had the opportunity to either succeed or fail, since after about six months GE decided to terminate all of its computer activities including Medinet. Although Medinet was not given the opportunity to implement a working demonstration of the proposed language, known as Filecomp, the specifications for the language were most intriguing in that they included the initial structure for a hierarchical global file structure.

The main character of the next flashback chapter is one of the most imaginative and productive computer scientists it has been my privilege to know—Neil Pappalardo. I first knew Neil when he was a student of mine at MIT and did his senior thesis in my cardiovascular laboratory. He and Curt Marble, a fellow MIT student, joined me after their graduation from MIT as research assistants studying cardiovascular system control. We were using mathematical models to analyze the feedback control of cardiovascular function and became heavily involved in the use of computers—first a PDP-4, then a PDP-7. In about 1965–1966, Neil and Curt tried to persuade me that we could develop a programming system that would support the development of medical information systems at MGH. For some months, I tried to discourage them from what I felt to be a radical and obviously unproductive activ-

FIGURE 2
The MUMPS global
explained

MUMPS SYSTEM

The file structure of MUMPS lends itself to hierarchical organization of data. As an example, a possible way to store laboratory test results might be as follows: (1) the top level node is a patient ID number, (2) below it are successive dates for which results exist, and (3) below a data node are test names and results for that date. The structure looks as follows:

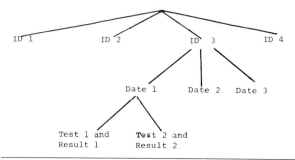

FIGURE 3
Sample of early
MUMPS code

A simple program which accepts results entered by a laboratory technician and stores them in the way shown below.

```
1.1Ø READ !,"PATIENT ID # ",ID IF ID='''' QUIT
1.15 IF 'ID:3N"-"2N TYPE "  ILLEGAL ID FORMAT" GOTO 1.1
1.2Ø SET IDA=$PIECE(ID-1),IDB=$PIECE(ID-2)
1.3Ø SET ID=$VALUE(IDA)+$VALUE(IDB)/1ØØ
1.4Ø READ !,"TEST NAME ",TN
1.5Ø SET TNN=$BOOLEAN(TN="NA",1;TN="K",2;TN="CL",3;TN="BUN",4;1,Ø)
1.6Ø IF TNN=Ø TYPE " TEST NOT IN DIRECTORY"  GOTO 1.4
1.7Ø READ !,"RESULT ",RST
1.8Ø SET D=$DATE,DA=$EXTRACT(D,3,4),DB=$EXTRACT(D,5,6)
1.85 SET DAT=$VALUE(DA)+$VALUE(DB)/1ØØ
1.9Ø OPEN ↑Z SET ↑Z(ID,DAT,TNN)=TN.",".RST CLOSE
```

ity—after all, what competence and experience did a hospital-based group have in comparison with the giants in the field who were not yet able to provide a viable, reasonably inexpensive, easy to program, time-sharing system. Neil, however ignored my guidance, as was his usual habit, proceeded with the development of MUMPS, and in a few months, had a system that was exciting and promising. To this day, I have not been able to trace who first thought of that name, or why we did not come up with a more dignified title. Some early descriptive examples are shown in Figures 2 and 3.

The development and use of MUMPS quickly became a dominant theme of our Laboratory. Indeed, it is my impression that one of the important reasons that MUMPS evolved into a powerful and easy-to-use language was that the development was carried out in an environment where there was very close communication between the potential users and the system designers. In our small group, there were no system analysts, no application programmers, no systems programmers—

we were all problem solvers trying to develop a working system. In addition, we had the fortunate luxury of relatively stable support—NIH was at first not overly supportive of our work in creating the language, but because their investment in the MGH project was so large, and because they had no good alternatives for application development, they provided the funding to allow us to proceed.

The technical details of the first MUMPS implementation on a PDP-7 are of interest in comparison with the technology now available. The PDP-7 had 8K of memory (18-bit words) with three Teletypes and a 256K fixed-head disk. The complete MUMPS interpreter with input/output routines and buffers occupied 4K with active user programs residing in one of the 2K partitions. A major breakthrough occurred when we obtained our first PDP-9 computer which utilized a 24K memory. The initial MUMPS systems were constructed before we had developed the global file-handling system, and DEC tapes were used extensively for data storage. One of our first ambulatory medical record systems had an active database stored on over 100 different DEC tapes—not exactly a computer operator's dream. The development of the global system and the expanded core memory on the PDP-9 made it possible to undertake much more challenging applications. In the 24K version of the PDP-9, we were able to have 16 users running simultaneously—albeit slowly.

The years of 1967 to 1972 were exciting times in the Laboratory. We were able to implement operational information systems in a variety of areas and undertook initial developments in a host of challenging medical applications. The major organizing principle of our development was a "modular" approach. We argued that because of the difficulty in formulating a "total systems" plan, it was more productive to focus on identifying functional information processing units of medical activity and to provide well-defined and clearly bounded computer systems that could be explicitly integrated into the real and concrete medical needs of operating departments of the hospital. This modular approach made it easier to obtain agreement and cooperation at the departmental level, sharply limited the initial start-up costs, and simplified the cost-benefit analysis since the computer program was closely linked to one specific operations unit. An additional advantage, which proved of great value, was that this modular approach resulted in a "domino effect": Success in one department served as an attractive role model for development of modules for other departments. Lastly, a major advantage of the modular approach was that it facilitated flexibility and graceful evolution since we could make specific changes to one module without having a large, unforeseen or negative impact on other activities. Figure 4 illustrates how we presented this view at the time.

The first two major hospital systems we implemented were the Chemistry Laboratory test reporting system and the Bacteriology test

FIGURE 4
Statement of goals

```
A research group concerned with the development of information
processing systems for patient care must not only be concerned
with the definition of the particular medical care problem but
also with the availability of appropriate computer technology.
We feel that R and D in the latter field is an essential part
of the overall problem.  Our group has chosen the course of
developing a "total" Hospital Information System in terms of a
series of functional modules.  These modules consist of moderate-
sized, remote-access, dedicated-function, time-sharing computer
systems.  The enclosed documentation describes such a module.

                                    G. Octo Barnett, M.D.
                                    A. Neil Pappalardo
                                    Robert A. Greenes, M.D.
                                    Curtis W. Marble
```

reporting system. The first part of the Chemistry Laboratory system was implemented in 1968 and has been operational since that time, 7 days per week, 24 hours per day with a downtime of less than 0.2% for the past 20 years. This system has been extended, patched, enhanced, modified, expanded, and marginally rewritten by dozens of programmers during the last two decades. This year, we are finally being forced to rewrite the system and discard the old programs. I doubt that there are many systems with this longevity; if there were a NLM archives for old code, I would nominate these Chemistry Laboratory Reporting programs.

Two of the early postdoctoral trainees at the Laboratory were Bob Greenes (now director of the Decisions Systems Laboratory of the Brigham and Women's Hospital) and Jerry Grossman (now president and director of the New England Medical Center). Bob Greenes played an active role in the early creation of MUMPS and, in addition, was the lead developer of a computer-based system using a dialogue between the physician and a computer-controlled display screen. His system for using this to collect progress notes in a hypertensive clinic was the subject of his PhD thesis in computer science at Harvard—one of the first PhDs awarded in what we now call medical informatics. It is of historical interest that Ted Shortliffe worked in the Laboratory on this project while he was a undergraduate student at Harvard College. There were no commercially available light pens at that time, so we had to invent our own touch-sensitive receptors—a series of metallic strips overlying the CRT screen. These metallic strips were part of a tuned circuit which had a frequency shift induced by a change in capacitance when touched. One annoying problem occurred in conditions of high humidity or when the users fingers were overly moist—in such circumstances the user would occasionally receive a mild shock. This Pavlovian reinforcement did tend to keep down the length of the notes that were generated with the system.

Jerry Grossman was one of the key figures in the Laboratory's first efforts in developing a computer-based ambulatory medical record. When the Harvard Community Health Plan was first planned by the Harvard Medical School dean in the late sixties, we were asked to work together to develop a computer-based medical record system. When the plan opened its doors, our computer-based record system was in place—though not heavily loaded since there were only eight patients enrolled. It was in large part a tribute to Jerry's enormous energy and commitment that COSTAR survived through the growing pains of both HCHP and the changes in the information system. He guided COSTAR through a number of rewrites and extensions—for a time, he even acted as the Medical Record Room supervisor for HCHP. COSTAR was our first major effort to develop a system that could be made available to the community as a public-domain supported product; probably the most amazing observation is that the system is still being actively used and supported and extended by over 100 different sites. A snapshot of the COSTAR Patient Status Reprint from 1971 is shown in Figure 5. Since the code was written by over 40 different programmers over the past 20 years, you can imagine that this system sets a new record for "spaghetti code."

FIGURE 5
An Early COSTAR
Report

```
                        PATIENT STATUS REPORT                    PAGE 1

       BARTON, WILMA SAMPLE
       HCHP PT 00-00-00

       MARRIED FEMALE DOB: 04/13/40
       77 MASS AVE, CAMBRIDGE, MA
       TEL:  864-6900


       DIAGNOSES AND PROBLEMS

             ABDOMINAL PAIN [K991]              B. WALTERS, M.D. (09/23/71)

             CHRONIC DEPRESSION [P120]          S. FRENCH, R.N.  (03/15/71)

             MONILIASIS [M191]                  F. WELLER, M.D. (10/20/70)

             PENICILLIN ALLERGY [A113]
                SKIN RASH                       B. WALTERS, M.D. (07/06/70)

             ASTHMA [G100]
                MODERATE, NEEDS REASSURANCE     B. WALTERS, M.D. (07/06/70)


       TEST RESULTS

             09/23/71    HCT              41

             10/20/70    VAGINAL CULTURE  CANDIDA ALBICANS
```

During the entire history of the Laboratory's existence I have enjoyed participating as a faculty member in the Department of Electrical Engineering and Computer Science at MIT. I have learned much from the students whom I have met in the different courses with which I have been associated. One of the most important opportunities I had was being one of the supervisors on the PhD thesis of Tony Gorry (now vice-president for Institutional Development of Baylor College of Medicine.) Tony and I were fascinated by Homer Warner's early work on using Bayes's rule in computer-aided medical diagnosis. We became interested in using mathematical models to assist in clinical decision making. Homer was very generous in sharing a large data set of clinical findings in congenital heart disease. Tony demonstrated that a program could employ sequential decision-making to balance the risk of making a diagnosis against the cost of further testing and the value of the evidence which could be obtained. His work in 1967 to 1968 was one of the first efforts to give explicit consideration to the potential value of information when deciding whether to collect further data. Tony's work was an important stimulus to my interest in sequential decision-making and to the potential role of computer programs in medical education. In fact, some of the most sophisticated computer-based medical education programs which we now write are still strongly influenced by my early collaboration with Tony.

The Laboratory is now almost 25 years old and much has changed since those early years. In the intervening years many wonderful individuals have worked on a variety of projects ranging from an automated medication system, to a number of laboratory and radiology information systems, to medical education programs, to different ambulatory medical record systems. I have been fortunate to be working in a hospital that has been very supportive and provided challenging opportunities and outstanding colleagues. I have also been fortunate in the support and encouragement that has been provided by the different funding agencies. Perhaps someday we will have a conference on what happened during the second and third decades of the development of medical information systems.

It is very tempting to become overly sentimental in recalling the history of the Laboratory. Flashbacks follow flashbacks follow flashbacks—memories become rose-colored with distance; I tend to remember the good and reinterpret the bad. However, preparing this paper does give me one opportunity I greatly treasure, and that is to thank those of you who have been so important in providing stimulation, leadership, support, guidance, wisdom and, most of all, fellowship over the years. I have always deeply enjoyed the many different experiences we have had, the site visits to Peoria and Columbia, the study section and committee work, the reports we have worked on together. A number of you in the audience I count as personal friends, as individuals who have been vitally important in both my professional and personal life. For all that you have meant to me, I can only express my deepest appreciation, and for the years ahead, I look forward to more of the same. I hope that I can pass on to the younger generation some of the excitement and fun and fellowship we have shared together.

Acknowledgments

The author would like to acknowledge the *New England Journal of Medicine* for permission to reprint material from my article "Computer and Patient Care," *NEJM* 279:1321–1327, 1968; and the New York Academy of Scinece for reproduction of material from "Interface Aspects of a Hospital Information System," by myself and R.A. Greenes, *Ann. NY Acad. Science* 161: 756–768, 1969.

References

1. Barnett, G.O. Computers and patient care. *NEJM* 279:1321–1327, 1968.

2. Barnett, G.O. and Greenes, R.A. Interface aspects of a hospital information system. *Ann. NY Acad. Science* 161:756–768, 1969.

3. Barnett, G.O. and Castleman, P.A. A time-sharing computer system for patient care activities. *Comp Biomed Research* 1:41–50, 1967.

4. Greenes, R.A., Pappalardo, A.N., Marble, C.W., and Barnett, G.O. Design and implementation of a clinical data management system. *Comp Biomed Research* 2:469–485, 1969.

5. Greenes, R.A., Barnett, G.O., Klein, S.W., Robbins, A., and Prior, R.E. Recording, retrieval and review of medical data by physician/computer interaction. *NEJM* 282:307–315, 1970.

6. Grossman, J.H., Barnett, G.O., Kospell, R.D., Nesson, H.R., Dorsey, J.L., and Phillips, R.R. An automated medical record system for a prepaid group practice. *JAMA* 224:1616–1621, 1973.

7. Gorry, G.A. and Barnett, G.O. Sequential diagnosis by computer. *JAMA* 205:849–854, 1968.

Participants' Discussion

Helmuth Orthner   In the olden days, whatever was produced under a government grant was in the public domain. In that sense the MUMPS language is in the public domain, and the government is now compensated for its investment by using MUMPS in the Veterans Administration—perhaps ten times what it originally invested in that language. But the situation has changed. Now the investigators can keep some of the technology. What will that do to the dissemination of research results and research developments that are being carried out in various laboratories such as yours?

Octo Barnett   My impression is that one of the significant failures we've had in the area of medical informatics has been the difficulty in finding the right types of relationships with private industry. I am very well aware now of the limitations of a laboratory like mine that are involved with the dissemination of a product. I think that public domain is almost a fatuous idea. It took us five to seven years to get Digital Equipment Corporation to be even interested in MUMPS. COSTAR would have been much better off if we had accepted the responsibility of supporting and maintaining it in it's initial years. I think that most individuals are responsible enough to realize there is a cost involved in acquiring a product and supporting it. The idea of getting something for free, I think, is really a very misleading type of idea.

    Now, what type of mechanisms can operate today, and how do we develop the various alternatives? It is very important that we try to deal with that because there are very few products that will not need changing a week after they leave the door. You are never going to get rich selling software but, you've got to find some mechanisms so you can provide continuing support and a continuing evolution of those products.

    I must say there have been 12 companies founded by people that have left the Laboratory that have done a fair bit better than the MGH Laboratory.

Morris Collen   Octo Barnett has been very modest and very generous in crediting others, but on my first visit to MGH I learned something that I've never

154

forgotten—that is, how well you can use nurses as systems people. I went home and implemented that idea. I think that nurses have not received their due recognition in implementing medical computing systems. They are finally now getting their due in nursing information systems, but I think history should credit Octo as being the first one to recognize that.

Octo Barnett   I still find some problem with getting the nurses to identify themselves as medical informatics individuals rather than as nurses. We have this tension that goes back and forth. I tend to be very sexist and exploit the great exploitable segment of our population because basically, most of my very good programmers and project managers have been females. I'm never quite sure I understand why that is. I quite agree there are tremendously good individuals in the nursing profession that could participate a great deal more in medical informatics.

Carlos Vallbona   The presentation from Dr. Barnett has brought up one point which I believe is unique to the history of medical informatics in this country, and that is this event which we have called the site visit. You alluded to the impact that one of your site visits made on the eventual development of MUMPS. Site visits can be a pain in the neck of those who are at one side of the table, but they can be very stimulating to those who are at the other side of the table. I believe that we should make it clear in the history of medical informatics the impact that site visits have had—both positive and negative.

Thelma Estrin   In teaching, I use a slide of Larry Weed's (Figure 1, next page) that shows a medical record. At the top of the page it states: "A physician's notes from a medical record in an American medical center." At the bottom of the page it says, "Society can only be understood through a study of the messages and communication facilities which belong to it." With that I would like to close our session. I'm one of those people who always thinks the future is the present, but in the next 25 years we will really automate the medical record. Twenty-five years ago I made the same prediction, and we now have the technology to make it happen—technology we did not have over two decades ago.[1]

---

[1] For a history of the automated medical record, see W.W. Stead, A quarter-century of computer-based medical records, *M.D. Computer*, (6,2):74–87, 1989.

FIGURE 6
A physician's notes
from a medical rec-
ord in an American
medical center

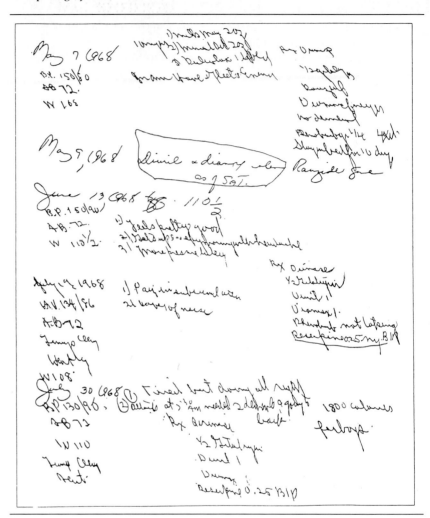

The UCLA Brain Research Institute Data Processing Laboratory

Thelma Estrin, PhD
School of Engineering, University of California, Los Angeles

Introduction

My personal interest in brain waves stems from my position as an electrical engineer in the electroencephalographic department of the Neurological Institute in New York City in 1951. At that time, I had just received my PhD in electrical engineering from the University of Wisconsin, and my husband had obtained his PhD in the same field. He was employed at the Institute for Advanced Study (IAS) in Princeton on their Electronic Computer Project. I also worked on the IAS computer project for several months, but sought a position using my electrical engineering background more directly. I had trouble obtaining traditional employment as an electrical engineer because my commitment was not taken seriously; a common attitude towards women's careers in the fifties.

During my graduate days at Wisconsin, I had heard a talk about the electroencephalogram and believed that the study of this electrical phenomenon should be of interest to an electrical engineer. When I couldn't find traditional employment in academia or industry, a friend helped me locate a position in the electroencephalography (EEG) department of the Neurological Institute in New York City. I was responsible for assuring the reliability of the clinical EEG equipment and was also given the opportunity to do research and collaborate with physicians on EEG and EMG studies. At that time I was as much a rarity among engineers for my technical work as I was for my sex, for biomedical engineering had not yet become a field of engineering. One of the compensations for the daily four-hour commute between my home in Princeton, New Jersey, and my work in New York City, was being able to participate in the social and intellectual life of the Institute for Advanced Study (IAS) where the computing machine, called the Johniac, was being built under the leadership of John von Neumann. Frequently we went out to dinner with the von Neumanns, and Johnny, as everyone called him, always queried me about the status of my EEG research. Johnny's interest in the brain stemmed from his interest in automata. In 1954 we had the opportunity to go to Israel to build a

157

version of the Johniac, and my computer experience continued at the Weizmann Institute of Science, where I was a computer engineer {1}.

While employed at the Neurological Institute, I had redesigned an electronic frequency analyzer for bioelectric signals. The frustrations of adjusting analog filter circuits in the early fifties, coupled with my new experiences in digital logic design, put me in a good position to introduce 006235 electronic digital techniques for recording the impulse firing pattern of neurons in 1960 {2}. My electroencephalogram and computer experiences were a good combination for introducing the use of computers to the neurophysiological community, and in 1960 I joined the Brain Research Institute at UCLA.

Historical Background

The Brain Research Institute is an interdisciplinary research unit of the UCLA Medical School, supporting basic research in fields that contribute to an understanding of brain mechanisms and behavior. In 1960 the School of Medicine was relatively young, having graduated its first class in 1955. Among the early professors to affiliate with the new medical school was Dr. H.W. Magoun, whose own research interests were in the nervous system. Under his leadership, a formal proposal was prepared requesting the University of California to establish a Brain Research Institute (BRI). The proposal was approved in December 1959 and by mid-1961, 67 members from 14 university departments (12 in the Medical School) moved into a new BRI building contiguous with the Medical School, and the Neuropsychiatric Institute.

When the Brain Research Institute at UCLA was planned in the mid-fifties, very few scientists of any discipline recognized the potential of automated data processing as a research tool, and the use of computers by neurophysiologists seemed like science fiction. Dr. Ross Adey, a physician, professor of anatomy, and a ham radio operator, understood the potential of the computer. Adey convinced Magoun and Dr. Jack French, the BRI's new director, that the computer revolution would bring enormous changes to neurophysiology. In 1960, the Institute made a commitment to obtain funding from NIH to pursue computing research, and I was the electrical engineer who wrote the engineering aspects of our proposal: to establish a Data Processing Laboratory whose major focus was the design and installation of a small general purpose computer facility centered around an automated analog–digital conversion center. By the time the Institute officially opened in 1961, the BRI was awaiting funding from the Institute of Neurological Diseases and Blindness (NINDB) for its successful grant application, "The Application of Computing Techniques to Brain Function, " to develop new computer methods for treating data derived from brain study. This was the first support of computer research that NINDB had funded, and there was much controversy at NIH over the size of the grant, which was about $290,000.

The goal of the grant was to introduce computing techniques to analyze electrical activity recorded from nervous structures in a variety of living forms ranging from invertebrate to man. The BRI had 90 projects and, in over half of the laboratories, electrical signals of nervous activity were observed and recorded. Electrical activity recorded from nervous tissue was classified as "spikes" or "waves." The term "spike" referred to the fast electrical action potentials of discharging nerve cells, called neurons. "Waves" were slow rhythmic potential changes as seen in the electroencephalogram (EEG), which represented ongoing oscillations from the brain. The goals of investigators studying these signals were varied and included:

- relating electrical events in single nerve fibers to the physicochemical processes that occur in the transmission of the nerve signal;

- monitoring electrical events in order to map pathways in the nervous system;

- correlating EEG changes in electrical activity with different behavioral or physiological states;

- classifying characteristic EEG patterns for clinical diagnosis; and

- monitoring electrical activity during different stages of sleep, conditioning or learning

to cite a few. All of these experiments were characterized by great masses of data that were largely assessed by the naked eye. The digital computer could provide a powerful tool for neurophysiologists to study these phenomena, but the incompatibility between the continuously time-variant nature of these physiological quantities and the discrete character code of the digital computer were major obstacles. Our immediate aim in designing the laboratory was to provide a facility to computerize the collecting, editing, and processing of these data.

The newly formed Data Processing Laboratory of the Brain Research Institute was specifically designed to make the latest high-speed computing techniques available in the BRI. But an analog–digital conversion system was needed to bridge the gap. In 1961, to make use of digital computers, the recorded analog data had to be digitized and stored on digital magnetic tape in computer-readable format. We decided to make several analog magnetic tape recorders available for lending to individual laboratories and to have a central facility, in DPL, with a versatile conversion system able to produce data tapes in IBM format. We wanted to enable our investigators to utilize the very advanced computing facilities available to the UCLA community at the time. We also planned to equip a small, digital techniques laboratory to develop special purpose devices to investigate digitizing data at the source and to implement the remote transmission of data stored on digital magnetic tape, between laboratories and computers. Additionally, we decided to rent a small general-purpose computer and investigate the application of "on-line" computing techniques to neurophysiological data.

UCLA has had a long and established history in the field of computing, dating back to 1949 when the National Bureau of Standards supported design and construction of the Standard's Western Automatic Computer (SWAC) electronic digital equipment on campus (which continued in service until 1966). In 1956 the Western Data Processing Center was created under the joint sponsorship of the University and IBM. A 709 computer was installed in the Graduate School of Management to support research and education in the application of computing to business management. In the same period, the School of Engineering and the Department of Mathematics recruited Dr. Gerald Estrin to initiate a computer engineering program and to help expand scientific computing at UCLA. With the aid of a grant from the National Science Foundation the University established the Campus Computing Facility in 1961. In fact, in 1961, three IBM 7090 computers arrived at UCLA: one for the Western Data Processing Center, one for the Campus Computing Center, and one for a new Health Science Computing Center. Dr. Wilfred J. Dixon, professor of Biostatistics in the Medical Center, had also obtained support from NIH for computation on medical data, and obtained a large mainframe to be housed in the Medical School. These three computers attracted the attention of the Defense Advanced Research Project Agency (DARPA) and generated the early research that led to the now-famous ARPA network. I recall from conversations with Dr. Dixon that the campus mainframe providers were very disturbed by the vast quantities of input and output data the biologists and medical people used. They believed that only small amounts of input or output data were required by scientists, assuming that the computer's speed and sophistication made appropriate use of clever algorithms. This was just prior to business applications of high-speed computers, and most physical scientists believed at that time that the medical people were asking the wrong questions or did not have a discipline that was suitable for computation!

In 1960 to 1961, the largest laboratory in the BRI was the Space Biology Laboratory (SBL), which pioneered the development of data acquisition and computing techniques. SBL programs planned to study the effects of environmental stresses likely to be encountered in space flight on the brain mechanisms of animals and man. In addition to having written the neurophysiological sections of the DPL grant to NIH, Dr. Adey also obtained support from the Air Force and the National Aeronautics and Space Administration to establish SBL for studying information storage mechanisms in brain systems tested under conditions of simulated ballistic flight. A major segment of the SBL program studied the electrophysiological correlates of behavior by means of electrodes implanted chronically in normal-behaving animals. Dr. Adey's aim was to find the EEG relationship to behavioral states of wakefulness, alertness, and decision making. The Data Processing Laboratory was designated as the computation center to support activities of the SBL staff.

In 1961, another new program for the BRI was the Clinical Neurophysiology Unit. On a mandate from Congress, NIH had set up a program designed to support facilities in which the techniques of basic research could be applied to clinical practice. In response, the National Institute of Neurological Diseases and Blindness funded the BRI to investigate basic neurophysiological methods suitable for human patients who could receive therapeutic intervention in the nervous system for temporal lobe epilepsy. In this program the techniques of basic neurophysiology, as developed in animal experimentation, were used to study patients with neurological and psychiatric disorders. There was particular interest in correlating recordings obtained from electrodes placed on the skull of patients, with activity recorded from the cortex and deep brain structures. An operating theater, 10-bed suite, electrophysiological recording unit, and the basic facilities of the Brain Research Institute were made available. In particular, the computerization of patient records would make possible studies of implanted electrodes from human patients by Dr. Mary A.B. Brazier, who had joined the BRI at that time. Dr. Brazier had been an electroencephalographer at the Massachusetts General Hospital, and had frequent contact with her colleagues at MIT. In the early days of DPL we had frequent visits with members of the Communications Biophysics Group of the MIT Research Laboratory of Electronics {3, 4}.

DPL was the first integrated electronic and computer laboratory established for the express purpose of developing automated technology for nervous system research. DPL was designed to be a resource for the conception and implementation of new computer-based methods by neurophysiologists and engineers in the BRI. I was driven by the need to make computer systems easier to use by medical scientists, rather than by "hacker" motivation; i.e., the need to program computers in the most clever or economical way possible. I wanted to bring computer technology to bear on the problems of neurophysiology and wanted a DPL that would enable experimenters to gain research strength and perspective from the large computing installations on our campus. This approach to computing systems was rare in 1960 and stemmed from my engineering education in which I was sensitized to a systems engineering approach to problem solving. Of course, the problem of asking meaningful neurophysiological questions still remained, and I was very dependent on my colleagues in physiology.

When the NINDB awarded the Brain Research Institute our first computer grant, it included funding for my proposal: to design and implement an analog–digital conversion system for DPL. This system had the versatility to digitize both ongoing electrical activity amplitudes and the time interval between neuronal discharges. Both EEG and spike train investigators could make analog data tapes to format into IBM digital tapes for analysis at the Health Science Computing Facility. The facilities and capabilities of the DPL in the early sixties are described in {5}. Renewals of this grant by NINDB provided 18 years of continuous support and enabled DPL to consistently remain a leader in the development of computer methods for neurophysiological research.

During the years 1960 to 1975, the period covered by this conference, DPL made pioneering contributions in the areas of: analog–digital conversion; automated data acquisition and preprocessing; signal analysis, interactive graphics, modeling and simulation, laboratory computer systems, and distributed processing systems. Throughout those years, over 100 investigators consulted with DPL staff on the introduction of computing techniques, and DPL activities contributed to the computer awareness of many more. During this period, nervous system research evolved from a fragmented quantitative descriptive discipline to an interdisciplinary neuroscience. In the next paragraphs, I will elaborate further on the type of computing system research done in the BRI-DPL during the three five-year periods between 1960 and 1975. In my review, I will not dwell on the computer technology of the system, details of which can be found in my references. The neurophysiological questions addressed by BRI investigators, and the role of computers as a tool in seeking answers, can be reviewed in the BRI Annual Reports {6}. A brief overview of the major advancements of the laboratory follows.

1960–1965: Analog–Digital Conversion

The first high-speed analog–digital conversion system on the UCLA campus was housed in DPL. In 1961, we purchased an analog–digital (A–D) conversion unit, built by the Airborne Instruments Laboratory, to meet DPL design specifications. Our original choice was to rent a computer from the Digital Equipment Corporation, because of DEC's ability to input analog data. But DEC would not rent equipment, and our budget did not allow us to purchase. Our conversion system included an analog tape playback unit, the 16-channel A–D multiplexer and converter, a storage unit, and a digital output tape, all integrated into a system by DPL staff. A storage device was necessary to hold data read from an analog tape, as the digital tape was stopped and started to prepare the spaces and format required by logical records and files. We decided to use a small computer as the storage device, because a computer both controlled data flow and wrote computer programs. We rented a Control Data Corporation 160a which provided the mass storage to allow the timing and tape format required for IBM-compatible digital tapes which we processed on the Health Sciences 7090. In a typical off-line operation, the computer controlled a tape-to-tape conversion system by sampling and quantifying information recorded on analog magnetic tape and assembling it into a series of IBM characters, which were recorded 200 bits per inch on digital magnetic tape. To digitize the analog data properly, rules of sampling theory were observed involving appropriate regard for the frequency spectrum of the original data, and the information to be extracted. These factors dictated such converter requirements as sampling rate, sampling aperture, and quantization level. A control unit supplied the timing and control signals and the logic that provided the system with flexibility to handle either EEG or spike electrical activity {7}.

The system was designed to serve the needs of many investigators employing different data acquisition methods and assumed that suitable record and playback equipment existed to reproduce their recorded signals. There were three primary off-line modes of operation: for spectral analyses, averaging responses, and interspike interval computing. The spectral analysis mode was heavily used by programs for correlation and spectral analysis, which were all done on the IBM 7090. The use of the power spectrum was introduced to the study of the electroencephalogram in 1962 by Dr. Don Walter, a significant contributor to DPL throughout its history. EEG data typically covered frequencies from 3 to 40 cps, in the 20 to 100 microvolt range and was amplified by recording amplifiers. With the advent of the fast Fourier transform (FFT), devised by Cooley and Tukey {8}, spectral calculations became quicker and easier, and became used extensively in studying the structure of EEG data {9, 10}. The measures that we normally calculated were the autospectrum, cross-spectrum (both amplitude and phase), and coherence. These measures allowed estimates of the distribution of power or variance as a function of frequency and of the interrelationships of activity in given frequency bands among different signals to be assessed.

The small memory size and relatively slow speed of the CDC 160a was a limiting factor for spectral problems that required very high-speed computing, but the computer was programmed to operate in an on-line fashion for average response calculations or for microelectrode studies. Microelectrode techniques recorded electrical activity from single nerve cells surrounding the electrode. The difference in recorded amplitudes of pulses in a spike train were the basis for discriminating between several discharging neurons recorded by the same electrode. These "spike" signals were in the millivolt range and required a frequency response to 30 kc/s to reproduce accurately their waveshape; however, bandwidths of 5 or 10 kc/s were sufficient to extract information as to firing pattern. It had been hypothesized that the temporal distribution of spikes represented a coding of information. Precise information on how nerves conducted signals had come from microelectrode studies in the peripheral nervous system, where neurons increased their firing rate as a function of stimulus intensity. Microelectrode studies were also made from deep brain structures, the electrodes were positioned by geometrical coordinates as with gross electrodes. It was of great interest to know whether the subtle variations in the response of brain cells to different modes of stimuli were the equivalent of some "coding" process, and much activity was directed toward obtaining interspike interval histograms of the nerve discharge pattern.

By 1963, over 20 investigators used the laboratory on a regular basis for two shifts a day. At that time, Mr. Dan Brown, manager of the laboratory, suggested we change to a Scientific Data Systems 930 computer which had a built-in A–D conversion system; we followed his advice.

1965–1970: Intelligent Peripheral Processors

Due to increased demands on DPL by a growing number of investigators, a program of hardware expansion resulted in the replacement of the SDS 930 with 12,000 memory locations by an SDS 9300 computer with 32,000 words of memory. In the 1966 to 1967 academic year, the Health Science Computing Facility also switched from an IBM 7090 to a 360-75. DPL staff designed and installed an adapter which permitted direct connection between the 360-75 and the SDS 9300, providing a two-way, high-speed information path between the two computers. Of course, with each change of computer hardware, much additional software had to be written.

During this time period, "dumb" terminals as input and output devices of remote, medium or large general-purpose computers were increasing rapidly in the commercial world. However, the use of "intelligent processors" with their own degree of independent processing was still in the pioneering stage. DPL undertook three projects which required these intelligent devices as input and output to a larger mainframe: a hardware software system known as SLEP; an A–D system *remotely* situated from the 9300 computer; and an IMLAC graphics processor interfaced to the 7091 mainframe. In accordance with the philosophy that the greatest assistance a computer could offer to research was real-time processing, the DPL had been working to extend the accessibility of the computer directly into the user's laboratory. This required a method for providing input and output capability throughout the BRI. In pursuit of this objective, the DPL installed a central cable facility extending from the basement computer room to all 10 levels of the BRI. For users, their respective intelligent processing input or output device connected them to the large computer and they were unaffected by others who were simultaneously using the same large mainframe. During this period, and for the next decade, Mr. Lazlo Betyar and Mr. Lionel Rovner were in charge of software and hardware engineering design.

A Shared Laboratory Interpretive Processor (SLIP) was designed in DPL to retrieve, operate on, and view data on a storage scope via a hardware-software system patterned after the Culler-Fried On Line System, which was designed to provide a convenient and rapid means for human interaction with a large digital computer {11}. Their system was useful for problems requiring repeated communication between user and computer, and was best suited for users who needed to experiment with different formulations, methods of solution, or various types of numerical analysis. The SLIP system extended the capability of Culler-Fried to control input/output devices, necessary for handling the large quantities of data generated by neurophysiological experiments. The hardware of SLIP consisted of a keyboard and storage scope referred to jointly as the console. From the users point of view, operations on the console proceeded as if each user had a machine containing a single accumulator able to handle 144 elements with each element able to represent a 24 binary-digit operand. Each of the 144 values of the accumulator could represent a different subroutine, or could be considered to be one vector with 144 components {12, 13}. SLIP provided a rapid means of interaction with the 9300 computer system on a priority interrupt basis. By 1968, DPL had six SLIP consoles, and three more were planned for additional neurophysiological laboratories. The system was intended to avoid the need for neurophysiologists to become programmers, and to encourage them to use the easier, data-oriented, time-shared SLIP system. These consoles offered the investigator the opportunity to modify analytic programs being applied to data and to create new options; in addition, they could be programmed to function as the entire input/output control point for an investigator's digitization, experiment control, data analysis, data editing, and graphics display.

The consoles and the cable system throughout the BRI could connect any laboratory to the medium-sized computer in the DPL, and from the DPL to the new HSCF IBM 360-91 through a tie-line. Digitized data could be sent over the tie-line and subjected to spectral and discriminant analyses, with the results sent back to the 9300 where a graph of spectra or lists of discriminant results were displayed on a SLIP con-

FIGURE 1
Typical computer
displays photo-
graphed from the
CRT

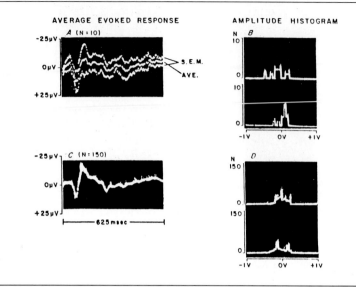

sole. The SLIP console was very useful for investigators working with neuronal spike data. The conceptualization of bioelectric signals as stochastic processes provided an analytical framework for the investigation of hypotheses concerning both the generation of the observed signals and the interrelationships between the multiple observed signals. Dr. Jose Segundo and his collaborators created a flexible system for on-line analysis of neuronal spike trains, using the SLIP system, and applied it to their studies of aplysia to provide numerous forms of statistical analysis of specific trains and their relationships

With the new medium-sized computer in the DPL, the possibility of time-shared on-line use in the neurophysiological laboratory had become a reality. A unique feature of the SDS system at the time was its 16-channel priority interrupt system essential for the real-time, multi-user environment we were building. In mid-1965, the first remote A–D conversion system and a SLIP console was installed in the EEG laboratory of Dr. Brazier. Brain waves were digitized from patients in her laboratory and transmitted to the remote SDS computer eight floors below. Computed results were returned to the EEG laboratory and viewed on a storage scope. The use of the equipment was to initially convert analog EEG information to digital form for immediate transmission to the SDS 9300 and then to the HSCF IBM computer for spectral analysis. Graphic displays from these computers were returned to her laboratory. Another use was to transmit data for analysis on the 9300 and get statistical outputs related to average response computing,

FIGURE 2
Processing overview,
filmed analysis of
EEG

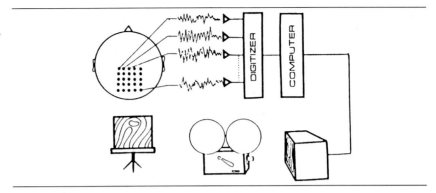

e.g., to obtain information on the influence of variance on the build up of an average response {14}.

In Figure 1, curves A through D represent one typical computer display photographed from a 4" by 5" CRT. The figure displays the results of an experiment in which a human subject was flashed 150 times at 1 f/sec. Figure 1A exhibits the average response banded by the standard error of the mean computer for flashes 140–150. Figure 1B exhibits the amplitude distribution of the last 10 flashes only. Figure 1C is the averaged evoked response, and 1D the amplitude distribution for 150 flashes where the standard error of the mean has become so small it was not resolvable.

A third intelligent input/output device was the IMLAC graphics processor used to support a new technique to compute and display the electroencephalogram (EEG) as a spatiotemporal phenomenon. In this technique, a position on the screen of a CRT was congruent with a position in a recording array of electrodes on the subject's head. The potential distribution over the area of the head covered by the assay was then computed and displayed as a contour map on the face of the tube. Succeeding displays represented distributions at successive instances of time and were photographed by a motion picture camera. The projected film recreated a time history of the potential field. In conventional electroencephalography, potential differences recorded between pairs of electrodes on the scalp were displayed as a parallel array of time functions, usually 8 or 16 traces at a time. Advances in A–D conversion, high-speed computing, and graphic display terminals enabled us to develop a new method for automatic computerized display of the EEG.

In Figure 2, the continuous electrical activity recorded by the electrode array was digitized and stored on magnetic tape. The digital tape data was interpolated by the computer to produce a contour map which represented, for one time instant, the potential distribution over the area of the head covered by the array. This map was displayed on a

FIGURE 3
Sample frames in
the time history of
the potential field

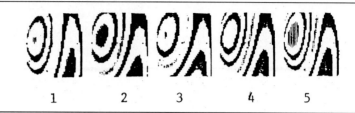

1   2   3   4   5

CRT and photographed under computer control. Figure 3 is an enlargement of five successive displays representing the potential distributions at instances five milliseconds apart. The complete projected film, illustrated by the film screen in the lower left, recreates in slow motion the time history of the potential field {15}.

1970–1975: A Distributed Processors Network

By 1970, minicomputers were gaining popularity as a moderately priced computing machine. The DEC PDP-12 was available, and the PDP-11 was to be produced shortly. At the BRI, we realized that our time-sharing system had become too costly to maintain. DPL had grown from two employees in 1961 to a staff of 40. We consulted with individual laboratories advising them to purchase new minicomputers if their computing needs required extensive hardware. For investigators whose computing needs only required A–D conversion, DPL planned to transport their activities to a night shift off-line facility to produce IBM formatted digital tapes. At this time, NIH also cautioned the BRI that if our computing grant was to continue, DPL had to obtain a full-time director and become an interdisciplinary center with more emphasis on neurophysiological or medical goals. I was appointed director of the laboratory in 1970 and by the end of the year, the SDS 9300 computer had been removed and replaced by a PDP-12; three neurophysiological laboratories had also acquired PDP-12 computers.

Early in this period our Data Processing Laboratory interconnected three available computers: a DEC PDP-12 and an IMLAC PDS-1D in the DPL, and an IBM 360-91 in the HSCF to form a network of distributed processors for interactive graphics programs. This network utilized the strengths of each of the processors. The PDP-12 laboratory computer was well suited for acquisition and preprocessing of neurophysiological data and for the generation of edited data sets. The IMLAC graphics terminal, with keyboard and light pen, provided a control processor for the transmission of edited data sets from the PDP-12 to the large scale IBM 360-91, and was also an interactive display terminal for the PDP-12 or the 360-91. The IMLAC had two instruction

FIGURE 4
Interactive graphics
system network

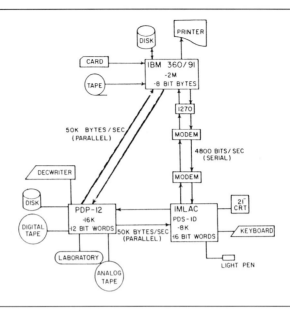

processors, one to control the display and the other a 16-bit minicomputer with a 4K word memory. The minicomputer controlled a serial communication interface which could link to a remote host by direct-dial phone. The IMLAC PDP-12 interface design included a simplified scheme for 1/0 bus construction on the PDP-12 and a software system for assembling and loading IMLAC programs and brain map data for the PDP-12. An important application of this system performed with Dr. R.I. Sclabassi was to facilitate the investigation of complex relationships between experimental and theoretical data in the spike activity of neurons {16}. Dr. Ronald Harper was a neuroscientist who also joined our laboratory in 1971 and used this system extensively in a comprehensive sleep study on the sudden infant death syndrome. Figure 4 illustrates the hardware of the three processor network utilized in our interactive graphics system.

When I became the director of the laboratory and PI on our NIH renewal, my personal research involved novel uses of interactive graphics as a tool for brain researchers. I worked with an innovative use of the network for a simulation program we called BRAINMAPS, to aid the surgeon-user of a stereotaxic device to determine the best trajectory for approaching a targeted brain structure. In the early seventies, CAT scanning had just emerged, and NMR images were still far away. The use of computer-generated brain maps to combine diagnostic information from radiological scanning of a patient's head with general neuroanatomical information from brain atlases seemed like a useful idea. Brain atlases presented macroscopic cross-sectional maps of the human brain and provided indispensable localizing anatomical information to those neurosurgeons who used stereotaxic techniques. However, the large variability in the dimensions of human brain structures limited the usefulness of the standard atlas. Dr. Paul Crandall, neurosurgeon, did clinical research on partial epilepsies and stereotaxically implanted electrodes for chronic EEG recording to help lateralize the discharging focus. The purpose of the computer program was to develop a prototype to aid in the placement of multiple electrodes in the temporal lobe. Neuroanatomical maps, scaled for the individual patient, based on measurements obtained from his pneumoencephalogram, were used to provide stereotaxic coordinates. The recent introduction of computerized tomography made it possible to obtain the measurements required for stereotaxic surgery without the injection of air as a contrast material. An interactive computer graphics system was implemented to scale and display brain maps, and a pilot study to evaluate its potential as an aid to better localization during stereotaxic placement was in progress. The system could serve the neurosurgeon by contracted or expanded standardized brain sections on the basis of X ray data from the patient. During surgery the computer, by simulation, could monitor and display the position of the electrodes relative to neuronal structures as the array moved along a path to its ultimate site. Figure 5 is a Cal-Comp plot of thalamic region from the Schaltenbrand and Bailey Atlas {17}. Neuroscientists also experimented with the system in their research with animal subjects {18}.

Another interactive application involved a computer network that was established between UCLA and the University of California at Davis for the purpose of gaining access to MUMPS, a popular computer language in the clinical medicine community. MUMPS is a multiprogramming utility system developed at the Massachusetts General Hospital for medical applications; a MUMPS interpreter was part of the software supported by the Davis computing center and was not available through the computing centers at UCLA. Mr. Richard Buchness, a DPL programmer, required access to MUMPS in order to write a CAI program for a pilot project on cancer education. We were able to complete the pilot program within several weeks because of our mini-network of distributed processors and the associated software that had been built by our programmers. Our use of MUMPS resulted in the only addition of a graphics capability to the MUMPS language that we knew about at that time. MUMPS could be used for interactive graphics when the graphics commands were encoded as character strings. The string manipulation features of MUMPS then allowed graphics information to be handled like any other MUMPS string. A host-independent graphics program called GRIP ran on the IMLAC minicomputer. This program contained both an alphanumeric scrolling editor and a

FIGURE 5
Plot of thalamic region

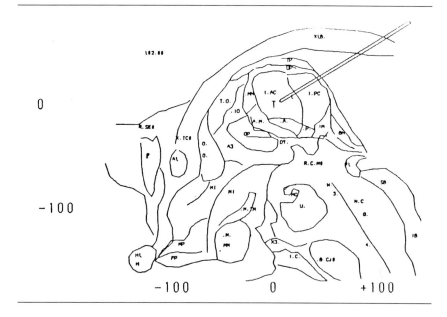

graphics interpreter. The interpreter decoded specially framed graphics commands created by MUMPS subroutines at the remote host. We had a library of such routines for generation of points, lines, characters, and beam position. Using this design, no modification of the MUMPS language was required to enable graphics programming for an IMLAC intelligent graphics terminal. The IMLAC terminal provided the user with vector and character generation, a light pen, and both alphanumeric and function keyboards. We used the MUMPS interpreter running on the Burroughs B6700 at the UC Davis campus, 500 miles away. Our use of graphics was not limited to figures composed of points and line segments, but also included the presentation of items for selection in the form of menus, independent of the scrolling editor which could remain on the screen for any period. The user interacted with the menu via keyboard, function key, or light pen. Presenting lists of choices via menus as opposed to presenting successive displays increased the rate of flow of information between the user and the program {19}.

Conclusion

Despite the significant "firsts" identified in this paper, the DPL ceased to function in 1979. Why? In 1979, DPL applied for an NIH renewal to institute a microcomputer network. Our grant was approved but not funded, and we were encouraged to apply again. The computer research study section had been disbanded, and our reviewers were primarily neuroscientists who did not understand microcomputers. The grant application refusal, coupled with the emergence of neurobiology as a central factor requiring BRI space caused us to give up our DPL housing. But perhaps most important was the lack of recruitment of mathematically or computer-oriented neuroscientists by the BRI. After most of our strong supporters had moved or retired, BRI did recruit first-rate neuroscientists; however, their interest in computer research was minimal.

On a larger scale, the application of real-time computing for neuroscientists and medical diagnosticians is still in its infancy, though more than a quarter-century has passed since DPL and its missions were organized. The lack of progress has been threefold: financial costs, simplicity of use, and people's attitudes toward changing their methods of work. The past year has seen the personal workstation applied as a tool for all intellectual personnel. The cost and ease of use have been significantly improved to meet market needs, thanks to the microprocessor and associated software. Users will have easier access to computer networks with increased power for data and program change, as well as immediate access to high speed visual displays, due to the emergence of portable graphics, supercomputers, standard software, and fiber optical devices for rapid transfer of data. Those scientists who use the computer as an indispensable tool for their research or practice will have a significant payoff, and they will encourage other investigators to think in computer-structured terms. In the next quarter-century the advances in neuroscience, cognitive science, and artificial intelligence should make medical informatics a household term.

References

1. Estrin, T. Computers, neuroscience and women: (1949–1999). *Proc. of the Annual Conference IEEE Engineering in Medicine and Biology Soc.*, 1984, pp. 831–836.

2. Estrin, T. Recording the impulse firing pattern of neurons utilizing digital techniques. *Digest of the 1961 International Conference on Medical Electronics*, 1961, p. 9.

3. Communications Biophysics Group of Research Laboratory of Electronics and Siebert, W.M. Processing neuroelectric data. Massachusetts Instit. Technol., Tech. Rep. 351. Cambridge: Technology Press, 1959, p. 121.

4. Brazier, M.A.B., (ed.). Computer techniques in EEG analysis. *Electroenceph. Clin. Neurophysiol.*, 1962, Suppl. 20, p. 108.

5. Estrin, T., Adey, W. R., Brazier, M.A.B., and Kado, R.T. Facilities in a brain research institute for acquisition, processing and digital computation of neurophysiological data. *Proceedings of the Conference on Data Acquisition and Processing in Biology and Medicine*. Pergamon Press, 1963, pp. 191–207.

6. Brain Research Institute, University of California, Los Angeles, Annual Reports 1–15, July 1961–June 1976.

7. Estrin, T. A conversion system for neuroelectric data. *Electroencephalography and Clinical Neurophysiology*, Vol. 14, 1962, pp. 414–416.

8. Cooley, J.W. and Tukey, J.W. An algorithm for the machine calculation of complex Fourier series. *Math. Comput.*, Vol. 19, 1965, p. 297.

9. Brazier, M.A.B. and Walter, D.O., (eds.). Evaluation of bioelectrical data from brain nerve and muscle, II. Part A. Frequency and correlation analysis. *Handbook of Electroencephalography and Clinical Neurophysiology*, Vol. 5, 1973.

10. Dummermuth, G., Walz, W., Scollo-Lauizzari, G., and Kleiner, B. Spectral analysis of EEG activity in different sleep stages in normal adults. *Eur. Neurol.* Vol. 7, 1972, pp. 265–296.

11. Culler, G.J. and Fried, B.D. The TRW two-station, on-line scientific computer. *TRW Space Technology Laboratories*, Vol. III, 1964.

12. Estrin, T. Neurophysiological research using a remote time-shared computer. *Data Acquisition and Processing in Biology and Medicine*, Vol. 5, Pergamon Press, 1966, pp. 117–135.

13. Betyar, L. A user-oriented time-shared on-line system. *CACM* Vol. 10, 1967, pp. 413–419.

14. Estrin, T. On-line electroencephalographic digital computing system. *Electroenceph. Clin. Neurophysiol.* Vol. 19, 1965, pp. 524–526.

15. Estrin, T. and Uzgalis, R. Computerized display of spatio-temporal EEG patterns. *IEEE Transactions on Bio-Medical Engineering*, Vol. BME-16, No. 3, 1969, pp. 192–196.

16. Sclabassi, R.J., Buchness, R., and Estrin, T. Interactive graphics in the analysis of neuronal spike train data. *Computers in Biology and Medicine*, Vol. 6, 1976, pp. 163–178.

17. Estrin, T., Sclabassi, R., and Buchness, R. Computer graphic applications to neurosurgery. *Proc. First World Conference on Medical Information* (MEDINFO), North Holland Publishing Co., 1974, pp. 831–836.

18. Estrin, T., Wegner, J.V., and Bettinger, R. Computer generated brain maps. *Proceedings San Diego Biomedical Symposium*, 1975, pp. 369–374.

19. Buchness, R., Estrin, T., and Sue, J. Use of MUMPS for interactive graphics. 1975 MUMPS Users' Group Meeting.

SIGNAL AND IMAGE PROCESSING

Some of the earliest computer applications were in the field of signal and image processing; many of these investigations now would be considered biomedical engineering. In this session, Judith M.S. Prewitt, PhD introduced both speakers and concluded with some observations about her own work in microscopy and pattern recognition.

Gwilym S. Lodwick, MD was the first presenter. His introduction to the use of computers in the interpretation of radiological images came—not from an interest in the technology—but from the challenge of a problem and the availability of a large database with which to build a model. In his talk, he described his personal development as well as his interactions with some of the other conference attendees. The paper in this volume is an expansion of his earlier paper.

Jerome R. Cox, Jr., DSc chose to offer selected anecdotes together with a photographic record. Keeping within the 1975 time period, Dr. Cox told of HAVOC, the PC, Aztec, and Argus. In this case, PC stood for Programmed Console; it was used for radiation therapy planning, but it also could play Hyperspace. Dr. Cox observed that they failed to recognize the commercial potential of the latter. His paper also has been expanded, and many of his slides are included as illustrations.

SPEAKERS

Gwilym S. Lodwick The History of the Use of Computers in the
                     Interpretation of Radiological Images
Jerome R. Cox, Jr. Recollections on the Processing of Biomedical Signals
Judith M.S. Prewitt Discussant

Gwilym S. Lodwick, MD is Professor Emeritus, Department of Radiology, University of Missouri School of Medicine and Visiting Professor, Department of Radiology, Harvard Medical School (both since 1983). He received the BS and MD degrees from the University of Iowa in 1939 and 1943. He has been affiliated with the University of Missouri since 1956 and has had appointments in both radiology and bioengineering. He received the Gold Medal for Outstanding Contributions to Radiology, XIII International Congress of Radiology (1973) and is on the editorial board of seven journals including *CRC Reviews in Medical Informatics* and *Journal of Medical Systems.*

Jerome R. Cox, Jr., DSc is chairman and professor, Department of Computer Science, Washington University (since 1975). He also holds the appointments of associate, Division of Health Care Research (since 1973) and senior research associate, Biomedical Computer Laboratory (since 1975). He received the SB, SM, and DSc degrees in electrical engineering from the Massachusetts Institute of Technology in 1947, 1949 and 1954. After graduation he joined the faculty of Washington University. He is a past chairman, DCRT Review Committee (1983–1984) and has been an associate editor or on the editorial board of five journals including *Computers and Biomedical Research* and *IEEE Transactions on Biomedical Engineering.*

Judith M.S. Prewitt, PhD is president of MEDIMATICS and Intelligence, Inc., consulting companies that provide services in systems design, strategic planning, and technology risk management for medical informatics and telematics applications. She received a BA degree from Swarthmore College in 1957, an MA degree from the University of Pennsylvania in 1959, and a PhD degree from Uppsala University in 1978. Her career spans academia, industry, and government service. She joined the faculty of the University of Pennsylvania School of Medicine in 1962. From 1971 through 1983, she was in the Office of the Director, DCRT, NIH, spending a sabbatical year as Stoker Visiting Professor, Ohio University. She then joined AT&T Bell Laboratories with responsibilities for the company's new medical ventures (1984–1986). She is on the editorial board of several journals and has held numerous posts in the IEEE organization. She was elected a fellow of the IEEE in recognition of her contributions to applying image processing techniques to automated medical diagnostics.

The History of the Use of Computers in the Interpretation of Radiological Images

Gwilym S. Lodwick, MD
University of Missouri and Harvard Medical School

Introduction

Throughout its history, diagnosis with a computer has been the target of the medical cartoonist, who displays humorous situations where the doctor, consulting his ridiculously large computer, gravely reports inappropriate diagnoses to his disbelieving patient. We laugh at this, yet, through lack of insight, computers do make inappropriate diagnoses, and despite years of polishing, most diagnostic programs are still experimental and await a serious role in the diagnostic armamentarium.

Radiological diagnosis with a computer involves the development of complex models intended to simulate and improve on human performance. There is a real need for such an effort since the frequency of human error in diagnostic decision making generally, and in the interpretation of x-ray images specifically, is astonishingly high (est. 20% detection, 10% to 50% diagnosis {1}. This high rate of error is largely unsuspected. Despite advances in imaging technologies with improved spatial, contrast, and temporal resolution, a high rate of human error persists. A major element of this error lies in the failure of the reader to detect signs of disease, which so often are embedded in a background of structured and statistical noise. The solution to this problem is complex and unresolved. Yet another source of error is in matching perceived sign information to the appropriate diagnostic classification.

In more than 25 years of trying to use a computer to improve on human performance, I have had both successes and failures. In this presentation I will focus almost entirely on personal experiences in developing computer-assisted interpretation of images and how I came to be involved with computers in the first place. Also I will discuss some of the advantages and disadvantages of computer-assisted interpretation and where I think this technology will ultimately lead.

The Beginning

In late 1946 I left the Army Medical Corps to find a residency in radiology. My hopes were to be accepted in the program at the University of

Iowa, where as a medical student I was fascinated with the magic of making medical decisions from images, especially as performed by Professor Carl Gillies. However, I found that I was at the end of a long queue of applicants and accepted instead the post of resident physician in pathology, until the position of my choice became available in the summer of 1948. This detour proved to be very important to my future career, since pathologic anatomy was just the ticket for a better understanding of clinical radiology. My experience in pathology made me look good enough to be invited to join the academic staff when I had "completed my training." Parenthetically, even now I seem still to be completing my training; but then, the process entailed a fellowship at the Armed Forces Institute of Pathology (AFIP) in Washington, D.C., to last until I was formally appointed to my new position of chief of the Radiological Services, Veteran's Administration Hospital, Iowa City. Arriving in Washington with my family, and waving a brand new certificate of The American Board of Radiology, I was greeted by my new chief, Col. William Thompson, and by Dr. Aubrey O. Hampton, a distinguished radiologist then in private practice and consultant to the Registry of Radiologic Pathology. Having been asked to watch out for me, Dr. Hampton introduced me to Dr. Lent C. Johnson, chief of the Registry of Orthopedic Pathology, who promptly put me to work on the task that has proved to be a consuming interest.

Lent Johnson was an extraordinary pathologist. Brilliant, controversial, intuitive, intellectually organized, and unrestrained by the conventional thinking of his peers, Lent was highly respected by his friends and students. Lent's opinions about structure and process were exciting fare. A workaholic, he had integrated tumor histology and location with age and the physiology of bone growth into an exciting hypothesis on the origin of bone tumors, published as "A General Theory of Bone Tumors" {2}. Lent was as skilled as any in the radiologic interpretation of bone disease, even though the state of knowledge of how to interpret X rays of bone neoplasms was far from perfect. While a few signs such as "moth-eaten" and "Codman's triangle" were commonly used, their diagnostic and prognostic meanings were unknown. So it was agreed between Aubrey Hampton, Col. William Thompson, and Lent Johnson that my mission would be to organize an exhibit that would display the radiological patterns of the common bone tumors correlated with gross and microscopic findings. At the fall 1951 meeting of the American Roentgen Ray Society our exhibit was awarded the bronze medal.

This modest success was not the end of my relationship with Lent Johnson. During our year of working together, too many unanswered questions had been asked, and too many issues were left unsettled, to leave either of us satisfied. We still did not know the meaning of the few radiological signs that had been described and realized that the solution to developing this information was a detailed analysis of the radiologic images of a large collection where the outcome was known. The case material of the AFIP, while abundant, was of military origin, where follow-up was difficult. The only collection of bone tumors we knew to have ample documentation and follow-up was The Bone Sarcoma Registry of the American College of Surgeons, then in residence at the University of Chicago. With my fellowship drawing to a close, I was anxious to begin the challenge of my new position. So, late in the fall of 1951, with an invitation to return to the AFIP at any time, I returned to Iowa City. In early 1954 I received a call from Dr. Johnson telling me of the news that the Codman Registry of more than 2000 primary bone tumors was now in file at the AFIP, and would I like to come to Washington to carry out the detailed analysis that we had dreamed of? With a three-month leave of absence from the Veterans Administration, my wife and family reluctantly saw me off to Washington to begin the most intensive work episode of my life.

Modeling the Image

At this point, the research goals were defined and the source of the data established. Now began the task of building a model that would be used to extract the standardized clinical and radiographic data from each case in the Registry. The clinical data were relatively easy; they were numerical, consisting of months of delay before diagnosis and length of survival after treatment. Kinds of treatment were also captured. I was to review the histologic material on each case in the context of the diagnostic summaries that had been recorded by such luminaries as Ewing, Codman, and Phemister. Lent Johnson was to review atypical cases with me. The difficult part was to identify and decide which sign information should be included in the model. There we were exploring the unknown. I ultimately used a rather primitive consensus model that we had evolved to analyze the entire data set, and made a detailed pencil sketch of the X ray of each tumor. Drawing images was tedious but led to my seeing the subtle changes in bone more clearly. With time it became apparent that the identity of the signs we had agreed on fit less and less well with what I was seeing, and subconsciously I depended more heavily on sketching signs as an alternative way of recording information. This was no time to go back and change the model. My workday averaged 16 hours, including weekends. Ultimately, the initial phase of this grueling task was completed, and the data, with drawings and some copies of X rays, were packed in a large trunk which accompanied me to Iowa City.

Then began the analysis. Given that there were more than 1500 cases with more than 20 radiographic variables for each, the length and numbers of summary sheets became impossible to manage. A better mechanism for data analysis was obviously necessary. It turned out that the United States government was beginning to introduce machine record inventory controls into the VAH system, and I was given access to the IBM keypunch machines for processing my data. Of necessity I became a semi-expert keypunch operator and personally encoded the data from each case on a single card. Now, developing composite survival characteristics for individual signs was easily possible.

The fibrosarcomas of bone were an especially valuable histologic type for sign and pattern analysis. Their radiographic patterns of bone destruction were a composite of the patterns seen in all histologic classes of tumors. Also, since fibrosarcoma has a paucity of tumor bone and of reactive response, which tend to obscure fine detail in radiographs, bone destruction was unusually clearly displayed. Experimenting, I separated cases of fibrosarcoma of bone into three data sets based on one of three patterns: 1) cystic destruction with sclerotic margins, 2) cystic destruction with ragged or invasive margins, and 3) moth-eaten or permeated bone destruction. The five-year survival statistics for these three groups were startling; 52% for the first group, intermediate for the second, and 7.5% for the third! Equally startling were times for delay before diagnosis: nearly 50 months for the first group and six months for the third.

These results were exciting to both of us. Lent Johnson undertook to reorganize the basic structure of the model along lines that integrated pathology with the kinds of radiographic patterns, (location, size, and shape; bone destruction; reactive new bone formation; and tumor bone). I focused on sharpening the identity and descriptions of the individual signs and extending the collection of survival statistics. The drawings and duplicate copies of X rays were essential to accomplishing this task. Periodically we met at the AFIP to compare notes and to iron out conceptual differences. New modeling concepts began to emerge. It was agreed that theoretically the model should be so complete that the encoded descriptors of a case should be sufficient to reconstruct the original image. This concept was tested with one of my residents (Dr. James Bauer) who sketched images from data I had encoded on several cases. His reconstructions were impressively similar to the original images. It was accepted that there were three basic patterns of bone destruction: geographic, moth-eaten, and permeated. The concept of analyzing for location, size, and shape helped to implement several concepts of Johnson's general theory, especially those concern-

FIGURE 1
Dr. Lodwick explaining a bone tumor diagnosis (1968)

ing the location of the tumor in relation to its histologic type. Size became a valued predictor. Since the time of this reorganization, the bone model has remained a stable yet dynamic concept; significant signs, such as burrowing in the presence of infection, are still being added.

Effective modeling of the radiographic image of a major disease class is a tedious iterative procedure and is subject to many design errors. An especially troublesome error involved measurement, where instead of recording actual measurements, we broke up measurements into broad ranges, such as 1 to 4 cm, 4 to 8 cm, etc. In so doing, we lost our flexibility to determine the exact point at which a measurement became significant.

Now there was much to publish. However, Lent Johnson was a perfectionist and unwilling to submit a manuscript for publication until he could see no possibility of further improvement. I, on the other hand, felt that I faced publishing or perishing and, with such a large investment of time and excellent results, was anxious to publish even in preliminary form. The extent of this conflict was such that it was never possible for us to publish any of our work together. Once, after I became professor and chairman at the University of Missouri in 1956, I was so bold as to submit a manuscript under both of our names to a major radiological journal, which accepted it as a lead article. I later withdrew it at Dr. Johnson's insistence.

Because I considered the concept of modeling images so important and was unable to publish the bone model, I similarly modeled a collection of lung cancers provided by Professor Hans Ehrenhaft of the University of Iowa. This new model, applied to the lung cancer database, replicated the success of the bone tumor model {3, 4}. Presentations I later made on systematic analysis of bone tumors were published as chapters in a book {5, 6}. Finally, the details of the bone model were published in a monograph in 1971 {7}.

Computer-aided Diagnosis from Images

An important by-product of the bone tumor data analysis was the stack of Hollerith cards that held the encoded data from the Codman Registry. I analyzed the data on these cards in many different combinations in order to learn whatever I could about tumor behavior. Handling these cards was a regular event, and quite coincidentally, I discovered that cards representing data from tumors of the same type often looked alike in that they bore holes in similar locations. It seemed that automated pattern recognition of such data should be possible, given the right decision model. At about this time Lee Lusted, who I had come to know through mutual friends, showed me an article which he and Ledley had published in *Science* {8}. This very timely paper dealt with the logical basis of medical decision making and obviously was of great importance to me. However, at just that time I was appointed acting dean of the medical school at Columbia, where, as in most new schools, a crisis atmosphere prevailed. By the time that things had settled down, Homer Warner had successfully applied Bayesian logic to the diagnosis of congenital heart disease {9}.

Nonetheless, all of the parts of a computer diagnostic model for bone tumors were there awaiting application. Lee Lusted had become the chairman of the newly formed NIH Committee on Computers and was looking for suitable research to review. I submitted an application entitled "Computer Analysis of Tumor Roentgenograms," and later was delighted to receive notice from the National Cancer Institute of a research award, effective January 1962. This research award was a key event in that it strengthened my interests in research and clinical radiology and diminished my interest in the Dean's Office. It also permitted me for the first time to recruit substantial programming assistance. I had the good fortune at that time, and later, to have the enthusiastic support of research colleagues of great competence, whose creativity, drive, and dedication more than matched my own.

The first product of this research grant was in the domain of computer-aided diagnosis (CAD), a diagnostic system where a human scans the image, identifies the sign information, and enters it into the computer. By contrast, automated image diagnosis is a system where the image is scanned under computer control, and the sign information is identified through the use of algorithms specific to each problem. In either system the predictive data from a case are the input into a program that uses decision rules functionally equivalent to those used by an expert. After analyzing the data, the program produces output in a format convenient to the user. The data input may be signs, symptoms, laboratory results, or whatever the diagnosis requires. Developing such a program may involve a dialogue between the expert and the programmer in order to code the rules that the expert is using in the flow of the logic. To gain more experience, additional cases are run, and solutions to wrong responses are agreed on. The iterative process is continued until the results are optimized. This basic process can be improved by substituting a generalized program with the rules not being a part of the program itself, but rather as a separate source of input. This means that the expert can modify the program by simply plugging in a new set of rules.

BAYES'S THEOREM AS A DECISION RULE {10}

We found that we had the choice of using one of two methods of implementing Bayes's theorem, which had been evolved for purposes of diagnosis. The first, which deals with symptom patterns, was described by Maxwell {11} and by Ledley {12}. It has the advantage of taking into account the interrelationships of the predictor variables. They need not be independent. It has the considerable disadvantage that, if the number of variables is large, an unwieldy number of possible symptom patterns must be considered. The second approach, which we used, is due to Warner and his associates {9}. It is a much simpler method to implement, but requires that the predictor variables must be independent. I have had good results with the latter method even though not all variables meet the prescribed requirement of independence.

In order to implement this latter approach, a prior probability matrix was assembled, which consisted of the relative frequency of each binary variable, compiled separately for each disease. Preparation of a probability matrix is a major task and heavily dependent on the integrity of signs. Also, it is dependent on several other factors, including the adequacy of the population on which it is based and the accuracy of the pathologist's classification, on the basis of which each case is assigned to a disease class. However, such empirically derived, prior probability matrices need not be considered as sacrosanct. Maxwell {11} sets forth a method whereby, in the light of statistical decision theory, equal prior probabilities may be assumed and then be suitably adjusted on the basis of the errors of misclassification to which their use led. By whatever method they are derived, the prior probabilities are at the heart of the Bayesian diagnostic process.

The Identity and Meaning of Signs

The quality of the sign input into this system is extremely important. When I was first identifying the signs to create the bone model, I had my own idiosyncratic meanings for the sign information that I used. This collection of signs was my personal model. However, there is a broader concept that must be observed for a radiologic sign to be effectively used. Each sign should be a reflection of a unique morphologic event. Once the sign is recognized, this uniqueness must be described, illustrated, and correlated with the anatomic changes that the sign reflects, so that when your colleagues recognize the sign, they receive a useful message, such as "I represent calcified neoplastic cartilage." At this point the sign has earned inclusion in what is known as the *public model*.

The other important attribute of a sign is its conditional probability. For example, take the relationship of permeated bone destruction, an easily recognizable sign that implies a rapid rate of growth, to each of four common tumors of bone. This sign may be found in 95% of Ewing's sarcomas, 20% of chondrosarcomas, 5% of eosinophilic granulomas, and 0% of osteoid osteomas. Given an unknown tumor of one of these four classes, it is clear that the most probable diagnosis, based on this sign alone, would be Ewing's sarcoma. The possibility of osteoid osteoma would be totally excluded. Most skeletal radiologists have an intuitive understanding of conditional probability and, based on their personal experience, can assemble a quite creditable probability matrix for the signs related to musculoskeletal diseases.

Our first paper on CAD of bone tumors was presented at the meeting of the Radiological Society of North America in the fall of 1962 {13}. Seventy-seven cases with eight different diagnoses were diagnosed with 77.9% accuracy. Other papers followed in succession {14, 15, 16, 17, 18}. For the fall 1964 meeting of the same society, Lee Lusted and I teamed up to take a small IBM computer, key punch, and printer onto the scientific exhibition floor of the Palmer House in Chicago. There we variously amused and astonished our audience by performing on-line diagnoses "on the spot," receiving the *magna cum laude* award. In 1965, we took the same show to the International Congress of Radiology in Rome.

Improving the Performance of CAD Programs

For human interaction with the computer, the response time must be fast, and the questions limited to a number that is acceptable by the user. No one likes to use a CAD program that repeatedly asks for the same information as if it had no memory. For these reasons, we have found automatic answer vectors to be necessary for eliminating the possibility of asking questions that are illogical in a given situation or have been previously answered in another way. In this manner, the computer interaction of the human scanning the image can be made clean, neat, and brief.

We have found decision trees to be very useful in developing the logic of a diagnostic situation. We designed an extensive set of decision trees for the purpose of reducing the number of possible diagnoses prior to carrying out Bayesian analysis. Surprisingly, we have found that humans make errors in following even the most simplistic decision trees. Further, we found that an error involving taking the wrong branch on a decision tree resulted in the wrong diagnosis 48% of the time. This has cooled our enthusiasm for decision trees, since an alternative logic is available for use.

Further, we have found through testing that humans make many errors in identifying signs. For establishing an experimental database that reflects the gold standard of signs, the truth of each sign can be established by double reading, with a third reader to break ties. Signs so confirmed are called "book signs." In a recent study of a test set of 245 cases of histologically proven bone tumors, where we used 40 signs to differentiate between 30 diagnostic possibilities, a first-choice accuracy of 79.6% was obtained with CAD and book signs. An accuracy of 93.1% was achieved where the criterion was that the correct diagnosis is one of the three highest probabilities listed by the computer. This is to be compared with an average sight reading accuracy of 55.4% for four experimental readers and, when the readers selected the signs, 59.3% for CAD. These significant differences show that inaccuracy of human interpretation of signs is a major cause of diagnostic error in CAD. For this reason, it is of critical importance that signs be meticulously defined and illustrated and that critical decision points are not based on differentiating two signs that are so similar they are likely to be confused with each other.

COMMENT

Despite these problems in human performance of sign identification, it has long been my experience that CAD effectively illustrates the sensitive relationships between signs and diagnosis and that CAD is an enormously effective teacher of the meaning of signs and of how the diagnostic process works. Recently, I have found CAD valuable for recording and evaluating radiologist performance in sign recognition.

Radiological Assessment of Growth Rate

Most experienced radiologists develop an intuitive feeling as to whether the radiologic image is that of a benign or a malignant bone tumor. In testing the signs and measurements that make up the radiologic model of bone tumors, it is clear that most such variables are related more to the aggressiveness of tumor growth than to histologic type. Indeed, diagnosis of tumors from radiographic information is so difficult because it is a diagnosis of inference and based on secondary evidence of histologic type. That is, Ewing's sarcoma is inferred to be Ewing's sarcoma because of the tumor's typical location and size, its permeated pattern of bone destruction, and its absence of tumor bone formation; not because the radiologist is permitted to see and recognize the particular cells of Ewing's sarcoma. The pathologist, on the other hand, does see the abnormal, highly cellular structure characteristic of Ewing's sarcoma, but little of the evidence of growth rate which characterize the radiographic image. The two kinds of evidence, radiologic and histologic, complement each other extraordinarily well, yet neither may be regarded as a total substitute for the other.

In recognition of this direct relationship between the radiographic image and the growth rate of a focal lesion of bone, I constructed an algorithm to grade aggressiveness into one of five different rates: 1A, slow or static; 1B, moderately slow; 1C, intermediate; II, moderately fast; and III, fast {19, 20, 21}. The algorithm for determining rate of growth is effective for grading particularly those lesions where destruction of bone is present and is deceptively simple, requiring binary decisions on only six signs in combinations of three or less for each grade. The logic of the grading sequence is based on the known predictive values of each sign and is such that failure to recognize a sign biases grade selection in favor of a more rapid estimate of growth. The performance of the algorithm has been extensively tested with the computer, its results statistically proved, and its design simplified in order to improve human performance in grade selection. The ultimate value of the radiologic grading system lies in its ease of human application and in its usefulness in evaluating the behavior of bone lesions in the clinical setting.

CRITIQUE

In perspective, two systems for diagnosing bone disease have evolved out of a study of the identity and meaning of radiological signs: One is a logical, computer-based, probabilistic methodology for diagnosing bone tumors; the other a computer-designed but human-mediated methodology for estimating rate of growth. The CAD system requires human interface with a computer, enough time to select and record the signs that are observed, and ultimately produces a product in minutes, which the user of the system is trained to produce in seconds, with his own logic and his own "built in computer." If the user of CAD can operate the system successfully, it is because he already has memorized the signs that are necessary for diagnostic decision making, and quite possibly he regards thinking on his feet as more effective and more fun than thinking with a computer.

On the other hand, the algorithm for assessing rate of growth provides a kind of information that is not otherwise available to the user. If a physician wishes to use an X ray to assess rate of growth, the logic for the computer and for the physician is exactly the same, and the results will be exactly the same. *There is no alternative logic to be used in accomplishing this objective.* The computer does not do it better, or faster, than the human. And because of its ease of application and its simple values, the use of radiologic grading of rate is a worldwide phenomenon.

Automated Image Analysis

During the early sixties, research in computer-aided diagnosis and the development and testing of The Missouri Automated Radiology System kept our program at Missouri exceedingly busy. During 1967 to 1968, I spent a sabbatical year at the Middlesex and the Royal National Orthopedic Hospitals in London, working on an atlas of tumors of bones and joints and learning more about orthopedic radiology. I had left the clinical department under the able leadership of Arch W. Templeton and computer research in the hands of Professor Peter Reichertz. I returned to find that the research program was progressing admirably, but that Arch Templeton's departure to the chairmanship of radiology at the University of Kansas had created a clinical void that could be filled only by me. Nevertheless, seeds planted in bioengineering before my departure had borne fruit, and I found that Samuel Dwyer and his colleagues had been working toward digitizing radiological images through the acquisition of suitable computing and image-scanning equipment. In view of my administrative responsibility to the clinical department as well as my commitments to complete a book and to direct substantial research and research training programs already funded, my further involvement in a major research program was a very risky business. Yet, the forward momentum was already there, and a great research opportunity would dissipate for lack of radiological leadership unless I stepped forward. At that time, no task seemed beyond accomplishment to me, so I joined with Dwyer in raising the funding for a program project entitled "Diagnostic Content and Redundancy in Radiant Images." A team headed by James Lehr had already made substantial progress in developing algorithms for the detection of abnormalities in brain scintigrams {22}. These results plus an impressive array of state-of-the-art technology convinced the site visiting team that we knew what we were doing, and as of September 1970 a program project research award was granted for support of automated image analysis. These were heady days, and, in retrospect, we really did know what we were doing but were doing it probably some 10 to 20 years ahead of clinical application.

FIGURE 2
Drs. James L. Lehr
and Gwilym
Lodwick

Our first major success was in the direct computer diagnosis of rheumatic heart disease, accepted for publication in September of 1971 {23}. This project, led by David L. Hall, a research trainee in radiology at Missouri, described the technical details of programs that identified the cardiac silhouette, measured its important parameters, and applied discriminant function analysis to decide whether the heart shadow was within limits of normal and, if not, which kind of rheumatic heart disease best fit the findings on the film. The computer had substantially greater success in classifying rheumatic heart disease than the radiologists had in viewing the same library of proved cases.

These accomplishments, along with technical proceedings dealing with the automated recognition of bone disease, were not unnoticed by either radiologists or the press. We had chosen to work in the domain of both chest and bone for the same reason that I had chosen to model images of both chest and bone; the contrast and spatial resolution inherent in the images of these regions are such that edges, shapes, and textures could be identified much more easily than in images of other anatomic regions. However, although I was a recognized expert in bone disease, I was treading on the turf of those who were more expert in the fields of vascular and pulmonary diseases, which was a sin that was difficult to forgive. The press responded by writing us up in the news magazines, while my vascular and chest radiological colleagues responded by attempting to shoot us down in the grants review process. Sam and I did our best to show that we were attempting to implement technology rather than to invade new turf, but the nature of our success in automating the process of clinical decision making was too threatening to be tolerated. So in the mid-seventies, at the time when we began to face stiff competition from computed tomography for the available research funds, we experienced an unsympathetic site visit and lost our support.

I turn now to two projects in the domain of automated diagnosis, which illustrate some important relationships between humans and computers.

Automated Diagnosis of Congenital Heart Disease

This first project deals with the evolution of the man-machine interface necessary to optimize success in computer recognition of six classes of disease in congenital heart disease. To establish a baseline of human diagnostic performance, three radiologists interpreted a data set of 387 cases, with an average human accuracy of 41%. The first task was to determine if the computer could do as well as the radiologists. Beyond carrying out the necessary preprocessing operations, just getting the computer to identify the heart seemed a monumental step. The task was made especially difficult because the films to be analyzed ranged in size from infants to adults. Next, the primitive tasks were to find edges, to trace contours, and to merge regions. A problem easy for humans but difficult for the computer was to find the left leaf of the diaphragm when there was a large bubble of air in the stomach under the diaphragm. Here the edge-finding algorithm followed the edge of the heart through the diaphragm into the stomach bubble, until a special "fix" was prepared.

The diagnostic predictors consisted largely of measurements and Fourier pairs, which contained information about edge shape. Given the outlines that the computer traced, computer accuracy was 40%, using the same films that the radiologists had examined {24}. To determine if hand-tracing edge information would yield more accurate results than if the computer found the edges on the films, we had the computer examine clear plastic overlays on which edges had been traced {25}. Diagnostic accuracy was improved by 25%. At this point further improvement was minimal until the radiologists called attention to the use of individual segments of the cardiac silhouette for clinical diagnosis, instead of the entire silhouette. A new computer model, which used Walsh descriptors for each of five cardiac segments, and with inflection points marked on the film by the radiologist, yielded an overall accuracy of 70%, nearly 75% better than the radiologists had achieved {26}.

CRITIQUE

Before we fully understood how human intervention would be needed to resolve the complexity of this problem in image analysis, the radiologist often felt a little like a spectator on the sideline, feeling outmoded by the machine and the engineers. An important lesson learned from this study is that humans and computers each have their special areas of competency, and that the goals of automated image analysis can be more rapidly furthered by a carefully designed symbiotic effort. To the radiologists, an attractive feature of this study is that results are not produced by computer magic—humans can understand the process that the computer is using to achieve results and, through experience, modify the process to provide better results.

Automated Analysis of Texture in Bone

We now turn to the second project, which deals with discrimination of textures, a topic vital to radiology. We are all aware of the adjectives spotted, honeycombed, fluffy, etc., in the radiologist's descriptive vocabulary. It is in the development of computer programs that differentiate between textures that the radiologist really finds himself in the role of a spectator on the sideline, as will become apparent later. However, as an orthopedic radiologist I had become expert in distinguishing between the textures of Paget's disease and diffuse neoplastic infiltration in spongy bone and was able to spell out the basic parameters of an interesting problem for texture identification. There are four such parameters, but the most important is the texture of spongy bone itself. A database of 163 cases was used for this study. Areas of interest, excluding cortex, that were selected by a radiologist were viewed or scanned through windows cut in opaque film. The radiologists participating in the experiment were asked to examine each case and to make a decision whether the trabecular structure reflected normal bone, Paget's, or carcinoma.

It is possible for the texture identification algorithm used here to differentiate mathematically different texture patterns that cannot be discriminated by a human observer. Computationally the heart of this spatial gray-level dependence method is a so-called spatial gray-level dependence matrix which is computed from the digital image along the directions 0°, 45°, 90°, and 135° from center, from each of which the second order probabilities of features of energy, entropy, correlation, local homogeneity, and inertia are derived. Five features extracted for each of four orientations give 20 measurements of texture, or even more if more than one intersampling distance is considered. Measurement selection technique consisted of a forward-sequential search algorithm judging each group of measurements by one of the following: 1) maximum overall probability of correct, 2) minimax probability of error, and 3) maximum 10% jackknife overall correct. The testing results for this study show overall accuracy roughly equivalent to human performance, but better than humans for identifying normal trabecular bone {27}.

CRITIQUE

These are regarded as excellent results, which probably could have been improved by increasing the size of the data set. From the engineers' perspective, there are problems with this methodology in that the engineers are unfamiliar with the clinical environment and with textures of bone, and the radiologists have little theory to offer them to guide the development of texture discrimination. The radiologists, on the other hand, can see the excellent experimental results but cannot causally relate these results to their own experience in recognizing textures. It would be helpful if the computer scientists were able to reconstruct the physical features of textures from the mathematically defined information derived from the test data, in order for the radiologist to be able to recognize such features and to improve his own skills in texture identification.

What of the Future?

I have unqualified enthusiasm for the future usefulness of automated image analysis but reserved enthusiasm for computer-aided diagnosis. The reasons are as follows:

1. The trend in diagnostic radiology is toward an increasing use of digital imaging. We are now beginning the use of prototype systems that provide chest and bone images in digital format *de novo*, with the implication that the preprocessing that formerly was necessary can largely be eliminated. Image information will be directly available for analysis.

2. Radiologists have learned to deal with digital images and displays on a daily basis. In my opinion they will welcome computer tools that can provide information that they need and cannot obtain in any other manner.

3. With the advent of digital image management systems, images will be accessible on displays at the radiologist's workstation. Image processing tools will become available first hand. Given the need for man-machine interface in solving some problems in pattern recognition, the radiologist's workstation may become a natural setting for such an interface.

4. There is a need for sophisticated programs to differentiate and qualitate textures. We know that some such programs can differentiate textures that look alike to humans. In my practice as a skeletal radiologist, I would like to have such programs now; I would use them to distinguish between Paget's disease, fibrous dysplasia, and chronic infection. I believe that chest radiologists need tools to differentiate textures in lung disease.

5. The need for programs to measure and calculate is limited only by the imagination.

6. CAD of images requires reliable data input; humans are inconsistent in identifying signs. Data entry can be tedious and time consuming. With the availability of the radiologist's workstation, the easy access to special programs may in time make CAD more acceptable.

7. The usefulness of CAD as a teaching aid has not been fully appreciated, and it needs to be further evaluated.

8. The role of artificial intelligence in enhancing decision making from images has not been sufficiently explored.

Acknowledgments

Through the years following the original award of support for computer analysis of tumor roentgenograms, major collaborative contributions were made by, among others, Cosmo Haun, Theodore E. Keats, Lee B. Lusted, James L. Lehr, Arch W. Templeton, Arch H. Turner, Jr., Peter L. Reichertz, Robert P. Covert, Jay Goldman, Samuel J. Dwyer, Robert W. Parkey, Charles A. Harlow, Corrine Farrell, Anthony Wilson, Timothy A. Salthouse, John J. Sterling, Roger A. Bauman, and Jaime Taaffe. These scientists participated in federally and otherwise-funded research projects on computer-aided diagnosis, simulation of patient and information flow in radiology departments, radiology information systems, automated image analysis, human processing of radiological information, research training in radiology, and clinical cancer training. The contributions of Peter Reichertz, James Lehr, and Sam Dwyer were of special importance because of their close relationship to me over a period of many years; theirs and the contributions of all others are gratefully acknowledged.

References

1. Garland, L.H., Miller, E.R., Swerling, H.B., Harkness, J.T., Hinshaw, H.C., Shipman, S.J., and Yerushalmy, J. Studies on value of serial films in estimating progress of pulmonary disease. *Radiology*, 58:161–177, 1952.

2. Johnson, L.C. A general theory of bone tumors. *Bulletin of the New York Academy of Medicine* 29:164–171, February 1953.

3. Lodwick, G.S., Keats, T.E., and Dorst, J.P. An evaluation of the significance of transverse hilar measurements in the diagnosis of primary lung cancer. *Radiology* 71:3:370–374, September 1958.

4. Lodwick, G.S., Keats, T.E., and Dorst, J.P. The coding of roentgen images for computer analysis as applied to lung cancer. *Radiology* 81:2:185–200, August 1963.

5. Lodwick, G.S. A systematic approach to the roentgen diagnosis of bone tumors. *Tumors of Bone and Soft Tissue*. Year Book Medical Publishers, Inc., 1963, pp. 49–68.

6. Lodwick, G.S. The radiologic diagnosis of metastatic cancerin bone. *Tumors of Bone and Soft Tissue*. Year Book Medical Publishers, Inc., 1963, pp. 253–268.

7. Lodwick, G.S. *An Atlas of "Tumors of Bones and Joints."* Year Book Medical Publishers, Inc., April, 1971.

8. Ledley, R.S. and Lusted, L.B. Reasoning foundations of medical practice. *Science* 130:9–21, July 3, 1959.

9. Warner, H.R., Toronto, A.F., Veasey, L.G., and Stephenson, R.E. A mathematical approach to medical diagnosis—application to congenital heart disease. *J. Am. Med. Assn.* 177, 1961.

10. Bayes, T. An essay toward solving a problem in the doctrine of chances, with Richard Price's forward and discussion. *Phil. Trans. Royal Soc.*, 1763, pp. 370–418.

11. Maxwell, A.E. Classification procedures based on Bayes's theorem and decision theory. *Analyzing Quantitative Data*. New York: Wiley, 1961, Chapter 10.

12. Ledley, R.S. Programming to achieve intelligence. *Programming and Utilizing Digital Computers*. New York: McGraw-Hill, 1962, Chapter 8.

13. Lodwick, G.S., Haun, C.L., Smith, W.E., Keller, R.F., and Robertson, E.D. Computer diagnosis of primary bone tumors: A preliminary report. *Radiology* 80:273–275, February 1963.

14. Lodwick, G.S., Turner, A.H. Jr., Lusted, L.B., and Templeton, A.W. Computer aided diagnosis of radiographic images. *J. of Chronic Diseases* 19:485–496, April 1966.

15. Lodwick, G.S. Solitary malignant tumors of bone: The application of predictor variables in diagnosis. *Seminars in Roentgenology* 1:3:293–313, July 1966.

16. Lodwick, G.S. and Reichertz, P. Computer assisted diagnosis of tumors and tumorlike lesions of bone. The limited-Bayes concept. *Proceedings of The Symposium Osseum*, London, April 1968, pp. 305–309.

17. Wilson, W.G., Templeton, A.W., Turner, A.H., and Lodwick, G.S. The computer analysis and diagnosis of gastric ulcer. *Radiology* 85:6: 1064–1073, December 1965.

18. Templeton, A.W., Jansen, C., Lehr, J.H., and Hufft, R. Solitary pulmonary lesions. Computer aided diagnosis and evaluation of mathematical methods. *Radiology* 89:605–613, 1967.

19. Lodwick, G.S. Radiographic diagnosis and grading of bone tumors, with comments on computer evaluation. *Proceedings of Fifth National Cancer Conference*. Philadelphia: J.B. Lippincott Co., Sept. 1964, pp. 369–380.

20. Lodwick, G.S., Wilson, A.J., Farrell, C., Virtama, P., and Dittrich, F. I—Determining growth rates of focal lesions of bone from radiographs. *Radiology* 134:3:577–583, March 1980.

21. Lodwick, G.S., Wilson, A.J., Farrell, C., Virtama, P., and Dittrich, F. II—Estimating rate of growth in lesions of bone. Observer performance and error. *Radiology* 134:3:585–590, March, 1980.

22. Lehr, J.L., Parkey, R.W., Garrotto, C.A., Harlow, C.A., and Lodwick, G.S. Computer algorithms for the detection of brain scintigram abnormalities. *Radiology* 97:2:269–276, November 1970.

23. Hall, D.L., Lodwick, G.S., Kruger, R.P., and Dwyer, S.J. Direct computer diagnosis of congenital heart disease. *Radiology* 101:497–509, December 1971.

24. Lehr, J.L., Schrunk, D.G., Lodwick, G.S., McFarland, W.D., Moore, G., Kahveci, A., Dwyer, S.J., Harlow, C.A., and Connors, R. Automated analysis of plain chest roentgenograms in congenital heart disease. *Proceedings of the San Diego Biomedical Symposium*, 1975, pp. 161–166.

25. Brooks, R.C. *Computer Diagnosis of Congenital Heart Disease Using Discriminant Functions*. A dissertation in fulfillment of the requirements for the degree Doctor of Philosophy, The Graduate School of the University of Missouri, Columbia, December 1973.

26. Lodwick, G.S., Harlow, C.A., and Cook, L.T. Fourier-Walsh shape descriptors and applications to radiographic image processing. *Proceedings of the Sixth Conference on Computer Applications in Radiology*, June 1979, Newport Beach, California, pp. 110–114.

27. Lodwick, G.S., Conners, R.W., and Harlow, C.A. Computer classification of normal, Paget's or metastatic carcinoma by tonal primitives. *Proceedings of the Sixth Conference on Computer Applications in Radiology*, June 1979, Newport Beach, California, pp. 122–128.

Participants' Discussion

Frawley McFarland How did you decide which computer decisions were wrong?

Gwilym Lodwick These are pathologically proved cases.

Recollections on the Processing of Biomedical Signals

Jerome R. Cox, Jr., DSc
Washington University, Saint Louis

Summary

The processing of biomedical signals took many steps forward in the two decades that followed the introduction of digital computers to the field in the late fifties. Along with my colleagues at the Central Institute for the Deaf and at the Biomedical Computer Laboratory, I was privileged to participate in this exciting early period of biomedical computing. Some of my experiences with projects, both successful and unsuccessful, in evoked response audiometry, neurophysiology, fetal electrocardiography, radiation treatment planning, electrocardiographic rhythm analysis, and ambulatory monitoring of electrocardiographic rhythms are described. These recollections give less attention to scientific results than they do to selected anecdotes and observations.

Introduction

These recollections stretch over 17 years of biomedical computing at the Washington University Medical Center, starting in 1958 at the Central Institute for the Deaf (CID), through the period 1964 to 1975 at the Biomedical Computer Laboratory (BCL). The period from 1975 on will not be covered for reasons I will try to explain. Since 1975 I have been at the Department of Computer Science, as chairman, and some projects started then are still underway. Since I want to try to report both successes and failures, and since achieving any degree of objectivity in these matters is difficult, no attempt will be made to report on recent events. In addition, these historical recollections provide an opportunity to report sidelights and difficulties that ordinarily do not find their way into the pages of the regular journals. I hope these touches of reality are useful to those whose picture of biomedical computing is drawn primarily from their reading of the scientific literature. With the perspective of the years such moments have softened, and I hope you will find them either interesting or amusing.

197

In keeping with my half of the theme of this session, these recollections are limited to signal processing, although I will take the liberty of finding an excuse to discuss one other project that provides some interesting sidelights.

AUDITORY EVOKED RESPONSES

My interest in biomedical computing had its beginning when Hallowell Davis, then director of research at CID, asked me to investigate methods for the measurement of the auditory evoked response in infants. The goal was to determine whether, despite their inability to communicate, these young children had hearing deficits. The experimental technique was that of Dawson {1} and required the averaging of scalp potentials synchronized to a repetitive auditory stimulus.

My background was electrical engineering and acoustics. In 1958 I was just beginning to learn about transistors and was completely unfamiliar with digital computers. Some study convinced me that the use of a special-purpose digital computer was the method of choice for the evoked response problem. Since a description of the first digital Average Response Computer (ARC) {2} was yet to be published and nothing was available commercially, I enlisted the help of three graduate students at CID, first Don Glaeser in 1958, Kirti Charan in 1959, and Maynard Engebretson in 1960. They tried three different approaches to the problem. One was a difficult design with excellent operational speed and low cost. The second seemed to be a quick and inexpensive design with tediously slow operational speed. The third required a substantial design effort and was not cheap, but did promise good operational speed.

It was neither the first nor the last time that I learned the hard way that the three competing objectives of rapid realization, low cost, and high speed cannot be achieved in a single design. If you are experienced in the area, you can get two out of the three. If you are inexperienced, as we were, you had better try for just one of the three objectives. The approach tried by Glaeser and me turned out to be extremely difficult, attempting as it did to achieve two of the three objectives. It was eventually abandoned, but more of that below. The approach I recommended to Charan, also an attempt to get two out of three, met a similar fate. Engebretson's approach attempted only one of the three objectives, high-speed, and a prototype was operational by late 1961 {3, 4}. A later version {5} incorporated the lessons learned from the prototype and by 1963 was in regular experimental use in Davis's new auditory evoked response laboratory where it met all the technical goals set for it.

FIGURE 1
HAVOC, a special purpose computer designed for recording evoked average responses from infants to ascertain the amount of hearing deficit. HAVOC first operated in late 1961.

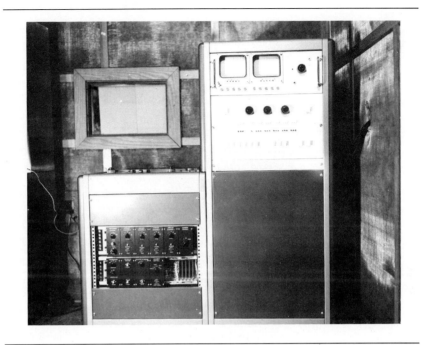

Taking only slightly less time than the design itself was the selection of a suitable acronym for Engebretson's special purpose computer. We settled on HAVOC for Histogram, Average, and Ogive Calculator. Once having gotten the hang of finite state machine design, we decided to incorporate the tabulation of frequency distributions (*histograms*) and integrals of frequency distributions (*ogives*) although little use was to be made of these two modes of operation throughout the years. Davis used HAVOC's *average* mode to create the field of auditory evoked response audiometry, now a standard technique in the evaluation of infants with possible auditory deficits {6, 7}. HAVOC was last used in 1982, after almost 20 years of productive service {8}.

NEUROPHYSIOLOGICAL SIGNALS

Hallowell Davis's auditory physiology laboratory at CID contained a Grass camera and a variety of amplifiers for the low-voltage electrical signals that he and Donald Eldredge recorded from guinea pigs and chinchillas. The camera was used to record photographically multiple simultaneous waveforms obtained from microelectrodes inserted in the experimental animal's inner ear.

FIGURE 2
Hallowell Davis and
Jerry Cox in front of
HAVOC at the time
of the computer's re-
tirement in 1982

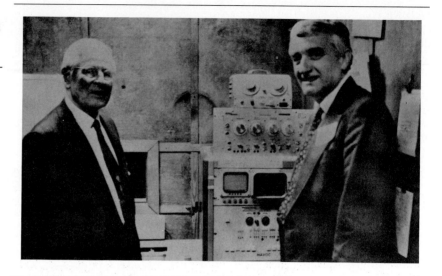

The first design mentioned above was to not only process auditory evoked responses, but also serve as a data acquisition system for the neurophysiology laboratory. To meet these objectives Glaeser and I attempted to build a high-speed average response computer based on a magnetic drum memory. The goal was to obtain increased storage at lower cost than was possible with the ferrite core memories of the day. It was a very educational experience for me, but the system never arrived in the laboratory. Timing constraints imposed by the rotating drum and high sampling rates required by the neurophysiological signals combined to increase the complexity of the design beyond what I could manage. We learned how to design a high-performance analog–digital converter {9}, we learned about fast digital circuitry, and I learned that Nature abhors a magnetic drum. Finally, I learned the importance of upbeat acronyms. DARC, standing for Drum Average Response Computer, never had the appeal of the more neutral ARC or even the somewhat chaotic sounding HAVOC.

THE LINC

Now that is an example of a high-class acronym, the Laboratory Instrument Computer. It was to change my life and to change biomedical computing. My part of this story begins during the design and construction of DARC. I had become aware of a new digital module manufacturer in Maynard, Massachusetts, and decided to visit the plant to see if their products lived up to the attractive literature circulated by this "new start," Digital Equipment Corporation. Ken Olson was available to this visitor from St. Louis, who just happened in off the street that spring morning in 1962, and we talked about DARC and a new stored program computer that I had in mind for the CID neurophysiology laboratory. He suggested that I drive over to Lincoln Laboratory to visit Wes Clark who was working on a similar project called the LINC {10}.

I did just that and found that the Lincoln Laboratory group was well ahead of my thoughts on laboratory computers. Not only had Clark designed a computer that for its day was ideally suited to the neurophysiology laboratory, but his group had a prototype running, and I was able to try some simple graphic routines. The console was a delight to use and the logic and timing drawings were elegant and easy to understand (apparently a lost art). It was a tremendously exciting afternoon. More or less on the spot, I decided to abandon my efforts to design a stored program computer for CID and instead to join forces with the Lincoln Laboratory group. They were to move shortly thereafter to MIT, at Kendall Square, to carry out the LINC Evaluation Program, an NIH/NASA sponsored program for the construction of a dozen machines for biomedical scientists at as many institutions throughout the nation {11}.

By the fall of 1963 we had a running LINC at CID assembled from one of 10 or so sets of parts acquired for a series of phantom machines

FIGURE 3
Maynard Engebretson at the LINC installed in the CID Physiology Laboratory in 1963

FIGURE 4
The CID LINC in the
Physiology Labora-
tory toward the end
of its useful life in
1980

purchased in parallel with the 12 legitimate machines for the LINC
Evaluation Program. Norm Kinch, drawing on his Navy Chief experience, had arranged for the phantom machines through creative purchasing, all for the benefit of the other organizations outside the
Evaluation Program who, like CID, saw the advantages of the LINC
and wanted to participate in the revolution in laboratory computing it
represented.

The LINC was installed in the CID physiology laboratory, now
under Eldredge's supervision as Davis was spending most of his time
with HAVOC in his new auditory evoked response laboratory.
Eldredge and a succession of collaborators used the LINC in their work
until 1980, when it was finally retired after 17 years of nearly trouble-
free service.

THE BEGINNING OF BCL

In 1962 I was asked to serve on the NIH Computer Study Section with
Lee Lusted as chairman and Bruce Waxman as executive secretary. One
day after the study section business was done, Lee asked me whether I
might have an interest in starting a research resource in biomedical
computing at Washington University. The Research Resource Program
was a new initiative of the Institute for General Medical Sciences of

FIGURE 5
Aerial photograph of the Washington University Medical Center taken about 1974. Nurses' quarters that became home for BCL is shown within circle.

NIH. The atmosphere was expansive and optimistic, a contrast to the character of the NIH grant process today. Soon the program was taken over by the newly formed Division of Research Resources operating out of rented quarters in North Bethesda. Dazzled by these developments I prepared, with considerable enthusiasm, a grant application for a new Biomedical Computer Laboratory at the Washington University School of Medicine.

During the period 1958 to 1963, I had assembled a group of graduate students at CID interested in biomedical computing that included Don Glaeser, Maynard Engebretson, and Floyd Nolle. When the BCL grant was funded there was no home for a new computer laboratory at the School of Medicine. We looked around the Medical Center and found nothing but an old garage building about four blocks away from where we expected to find our collaborators. With heavy heart we took steps to complete arrangements to renovate the garage so that it could accommodate our new laboratory, but at the last possible moment an excellent location, the old Shriner's Hospital, was acquired by the Medical Center. Renovations were still in order, since the buildings were about 40 years old and in poor repair. While remodeling proceeded, CID generously allowed us to continue to work in their research space.

FIGURE 6
Basement of old Shriner's Hospital nurses' quarters before renovation (ca. 1964)

FIGURE 7
Dan Glasser demonstrating LINC to visitors at BCL open house (1964)

During this period our small group was joined by several full-time staff members including Sharon Davisson, Mike McDonald, Bob Kimack, and Fred Francis. Finally, on April 15, 1964, eight of us moved into freshly painted laboratory space at the old Shriner's Hospital nurses quarters, 700 South Euclid Avenue, where BCL continues to operate today.

Less than three months after BCL opened, Bill Papian, Wes Clark, and members of the LINC design team moved to Washington University from MIT. Norm Kinch joined the group after a year spent in the southwest and Charles Molnar, codesigner of the LINC, moved to St. Louis from Boston two years later. A sister organization to BCL was formed, which is now known as the Computer Systems Laboratory. Thus began a long and fruitful collaboration between the two laboratories.

FETAL ELECTROCARDIOGRAPHY

One of the first projects to be initiated at BCL was a collaboration between Remsen Behrer, a pediatric cardiologist, and Don Glaeser in which signal processing techniques were used to recover the fetal electrocardiogram (ECG) from electrodes on the mother's abdomen. Nor-

FIGURE 8
Fred Francis (left), Don Glaeser (center), and Ramson Behrer in the fetal electrocardiography laboratory. LINC can be seen at right rear.

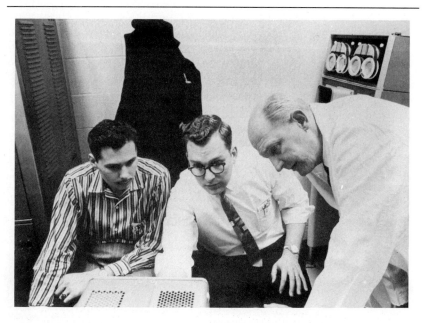

mally the maternal ECG is many times larger than the fetal ECG, making it difficult to recognize abnormalities in the fetal heartbeat. The LINC was used to obtain a representative maternal ECG waveform by calculating a running average synchronized with a signal obtained from shoulder leads. This representative maternal ECG waveform was then subtracted from the total abdominal signal leaving the fetal ECG waveform.

Was the project successful? From an engineering point of view it was, but from a clinical point of view it was clumsy, ahead of its time, and not useful during labor. Positive scientific results were reported {12}, but the technique did not find popular clinical support. With the fetal ECG team in attendance the LINC produced results rapidly, but the patient had to be brought to a special laboratory at a scheduled time. It was not clear then that the value of the test was great enough to overcome this inconvenience. Both Behrer and Glaeser left Washington University to follow other career opportunities.

Ivan Sutherland years ago described the wheel of reincarnation in display technology. Perhaps he will pardon my application of his

FIGURE 9
Wes Clark (left) and Jerry Cox in Clark's office. Probably taken shortly after 1965 collaboration on computer design class.

FIGURE 10
Jerry Cox (left) and Severo Ornstein (right), both framed by the relay rack that held one of the two 4W2s built by the computer design class, April and May 1965. Several members of the class are grouped around the machine.

FIGURE 11
Cox describing the PC to the participants in the Radiation Treatment Plannning Program in 1967. The PC keyboard and console can be seen in the center foreground.

phrase to a different situation: Good ideas get reinvented periodically until some combination of circumstances (convenience, cost, need) causes the invention to become widely accepted. The idea presented in 1968 by Behrer, *et al.* had important and novel features, but recording the fetal ECG was not new {13}. It was the best version of the technique up to that time, since it required no vaginal electrode, but even today the idea continues to be reintroduced. Do we want to increase our vigilance to prevent journals from publishing another turn of the wheel of reincarnation? I think not. Circumstances change and an old idea may become practical in a new environment or with a new twist.

THE PROGRAMMED CONSOLE

The Programmed Console (PC) grew out of a computer design class that Wes Clark and I taught in the spring of 1965. The design was less powerful, but in many other ways much like that of the LINC. An important distinction was that the PC incorporated as a standard feature a modem for data communication with a host computer and thus became an early workstation (although we did not know the term in those days) sharing the computational load with the host.

After the class had finished, I redesigned the PC with help from Bill Gerth for a major DRR-supported project in radiation treatment planning. The idea for the project occurred during a meeting with

Bruce Waxman held in the summer of 1965. Bruce was then head of the Biotechnology Resources Program at DRR, and I showed him some photographs of radiation isodose contours Bill Gerth had produced to show off the PC's graphic ability. He became interested, and we planned an evaluation program that would place the PC in a few leading institutions. Competitive bidding lead to a contract with Spear, Inc., Waltham, Massachusetts, for the construction of six PCs, one for radiation therapy at Washington University, four for other therapy units in the U.S., and one for the Ontario Cancer Institute.

This radiation treatment planning project had nothing to do with signal processing, but is introduced here because it bears on the next topic and also because it gives me an opportunity to relate several stories that may provide interesting historical sidelights. The origin of the name PC is one such sidelight. During the last frantic weeks of the spring 1965 class we had dubbed the two machines being designed and built by the class "The Four-Week Wonders" or, following the lead of a then popular television program, the 4W2.[1] When it was clear that the 4W2 was going beyond the end of the spring 1965 semester, Bob Ellis, a participant in the class, suggested that we needed a more dignified name. He proposed "Programmed Console," since the machine we had designed was like a computer console (or terminal) but yet it was programmed. Little did we know that 16 years later the two letters "PC" would be appropriated to play a fateful role in a new era in computing.

The second story concerns an unexpected development on the machine delivered to Jack Cunningham at the Ontario Cancer Institute. One of Jack's research assistants, Joe Milan, wrote a space-war program for the PC over a couple of weekends shortly after the machine was delivered to Toronto in 1967. Joe called the program Hyperspace because in this version of the famous computer game missiles and spacecraft could fly out one side of the display and immediately reappear flying into the display on the opposite side. Hyperspace was provided to all six PC sites and somehow appeared on all the development machines at BCL. Because the CRT display was an integral part of the PC, the responsiveness of the space-war game was excellent, and it became an instant hit within the PC community.

The first indication to me of how pervasive Hyperspace had become was a plague that was visited on a pair of keys on the PC keyboard. It turned out that the keys were failing so often because they were used as the two missile-firing keys in Hyperspace. Bill Gerth and I realized that we were witnessing an important phenomenon, but we had done an inadequate job in our market analysis. We considered putting PCs into airports but figured we would have to charge at least

---

[1] For the youngsters among us, a popular 1965 comedy news show was titled, "That Was The Week That Was" or TW3.

FIGURE 12
Helen Fortenas, a radiation physics technician, at the PC keyboard preparing a treatment plan (1970).

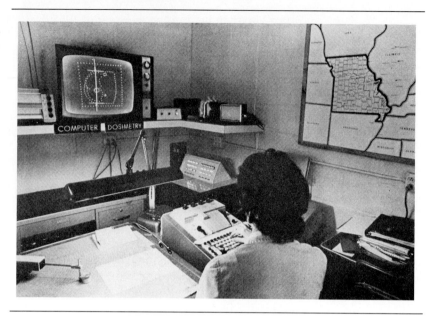

$0.50 a play and, after all, who would be foolish enough to continue to pump quarters into a computer game?

The final story concerning the PC had its denouement just this year. In addition to the superb stand-alone external beam treatment planning programs developed by Bill Holmes, the modem on the PC allowed us to send data to the host computer for the calculation of the dosage pattern from interstitial radioactive implants. Through communication programs developed by Liz Van Patten and Dave Bridger, the PC functioned as a data-entry device instead of the keypunch that had been used previously. It was no longer necessary to transport cards to the central computing facility and, furthermore, results could be returned promptly via the same modem connection to be displayed or plotted by the PC. All of this was operating by February of 1967, reported in the literature {14} and preserved on motion picture film.

In 1973 a patent was granted to a firm that is now defunct, claiming as an invention a similar system for data entry. In the mid-sixties none of us gave a second thought to patenting the PC because we felt the technology was obvious in the light of the development of the LINC. Over the last decade the present owner of the 1973 patent has sued several manufacturers of smart terminals for an aggregate well into nine figures. Wes Clark and I recently appeared as witnesses for the defense in the latest of these cases. We supported the position that the PC and the LINC anticipated the patent and compromised the validity of the 1969 filing and the subsequent 1973 patent. The judge will soon decide whether that position is correct, but however he rules there is a significant point for biomedical computing: Biomedically inspired research and development can lead the way for technology in general. Clearly the LINC was such a pioneering development and so too, in its own area, was the PC.

ELECTROCARDIOGRAPHIC RHYTHM ANALYSIS

One of the advantages of a major project like the development of a computer system for radiation treatment is that the design group is likely to have a few extra machines around before it's all over. Our prototype PCs were not as fast as the Spear PCs and were much less attractive. We felt they were inappropriate for our radiology collaborators at other institutions and thus were ripe for application to another project at BCL. Such a project was the automatic detection of cardiac arrhythmias, which had begun in 1965 on the LINC but by the fall of

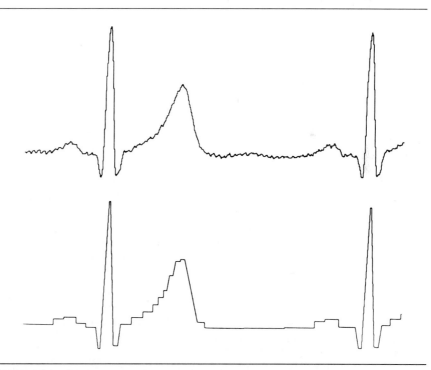

FIGURE 13

A segment of an electrocardiogram (upper trace) showing two successive QRS-complexes and an intervening T-wave. The Aztec processed waveform (lower trace) shows the stepped T-wave that could be likened to an Aztec temple, accounting for the choice of the name.

1966 had been transferred to two prototype PCs that were subsequently dedicated to the project.

In fact, our original objective had been to develop a system for the diagnosis of 12-lead ECGs, but in 1965 that seemed excessively difficult for a first venture into pattern recognition. Harry Fozzard, who was our initial cardiological collaborator, Floyd Nolle, and I thought we would first spend a year or two warming up our skills on a much simpler problem: the detection of cardiac arrhythmias from a single chest lead. Actually BCL has spent more than 20 years on the arrhythmia problem, and we never did get around to the diagnostic ECG problem. So much for planning in research.

The first step in our rhythm analysis project was Floyd Nolle's invention of a preprocessing routine that reduced the input data rate to the analysis programs but retained enough information for them to carry out an accurate rhythm diagnosis. The program transformed the sampled ECG data to a series of horizontal and sloping line segments. I think it was Charles Oliver, a second cardiological collaborator who joined the project in 1966, who looked at the preprocessor output and commented that it looked like a profile view of an Aztec temple. It did, and so we began an intense effort to find a good acronym expansion. After rejecting many names as unimaginative or baroque, I began an exhaustive search of appropriate sections of the unabridged dictionary and ultimately decided on "amplitude zone, Time-Epoch Coding," a name that fit the algorithm tolerably well.

Aztec worked well on ECG data, producing a compression of about 10:1 with enhancement of the waveform components needed for later analysis. We were eager to publish our results and thought a letter in *Science* would reach the right group of readers. It was, alas, rejected because it was "of interest to only a limited audience." Later published in the *IEEE Transactions on Biomedical Engineering* {15}, it has been cited widely for over a decade and more recently appears without citation having become a part of the language of rhythm analysis.

In the fall of 1969 the Barnes Hospital Coronary Care Unit (CCU) opened under the direction of Gerald Wolff. Floyd Nolle, Charles Oliver, and I had worked hard during the previous two years to develop an ECG monitoring system called Argus[2] (ARrhythmia GUard System) that could be used 24 hours a day to alert CCU staff to life-threatening arrhythmias {16, 17}. The early experience with Argus was exciting and rewarding as a result of the exceptional support we received from Gerry Wolff and several members of his new nursing staff.

---

[2] According to *Websters Third New International Dictionary,* Argus was a "mythological being with many eyes some of which were always open, known as a zealous watchman." The choice of this acronym was due to Charles Oliver.

FIGURE 14
Floyd Nolle (left), principal developer of Aztec and Argus, in the computer room of the Barnes Hospital Coronary Care Unit. The two PCs used to monitor electrocardiograms are at the extreme left above Nolle's head (1970).

An example of the excitement occurred not long after the unit had opened. A patient that the monitoring equipment indicated to be in ventricular fibrillation was observed by the responding "code" team to be sitting up in bed eating lunch with no signs of a life-threatening arrhythmia. How could this be?

The mystery was solved by Floyd and Dieter Ambos who discovered that a nurse walking on the CCU's special antistatic carpet caused the thin conducting wires embedded in the weave to modulate the signal from a nearby TV station. This fluctuating signal carried by the carpet's conducting wires was rebroadcast particularly strongly inside one patient's room; was picked up by the monitoring leads there; was accidentally demodulated by special loose-lead circuitry, the latest "improvement" in the ECG monitoring amplifiers; and simulated with surprising faithfulness ventricular fibrillation on the monitor's screen and in the monitor's circuitry itself.

The ability of the "code" team to detect absurdity is, thankfully, much better than it can be in any computer and no harm was done by this highly improbable combination of circumstances. The episode does emphasize the inability of even the most careful designers to think of all possible contingencies. Staff who distrust equipment and think for themselves are essential to avoid serious consequences during the initial period of use of automated equipment in a clinical environment. Only after considerable experience and a careful cataloging of the modes of equipment malfunction should the staff become comfortable enough to suspend their adversarial relationship with the equipment.

A clinical evaluation of the operational impact of Argus was carried out in the CCU in 1971 and 1972 by a team led by Charles Oliver. The results {18} showed that for one group of CCU patients Argus produced more than twice as many treatment actions as observed in an equivalent control group. The only difference between the two groups was that the output of Argus was available to the CCU staff in the study group, but withheld in the control group.

If treatment actions, such as the administration of lidocaine, can be beneficial to the patient, should we deduce from these results that computer monitoring is beneficial? Each therapeutic treatment has its associated medical risks and benefits that our clinical study made no attempt to address. These are medical questions that require a clinical study well beyond the scope of ours, dealing as it did with only the operational impact of Argus.

There were no deaths in either the study or control groups during the investigation. In fact, it would take a very large multicenter clinical trial to reliably estimate the effects of different levels of each of the treatment actions on mortality. Had we those results it would have been possible to evaluate the therapeutic efficacy of Argus.

It is not unusual for unanswered and deep medical questions to intrude on the evaluation of medical technology. Our only choice as designers of such equipment is to assume that current views about "good medical practice" are valid, but be alert to the results of clinical research that may change these views. Computer monitoring in the CCU has grown into a substantial industry since 1969, now exceeding $100 million per year worldwide. We still have no scientific evaluation of the therapeutic efficacy of such systems, but the clinical judgement of CCU directors seems to be that the systems help their staff deliver high-quality medical care.

AMBULATORY MONITORING OF ELECTROCARDIOGRAPHIC RHYTHMS

Portable recorders became available in the 1960s, designed to store 24 hours of an ambulatory patient's electrocardiogram on a single tape. The job of analyzing these tapes became a growing burden to clinical investigators, and the new rhythm monitoring algorithms developed for the CCU seemed an obvious solution to the problem. Thus, in 1971, we began to develop a high-speed version of Argus to analyze monitoring tapes for a project on the relationship of ventricular arrhythmias to sudden death in ambulatory survivors of myocardial infarction.

Argus needed to be speeded up considerably, since we wished to analyze the tape recordings at 60 times faster than their recording speed. One hour of the patient's ECG would be analyzed in one minute of processing time. It took many years to reach this goal, with part of the increase in speed coming from faster equipment and part coming from algorithmic improvements. In the early 1970s Floyd Nolle, Dieter Ambos, and Ken Clark did most of the software and hardware development toward this goal. Charles Oliver led a clinical team that organized the patients to be studied and analyzed the data produced by our high-speed version of Argus.

Floyd was trying to organize the ECG patterns for many different types of heartbeats into families with similar characteristics {17, 19}. He used a stick figure that summarized the several features extracted from each ECG pattern. The walls and desk in our office at the CCU were covered with plotter output showing the seemingly infinite variety of these stick figures. His observation that it would be much easier to teach a pigeon to recognize these stick figures than it would be to program a computer to do the job was immediately recognized by Ken and Dieter as a rare opportunity.

They investigated a suburban pigeonry and found the proprietor had two classes of homing pigeons, one at $2 and a second class at $0.50 each. The difference was that the $2 birds would return to the pigeonry in suburban St. Louis, and the cheaper birds returned to Crystal City, about 50 miles to the south. They purchased one of the economy birds.

Floyd tended to the pigeon during the week and my secretary, Shirley Gonzalez-Rubio took care of it over the weekend. It did not learn to recognize stick figures, it did provide a good bit of comic relief flapping around BCL's basement and Shirley's bathroom, and perhaps it gave Floyd some new ideas for algorithms before it was released to find its way back to Crystal City, where we assume it lived in Argus-free bliss ever after.

In the fall of 1972, Charles Feldman, of Worcester Polytechnic Institute, organized an Evaluation Group for Arrhythmia Detectors (EGAD) at the Dallas meeting of the American Heart Association. The purpose of this organization was to try to set up methods and procedures to assist in the objective evaluation of the growing number of computer-based arrhythmia detection systems. I was happy to place the resources of BCL behind this project because of its importance to the systematic development of the field.

It was to take more than a decade, but finally in 1984, Russ Hermes of BCL completed the last of a set of carefully annotated digital tapes for commercial sale to arrhythmia system developers {20}. Known as the AHA database, it had the benefit of careful review and annotation by some of the nation's most prestigious electrocardiographers. The effect of this database and its companion from MIT {21} was to bring research and development in arrhythmia detectors from a state of chaos to one of cooperative progress. With an objective method to compare the performance of detection systems, it became much easier to recognize which methods were successful and which were not. A convergence on the successful methods ensued, and the value of this kind of database in pattern recognition problems was demonstrated once again. The development of the AHA database was an important factor in improving the performance of several commercially available, high-speed analysis systems for ambulatory ECG recordings.

Conclusion

Hal Davis has retired and at 91 continues to receive the scientific acclaim he so richly deserves. Don Glaeser, Floyd Nolle, and Maynard Engebretson, the three graduate students who helped me form BCL, went on to their doctorates through their work at BCL and then to highly productive careers in biomedical computing. Bill Gerth recently left St. Louis to join the family business in Nashville. Ken Clark and Russ Hermes are stalwarts at BCL. Dieter Ambos is a research associate professor at Washington University. Wes Clark left Washington University in 1972 and was succeeded as director of the Computer Systems Laboratory by Charlie Molnar. In 1984, Charlie founded and became the first director of the Institute for Biomedical Computing, which brought the two sister laboratories together within a single organization.

My years at CID and BCL were certainly exciting. I was privileged to be a part of it and to have had the friendship and support of those mentioned in these few stories and the many more who over the years have helped in important ways. I do not have any important wisdom to impart. Maybe it is worthwhile to say that perseverance and getting down to basics should be valued more than they are. It often seemed that we should abandon a research direction because other laboratories elsewhere were doing astonishing work, but in the end we persevered and nothing seems to endure like endurance.

Acknowledgments

The work described was largely sponsored by the National Institutes of Health through a variety of grants and contracts. The principal ones were B2302, RG8160, FR00161, RR00396 and HV12481. The grant from the Division of Research Resources (RR00396) was the most long-lived, extending from 1967 through 1981. Without this patient and generous support neither BCL nor the achievements alluded to in this paper would have been possible.

I also want to acknowledge the work of many friends and colleagues at CID and BCL not associated with the topics covered in these reflections. Because of the limitations of my title and a requirement for some restraint with respect to space, I have had to skip over many whose contributions to projects that I directed were significant. Of those not mentioned, I must recognize four special friends from the BCL years: Lew Thomas, who took over the laboratory when I went to Computer Science; Don Snyder, who taught me about point processes and much more; Jim Blaine, who worked closely with me from the time he came to BCL in 1967 until the present; and Virginia Bixon, who as laboratory business manager, has kept us all out of financial mischief.

References

1. Dawson, G.D. A summation technique for the detection of small evoked potentials. *Electroencephalography and Clinical Neurophysiology* 6:65–84, 1954.

2. Clark, W.A., Brown, R.M., Goldstein, M.H., Molnar, C.E., O'Brien, D.F. , and Zieman, H.F. The Average Response Computer (ARC)—A digital device for computing averages and amplitude and time histograms of electrophysiological responses. *IRE Trans. Biomedical Electronics* BME-8:46–51, 1961.

3. Cox, J.R. Special purpose digital computers in biology. *Computers in Biomedical Research II*. Stacy, R.W. and Waxman, B.D., (eds.). New York: Academic Press, 1965, Chapter 3.

4. Periodic Progress Report No. 5. Central Institute for the Deaf, St. Louis, Missouri, 1962, p. 25.

5. Engebretson, A.M. *Digital Computer for Analyzing Bioelectric Signals*. Masters Thesis, Washington University, St. Louis, Missouri, 1963.

6. Davis, H., Engebretson, A.M., Lowell, E.L., Mast, T., Satterfield, J., and Yoshie, N. Evoked responses to clicks recorded from the human scalp. *Ann. N.Y. Acad. Sci.* 112:224–225, 1964.

7. Galambos, R. Hallowell Davis: Father of the AER. *Hearing and Davis: Essays Honoring Hallowell Davis*. Hirsh, S.K., Eldredge, D.H., Hirsh, I.J., and Silverman, S.R. (eds.). St. Louis: Washington University Press, 1976, pp. 381–391.

8. Eldredge, D.H. Personal communication, 1987.

9. Cox, J.R. and Glaeser, D.H. A quantizing encoder. *IEEE Trans. Electronic Computers* EC-13:250–254, 1964.

10. The LINC computer. Quarterly Progress Report, Div. 5, The Lincoln Laboratory, Massachusetts Institute of Technology, Lexington, Massachusetts, September 15, 1961, p. 1.

11. Clark, W.A. The LINC was early and small. *Proc. of the ACM Conference on the History of Personal Workstations*, January 1986, pp. 133–155.

12. Behrer, M.R., Glaeser, D.H., Cox, J.R., and Woolf, R.B. Quantification of the fetal electrocardiogram through LINC computer processing. *American Journal of Obstetrics and Gynecology* 102:4:537–548, October 1968.

13. Hon, E.H. Instrumentation of fetal heart rate and fetal electrocardiography. *Am. J. Obst. and Gynec.* 86:6:772–784, 1963.

14. Cox, J.R., Gallagher, T.L., Holmes, W.F., and Powers, W.E. Programmed console: An aid to radiation treatment planning. *Proc. Eighth IBM Medical Symposium*, April 1967, p. 179–188.

15. Cox, J.R., Fozzard, H.A., Nolle, F.M., and Oliver, G.C. AZTEC, a preprocessing program for real-time rhythm analysis. *IEEE Trans. on Biomedical Engr.* BME-15:2:128–129, April 1968.

16. Cox, J.R., Fozzard, H.A., Nolle, F.M., and Oliver, G.C. Some data transformations useful in electrocardiography. *Computers in Biomedical Research III*, Stacy, R.W. and Waxman, B.D., (eds.). New York: Academic Press, 1969, pp. 181–206.

17. Nolle, F.M. and Clark, K.W. Detection of premature ventricular contractions using an algorithm for cataloging QRS complexes. *Proc. of the San Diego Biomedical Symposium*, 10:85–97, March 1971.

18. Oliver, G.C., Nolle, F.M., Tiefenbrunn, A.J., and Clark, K.W. A study of the effect of the Argus computer system on treatment actions in a coronary care unit. *The American Journal of Cardiology* 29:284, 1972.

19. Cox, J.R., Nolle, F.M., and Arthur, R.M. Digital analysis of the electroencephalogram, the blood pressure wave, and the electrocardiogram. *Proc. of the IEEE* 60:1137–1164, 1972.

20. Hermes, R.E. and Oliver, G.C. Use of the American Heart Association database. *Ambulatory Electrocardiographic Recording*. Wenger, N.K.,

Mock, M.B., and Ringquist, I., (eds.). Chicago: Year Book Medical Publishers, 1981, pp. 165–181.

21. Chernoff, D., Lee, T., Moody, G., and Mark, R. Evaluation of R-R interval predictors using an annotated ECG database. *Proc. of Computer in Cardiology*, 1981, pp. 359–362.

Participants' Discussion

Octo Barnett	In hindsight, what would you say were the most important opportunities you failed to understand the importance of, or take advantage of, in your long career?
Jerry Cox	Well, we tried to get radiation oncologists to communicate with each other by means of a network back in the early 1970s. We thought it would be a good idea to have a network of radiation oncologists sharing their data. There were problems that I didn't anticipate having to do with sensitivities about letting data out of their hands before they'd skimmed off all the cream. Maybe if I'd persevered a little longer we could have made some progress on that front. I still think that's an important area.
Donald Lindberg	How did macro modules come to St. Louis?
Jerry Cox	They came because Wes Clark and Charlie Molnar came to St. Louis. Wes, can you tell us?
Wesley Clark	Charlie and I had formulated the general idea of macro modules while we were at MIT. After we went to St. Louis, we worked together on the macro module project for seven years. It was funded by both NIH and ARPA at the level of $1.5 million per year, so it was a big project. The objective was to develop a set of hardware building blocks that would work together in a system the way programmers put software programming modules together. The idea was that the engineering problems would be pre-solved in the macro modules, which would then be used to build systems. If the system design were logically correct, then the system would work.
	We built several hundred of the modules, in less than a dozen types. They were the size of a large brick, and a system built from them could be any size. Over the seven years, we built hundreds of systems of different kinds. They were easy to assemble and disassemble, so the modules could be used again.
	After I left, Charlie had the same funding for two more years. The modules were redesigned, then the project was terminated. The work is

now resurfacing in integrated circuit technology where VLSI is achieved by putting integrated circuits together out of a library of standard cells. The standard cells are updated macro modules.

Our biggest problem was timing and synchronization among the modules, and our work on synchronization was a major contribution to the field. If you want to find out more about macro modules, Stacy and Waxman's *Computers in Biomedical Research*, volume 4, has a key paper by Charlie and me. There's also an interesting paper by Jerry Cox on the use of macro modules in cardiac arrhythmia studies. Jerry actually built a system using macro modules for this purpose.

BANQUET ADDRESS

The conference was held in the National Library of Medicine, and there were no facilities for a large sit-down dinner. Consequently, the banquet was held at a Holiday Inn that the organizers said was within walking distance but, in reality, was a comfortable ride away.

The banquet speaker was Lawrence L. Weed, MD. Prior to the banquet, there was a half-hour presentation by Dr. Weed in the Lister Hill Center Auditorium. There were two reasons for this. First, we felt that it would be instructive for the attendees to understand Dr. Weed's current thinking so that they could see how his earlier work evolved. Second, this seemed like a pleasant interlude before cocktails.

Following a live demonstration of the Problem-Knowledge Coupler, the attendees assembled for cocktails and hors d'oeuvres. We then retired to the dining room for the banquet and address. The paper in this volume is an extension of the one included in the proceedings.

SPEAKER

Lawrence L. Weed The Premises and Tools of Medical Care and Medical Education: Perspectives Over 40 Years

Lawrence L. Weed, MD is Professor of Medicine Emeritus, University of Vermont (professor of Medicine 1969–1984). He currently works full time as president, PKC Corporation, a small software company that markets microcomputer-based medical software aids to clinical decision-making (the Problem-Knowledge Coupler). He received a BA degree from Hamilton College in 1943 and an MD degree from Columbia University in 1947. From 1961 to 1969 he was on the faculty of Case Western Reserve University. He joined the University of Vermont in 1969 as professor of Medicine, professor of Community Medicine (until 1979), and director of PROMIS Laboratory (until 1981).

The Premises and Tools of Medical Care and Medical Education: Perspectives Over Forty Years[1]

Lawrence L. Weed, MD
University of Vermont and PKC Corporation, South Burlington, Vermont

It has been said by some psychiatrists that there are just three categories of patients—"Poor me," "If it weren't for him" or "If it weren't for her," and "Change that kid, but don't change me." Well, when it comes to thinking about the past, each of us falls into one of another three categories. Of all the tapes we have in our memory banks, there are those who play only the bitter stories and the sad music; there are those play only the happy tunes and the triumphs, big or small; and there are those—and they are very rare—who play a balanced sample with an amazing objectivity and calm. And of course, we all occasionally play a tape that got into the collection by way of our imagination, not through any reality that anyone else can recall. The lost or damaged tapes never get played at all. For after all, as Santayana has said, for most of us, going through life is a slow movement from the forgotten to the unexpected.

Recognizing these ways in which we all function, I thought the best thing for me to do is to structure my recollections around a series of beliefs—those that I had when I entered medical school in the early 1940s and the parallel and very different set that I hold now in 1987. After I do this, I shall try to describe and explain some of the events that led to the changes. I shall conclude with some implications of these changes.

Before proceeding to the old and new beliefs, I should state at the outset a deeply held conviction that underlies everything that follows. Our study of the science of medical practice must now match in rigor and in elegance what has been our study of the science of disease. "Informatics" is the basic science of that effort. We must overcome the enormous "voltage drop" from the best that is known in medical science to what the average patient receives on the average encounter in the daily practice of medicine. If the information transfer from DNA to the working machinery of the cell were as disorganized and chaotic as it is across human minds and actions in the medical care system, many organisms would not survive, and those that did would be ridden with

---

[1] This paper includes several additions, some of which are new, and others of which are derived from articles written in the two years since the conference.

224

all sorts of malfunctions. "Basic science" for medical students, up until now, has been mainly involved with understanding how nature runs *its* information system; scientists are just now beginning to try to affect that system when errors arise. Whereas in medical practice, we must not only understand, but also conceive and implement, our own information system, one that rigorously couples the fruits of scholarly effort and research to the everyday actions of us all. We ourselves are the engine of our own extrasomatic evolution. Physical man has changed little over thousands of years. It is has been his tools and his beliefs that have enabled our civilization to develop. After 40 years I have come to the realization that the present premises and tools of medical education and medical care cannot support or even allow the proper evolutionary steps to take place. Much of our frustration after so much hard work has its roots in those flawed premises and inadequate tools. We can no longer take pride in only highly focused, brilliant efforts in research and take refuge in phrases like "pure science," dismissing the medical care system for all the people as "applied science" for lesser minds working in an environment of less intellectual rigor and discipline. The most difficult of intellectual challenges now lies ahead—developing a framework in which the brilliant pieces of understanding are routinely assembled into a working unit of social machinery that is as coherent and as error-free as possible—a challenge in which we ourselves are among the moving parts to be organized and brought under control. As Bertrand Russell said, "Not only will men of science have to grapple with the sciences that deal with man, but—and this is a far more difficult matter—they will have to persuade the world to listen to what they have discovered." And now on to the old and new beliefs.

1. As I entered medical school I believed that a core of knowledge must be taught and memorized.

   I now believe that a core of behavior, not a core of knowledge, must be inculcated. A person must be thorough, reliable, capable of defending the logic of his actions, and efficient in completing the tasks for which he or she is responsible. As John Ruskin said a century ago, "Education is not teaching people to know what they do not know. It is teaching them to behave as they do not behave."

2. I once believed it was possible to recall and process all the necessary variables at the bedside or in the clinic at the time of clinical action after one had mastered a core of knowledge.

   I now believe that we need electronic extensions of the human memory and analytical capacity at the time of action, just as we need X rays to extend the human eyes. Physicians should rely on such tools just as a traveler relies on maps instead of memorizing trips in geography courses. Faculties and researchers should keep the tools up-to-date.

3. I once believed that passing National Board and Specialty Board examinations could be used as an indicator of one's capacity to fulfill responsibility to patients over a lifetime.

I now believe that good medical practice can only be assured through a random audit of performance in the real world and that such an audit requires a defined system of care and the availability of up-to-date information tools.

4. I once believed that you could divide knowledge into academic packages—courses—and that defects in performance such as unethical behavior could be remedied by adding a new course to the curriculum.

I now believe that real problems in the real world—practical or theoretical problems—do not fit neatly into academic boundaries, and it is dangerous for professions serving real people to try to make them fit. Academic boundaries and specialties make us focus on the few things that patients with a given disease have in common; whereas the thousands of things they do not have in common may have far more to do with what action should be taken and what the outcome will be. Defects in the care process should be corrected either by updating the information tools provided for use at the time of care or by demanding a more disciplined use of the proper tools at the time of action. What is in the information tools will be determined by what the problem requires, regardless of the old classification systems for knowledge such as science, humanities, ethics, surgery, medicine, etc.

5. I once believed that physicians should be the principal force in choosing among diagnostic and therapeutic options for the patients.

I now believe that the patients themselves and their families should be the principal force and that they should always have a copy of their own problem-oriented records and use the up-to-date information tools in partnership with all medical personnel.

Let me go back 40 years and consider what might have led to these changes. The thing I most remember about those early years is not the actual material that we had to memorize, but simply the fact that we had so much to memorize—so much to regurgitate—so much to forget. Life for those first two years was a series of weekly quizzes, monthly exams, and finals in biochemistry, anatomy, physiology, etc.—the so-called basic sciences. Who could ever forget those after-lunch, numbing sessions in darkened lecture halls when neuroanatomy cross-section lantern slides went on day after day? Long after the details on those slides have been forgotten, stories about the experience remain forever. A friend told me that one day in his school he was wakened from a heavy sleep in just such a lecture by the crash of a student's body hitting the floor of the upper tier aisle of a steep, old-fashioned lecture hall. The side of his chair had broken, and the #8 billiard ball that he carried, as Linus carried his blanket, slipped from his hand and noisily went step by step to the feet of the elderly lecturer. As the whole class came out of its postprandial nap, the droning old professor went over and turned on the lights, bent over and picked up the billiard ball, and said with his thin, elderly, high-pitched voice, and with a rare wit that up until now had been hidden from the students, "Would the gentleman who just lost his head, kindly retrieve it."

And the memory game did not stop when we reached the clinical years. Anecdotes about feats of memory or embarrassing failures of memory were standard fare at the dinner table or in dormitory bull sessions. We were all so impressed when Dr. Loeb would walk onto a ward, see the face of a recently admitted patient, immediately recall her name and say her BUN in 1938 was 87 or some equally precise figure. And how vividly I remember the presentations we were expected to give from memory. One night I was up all night working up two new patients who were very sick and had very thick, old charts. I knew I would have to present to Dr. Loeb the next morning on metabolism rounds—I would have to say all the right things—say them from memory and not take too long. Tony, my patient, was in his teens, had Addison's disease, and was in an impending crisis. I began my presentation with: "Tony's disease began in early childhood, the pigmentation first being noted at age 7"—at which point that familiar voice of Dr. Loeb interrupted, saying "Weed, are you sure it was not at age 5?" You can imagine what that did to the programs and the files that I carried in my little personal computer of the 1940s—that little weary, up-all-night brain. The programs and the files were pretty messy to begin with—but after that interruption they were chaotic. It seemed that no debugging operation known to man could save the situation. But I did pull myself together and say, "Well, sir, I am sure I could be wrong, but age 7 must be somewhere in those thick charts—I would not just fabricate a figure for a presentation. Should we take the time to stop here and look through them?" Dr. Loeb said—"Well, Weed, that would take a lot of time, and I am not sure that is necessary." At that point a demon—indeed the devil himself—entered my weary, exhausted mind and body, and I said, "I have an idea Dr. Loeb. Let us ask Tony—he has heard his presentation so many times after so many admissions"—at which point that unforgettable smile of Dr. Loeb's came across his face, and he exclaimed, "Darn good idea, Weed," and he turned to Tony and asked him, "When did your skin start to get darker?" The answer was wonderful. Tony looked up, and with an unforgettable smile of his own, he said, "It began somewhere between the ages of 4 and 8." That broke up the assembled entourage, and Dr. Loeb said without hesitation, "We shall proceed; that point will not be pursued further."

I could go on for the rest of the evening with anecdotes over the next 40 years in seven different medical schools. But the striking thing in those early years was the almost total lack of discussion of the very nature of the vast reservoir of medical knowledge itself. How should its boundaries be defined? What should be put into courses? And what was the evidence that what had been chosen for courses actually related in rigorous ways to the care of patients? And even if it did, what evidence was there that our tired and bewildered minds could recall and process the almost infinite variety of facts and variables that highly specialized faculty members were forever pouring into our brains? How come we had a "basic science course" in biochemistry filled with intricate details about the Kreb's cycle, but we had no such course in basic psychology, when many, if not the majority of our patients, to say nothing of many of the students and faculty themselves, were beset with psychological problems and normal limitations on what the human mind can actually achieve. Think of how devastating it would be to the whole curriculum and all its pretentious board exams as a basis for licensure, if the students were reading papers by Tversky, *et al.* {1} and Kern, *et al.* {2} and books such as that of Wason and Johnson-Laird {3}, in which findings were neatly documented that provide a basis for the following assertions:

1. The human mind will start generating hypotheses in the earliest moments of encounters with patients and thereby prematurely bias the remaining steps in the search for data.

2. The mind will limit the number of hypotheses it generates to a number far smaller than the problem requires. We therefore do not fulfill our responsibility to the patients with the rare disorders. As Wason and Johnson-Laird state: "When the individual mind's logical ability is restricted, it will operate within heuristic or hit-or-miss procedures which do not guarantee a solution."

3. The mind will underestimate the complexity of problems, and it will overinterpret the data it does collect. It will indulge in the categorical reasoning of the expert.

4. The mind will take the probability information based on the studies of a very limited number of variables on large populations and let it supersede highly improbable but correct information on a very large number of variables on a unique patient, thereby often

getting the patient into trouble. The mind also applies inappropriate prevalence data in many of its calculations, placing a patina of quantitative and numerical respectability on to a not-so-respectable foundation of misguided and inaccurate estimations.

As Wason and Johnson-Laird have said:

> We like to think the educated human mind is capable of thinking in terms of propositions which take into account the possible and the hypothetical, and that the mind will be able to isolate the variables in the problem and subject them to combinatorial analysis which nicely exhausts the possibilities. {3}

But this of course as Wason, *et al.* point out, is exactly what most of their subjects failed to do.

And even more devastating to a curriculum committee would be to have one of their meetings interrupted by a poet coming back to life and reading one of her sonnets. Edna St. Vincent Millay wrote long ago (Sonnet 137):

> Upon this age that never speaks its mind,
> This furtive age, this age endowed with power
> To wake the moon with footsteps, fit an oar
> Into the rowlocks of the wind, and find
> What swims before its prow, what swirls behind —
> Upon this gifted age, in its dark hour.
> Rains from the sky a meteoric shower
> Of facts ... they lie unquestioned, uncombined.
> Wisdom enough to leech us of our ill
> Is daily spun, but there exists no loom
> To weave it into fabric.

Nor was anyone in the medical school ever suggesting that what the Tillichs and the Niebuhrs and even the Norman Vincent Peales were, in those days, saying in a different part of town may have as much to do with understanding the medical plight of our patients as anything that PhDs in anatomy and physiology were saying. As I think back on my early days in medicine, I am troubled not only at how much I was a prisoner of conventional wisdom, but also how unaware I was of the arbitrary nature and inherent ambiguities in much of what I was required to learn. Nor was I aware of how arbitrary were the boundaries between what I was preparing for and what others were doing in different fields. For example, as a student when we used to work over the CPCs in the New England Journal, week after week, no one told me (nor did I discover on my own) that the great Dr. Cabot who started the CPCs also wrote a book in 1926 entitled *The Adventures on the Borderland of Ethics*. In 1931 he was elected the president of the National Conference on Social Work, and in 1933 he wrote on "The Meaning of Right and Wrong" and in 1938 a book entitled *Honesty*. And of course Dr. Cabot can never know that a half-century later President Bok of Harvard would be lamenting in his article "Needed: A New Way to Train Doctors" {4} that a study of 400 medical students showed that 88% admitted having cheated at least once in college.

Among all the books that had been assigned to me, there was not included a little book called *A Study in Hospital Efficiency* by E.A. Codman {5}. We as medical students had no way of knowing that a physician up in Boston had, in 1918, written about all the problems that were bothering us—and furthermore, he offered some very concrete solutions. He stated at that time, "It is not idle to say that we have not already much truth at our disposal, but it can be said that we should find more truthful ways in which to use it." Not only was his book not known to the medical students, it was not in a standard publication. He had to publish it himself, and his reasons for having to do so tell us much about the problems he faced with the university, the journals, and the hospitals. In that day, medical students were insulated from the political controversies that swirled around them, and they are insulated today. And that insulation will continue as long as the students are burdened with courses, computer simulations of, and examinations on accumulated wisdom. Only real and current problems, honestly confronted, can immunize the students against the misconceptions and generalizations of those who teach. And like all immunizations, they only work if you get there before the invasion and the damage have taken place.

We were so busy memorizing and regurgitating—going over hurdle after hurdle—that there was no time left to reflect and think philosophically about the system we found ourselves in. We were so consumed with doing the thing right, that we had neither the time nor the courage to ask, "Are we doing the right thing?" Indeed, the basic premises that underlie most human endeavors are rarely surfaced and brought into question until there is a crisis. Our instinct for survival under somebody else's rules and our capacity for compartmentalization in our tired minds is phenomenal. Nor were the premedical years, in even the best colleges, considered a golden opportunity to think about what the practice of medicine was all about. Premedical students seemed almost more consumed by mindless preoccupation with high grades in chemistry and biology prerequisites than were the sheep-like, unquestioning medical students.

I was one of those highly compartmentalized medical students. When, I have often asked myself, did my vague unease with the system begin to crystallize into sharp and clear perceptions? In that first very unhappy year of medical school, I remarked to Dr. Sherry Washburn, the distinguished physical anthropologist and at that time one of our anatomy teachers, that I wish I could work with real tissues that were not some hardened-with-formalin cadaver, and take a surgical anatomy book and just do operations—take out kidneys, etc.—so that I could get a feel for the real thing. He found me a little room, and he would give me cats and dogs and an occasional primate left over from ongoing experiments in departments in the medical school and university. It saved my life. At least for part of the day I was in the driver's seat—not a slave to the syllabi and schedules of a content-driven basic science faculty. He then asked me to help teach the human anatomy part of an anthropology course he was to give that summer.

I was determined that I would not make others suffer the way I had felt I was suffering in that first year in medical school. The first thing I did was to tell the students that no one should buy a book until I gave the go-ahead. I then showed each individually how to use a scalpel, what arteries, veins, muscles, nerves, and visceral organs looked like—and then said make believe you are Vesalius—begin to dissect and explore—putting your own names on things and guessing what the functions of a given muscle might be. After a few weeks had gone by and they were intellectually in charge of their own situations, I said, "Now buy a book and see what Spalteholtz or some other great anatomist thinks." It was at that point that I was beginning to realize that the first two years of medical school were so devastating because one was forever memorizing observations which one had never made and memorizing answers to questions which one had never asked. Years were to go by before I realized how toxic to the healthy mind memory-based credentialing systems can be. For many medical students, the damage seems almost irreversible. Indeed, it was at the end of that summer during the war that I thought of leaving medical school, but I was in a Navy program, and the officer in charge said, "We have reviewed your college record; you are capable of meeting the requirements. Stop bitching and get to work. If you flunk out I personally shall see that you shall not follow your brother and your father to the Far Eastern theater of war, but you will wash dishes in the Brooklyn Navy Yard or be tied to a desk in some recruiting station in the Bronx." And so I labored on.

After several clinical years I wanted to try my hand at some basic research in biochemistry—particularly in nucleic acid chemistry. I went to Dr. Palmer, the chief of Medicine at Columbia at the time, and we talked about the great things going on in the biochemistry department at the University of Pennsylvania. He said he would call Dr. Wilson (the department chairman) and recommend me, but they may want me to do nothing but biochemistry—no dabbling a day a week in the clinic or running off to grand rounds. "You know," Dr. Palmer said to me, "the sad part about all this is, if you are very good in research you will probably never come back to clinical medicine, and if you are bad or mediocre you will come back—so sometimes I am not so sure about the end result of such recommendations"—but, nevertheless, he got me settled in that land where the great Meyerhof was still giving seminars, the new isotope methods were opening up all sorts of exciting matters in intermediary metabolism, and best of all, the very character and integrity of Dr. Wilson himself permeated the atmosphere of the lab I worked in. I learned then that ethics is not a series of abstractions in some course, but it is what you feel and hear and see among your leaders as you work every day.

It was in this period, when I was working day after day with PhDs and graduate students in biochemistry, that I began to see the world in a very different way than I had seen it as a medical student. PhDs worked on one or two problems at a time—they lived and breathed a single problem—they read extensively about the problem—they wrote papers on it. In their lives, time and tasks were variables and achievement the constant. One or two tasks at a time—and the necessary time and grant money were made available until peers reviewed the work, and it was published. Experiments could be carefully designed and variables could be controlled. In contrast, a doctor or a medical student did not have one problem—one patient could have five problems and there were 30 patients on the ward and hundreds on the rolls of the clinic. Time was not set by the doctor—the appendix would perforate on its timetable, not the doctor's. There was nothing in the life of the PhD that would equip him to prepare medical students for a world of multiple tasks in limited time with widely varying levels of achievement, with the lives and comfort of real human beings involved at every step. Basic science faculty had been led to believe that somehow, if they could just get the facts into a medical student's head, he would always be able to recall them and would be able to integrate them properly into the complex problem situations that he would confront day after day. The medical students were being stuffed with the facts of basic science, but could it be that the behavior of a scientist was escaping them—indeed would it not be impossible for anyone to exhibit good scientific behavior under the conditions of modern medical education—multiple PhDs and MDs converging on the single mind of medical student—all under the premise that a mind so exposed could store, recall, and process all the appropriate variables at the time of problem solving in the real world.

Medical education and care, with their board exams and licenses based on them, were also contradictory to the world of the professional musician, the professional athlete, the vigorous business man, or the research scientist. For them, quality has always been defined as the excellence with which a well-defined function is performed. In medicine, quality has been defined as that which people with credentials do, and only others with credentials have a right to judge it—even though everyone knows those credentials may represent nothing more than a passing grade on an examination taken many years ago. Furthermore, examination results had never been shown to consistently reveal what the examinee would do when confronted with a real problem in the real world under all sorts of conditions. Suppose some regulatory agency had scrutinized the credentialing process of the human mind with the same rigor that the Food and Drug Administration looks at a new drug or a new instrument. Had they done so they would have found that the production standards and the requirements for ongoing quality control of the output of the credentialed human mind are far below any standards we use for any drug or instrument. How ironic, for it is the "educated, credentialed" human mind that orders the drugs and makes all the decisions that set all the various technologies into motion.

Thoughts similar to the above came to me with a special force after finishing my time in biochemistry at Penn and after a stay in the army and clinical time at Johns Hopkins. In a joint appointment in pharmacology and medicine at Yale I lived in three worlds: the world of clinical medicine, the world of nucleic acid research, and the world of teaching the endless details about drugs to medical students. On one occasion, after dumping a particularly large load of pharmacology details on the heads of the second year class, my mind, without warning, brought to the surface recollections from George Eliot's *Middlemarch*. In a small English town, there was this lovely young girl who aspired to higher things, and, to her, an opportunity to assist and work with the local scholarly bachelor, Mr. Casaubon, was everything an ambitious young lady could hope for. He had a large house, a large library, and many scholarly pursuits. He was always working on his store of knowledge and was in Eliot's words "as genuine a character as any ruminant animal, and he had not actively assisted in creating any illusions about himself." Eventually, as they worked together, the less scholarly aspects of Mr. Casaubon's physiology were awakened, a courtship ensued, and marriage took place. And it was several weeks after the marriage that, in Eliot's words, "Dorothea had not distinctly observed but felt with a stifling depression, that the large vistas and wide fresh air which she had dreamed of finding in her husband's mind were replaced by anterooms and winding passages which seemed to lead nowhither." Were the minds of these medical students just mindlessly collecting undigested facts in dim dark corridors that would lead to nowhere—nowhere but to depression and bad habits of thought? What was I doing to the students' minds? What would their minds eventually do to the patients? Was all this "educational malpractice" that someday would lead to "medical malpractice," with the patients and the students becoming the ultimate victims, and we, the faculty, escaping unharmed and totally unaware that we were the root of the problem?

And from that world of teaching facts, one day I walked onto the ward as an attending physician and said, "Do not present a new patient in the usual fashion. I want to know where we stand on each of the problems we discussed on my last visit—and be like a good graduate student, bring me your manuscript and notebooks—I want to see the problems, the data, and the conclusions and all subsequent actions on the problems." "What notebook?" they asked. And I said, "Your notebook must be the patient's chart. Bring it to me—the chart on the patient we discussed last time." And suddenly I realized that there is no complete list of problems, just a few "impressions" written on the night of admission and never updated. The plans we had discussed on the previous visit were not unambiguously recorded for each problem, and there were no problem-oriented progress notes and no flow sheets to reveal to us the logic and the results of what we as doctors and scientists were trying to do. How could we define quality as the excellence with which a well-defined function is performed when we never defined clearly what medical care should be—how defined and how recorded. We simply measured what people knew on an arbitrary examination at one moment in time and equated it with good care over a lifetime and gave the person a license.

And so I left Yale to become the director of Medical Education at the Eastern Maine General Hospital in Bangor, Maine. The first order of business was to develop a problem-oriented medical record as the very basis for treating an intern as a graduate student and for evaluating the quality of the care provided by the staff. The second chore was to get an adequate library so that the physicians could look things up when they did not know. And my job was to be the reader and the auditor of the records—the scientific manuscripts that represented the efforts in medical care. We would no longer teach a core of knowledge—we would teach a core of behavior. Was the physician thorough—was the database defined and complete, was every problem on the list, was there a plan for each of the problems, and did progress notes, titled with a specific problem, show that the plan was carried out? Was the physician reliable—were the findings in the chart accurate? Was the physician analytically sound—could he defend every plan within the context of the other problems and with references or common knowledge in the basic sciences? As the actual data unfolded in the progress notes and on the flow sheets, did the physician draw logical conclusions and make reasonable adjustments? Was the physician efficient as he cared for the patients in such a defined system?[2]

No matter where I went in American medicine, from the most prestigious medical centers to the most isolated solo physician, we found that few could meet the standards that their credentials suggested and that a well-defined system of problem-oriented care required. Memory-based, credentialed specialists had become chairmen of departments and deans; they had formed their own fiefdoms with their own provincial ways of keeping records, setting fees, and teaching students and residents. To this day, most of them have not worked together to establish a single, problem-oriented, computerized medical record system throughout an institution and a community, with the patient, at all times, having a copy of that record in his or her own hands. It is like the situation that existed over a century-and-a-half ago when the great railroad barons and tycoons had trouble agreeing on a single gauge track that would have effected enormous efficiencies in the transportation of all sorts of materials over a broad geographic area.

But it was with just such a grand scheme in mind, that we undertook the development of the PROMIS computerized system to support the human memory and to help in the coordination of the many providers working on a single patient. It is not possible to review here the many years covered by the PROMIS experience.[3] Suffice it to say for now that the PROMIS system soon revealed that when you solve the memory problem of the human mind, you uncover a processing limitation that is even worse than the memory limitation. That is to say, with 55,000 displays of medical details instantly available at the doctor's fingertips, he could be overwhelmed by the task of integrating the relevant details from the unique patient with the relevant details now so instantly available on a computer screen. We came face-to-face with the realities and complexities in decision making that had been hidden under terms such as "clinical judgment" and "intuition" and "experience." The hallucinatory fulfillment for students and faculty alike was rudely interrupted. Ian Lawson, in a commentary on the problem-oriented medical record he wrote some years ago, captured the essence of much that was becoming apparent in the presence of new tools and new premises. As he stated,

[2]   References on the Problem-Oriented Medical Record System will be found in {6–11, 16}. The references to Bjorn and Cross and Hurst were chosen from the many available because their efforts and leadership played such a crucial role in the early days.

[3]   The reader may begin an exploration of that period with articles by Schultz on "A History of the PROMIS Technology"; by Cantrill on the "Computerization of the problem-oriented record"; by Hertzberg, Schultz, and Wanner on, "The PROMIS Network"; and by Weed on, "The Representation of Medical Knowledge" {12–14, 32}. In the latter paper I included the names of all the PROMIS staff that were involved in that broad collaborative effort over many years.

> The POMR sets out to affect the basic attitudes of professionals toward people problems, as well as their formal logic in patient care. It compels relationships and interdependencies as conditions of physician conduct. And, now, through computer technology, it draws us into a thoroughgoing consistency, which is unfamiliar to most natures and threatening to our tolerated caprices. {15}

We all knew in a commonsense way that decisions could go wrong if you were making them without enough information to start with or if the so-called facts in the situation were not accurate. The decision could also go wrong if you did not know how to interpret the facts. Medical training, as most of us had known it, had not equipped us to come to terms with this difficult situation. Some turned to mathematicians, psychologists, and computer scientists for help. Many of those people, in turn, focused mainly on the intelligent manipulation of the facts that their medical colleagues gave to them—paying little attention to the inaccuracy and incompleteness and highly provincial nature of the data that was flowing from a deeply flawed medical care system. The data came from a memory-based, credential-oriented group of medical providers—many of whom were specialists who were not linked to one another in a highly disciplined fashion and who, in many cases, kept sloppy medical records. Such records and a medical literature system that has been severely criticized for its lack of quality control standards have been the underlying basis for their "expert" opinions and uninhibited intuitive leaps to conclusions about diagnoses and management options.

All of this has led to much magnificent navigation to the wrong port. There were calculations of probabilities before many relevant and easily available variables had been isolated and taken into account. There seemed to be a disregard of the idea that one uses probabilities in direct proportion to one's ignorance of the uniqueness of the situation. Combinatorial thinking, on the other hand, that seeks out the uniqueness of a situation and that exhausts all the possibilities in a complex diagnostic or management situation is as much beyond the unaided mind as modern astronomy is beyond the unaided human eye. And yet here we are in 1987 still examining students on what they know instead of on how gracefully and effectively they interface with the areas of their ignorance when others are trusting them to solve a problem. Patients are not interested in what is probable among large numbers of patients based on a few variables—nor are they interested primarily in what the "expert" knows—they are interested in what is wrong with them—no matter how improbable and unique their situation might be. And knowing the power of uniqueness in making wise choices among diagnostic and management options, we realize how serious have been the consequences of our neglect of all the details in the complex lives of patients—how easy it was to operate on a meager set of facts that we could hold in the memory or elicit from an incomplete and disorganized medical record. And how easy it was to neglect the patient's role in his own behalf. If the patient and the families do not understand and do not have the right tools to work with, then the most sophisticated efforts in the information sciences may come to naught {16}.

In that regard, I remember one day when I was the attending physician on the computerized ward with all the displays and incredible electronic linkages to other services, they wanted to present a patient to me. I said, "Do not present a new patient; tell me who is going home today." The nurse volunteered the name of a middle-aged woman who had lupus for 10 years. I suggested they give me 15 minutes with the patient and then they could return for discussion. I asked the patient to tell me all she knew about each of her problems. She knew very little.

"Do you have a copy of your own medical record?"

" No."

"Are all your medications in the bedside stand, and does the nurse come around at regular intervals to see if you are taking the right ones at the right time?"

"No. The nurse just comes with little paper cups with pills in them and I swallow whatever is there."

"Do you know what a flow sheet is—what parameters we are trying to follow—what endpoints we are trying to reach?"

"No."

At this point I called the staff back together and told them what I had found. Their reactions were:

"We never give patients their records."

"We do not have the time to give her medicines that way, and besides it would not be safe to leave her with them unattended—she is on many powerful drugs."

"The patient is not very well educated, and I do not think she could do all the things your questions imply."

"But," I said, "you said she is going home. She lives alone. At 2 P.M. you will put her in a wheelchair, give her a paper bag full of drugs, and send her out the door. Are you going home with her?"

"*No*! Is her management at home our problem?"

"You just said she could not handle it—who will do it? The patient may not be very well educated or seem very bright to you—but how could anything be more stupid than what we are doing?"

We must think of the *whole* information system and not just infinitely elaborate on the parts that interest us or fit a given specialty.

Patients do not specialize, and they or their families are in charge of all of the relevant variables—they are the most neglected source of better quality and savings in the whole health care system. After all:

1. They are highly motivated (and if they are not, nothing works in the long run anyway).
2. They do not charge, they even pay to help.
3. There is one for every member of the population.

In the time remaining, we could go into greater depth on any one of the aspects mentioned above or on the details of how a "knowledge-coupling" system was developed on microcomputers (by Richard Hertzberg, Christopher Weed, Laura Weed, and myself) for overcoming the "voltage drop" from the best that is known for solving a specific problem to what is actually done for the average patient on the average encounter in American medicine {17–21}. There has already been enough experience with the new tools in medical practice to show that they are practical and that it is realistic to operate under new premises. Let it suffice for this evening to summarize what a Knowledge Coupler can do for a practitioner:

1. It reminds him of the appropriate things to elicit on the history and physical examination, given a specific problem.
2. A list of the positive findings is immediately available on a screen or on paper for both provider and patient.
3. It organizes the findings in terms of possible causes (or Management Options in the Management Coupler) and in some Couplers also in terms of physiological function.

How well the findings in the unique patient "match" the causes or Management Options in the system are immediately apparent to the user.

The Knowledge Coupler software does not do any mathematical manipulations and present the user with calculated probabilities. This is not attempted because the exact "weight" to give for each finding for each cause is not known, since in medicine we have never kept records of the necessary quality. Furthermore, we do not know the prevalence of each of the possibilities in the population from which our patient comes, and finally we do not know where in the course of the disease the patient is. For example, in early appendicitis, there may be epigastric pain but no right lower quadrant pain; later in the disease the reverse may be true. Nor could any human "expert" know such details beforehand to insert into any computer program. In fact, differential weighting may be necessarily inappropriate in most cases if the findings and set of possible causes have been well chosen. Powerful support for this conclusion can be found in Dawes's work, *Linear Models in Decision Making* {29–31}. A Problem-Knowledge Coupler can be thought of as a set of linked linear models (one linear model per primary option). The models are linked in the sense that in general any two of them will employ some of the same finding variables and in the sense that all the primary options stand in a specific common relationship to the topic of the Coupler.

Having given a brief review of what a Knowledge Coupler is, I would like to use the remaining time to reflect on the devastating effects of wrong premises on the educational system {22} and to discuss how the present situation may have evolved and how new premises and new information tools can extricate us from the extraordinary difficulties in which we now find ourselves.

First of all, consider the evils of a memory-based system. Since knowledge is forever expanding, and since each specialist is bent on stuffing everything he knows into the students when he has them, the student has no opportunity to think about the nature of the task—the nature of the knowledge and the results of its usage. The student is literally consumed by the process of memorizing and regurgitating. It is as if all travelers must have a degree in geography, must have sat through lectures by specialists on every geographic region, and must travel from memory and have credentials based on passing exams on the territory they want to travel over. But the real world of transportation is not that way. Everyone can travel anywhere with a set of maps, minimal background, and no credentials.

As a medical student I never gave a thought to the nature of medical knowledge—the epistemology that was the basis of my whole career. In the whole matter of making a diagnosis, I never reflected much on the word itself—that it involved just a specialized classification system, and that great minds had struggled for decades, even hundreds of years, over the underlying principles of taxonomy, the science of classifying things. I passed my organic chemistry in college by memorizing and regurgitating a few formulas, but the whole field of evolutionary biology escaped me. Not only had I not read Darwin's musings in a very thoughtful manner, but in later years I was not reading authors like Sneath and Sokal, numerical taxonomists who were saying,

> It is the self-reinforcing circular arguments used to establish categories, which on repeated application invest the latter with the appearance of possessing objective and definable reality. This type of reasoning is, of course, not restricted to taxonomy—but it is no less fallacious on that account. A group assumes a degree of permanence and reality quite out of keeping with the tentative basis on which it was established {23}.

Tolstoy seemed to understand the essence of what they were saying when he wrote in *War and Peace*:

She could not eat or sleep, grew visibly thinner, coughed, and as the doctors made them feel, was in danger. They could not think of anything but how to help her. Doctors came to see her singly and in consultation, talked much in French, German and Latin, blamed one another, and prescribed a great variety of medicines for all the diseases known to them, but the simple fact never occurred to any of them, that they could not know the disease that Natasha was suffering from, as no disease suffered by a live man can be known, for every living person has his own peculiar, personal, novel, complicated disease unknown to medicine—not a disease of the lungs, liver, skin, heart, nerves, and so on, mentioned in medical books, but a disease consisting of one of the innumerable combinations of the maladies of those organs. This simple thought cannot occur to the doctors, as it cannot to the wizard who is unable to work his charms. {24}

Medical students are made to feel stupid, and patients made to feel guilty when they overhear themselves being identified as "turkeys" or "neurotic," as both patients and students struggle with the inconsistencies among experts, and when their unique situations do not match the textbook pictures and averages and do not yield neatly to the mathematical manipulations based on flawed premises and inadequate or unreliable data. In our training, we were always so busy meeting the demands of superiors, made according to their beliefs, that we never read about the history of people like Codman and the Mayo brothers who were locking horns with prestigious medical schools and the organized hierarchies of American medicine. We never demanded logical and rigorous connections between what we were memorizing and what we would someday do in the total context of patients lives. We just assumed that somehow a complete and evenly working system would evolve out of a group of scientists and specialists of all sorts making their living out of their chosen specialized part of the human body. It should have been in the middle of our medical development, instead of alone in some forgotten college course, that we should have heard the cynical belief of Malthus that we would always be victims of the insensible bias of situation and interest {25}. Medicine has had, and will always have, its counterparts to the Jay Goulds, the Andrew Carnegies, and the Whitneys of the business world {25}. They had, and physicians have, their apologists who translate unconscionable, even cutthroat behaviors, and unbalanced distribution of resources and rewards into words and phrases like thrift, dedication, and pure science. All people in medicine are subject to the passion that Karl Marx said was among the most violent to inhabit the human breast—the passion of self-interest.

As we now grapple with the relevance of the efforts of each individual to the whole health care enterprise with all of its humanitarian and scientific aspects, it is in the articulation of new premises for medical care and education and in the creation of new tools and information systems that all the pieces can be brought together into a meaningful whole—a framework for creative and productive activity in a science of medical practice. We no longer need to be, in Le Corbusier's phrase, "A spectacle of fragments of intention." We are now in a position to move much of medicine from the philosopher Karl Popper's World 2 to his World 3—from the world of our notions, our intuitions, our judgments, our mystique to a world of objective reality that is open to criticism and logical correction of defects as they appear. Memory-based, credential-oriented systems, with their "habits of certainty" and obscure dark corners of mystique must now be abandoned. Compassionate concern without competence and accountability is always in danger of becoming fraud and malpractice. Patients have to come to terms with the fact that on any single medical encounter, they have to assume that from time to time they will fall into the hands of persons who are the lowest common denominator of the system, and we all therefore should focus more on how that system runs. There will be more than enough room for the mystical aspects of human interactions in medicine to flourish once a sound base for those interactions is consistently and uniformly established—in fact, the "art" of medicine will just be moved to a much higher plane. As Beryl Markham said in her reminiscences about flying,

> After this era of great pilots is gone, as the era of great sea captains has gone—each nudged aside by the march of inventive genius, by steel cogs and copper discs and hair-thin wires on white faces that are dumb, but speak—it will be found, I think, that all the science of flying has been captured in the breadth of an instrument board, but not the religion of it.

Once we stop examining physicians on what they know and start examining them on how effectively they serve other human beings with modern information tools that have built into them the parameters of guidance and the currency of information for doing each job correctly in the context of an individual's life—then will we be able to return to that era of a century ago that Sloan the historian described—that era when moral philosophy was the most important course in the college curriculum {26}. It was usually taught by the college president. In Sloan's words, "It was the capstone of the curriculum—it aimed to pull together, to integrate, to give meaning and purpose to the student's entire college experience. Even more important, it sought to equip graduating seniors with the ethical sensitivity and insight needed to put their newly acquired knowledge to use in ways that would benefit themselves and the larger society. Intellectual unity was required as the essential safeguard against moral and cultural chaos." He quotes Horace Mann as saying that schools are "the balance wheel of the social machinery."

But what happened as the century came to a close and our own century began? Knowledge expanded, subject matter demanded to be included in the curriculum, and fragmentation was underway. You and I think of Adam Smith as the first great economist, but he was, first and foremost in his day, a professor of moral philosophy. In our time, his career and the courses he taught have splintered into political science, economics, philosophy, philosophical ethics, psychology, anthropology, and sociology. Fewer and fewer teachers could teach by the example of the breadth and moral concerns of their own lives. Sloan says, "Faculties became trained experts. And emphasis on ethics gave way to an emphasis on research and specialized training." Scholarly productivity consumed us all. And now what are some of the products of that objective, scientific scholarly activity? We have a massive mixture of the good and the bad—thalidomide and penicillin, Three Mile Island and relativity, modern plastics and undrinkable water supplies.

If we are ever to recapture the intellectual unity that is the "essential safeguard against moral and cultural chaos," and still not be nihilistic about the advancing technology and ever-expanding knowledge, we must change the premises of our educational system. The new tools for extending our minds at the time of action allow us to do that. But many of us just keep extolling the virtues of the modern information tools while we do nothing to change the premises that underlie the system in which they must operate. Suppose they had given the new printing press just to the monks so they alone could copy their manuscripts faster as opposed to letting it, in Thomas Carlyle's words, "cashier in kings and senates and introduce a whole new democratic world."

In many places, we have literally done little more than automate the chaos, or use the tools in ingenious ways to "pick up after" erratic, unaided human minds as they set all sorts of misguided clinical activities into motion, instead of guiding the actions in the first place. Our very use of phrases like "expert systems" and "artificial intelligence" suggested to many that we had yet to admit that many "experts" and many an unaided intelligence cannot do what patients and third-party payers had always assumed they could do. And knowing the studies in the literature, e.g., {1–3}, that have already demonstrated the limitations of the unaided mind, we still hear demands for controlled studies to prove that new tools are better than what we are now doing. When we introduced the X ray machine to extend the unaided human eye and ear, we did not talk about "artificial eyes" and evaluate the adequacy of X ray by comparing its results to the vision of "experts" in clinical medicine. Nor did we try to use X rays alone without the added modalities of stethoscopes and histories and physical examinations. Indeed, one professor said he thought computerized knowledge coupling tools may have some advantages, but he, with his broad experience, would only use them on the difficult case. How would we react if we heard a person say that he thinks the telescope is an interesting, even powerful idea, but because of his years of experience in looking at the sky, he would only use the telescope when he sees something unusual up there. When will we admit that the human capacity to recall and process many variables must be extended with new tools if the patients are ever to consistently receive the best that medical science has to offer? The veto power of credentialed "experts" is awesome because we have vested in them the power to counter logic, not with evidence and more logic, but with authority.

Were I teaching biochemistry or microbiology with these new tools in place, I would not be overwhelming students with tricky exams with multiple-choice questions about a thousand possible metabolic pathways; but I would ask them to stand back and notice all the things that a single *E. coli* can make (e.g., vitamins and amino acids) with just a little salt water and minimal nutrients thrown in, something that no human can do. I would also point out that the civilization of *E. coli* is not very sophisticated—just a division every 50 minutes. No single cell of a multicellular human being can stand alone quite as well as an *E. coli*, yet human cells working together in a highly organized environment form a higher organism which in turn has developed a higher civilization. As the cells came together to do bigger things, each gave up its autonomy in order to do its specialized functions better, but yet do them in the context of the other cells of the organism.

Now the time has come to think in more precise terms about how the single cells of society, human individuals, communicate to accomplish larger goals. Complexity demands that one have the right combination of people, tools, and philosophy to deal with that complexity in an effective and productive manner. Whole systems must be thought out in advance. One individual cannot, all at the same time, be the cartographer who makes maps and the busy traveler who uses them. And in medicine, the options on the medical landscape must be laid out in great detail and then made available to patients and providers alike at the time of action. Modern knowledge coupling tools are now available to do that {14–18}—we just must get on to using them. The expert cartographer cannot tell you what your trip should be—but neither can you make the best possible trip without his map. There are almost an infinite number of trips on the map, but each of them must be made within the restrictions of the rules of the road and the traveler's needs and destination. Quality of travel does not require that unique individuals make identical trips. Quality of total medical care to an individual will be the sum total of the legitimacy of the options used in his care and the assurance of adherence to the logical connections among the diagnostic and management options and unique character- istics and goals of the individual patient as defined by modern knowl- edge coupling tools as opposed to fallible human memories and processing capabilities. Quality of a provider's performance cannot be defined by outcomes since outcomes are due to more variables that the provider has control over. Providers can only be fairly judged against the rules of the system and those rules must be consistent with human capabilities. Outcomes are then used to judge and improve the system of care itself.

For society to grapple with its problems and with problem solving in all areas where complexity is overwhelming us, we need to evolve a nervous system that can precisely connect the parts—and that is exactly what our computer information systems are beginning to do. If the professors of moral philosophy of 150 years ago had had our tools, they would have been able to master and control details and construct cor- rective feedback loops without being swallowed up by the ugly, non- cumulative, stultifying process of memorizing, regurgitating, and forgetting—all in the name of higher education. We should at least call it lower education—reminding ourselves on a daily basis how back- ward we are. Students should be colleagues using these modern tools to build with us—recognizing by their daily efforts as John Dewey said, "There is an inseparable relationship between knowledge and action, research and its consequences, science and ethics, the natural world and human values." He proclaimed against the fallacy of selective em- phasis.

We are now in a position to heed, in very specific ways, Whitehead when he said that it is a misconception, particularly among educated people, that you can think about what you are doing at the time you are doing it in a complex task, or that civilization rises in direct propor- tion to its capacity to put complex tasks at the unconscious level.

Let me now express some concluding thoughts. It is true, as Boorstin {27} the historian has said, that often the enemy of new knowl- edge is old knowledge—scholars who knew Ptolemy's maps had greater difficulty recognizing a new continent than those who had never learned that America could not be there. And since modern infor- mation tools can do things that the unaided human mind cannot do, when we use such tools we may see a picture of medicine that we have not seen before. The most experienced, the most highly credentialed "experts" may be the ones who find it most difficult to accept the new ambiguities and the contradictions to our present "knowledge." John Milton found it difficult to accept the telescope. It presented a picture of the universe different from his own. Pride in one's knowledge can be one's worst enemy—particularly too much pride in the knowing itself. For when you become proud of what you know, you are in danger of becoming imprisoned by the boundaries of what your limited human mind can know, and you do not get on to the business of building, and using consistently, the tools you need to mobilize crucial knowledge at the time of problem solving in the real world. Never again should we judge people or empower people on the basis of what they know or once did know. We all should be judged on what we do. Nor should time and tasks be the constant and achievement the variable in education. Each human being is unique, and if each is to reach the highest level of achievement in what he does, then no two people can ever be expected to do the same number of tasks in the same amount of time to the same level of quality—and every individual should have at his disposal the best possible tools for doing one's work correctly.

Having changed basic premises and having introduced new tools, how then do we define a physician or a nurse? First of all, we should recognize that no one, no matter what the education, can acquire all possible technical skills in medicine, even if the best information tools are at one's fingertips. Nor can one be born with the patient, move out of town with the patient, or be available 24 hours a day, 7 days a week, all year round. The care of a human being over time is the efforts of many people, and the patient or the family should have a central role in coordinating all care. Although we all recognize the evils of specialization, for many of the tasks in medicine to be done at a high level of quality there is no alternative. The problem has been that the efforts of specialists have not been coordinated and in the context of the whole life of an individual. As Wendell Berry has said in the context of farming, "Specialization is thus seen to be a way of institutionalizing, justifying, and paying for a calamitous disintegration and scattering out of the various functions of character: workmanship, care, conscience, responsibility" {28}. Wendell Berry thinks of the modern one-crop farmer as an exploiter, whereas the old-fashioned, complete, ideal farmer is a nurturer. For him the standard of the exploiter is efficiency, the standard of the nurturer is health—his land's health, his own, his family's, his community's, his country's. Our goal must be to develop a system of medical care whereby each individual is the "nurturer" of his own health care, and where he has available to him the guidance of an overall information system and the skills of the best trained specialists. Until such a framework is in place, and the patient is in charge, our situation can only grow worse. The exploitive nature of the specialist will get out of control. In Berry's terms, "The specialists are profiting too well from the symptoms to be concerned about cures (prevention of the situation in the first place). The problems become the stock in trade of specialists."

The time I had this evening is limited, and so I neglected many aspects of my experiences in biochemistry, internal medicine, and computerized problem-oriented systems. As exciting and as profitable as many of the individual experiences were, it is my preoccupations with making the efforts of us all collaborative and cumulative that seems so important to me now. Once a defined system of medical care and education, based on a new set of premises, is in place, the following advantages may become apparent:

1. Patients and students will become productive members of the system as they move from a dependency state to being informed partners in the process. The energy that went into memorizing and regurgitating can now go into thoughtful analysis, useful work, and suggested improvements in the system.

2. As Knowledge Couplers immediately map the patient's unique problem and situation against known diagnostic and management options, students and all providers will learn to ask the question: "How well do present, arbitrarily defined classification systems and therapeutic interventions accommodate the unique combination of findings presented by the patient?" The focus will be as much on the fallibility and inadequacies of current knowledge as it will be on failures and inadequacies of patients and students.

3. Students and providers will shed their habits of certainty and associated intolerance, and cultivate instead a capacity to tolerate and to negotiate the ambiguities that inevitably appear when natural situations are honestly confronted. Each patient problem becomes a research challenge and not just another case to be run through the specialist's mill.

4. Creative people from all walks of life, as they interact with the medical care system, may offer very concrete suggestions for improving a given step in the very well defined processes of care. No longer will improvement of the system be just the province of medical researchers and members of the medical industries.

5. Since everyone will eventually be an informed, knowledgeable member of the medical care system, priorities can be fairly set and the economics of care openly discussed. No country's economy would ever be able to support the expectation of the best of medical care for all people, in all age groups, at all times.

And finally, each year that goes by, one recognizes more and more what a tiny cog you are in this massive civilization of ours—and how dependent you are not only on those that surround you but those who preceded you. It is not possible to remember and recognize everyone who has had a share in even the smallest contribution. To try is to run the risk of some serious and crucial omissions. I would like to say, however, what a privilege it has been to have worked with so many dedicated and talented people over the years.

References and Bibliography

1. Tversky, A. and Kahneman, P. Judgment under uncertainty: Heuristics and biases in medical decision-making. *Science* 185:1124–1131, 1974.

2. Kern, L. and Doherty, M.E. Pseudodiagnosticity in an idealized medical problem-solving environment. *J. Med. Education* 57:100–104, 1982.

3. Wason, P.C. and Johnson-Laird, P. *Psychology of Reasoning*. Cambridge: Harvard University Press, 1972.

4. Bok, D. Needed: A new way to train doctors. (President's report to the Harvard Board of Overseers for 1982–1983.) *Harvard Magazine* 86(5):32, May–June 1984.

5. Codman, E.A. *A Study in Hospital Efficiency, As Demonstrated by the Case Report of the First Five Years of a Private Hospital*. Privately published, 1918.

6. Weed, L.L. Medical records, patient care, and medical education. *Irish Journal of Medical Science* 6:271–282, 1964.

7. Weed, L.L. Medical records that guide and teach. *New Eng. J. Med.* 278:593–599 and 652–657, 1968.

8. Weed, L.L. *Medical Records, Medical Education, and Patient Care*. Cleveland: The Press of Case Western Reserve University, 1969.

9. Hurst, W. and Walker K., (eds.). *The Problem-Oriented System*. New York: MEDCOM Press, 1972.

10. Hurst, W. and Walker K., (eds.). *Applying the Problem-Oriented System*. New York: MEDCOM Press, 1973.

11. Bjorn, C.J. and Cross, H.D. *The Problem-Oriented Private Practice of Medicine, A System for Comprehensive Health Care*. Modern Hospital Press, 1970.

12. Schultz, J.R. A history of the PROMIS technology: An effective human interface. *A History of Personal Workstations*, Goldberg, A., (ed.). Reading, Mass: Addison-Wesley, 1988.

13. Hertzberg, R.Y., Schultz J.R., and Wanner, J.F. The PROMIS network. *Computer Networks* 4, 1980, pp. 215–228.

14. Weed, L.L. and PROMIS Laboratory. Representation of medical knowledge and PROMIS. *The Proceedings of the Second Annual Symposium in Computer Applications in Medical Care*, 1978, pp. 368–400.

15. Lawson, I. Comments on the POMR. *Problem-Directed and Medical Information Systems*, Driggs, M.F., (ed.). New York: Intercontinental Medical Book Corporation, 1974, p. 39.

16. Weed, L.L. *Your Health Care and How To Manage It*. Essex Junction, Vermont: Essex Publishing Co., 1975, revised 1978. (Currently available from PKC Corp., 10 Mary St., South Burlington, Vermont 05403.)

17. Weed, C.C. *Problem-Knowledge Couplers: Philosophy, Use, and Interpretation*, PKC Corp., 1982 (10 Mary St., South Burlington, Vermont 05403).

18. Weed, L.L. and Hertzberg, R.Y. The use and construction of problem-knowledge couplers, the knowledge-coupler editor, knowledge networks, and the problem-oriented medical record for the microcomputer. *IEEE Proceedings of the Seventh Annual Symposium on Computer Applications in Medical Care*, 1983, pp. 831–836.

19. Weed, L.L. Problem-knowledge coupling. *Mt. Sinai J. of Med.*, 52(#2): 94–98.

20. Weed, L.L. Knowledge coupling, medical education and patient care. *Crit. Rev. Med. Informatics* 1:55–79, 1986.

21. Weed, L.L. Flawed premises and educational malpractice: A view toward a more rational approach to medical practice. *The Jour. of Med. Practice Management* 2(#4):239–254, 1987.

22. Weed, L.L. Medical education and patient care: mistaken premises and inadequate tools. *Physicians and Computers*, Jan. 1987, pp. 30–33 and Feb. 1987, pp. 32–35.

23. Sneath, P.H.A. and Sokal, R. *Numerical Taxonomy; The Principles and Practice of Numerical Classification*. San Francisco: W.H. Freeman and Company, 1973.

24. Tolstoy, L. *War and Peace*. New York: Simon and Schuster, 1942.

25. Heilbroner, R.L. *The Worldly Philosophers: The Lives and Times and Ideas of the Great Economic Thinkers*. New York: Simon and Schuster, 1972.

26. Sloan, D. The Teaching of Ethics in the American Undergraduate Curriculum, 1876–1976. Hastings Center Report 9(#6):21, 1979.

27. Boorstin, D.J. *The Discoverers*. New York: Random House, 1983.

28. Berry, W. *The Unsettling of America: Culture and Agriculture*. San Francisco: Sierra Club, 1977.

29. Dawes, R.M. and Corrigan, B. Linear models in decision making. *Psychological Bulletin*, 1974, Vol. 81, No. 2, pp. 95–106. (Robyn M.

Dawes is currently a professor in the Department of Social and Decision Sciences at Carnegie-Mellon University.)

30. Dawes, R.M. The robust beauty of improper linear models in decision making. *American Psychologist*, July 1979, Vol. 34, No. 7, pp. 571–582.

31. Dawes, R.M., Faust, D., and Meehl, P.E. Clinical versus actuarial judgment. *Science*, 243:1668, 1989.

32. Cantrill, S.V. Computerisation of the problem orientated record. *The Problem Orientated Medical Record*. Petrie, J.C. and McIntyre, N., (eds.). New York: Churchill Livingstone, 1979.

CLINICAL DATA PROCESSING

The second day of the conference opened with a session on systems designed to process clinical data. Hubert V. Pipberger, MD was the discussant. Because of a massive traffic jam, he arrived a little late and was not able to introduce the first speaker. At the end of the session, however, he engaged the audience with some of his recollections and observations. These are included in his paper.

Cesar A. Caceres, MD was the first speaker. He told how he began working with computers in clinical medicine as a research project in computers and electrocardiography and eventually recognized how these same techniques could be of benefit in patient care. His talk included both a history of his early days, with its successes and disappointments, and a review of the current role of computers in his private practice. The paper has been prepared by Dr. Caceres and his colleagues.

The second presenter was Thomas L. Lincoln, MD, who provided a historical perspective on clinical laboratory information systems. Rather than offering a personal chronology, he elected to present an overview that captured the essence of this history. He drew on many images and aphorisms. (For example, the final slide was of a sailboat in a heavy breeze with a trailing spray. Dr. Lincoln observed that, just as the picture could only suggest the reality of sailing, he was able to convey just some of the excitement that he witnessed in the unfolding of medical informatics.) His paper lacks the illustrations, but it contains the substance of his talk.

SPEAKERS

Cesar A. Caceres   Models for Development of Clinical Data Systems
Thomas L. Lincoln   An Historical Perspective on Clinical Laboratory
Information Systems
Hubert V. Pipberger   The Present State of ECG Data Processing

Cesar A. Caceres, MD has maintained a private medical practice in internal medicine and cardiology since 1971. He also is the president of a consulting firm and directs the nonprofit Institute for Technology in Health Care. He received his BS and MD degrees from Georgetown University in 1949 and 1953. He joined the faculty of George Washington University in 1960 and later organized and served as chairman of the country's first department of "clinical engineering" (1969–1971). He has published nine books with others in preparation. Several have been the first texts in their respective fields.

Thomas L. Lincoln, MD is senior scientist, Systems Sciences Department, The RAND Corporation (since 1967). He also is professor, Research Pathology (since 1987), and chief, Clinical Information Systems (since 1977), at the Los Angeles County/University of Southern California Medical Center. He received a BS degree in zoology in 1955 and an MD degree in 1960, both from Yale University. His areas of research include medical information systems, medical system requirements, curriculum development, and biomedical modeling. He also serves as the medical editor for *Software in Healthcare*.

Hubert V. Pipberger, MD is Professor Emeritus of clinical engineering and of medicine, George Washington University (since 1982). He received a BA degree in 1938 and an MD degree from Rheinische Friedrich Wilhelms University in 1951. He joined the faculty of Georgetown University in 1956 and came to George Washington University in 1971 as professor of clinical engineering and of medicine. Among his honors are the IFIP Award of Distinction (1979) and the AHA Cardiologist of the Year (1981). He currently serves on the editorial board of four journals including *Computers and Biomedical Research* and *Methods of Information in Medicine*.

Models for Development of Clinical Data Systems[1]

Cesar A. Caceres, Donald Barnes, William Ayers, Sidney Abraham, and Jacqueline W. Schick, Washington, D.C.

The first complete model for clinical data systems development in the United States was the U.S. Public Health Service Medical Systems Development Laboratory (MSDL). In reviewing the accomplishments of the MSDL it is important that consideration be given to the non-technologic factors that interplayed with the laboratory's objectives and motivated its staff to the extent that two Department of Health, Education, and Welfare Superior Service Medals were awarded. In the late 1950s and early 1960s at least two major factors come to mind:

1. changing concepts about population equality and the right to health care; and,

2. developing demographics that showed chronic illnesses replacing the infectious diseases as targets of intervention.

What Makes a Health Care Policy Work?

When compared to these nontechnological factors, the frequent and, at times, spectacular breakthroughs that occurred in the areas of computerization and telecommunications of clinical data now seem more appropriately viewed as improvements in the lubrication used to drive the health care system. And perhaps these "lubricants" should be looked at now as a model to consider the "lubricants" needed today.

In 1958 Dr. Arthur Rickli of the Public Health Service realized that because of a) the growing number of physical and laboratory tests required by an increasing and aging population, b) the shortage of physicians and other health personnel, and c) awareness of the need for raising the quality of medical practice for all citizens, clinicians should utilize the precision and rapidity of computers. He asked one of us (CAC), after consultations with Dr. Robert P. Gran of the National Institutes of Health, to consider those viewpoints and to set up a laboratory using electrocardiography as a model.

[1] This paper was funded in part by The Institute for Technology in Health Care, Washington, D.C.

From that basic viewpoint, automated systems were considered by MSDL as tools in medical practice to keep up and not fall behind the vital battle to preserve health. Delegation of routine duties to automated systems was thought an ideal way for physicians to find more time for development and exercise of higher professional skills, and to provide leadership to the medical teams required in emerging perceptions of comprehensive health care.

We found computer programs could indeed increase the effective use of physicians' time, thereby allowing them to concentrate more time on patients. The use of a program maintains and improves the quality of physician service. If properly used, computer analysis could also speed the physicians' diagnostic procedures to shorten hospital time.

But there was, and there still is, delay in acceptance. In the late fifties, there were no clinical computer systems anywhere. Clinical computers are now more common, but the use of computers is a trend that many in health planning seem to be only just realizing. The early delay in the involvement by the medical community in the application of computer technologies has resulted in the loss of a window of opportunity that was uniquely available because of the nontechnologic factors mentioned earlier. The impetus given by the MSDL helped initially and needed continuation.

There is one other factor that deserves mention. That was the ever-present, but vacillating, political debate as to the merits of a decentralized federal health mission and the relative productivity of a federal civil service versus contract employment to achieve national objectives. In 1969 the stroke of a reorganization pen decided in favor of the latter, and the MSDL was abolished. An opportunity for a medical-user orientation in the design and development of health care delivery systems was eliminated by Drs. Paul Sanazaro and Bruce Waxman and their staffs. A decade of progress for clinical computers in real, "hands-on" patient care was lost due to lack of imagination of those in control.

The Framework of the ECG Project: An Ideal Model for Clinical Data

We can only highlight MSDL developments to suggest that updated protocols may be applicable today. The first need in the model system was for a commercially available data-acquisition system. The need for economic viability of computerized electrocardiography was recognized early, and hence data-acquisition units were contracted out. Such units were the first commercially produced, computer-assisted ECG devices and heralded the era of high-speed diagnostic information. The first units were analog. A later, fully digital version made by Beckman Instruments was the first medical system in the world to record data digitally on-line.

The data-acquisition consoles were operated by a conventional ECG technician. Each unit was similar to conventional electrocardiograph machines; essentially it was a tape recorder plus a conventional ECG machine. The data-acquisition unit included many unique features. On the analog units, patient and lead identification codes were recorded, like bar graphs used today, on the visible tracing and on analog magnetic tape inputs to a computer system. A binary-coded decimal signal was used to identify the patient, including age, sex, height, and weight. An automatic timer provided a standard metered length of recording.

The magnetic tape recording of the electrocardiogram was fed through the telephone by use of a data-telephone system, again the first developed for electrocardiograph data transmission, which could transfer the signal to any computer center. In the initial experiments, the MSDL, in Washington, D.C., received the data and fed it into an analog–digital converter in its unique developmental models. The converter sampled the continuous ECG waveform 500 times per second; the computer program then identified the peaks and valleys of the wave complex. The amplitudes and durations of the P, QRS, and T-waves was programmed with 14,000 instructions. Within 15 seconds the computer recognized the waveforms of all the leads, integrated the values, and printed out the interpretation. An interpretation a physician would normally have received from an electrocardiographer was received within seconds at the physician's office or hospital. The data was then stored on digital magnetic tape for future comparison, follow-up, or statistical analysis.

The error rate in the computer measurements was less than seven-tenths of one percent. A high degree of agreement between cardiologists and computer interpretation was achieved. Additionally, the computer showed that it could help physicians avoid missing significant data. In the first functional year of data processing, 40,000 ECGs were processed, using one-third of the system's capability.

DEDICATED COMPUTERS

The vision of small *dedicated medical computers* and especially their *networking*, as far as medicine is concerned, was enunciated first at the MSDL. Emphasis on the practical, clinical use was fostered by the selection of the *12-lead scalar* ECG, rather than the vector analysis favored by others. Over 20 years later, vectorcardiography is still not widely used.

However, it is important to point out that the MSDL helped fund the early vectorcardiographic research carried out at the Veterans Administration Hospital in Washington, D.C. Other areas of research were also funded; statistical analysis received emphasis. It was believed such research should blend in with the practicality of clinical work.

STATISTICAL ANALYSIS

The value of clinical electrocardiography depends on the accumulation of large amounts of clinical data and the association of that data to pathological conditions. The ECG is in fact a cryptogram. In view of the empirical basis of clinical electrocardiography, the diagnostic accuracy of the ECG to differentiate between normal and abnormal depends on the analysis of the distributions of electrocardiographic characteristics in "normal" and ill populations.

Among the simple descriptive measures that can be used are means, percentiles, and cumulative percent distributions. The purpose of such reduction of data is not only to enable description of populations as concisely and briefly as possible, but also to enable comparisons between populations. Such comparisons can be made by univariate and multivariate analysis. MSDL, with Charles Steinberg and Walter Tolles of Airborne Laboratories as an associate, was the first in the world to suggest and use multivariate analysis for ECG.

Significance of the difference of individual ECGs in the populations was evaluated by standard tests. The assignment of an individual on the basis of ECG variables using standard tests of significance is likely to be inadequate where existing knowledge implicates multiple variables. For multivariate analysis, for example, the significance of a specific ECG variable in a discriminant-function analysis was tested with regression methods. The results of the discriminant-function analysis place the selected minimum number of ECG variables in rank order of importance and provide regression coefficients that allow the variables to be weighed. From the equations containing the regression coefficients, scores were given to distribute the subjects into distinct populations. An unknown subject's data can then be inserted in the prediction equation and if the data's score falls within the previously determined range, then an unknown can be classified.

The automated electrocardiographic computer program provided quantitative measures of amplitude and duration of all the wave forms of a heart cycle, as well as the heart rate. These measurements were then used to describe numerically the distribution of each ECG variable. Comparisons between populations could be made through these calculations.

These descriptions could have begun a new era for ECG processes had MSDL continued. Academicians have lacked the imagination to continue in that direction based on a review of the literature revealing only 68 entries at the National Library of Medicine in computers and electrocardiography since 1982, and a bare handful dealing in the statistical areas.

MULTIDISCIPLINARY GROUPINGS

The ability to generate from the federal level an *industrial response* that was not dictated by the government was new. The response was the result of codevelopment by a federal liaison. This was an expression of the MSDL "Data Pool." A group interested in pooling data and, hence, in all required to achieve that goal. Because development was codirected with the private sector, funding issues could be addressed prospectively. The lack of a mechanism to evaluate new technology in a process that includes codevelopment may be partly responsible for escalating health care costs.

The concept of a hands-on *multi- and interdisciplinary medical group* within or outside of government was new then; engineers, mathematicians, statisticians, computer scientists, and young, not yet academic physicians were captured by the excitement of being at a cutting edge. What made it so was not just the glamor of supporting NASA's early attempts at in-flight monitoring of ECGs (interestingly, from monkey to astronaut flights, we found in one case the computer system told us, correctly, the leads had been reversed by one monkey) or the early use of communications satellites for sending and receiving intercontinental ECGs, but the ability to work with industry and nonfederal institutions in the cooperative setting of standards and criteria for fiducial software and hardware.

These observations are perhaps best defended by reviewing the groups of solicited and unsolicited participants that joined with MSDL to conceive, develop, test, demonstrate, and use the interrelated technologies that accommodate the delivery of health care.

In addition to the large presence of physician providers from all health care settings, medical researchers, computer scientists, and engineers, the care principals in this user-oriented development strategy included: medical equipment and auxiliary supplies, manufacturers, distributors, and investors; official agencies, such as the military, concerned with performance standards and portability; intelligence and other agencies, concerned with system adaptability, reliability, and miniaturization; along with local health agencies, concerned with record duplication and transfer; and a myriad of health overseers, anticipating benefits from the massage of shared data for the purposes of epidemiology, forecasting, or gaining new knowledge.

Other participants, particularly the almost 100 institutions that applied MSDL, developed technologies to their local settings and completed a feedback loop that ensured a user-oriented product. During 1965–1973, institutions in the "Data Pool" were linked to promote common objectives through the sharing of data, experiences, and expenses. As locally initiated and self-supporting, Data Pool member institutions avoided two causes for failure of federally funded demonstration projects since they had cost- and risk-sharing and the initiative associated with them.

Another group of Data Pool participants which should be mentioned is the entrepreneurs who worked with staff to achieve an economically viable and competitive health service delivery product despite the complex and difficult problems of marketing public domain-transferred technology.

THE SYSTEMS APPROACH

The ECG system led to other efforts. MSDL was one of the early, if not the first, developmental resources that looked on the entire infrastructure of specific medical technologies as within its mission to conduct research to increase access, reduce costs, and improve the quality of health care.

At times the outpouring of research publications, official statements of objectives, and publicity originating from the Laboratory seemed even broader than its title. However, it was in its interpretation of the word "systems" that the Laboratory's leadership and staff most stretched its resources and shaped its uniqueness and subsequent contributions. The comparable word that now comes to mind is "infrastructure."

The challenge of listing, some 20 years later, the accomplishments of the Laboratory is not unlike that confronting the town historian assessing the contribution of its public library. It is an easy task to count or list books and borrowers. It is several orders of magnitude more difficult to measure how, or even if the books were used and how they changed people, practices, and the community.

MSDL was a watering hole for thirsty, future-thinking health care planners, for technology-oriented researchers and providers, for gadget-minded practitioners, for expectant entrepreneurs, and for innovators at all levels of the health care system. Not everybody checked out a book. Some went to different libraries. Most subscribed long enough to benefit by the transfer of the basic technology that was being developed. Along with this technology many participants benefited from two more subtle but equally important accomplishments of the Laboratory; the user-oriented systems development model and the coordinated planning and development of large data banks.

The now-ubiquitous computer user groups with all of their data, software, and management-sharing adaptations may obviate any current need for physical plants such as MSDL. That is not to say, however, that medicine would not benefit from a renewed commitment to a total systems approach, including the infrastructure, to the development of a more equitable, fairer priced, and higher quality health care delivery system.

In the early sixties, discussing these problems and the effect of the computer systems in medical practice and research, the surgeon general said, "However much we may do to build schools and train more physicians, there is an immediate urgency to use the available human resources in medicine to the highest degree for which they have been trained. The physician should delegate as many of his duties as possible and reserve his time for the exercise of his highest professional skills." That still holds true today.

A Clinical Era

And that was the message one of us (CAC) took from the Public Health Service when he left in 1969 after 10 years of working in the MSDL environment. The new environment was purely clinical, working, in part, towards the development of multiphasic health delivery systems patterned after those of Dr. Collen, who had perfected such systems in California.

The medical community, to its detriment, has not accepted the multiphasic health delivery philosophy. Had the medical community embraced the concept of multiphasic health care systems, we would not have some of the cost reduction measures the federal government is attempting to thrust on medical care services today.

THE CONCEPT OF AUTOMATED MULTIPHASIC
HEALTH TESTING

MSDL had started to amplify from electrocardiograms to other data. It developed the first computerized, spirometric, electroencephalographic, and phonocardiographic analysis systems. It even developed a television opthalomoscopy system and a digital system for glaucoma analysis. MSDL had one of the first units for echocardiographic heart valve display and was ready to automate that.

Automated Multiphasic Health Testing (AMHT) is the use of automation to perform more than one medical or health test. Its origins are in the large scale industrial health screenings started in the 1940s by the Kaiser Foundation.

In the mid-1960s, the Public Health Service created four model AMHT centers. The goal was to determine if transfer of the techniques and programs of Kaiser could be achieved. Ultimately, the transfer failed due to health-planner mismanagement. The centers were allowed to alter the model according to their own whims. This built-in flexibility generated four centers that could not be compared and evaluated.

The private sector also began opening AMHT centers between 1968 and 1973. The following reasons for failures on the part of some centers have been cited:

1. Lack of physician support because AMHT centers are viewed as a threat to traditional medical practice and as recipients of patients the doctors would otherwise see.
2. Lack of government support for programs as demonstration projects.
3. Failure of government to provide referrals.
4. Failure of third-party payers and the Social Security Administration to reimburse for physicals of a nondiagnostic but preventive nature.
5. Inappropriate use of AMHT in areas that need a higher degree of personalization that it can provide, as evidenced by the basic physician criticism.
6. Lack of consideration for AMHT's most cost-effective role— routine data gathering, i.e., the patient database.
7. Lack of sponsoring agency expertise and capability in data acquisition, evaluation, and feedback methodology.

These reasons show failure not of AMHT, but of health planners in and out of government and the medical community!

As occurred with the MSDL, we lost another opportunity to truly evaluate the potential of automation to reduce health care costs and raise the quality of health care.

The ideal route for study of a new medical instrument or system must be a circular process that facilitates constant oversight and evaluation of the breadboard, prototype, and production models. The first step in the process is the formulation of a policy, based on the currently available data, which will guide the instrument's or system's progress through the early development and demonstration stages. After a product has been demonstrated and has received conditional or limited acceptance from the medical community, it must be produced commercially, if it is to become widely available. Without standardized objective data, open to critical analysis, the formulation of meaningful policy is difficult. As policy planning is invariably subject to political pressures, a lack of hard data or a preponderance of adverse anecdotal data can signal the end to implementation of any item, regardless of the item's potential utility to the community.

THE COST OF TIME

One primary impactor on costs is physician time. The utilization of nurse practitioners or physician assistants can dynamically reduce costs. The model offered by Collen demonstrated a $32 savings (in 1977 dollars) in health examinations when multiphasic health testing was used in conjunction with nurse practitioner follow-up.

Medical assistants, whose training has a different type of emphasis, are a logical extension of the nurse practitioner role. But they are only now being recognized as playing a useful role in cost reduction and improved quality of health care. However, it has been primarily the Health Maintenance Organizations that have utilized their skills, and they have misused them, attempting to substitute them for physicians, a most inappropriate utilization of "technology."

THE TRANSFER OF AUTOMATION TO TRADITIONAL PRIVATE PRACTICE SETTINGS

Implementation of automation requires that the physician: a) analyze what it is he or she does routinely and repetitiously, b) develop criteria, and c) stick to the criteria. It requires standardization on the part of the physician and the staff. This has been attempted in the senior author's private practice since 1970.

Sick patients are uncomfortable waiting to see the physician. Well patients are in a hurry to get on with their day. And waiting is one of the most frequent complaints patients have. While not every delay can be eliminated, appropriate technology applications can make the time spent in a physician's office productive in terms of health care delivered, and reduce unnecessary visits and phone calls.

Through proper, computer-assisted utilization of a) in-house laboratory services, b) appropriate utilization of medical-assistant–level employees, and c) implementation of multiphasic health testing, physicians can obtain desired data *prior to* their consultations with patients.

What is eliminated? Extra visits or phone calls to review results and provide prescriptions and unproductive waiting time.

What is gained? Five to 10 minutes of waiting time is saved, patients can discuss their health problems early in the visit with an appropriately trained individual. That individual serves in part to organize thoughts with the patient and to reduce data. Most importantly, the physician has the test results needed for diagnosis and treatment before he or she actually sees the patient. The consultation time with the physician is oriented not to discovering why the patient came to the office in the first place, but rather to discussing the patient's health concerns. Or, based on laboratory findings, what, perhaps, *should* be a patient's health concern!

Standardization does not imply a rigid, dehumanized approach. In fact, when properly implemented, the computer will free the physician and staff to address patient needs.

Computer applications in most medical offices are geared toward accounting needs, not patient care needs. Yet it is, in fact, patient care that determines the bill and the insurance claim. When the reasons for automation (whether it is a laboratory test panel, or complete office system) are re-examined, the following benefits are realized:

1. Complete, standardized, accurate documentation of the medical record (in a legible form);
2. Increased human time for patients;
3. Reduction (or possibly even elimination) of batched paper work by support staff;
4. Rapid (real-time) claims-processing and higher patient collections.

An Office System Model

On an initial visit to the senior author's office, the patient completes a questionnaire detailing his medical history and is then admitted to see a medical assistant, who goes over the history and performs the first physical examination.

The medical assistant enters information into a computer, along with his or her preliminary diagnosis and recommended laboratory tests, obtains a printout, and gives it to the technician in the in-house laboratory, where almost all the labwork for the practice is done.

After a short wait, the laboratory results are available and are entered into the computer; the patient is then admitted to see the physician with a listing of history, physical findings, and printout of lab results. The physician checks over and corrects any errors or oversights in the patient's workup, orders any necessary, additional tests, examines the patient, and devotes the rest of the visit to discussing the diagnosis and therapeutic approaches with the patient.

Purchasing the computer itself is not difficult any more. A doctor does not need the fanciest machine on the market, just something that is dependable and easy to use. In the senior author's office a simple Radio Shack TRS-80 Model II, hard disk, and a printer are the data acquisition unit, processor, and display all in one.

KEEPING OVERHEAD LOW

The major expense in hardware purchase does not even compare to the cost of personnel. In the senior author's system, terminals have been gradually added over the years—a total of 12 now—to develop a complete station-to-station system. But even in reference to hardware costs, incorporation of the computer into the practice has been accomplished by following one simple rule: Each computer expense must be made up through cost-savings elsewhere.

But there is limited choice of software packages available. Several programs have been developed by people with little knowledge of the day-to-day needs of practitioners.

Today, several years after the initial program was begun, the computer system does the work of three nonexistent secretaries and aids medical staff in every role.

The custom-made programs have enabled the computer to take over and expand many routine tasks that were once performed by office staff. Here are some of the time-consuming, and expensive, chores now performed electronically.

Billing

At the end of each visit, patients receive an itemized bill that includes a computer calculation of how much will not be covered by their insurance carrier. This helps us encourage them to pay their portion promptly, without waiting for the insurance company to come through. The system also processes the information needed to suit the specific requirements of each insurance carrier, then generates a claim form. All that is needed is to rubber stamp the signature and the claim is ready to mail.

At the end of the day, the computer tallies the receipts and prints the bank deposit form, which has been found to be quite acceptable by the bank tellers.

Patient Charts

Because our records are computer generated, we routinely provide patients with complete copies. At the end of a visit, they are given a printout describing their diagnosis, treatment, and most of the laboratory results. Any lab work that must be pending (outside laboratory tests, X ray results, etc.) is mailed to the patient later. That allows them to compile their own medical charts and track the care they receive.

Prescriptions

These are not handwritten. Instead, the appropriate medication is selected from a computer listing. The computer prints a script with complete information about dosage, some warnings, and refills. The physician simply signs it. Patients like receiving a copy of their prescription printout for their records, and pharmacists are less likely to misinterpret a typed prescription than one scrawled by hand. Our calls from pharmacists for interpretation and clarification of prescriptions have been eliminated!

MORE STAFF EFFICIENCY

When a referral is selected from the computer list, the system generates a letter giving the specialist complete information. Directions are included for the patient. The computer has also taken over all routine secretarial chores of composing and typing informational memos, return-to-work letters, and patient reminders about follow-up visits. The staff merely adds the necessary information to one of several form letters stored in the computer, then prints out a hard copy.

As a bonus, the computer takes on tasks that would be too burdensome for even the most efficient secretary. At the end of each day, for example, it provides a list of patients seen during office hours and the medications each received. By keeping the printout by the phone at night, one is well prepared for any late night phone calls.

MORE TIME FOR PATIENTS

While it is great to relegate the most mundane office work to a machine, some doctors worry that a computer will dehumanize their practice. But, in reality, the computer has encouraged many patients to take a more active role in their own health care. An illustration: Lectures about curbing alcohol consumption seemed to have little effect on one middle-aged patient. But when he received a computer printout that showed his elevated SGPT value along with an indication of possible liver malfunction, he cut down his drinking. Now the first thing he asks each visit is, "How are my liver functions doing?"

He is not an exception. Most patients enjoy studying their printouts, which describe the medical reasons for each lab test and how their rates compare to high and low limits. Patients themselves can now track a host of health indicators, even if they do not have a serious medical problem. It is no surprise when a patient greets the physician saying, "I'm expecting my cholesterol levels to be lower this time. I've really been watching my diet."

The computer system also makes the office friendlier—since the system is easy to run one can emphasize people skills in the staffers hired. One receptionist, for example, used to be a *maitre d'* in a local restaurant. He was not a champion typist, but he was a real pro at greeting patients and putting them at ease.

A FINAL THOUGHT

Overall, the senior author has experienced first-hand the transfer of technology from research to "hands-on" medical care. The background in the concept of systems development in electrodardiography, expanded to multiphasic testing, has allowed patients to benefit today in a standard, private practice patient setting. What else is there to say?

Bibliography

Caceres, C.A. *Bio-medical Telemetry*. New York: Academic Press, 1965.

Caceres, C.A. *Computer Analysis of Electrocardiograms—A Film*. Produced in cooperation with the Heart Disease Control Program, USPHS and Computer Instruments Corporation, Hempstead, NY, 1964.

Caceres, C.A., (ed.). *Management and Clinical Engineering*. Dedham, Mass.: Artech House, 1980.

Caceres, C.A. *The Management of Technology in Health Care*. Dedham, Mass.: Artech House, 1980.

Caceres, C.A. and Zara, A., (eds.). *The Practice of Clinical Engineering*. New York: Academic Press, 1977.

Caceres, C.A. and Dreifus, L.S., (eds.). *Clinical Electrocardiography and Computers*. New York: Academic Press, 1970. (Also published in the USSR in a Russian translation as *Computer Systems and Automated Diagnosis of Heart Disease*. Moscow: MIR Publishing House, 1974.)

Caceres, C.A. and Perry, L.W., (eds.). *The Innocent Murmur*. Boston: Little, Brown and Co., 1967.

Caceres, C.A. and Rikli, A.E. *Diagnostic Computers*. Springfield, Illinois: Charles C. Thomas, 1969. (American Lecture Series, No. 717.)

Caceres, C.A., Yolken, H.T., Jones, R.J., and Piehler, H.R., (eds.). *Medical Devices: Measurements, Quality Assurance, and Standards*. Philadelphia: ASTM, 1983.

Dallow, R.L. *Television Ophthalmoscopy Instrumentation and Medical Applications*. Foreword by C.A. Caceres, MD. Springfield, Illinois: Charles C. Thomas, 1970.

Eden, M. and Padwo, S., (eds.). *Federal Agency Development in Medical Engineering, Subcommitte on Interaction with Industry* (M. Eden, C.A. Caceres, T.P. Heuchling, J.H. Irving, D.G. Levitt, S. Padwo). National Academy of Engineering, Washington, D.C., 1972.

Schmitt, O.H. and Caceres, C.A. *Electronic and Computer-Assisted Studies of Biomedical Problems*. Springfield, Illinois: Charles C. Thomas, 1964.

Participants' Discussion

Robert Greenfield In one of your slides you showed a physician receiving information from the computer, and then you showed a decision diagram coming from the physician. So it looks like at that time you had a physician doing the decision making. What do you think about that today?

Cesar Caceres I like to think of data as something that is not processed by a human being, something before action, and information as human-processed data. It depends, then, on when in the process you make the decision. Early in the game the idea was to show that the computer could make a decision of a certain type and say that this patient has myocardial infarction. However, the physician still had to act on that data to convert it into useful information to give some sort of medicine for that infarct. Clearly the decisions that computer systems could make then were very simplistic.

   Now, with the use of multidimensional statistics, the decisions that could be made by automated systems would be far enhanced, and so would the decisions that the physician makes. Thus we should enhance the data received by the clinician so that he can operate at a far higher level than he is currently. There are decision points, but if you use computers, you are pushing the decisions to a far more significant level.

Robert Greenfield Your evolutionary answer is good. Do you make a sharper distinction today than you did earlier as to how much of the decision should be within the human mind and how much with the computer?

Cesar Caceres What I could say is that I'm disappointed that I'm still making decisions today that physicians were making 30 years ago and in almost the same fashion. That's really the problem, I think. We are wasting physicians' time by having them make certain decisions that could be made by others. The computer should make the first decisions, followed by the medical assistants. Then improved decisions by the computer and medical assistants would go on to the physician who is then making a judgement based on a triage-type system.

265

Helmuth Orthner   I have a question regarding the relationship of the automatic interpretation of the ECG to the regulatory affairs of the Food and Drug Administration. You have been a pioneer in the development of the automatic interpretation of the ECG, and you have stated that machines are interpreting better now than a physician does except in complex cases. How far should the regulatory agencies go in regulating these kinds of automatic interpreters?

Cesar Caceres   The people that select themselves for regulatory agency work unfortunately are not the same types of people that select themselves for clinical work, and they sometimes want to add regulation where there is no need. For a computer electrocardiographic system or a spirographic system or other systems of this type, the only need is simply that there be an agreement among, for instance, the American Heart Association, the National Institutes of Health, and the American College of Cardiology that these are suitable criteria that should be followed. Once it is decided what kind of signal indicates myocardial infarction for instance, all you have to do is tell a manufacturer what the machine should do when presented with this signal. You don't need a regulatory agency involved. The manufacturer will satisfy the group that is responsible for standards.

Working with the Association for Advancement of Medical Instrumentation, for example, we developed a standard three or four years ago for automated and regular blood pressure cuffs. There wasn't any government involvement in that standard, and there was no real need for it. All that is necessary is for the concerned organizations to join together and decide on a standard that should be followed. In order to sell the equipment, the manufacturers will do exactly what you wish. There could be some monitoring of compliance, but as a practical matter the medical groups should decide on the output standards.

Donald Lindberg   Cesar, I remember in the old days you did an ECG of Everett Dirkson on the floor of the Senate. Did that help the cause?

Cesar Caceres   That was a spirometry, and he didn't do very well, but you are quite right. It did help in increasing the budget.

An Historical Perspective on Clinical Laboratory Information Systems

Thomas L. Lincoln, MD
University of Southern California, Los Angeles; The RAND Corporation, Santa Monica

Summary

The clinical laboratory environment represents a microcosm in which practical solutions to operational problems in medical informatics have gone hand in hand with the development of laboratory instrumentation and computer technologies. These achievements follow a typical pattern in technological development, leading from the specific to the inclusive. The history of laboratory computing offers insights, not only for the past, but also for the future.

Introduction

I have been asked to present a history of laboratory information systems as one aspect of the short modern history of medical informatics. In this context, I must state my view that the key issues in the evolution of any technology cannot be captured by reciting a set of facts. Rather, as in the history of science, the turning points are related to insights—in this case insights into the logic of a particular kind of clinically related work—where the reward for understanding the process has been a good design as measured by the practical effectiveness of information use. This perspective suggests that there is an inverse to Gresham's law, in which good technology is presumed to drive out the bad through a marketplace of ideas tested by performance. For this interpretation, I am most directly indebted to Devendra Sahal and his *Patterns of Technological Innovation* {1} and to Richard Foster's *Innovation, the Attacker's Advantage* {2}. But the deepest support comes from Arnold Toynbee, who, in *A Study of History*, notes that "Technology is perhaps the one product of human activity in which there has been continuous progress" {3}. It is, in some sense, a favored arena in which we have tenaciously held onto what we have learned. Thus, like time's arrow, technology pushes us to fulfill the inscription above the National Archive: "What is Past is Prologue."

267

Underscoring that history need not face backward, Toynbee titles the last chapter of the last volume of *A Study of History*, "The Next Ledge," remarking that "The next ledge above, unlike the last ledge immediately below, is invisible to climbers who are striving to reach it" {4}.

Motivations and Materials

In laboratory information systems, and in medical informatics generally, we have climbed from ledge to ledge in the solution of demanding practical problems, but each discovery, once achieved, has almost immediately appeared obvious, so obvious, in fact, that these advances have generally escaped academic commentary and recognition.

The motivations for the climb have changed little in more than 20 years. The four reasons for automation, cited in the 1966 edition of the *Encyclopedia Britannica*, are the same today: "The decision to shift from manual to machine operation is usually determined by consideration of the following factors:

1. Saving of labor....

2. Saving of time....

3. Effects on personnel...[which may]...nullify anticipated savings in labor.

4. Need for accuracy." {5}

Furthermore, the same edition of the encyclopedia commented on the critical role that computers were already playing in society:

> Electronic computers...have now become the commonplace tools in data processing for government, business, and industry; in scheduling and control of manufacturing operations; in military systems;...and in scientific activities.... A whole new profession has arisen—the art of using and applying computers to problems of all types. Most college and university students now receive some training in the design and use of computers, and science and mathematics curricula are being revised in the secondary (and even elementary) schools to introduce the new concepts required {6}.

To the engineer, the clinical laboratory is a light industry where measurements and observations are made on a patient's blood or other body fluids at a physician's request and where the major visible products are the reports that contain these results. Addressing the issues of information automation in the early 1960s, laboratorians were not hampered by traditions and conventions from medicine's past because the clinical laboratory was coming into its own at the same time as the new computer technologies. Clinical laboratory science and the mechanization of laboratory measurement had progressed to a point where the challenge of computer automation was a natural extension of other developmental activities, so that laboratorians accepted the computer as another piece of instrumentation. They began by addressing problems that were close to the bench—data conversion from instrument data to clinical form and the calculation of measures such as standard error. Foresightful individuals, anticipating a flood of demand for new lab services, projected that computers would have broader uses in the organization, generation, and delivery of lab results. They were right. Today, a modern, fully featured system can handle an almost paperless flow of information throughout an entire laboratory complex. But such systems have more than 3000 separate (and hard-won) subroutines {7}! The dimensions of this problem were unsuspected by the pioneers.

Personnel

In the 1960s, the idea of laboratory computer automation was "in the air," but an attempt to identify the first steps and who carried them out would probably lead to much irrelevant dispute. We now understand the many roots of this common endeavor, so it is not surprising that, even at the beginning, the number of participants working on some aspect was very large. I will cite a few individuals whose energy and optimism will stand surrogate for all of the instrument automators, pattern recognizers, laboratory managers, medical technologists, vendors, programmers, and users that led the way. At one time or another at the NIH: Williams, Cotlov, Brecher, Bull, Dutcher, Pratt, and Prewitt; in England: Whitehead; in the middle west: Hicks, Strandjord, Rappaport, Ditto, Lindberg, and Tong; and elsewhere: Seligsohn, Straumfjord, Steward, Krieg, Wattenberg, Mitchel, Peebles...and many others. Moreover, in technology, unlike science, major contributions are often both widely distributed and nearly anonymous—a matter that has constantly plagued those with academic careers. Therefore, it took foresightful academic chairmen like Benson and Hutchins and Lucas, thoughtful NIH policy advisors like Kinney, and NIH administrators such as Stone to provide a level of academic support that would allow the field to grow in conceptual stature as it grew pragmatically.

Approaches and Early Results

Because much initial work focused on issues close to instrumentation, the limited capacities of the LINC, the DEC PDP-4 through -8, the IBM 1800, and the early transistorized calculators such as those by Wang and Olivetti were the most immediate limits to be overcome. Adequate performance generally required writing in an assembly language. Distinct operating systems were the domain of large machines, and there were few software tools. Most on-line debugging consisted of reviewing and manipulating binary code in the registers of the machines themselves. To be successful at all, a programming solution had to be focused and specific.

Every area had its unique problems. Chemistry became absorbed in translating analog signals into digital measurements, and the Skeggs autoanalyzer presented the same "peak picking" measurement problems as were present in electrocardiography. Designers, who set about automating the task of counting blood cells under a microscope to create a differential white count, encountered the now-familiar interface complexities associated with apparently simple professional tasks. The logic of cell recording by automated keypad was found to involve so many ins and outs that the process required a whole organization of its own. In cytology, the repetitive quality of observations focused attention on "canned" but modifiable reporting mechanisms, but brought up the linking of present specimens with past ones, and a cross linking to a surgical pathology database. Although the blood bank could be formulated as an inventory problem, the medical requirements were found to be so very complex and dynamic that they could not be solved by off-the-shelf inventory ideas from industry. Microbiology was faced with linking multistep diagnostic work sequences that extended over several days' time and with managing an encyclopedic set of bacterial alternatives with many potential synonyms and qualifications.

Immediate problems with machine capacity made it hard to appreciate the importance of unresolved issues involving human factors and medical logic. Each successful program offered the promise of a more general solution, but as new areas were tried, the parochial nature of the initial approach became evident. A logic that functioned very well in one area, when tried in another, was often found to boarder on the absurd. Thus, for example, chemistry systems that started with a numeric base lacked a data structure that could adequately handle the extensive text of microbiology. Such text-based observations could not be reduced to a coded numerical equivalent in any simple way because, unlike a chemical measurement, more than one answer could be required for any given field. Microbiology was not, however, somehow more general than chemistry, and attempts to reverse the direction of development ran into equal trouble. Because the logical differences often lay deep in the program design, and because these early programs were very rigid, unexpected limitations were difficult and expensive to overcome.

The Road to Solutions

The most compatible, separate areas were chemistry and hematology, and early successful prototypes of general laboratory systems began by combining these areas. One of the first and most ambitious was the system designed by Berkeley Scientific Laboratories in the late 1960s and first introduced at the NIH Clinical Center and then at the University of California, San Francisco. Abroad, Swedish and British developers were also at work.

As has often happened with medical computing, what were first presumed to be a simple set of engineering tasks were found to depend on clinical decision-making situations that had never been described in procedural terms. Consolidating data from separate laboratory sources into a single report led to the elusive search for the optimal reporting format—only to discover the obvious—that, given the multiple uses to which clinical data are put, all hard copy formats fall short in one manner or another. Not even the flexibility of electronic displays can resolve all such issues on a conventional terminal.

The hierarchical file structures of the 1960s were appropriate for patient-oriented files, but the unpredictability of what test would be asked for and what data would be collected made fixed-length record formats, such as those favored by Assembler, COBOL, and FORTRAN, very inefficient unless additional pointer structures were introduced. The retrieval of data across patients for various administrative purposes, such as laboratory quality control and workload statistics, required separate preplanned inverted files. Once again, the diversity of the activities in different laboratory sections made common conventions difficult. The sparse arrays and flexible field lengths of the Massachusetts General Hospital Utility Multiprogramming System (MUMPS) offered the first convenient prototyping environment that could respond to the wide variety of *ad hoc* changes that were needed to explore the many-sided and incompletely understood requirements of laboratory systems.

Looking Back

From the perspective of 1977, Professor T.P. Whitehead summed up the evolution of the field at the Second International Conference on Computing in Clinical Laboratories in Birmingham, England, as follows:

> Frequently there are four phases in the application of technological innovations in medicine. The overoptimistic introductory period lead by enthusiasts, a second phase of developing pessimism as the limitations and full costs of the innovation are realized. The third phase is a recovery

phase where the balancing of the claims of phases one and two are achieved, and finally the fourth phase where the innovation is applied at its correct level {8}.

Those who have studied the process of technological innovation as a general phenomenon of our time have found similar patterns representing discontinuous conceptual steps in many emerging technologies. Sahal and Foster {1, 2} identify an initial turbulent phase—fraught with optimism, pessimism, diversity, and absurdity—followed by a coming together of understanding and design around a benchmark configuration that serves as a guidepost for successful future implementations. The cited authors present extensive analyses. Both emphasize the dynamic nature of technology so that no company involved in manufacturing and selling a product, faced with the flux of new demands and new ways of doing things, can afford to stand still. But to develop new products is to incur new uncertainties. ...

Luckily, in the formative 1970s in the United States, the clinical laboratory was a profitable revenue center, which coincided with the need for capital to explore new technologies and to pursue computer-based information systems. There was, in effect, enough money to absorb the costs of development and accept the risks of failure.

These very real risks of the time were clearly presented by J. Lloyd Johnson and Associates in their 1975 study on *Achieving the Optimal Information System for the Laboratory* {9}. In this study, a successful system was considered to be one that had some of the instruments in chemistry and hematology on-line, with any three of the following functions:

- Test request entered through a video display terminal or by some more efficient manner,
- collection list with labels printed,
- test results entered without manual reentry of patient or other specified number,
- ward report printed, and
- cumulative summaries printed.

Their extensive review concluded that 25% of hospital laboratory systems had achieved satisfactory working status for less than $1000 per bed (recalculated in 1975 dollars and adjusted for hospital size), 25% required approximately double this amount, and, no matter how much was expended in money and effort, one-half of the hospitals could be expected to lose their entire investment! Looking backward, all strategies appeared risky, whether programmed in-house or supplied by vendors {10}. Success was felt to depend on the tautologous wisdom of "understanding one's needs," plus certain analytic skills to be provided by experienced consultants.

The Turning Point

Even as the Johnson study appeared, a turning point had been reached with the advent of the DEC-based CLINLAB and the Hicks LCI systems. Limited in scope and rigid in language, these systems were the necessary benchmark examples that illustrated how separate functions could be brought together using tables and indirection to provide flexibility. One might well suggest 1973 as the year when the interaction between a computer team and a clinical laboratory began to have more than a fifty–fifty chance of success. As a consequence, the period from 1970 to 1980 became one of growth and ferment for vendors, for programmers, and for laboratories, but also one of confusion for hospital decision makers. No sooner had an effective system been identified, than a more effective one appeared to outperform it. DEC-based assembly language systems were overtaken by the FORTRAN systems of MEDLAB and Community Health Computing. Toward the end of the decade, these in turn were challenged by the MUMPS-based systems of MEDITECH, SUNQUEST, and Medical Data Corp. There were many other players, and the clinical reference laboratories followed a pathway of their own with BIOSCIENCES using IBM equipment and RUBICON using MUMPS. Each new wave took advantage of a language that supported more flexibility than its predecessor, and new hardware came along to make up for the lack of speed introduced by the added complexity. However, at a deeper level, a consolidation of understanding was taking place that focused on the formal modular nature of these systems and on the complex relationships that linked the flow of patient specimens and data through the laboratory to the clinical caregivers and, secondarily, to the medical record and on to the billing office {11, 12}.

Some laboratory areas, such as blood banks, were so different that they were brought under a common framework later than others, and separate systems that serve this specific need remain viable today. But the attempt to automate the whole laboratory by a "mix-and-match" of computer systems from different vendors found the unified concerns of patient care a difficult taskmaster, and clinical demands mitigated against such fragmentation. The clinically satisfactory line of attack proved to be one of synthesis and consolidation of specific functions into an ever more inclusive configuration that remained under the control of those that used the system.

By 1980 laboratory systems had converged on an interactive design that placed a terminal at every workstation or instrument interface, that consolidated patient data in a common database, that viewed intra-laboratory task organization and communication as the key design parameters, and that used differentiated subroutines to carry out the specific laboratory information tasks of each department {13}. This mature design recognized the unique perspective of each laboratory section but managed to subsume these differences under a common framework that could take advantage of all of the major capabilities of computer systems: calculation, archiving, message transmission, and the support of workstations. Such systems have now become the broad-based backbone of effective laboratory operation.

Today, vendor product differentiation depends on service support, price, and special features rather than fundamental differences in scope and performance {14}. In 1987 one can expect a successful implementation of a well-tested system in better than 90% of the cases. Indeed, the functional requirements for most laboratory areas can now be stated with such self-evident clarity {15} that it is hard to think back to a time when these specifications were difficult to formulate. They were indeed so, before the present ledge was reached.

The Next Ledge

On our present "ledge" we still have some cleaning up to do. There are new areas of laboratory responsibility; there is uploading and downloading to personal computers, and there is remote but secure access from physician offices. But the major task still to be completed is bringing together laboratory computer systems with all of the other clinical systems that support patient care (hospital information systems, pharmacy systems, and the like) into one consistent, patient-oriented, organic whole. In this larger arena, we are today where we were in the laboratory 10 years ago: We must introduce consistency without sacrificing the diversity that is characteristic of productive professional work patterns.

The historical experience of the clinical laboratory overwhelmingly supports the power and practicality of bringing together the different perspectives of different work environments under the common logic in a single system design, but it also points to the difficulty and subtlety of doing so.

However, as we peer up toward the next ledge, we will have to come to terms with the clinically derived knowledge bases and expert systems that loom ahead. To the extent that these new systems, now in their infancy, must rest on real data acquired in real time, they will have to depend on robust and fully consistent information systems that can generate the necessary clinical archives from which these relationships can be constructed.

References

1. Sahal, D. *Patterns of Technological Innovation*. London: Addison-Wesley, 1981.

2. Foster, R. *Innovation, the Attacker's Advantage*. New York: Summit Books, 1986.

3. Toynbee, A.J. The transitional societies. *A Study of History, Vol. XII, Reconsiderations*. New York: Oxford University Press, 1961, Chap. IX, p. 331.

4. *Ibid*. The next ledge. Chap. XIX, p. 562.

5. Office machines and appliances. *Encyclopedia Britannica*, Vol. 6, Chicago: Benton, 1966, p. 24.

6. *Ibid*. Computing machines, Electronic. Vol. 16, p. 13.

7. Aller, R.D. Personal communication, Cottage Hospital, Santa Barbara, Calif.

8. Computing in clinical laboratories. *Proceedings of The Second International Conference*. Birmingham, England, 1977, p. 7.

9. J. Lloyd Johnson and Associates. *Achieving the Optimal Information System for the Laboratory*. Northbrook, Ill., 1975.

10. Liscouski, J.G., (ed.). *Computers in the Laboratory: Current Practice and Future Trends*. Boston: Digital Equipment Corp., 1983.

11. Lincoln, T.L. Computers in the clinical laboratory: What we have learned. *Medical Instrumentation*, Vol. 12, No. 4, July–August, 1978.

12. Krieg, A.F., *et al*. A definition and classification of clinical laboratory data processing. *Pathologist* 33:78–83, 1979.

13. Lincoln, T.L. and Korpman, R.A. Computers, health care, and medical information science. *Science*, Vol. 210, No. 4467, Oct. 17, 1980, pp. 257–263.

14. Aller, R.D. and Elevitch, F.R., (eds.). Symposium on computers in the clinical laboratory. *Clinics in Laboratory Medicine* No. 3: 1983, pp. 1–254.

15. Aller, R.D. and Elevitch, F.R. *The ABCs of LIS: Computerizing Your Laboratory Information System*. Chicago: American Society of Clinical Pathologists, 1986.

Participants' Discussion

Question   Over the years you have watched computer systems come and go and you have seen the organizational setting at which each of these projects succeeded or failed. I'd like to know whether you have studied the Veterans Administration's approach to automating their hospitals and whether you could or would comment on that?

Thomas Lincoln   Yes, I have studied the VA approach at least in part, because I was on an Office of Technology Assessment panel charged with reviewing some of the studies. The approach is very interesting. The options are either to put in a complete external hospital information system or to allow the homegrown internal development of such systems using the MUMPS-based FileManager. The dilemma, as stated in several of the reports, is that there is not a complete unanimity of judgment. But there was a broad unanimity of judgment on the panel that the FileManager internal approach has been more effective because of user commitment and the ability of the user to manage and express the needs of individual institutions. This solution has the danger of not having much of an overall business plan and structure, and indeed it is going to take some orchestration.

Judith Prewitt   Some of your earlier work was in mathematical modeling in cell kinetics. Would you comment on the relationship of that type of mathematical modeling to the clinical systems as they evolved?

Thomas Lincoln   There is a relationship. Pharmacokinetic systems of the Bishof-Dedrick type are a weave of flow parameters that constrain things. These are highly parametrized models that can't go off in all directions because they must obey the rules of biology. We are now working on some AIDS models that are similarly constrained.

   The connection in my mind is conceptual. I always try to think about internal consistency, whether it's in the organization of laboratory systems, or the flow of cells and the interaction of cells with chemotherapeutic agents, or the issues involved in the sociology of human interaction. The engineering perspective accepts a complexity of consis-

276

tent interactions that is generally avoided in administrative systems. The ability to encompass complexity is a critical ingredient for success.

Bonnie Kaplan   Tom, you have written in the past that laboratories represent a microcosm of what goes on in data processing in medical centers and hospitals, and you've drawn some conclusions from that today. But laboratories also represent one place where there has been more successful automation than elsewhere in the medical centers. Can you address some of the differences, some of the ways in which laboratories may not be a microcosm in that respect?

Thomas Lincoln   First of all, laboratories are generally under one departmental direction. They have a number of separate components that are quite diverse— chemistry, microbiology and the blood bank, for instance, all operate according to different information principles. The blood bank in particular dispenses blood, and other laboratories dispense reports and advice. But the parochialism of those groups is easier to weld together because there is a common culture of medical technologists and pathologists within the laboratory.

It has been fairly difficult in large institutions to weld together that common culture. The focus in the laboratory is closer and therefore not a complete model in that sense. But you still have the issues of administrative priorities, patient-focused priorities and distribution of patient values, responses, and so forth. Also, there are two separate professional priorities, namely that of the technologist and the pathologist. So I think it's actually quite a good model. It just has to be opened up and given more parameters. But then you get into the more complex three-body problem, and I think one has to be careful to allow enough flexibility.

The Present State of ECG Data Processing. What Has Been Accomplished in Thirty Years?

Hubert V. Pipberger, MD
George Washington University Medical Center, Washington, D.C.

This is the year of anniversaries. The U.S. Constitution is 200 years old. ECG data processing has been going on for 30 years. We cannot compare one with the other; but because we are dealing with a round figure, it is worthwhile to look back to see whether there is any reason for celebration.

It was in the spring of 1957 when Dr. Martin Cummings, who was then director of research of the Veterans Administration, approached me and asked whether I was interested in developing a computer system for automatic analysis of the electrocardiogram. I had heard about computers, but my knowledge of these monster machines was, at that time, almost zero. I had some background in electrocardiography and electrophysiology and, following very short consideration, I decided that this undertaking was probably worthwhile and might be a lot of fun. I started reading everything I could find about computers. But by July 1, 1975, when the project started officially, my knowledge and background in this new field were still far from profound.

With my friends and colleagues in electrocardiographic research, I discussed extensively the goals of ECG computer analysis, if such methods would ever become feasible, practical, and widely used. The most immediate aim was, of course, the elimination of the daily chore of reading and interpreting the dozens and dozens of records that need to be interpreted in daily hospital routine work. A second goal, which I considered most important in our research, was improvement in ECG interpretation. This second goal became clearer in the next years when more and more studies on ECG interpretation were performed, using independent, that is, non-ECG evidence, for documentation of diagnoses. I am thinking here mainly of investigations such as that of Simonson [1], which represented a landmark in this field. Later on, many investigators followed in the footsteps of Ernst Simonson with very similar results. In a nutshell, they found that the diagnostic performance of experienced electrocardiographers was usually between 50% and 60%. In practical terms, this means that the ECG interpretations that we obtain from the heart station are accurate only in approximately one-half of the cases. Based on my own experience, I did not find these results as shocking as many clinicians did. These studies reinforced my intention to try to improve ECG diagnosis by this new tool, the computer. In parallel with those plans, many biophysicists investigated the performance of ECG leads in terms of lead strength and lead direction. To summarize these studies, they found a great variability in lead performance and, furthermore, they found that much of the information recorded with conventional ECG leads is redundant. At the time, it was felt that three orthogonal leads contained all the information available from the body surface. It was thought that the heart as a current source can be represented by a fixed-location dipole with varying strength and direction. Such a current source can be completely described by an orthogonal lead system. It was shown later that this description is inadequate, and I will go into more detail on the various lead systems a little later. In 1957, we felt that an orthogonal lead system was adequate for recording the total information available. Such a system had the definite advantage of a small number of leads as compared to the conventional lead system made up of 12 leads, which is still in common use today. Because of its simplicity, we decided to apply the Frank orthogonal lead system {2}.

In order to convert the analog data recorded from the patients into digital form, we realized very early that we needed an analog–digital conversion system. For this reason, we made a contract with the National Bureau of Standards to develop such a system {3}. One has to realize that A–D conversion was a major undertaking in the early days of data processing. It took approximately one year to develop such a system (Figure 1). It included a monitoring facility that allowed us to view the ECG leads recorded from the patient and to select a proper part of the tracing before activating the A–D system proper. At the time, we felt very proud of this monster, but we soon realized that in order to perform a detailed ECG analysis we also needed a system that would locate the beginning and end of the various wave forms that form the electrocardiogram. The beginning and end of the P-wave, of the QRS complex, and the end of the T-wave were the landmarks which needed to be identified. One of the collaborating mathematicians, Dr. F. Stallmann, designed such a program for application on the SEAC.

The SEAC computer represented a problem by itself. Probably very few of you have seen this type of digital computer, which operated with tubes. Since the number of tubes was very large and the lifetime of tubes was limited, the downtime of the SEAC was horrendous. Later on, we switched to the IBM 704, which was much more reliable.

A first program to analyze electrocardiograms was executed on the SEAC. This was done by use of the ventricular gradient. This is a tech-

FIGURE 1
Early ECG monitoring system

nical ECG term, which indicates a time integral of a cardiac cycle including P, QRS, and T waves which do not need to be separated for this analysis. A crude separation between normal and abnormal records became possible with this procedure.

Early Contacts with Other Interested Research Teams

In the late 1950s, interest in medical data processing spread very rapidly. Through the introduction of digital computers, many investigators were able to think of new ways to solve research problems, particularly those that could be solved numerically. People like Otto Schmitt in Minneapolis, Ernest Frank in Philadelphia and later in Washington,

D.C., McFee, and many others showed an early interest that was welcomed in our group. Collaboration with these researchers lasted for many years, and an active exchange of ideas developed. Because of this growing interest, we decided in 1959 to organize an international conference on automatic data processing in electrocardiography entitled "Conference on Modern Concepts of Electrocardiography and Methods of ECG Data Processing."

In an attempt to stimulate a free exchange of ideas and in order to avoid lengthy presentations of computer dreams, we limited the speaking time for each participant to five minutes. The conference format proved a complete success, and Professor Rijlant from Brussels, Belgium, repeated many times in later years that this meeting was the most successful he had ever attended. In the following years, we became very popular and received a large number of requests for digitized ECG data, which we distributed freely. We were somewhat disappointed, however, when, in the following years, we saw some publications without any reference to the source of the data.

Automatic ECG Wave Recognition

As mentioned earlier, in a complete ECG analysis, one needs to identify exactly the beginning and end of the various wave forms. This problem proved relatively difficult because, in clinical practice, the ECG is usually superimposed by muscle noise, 60-cycle interference, and many other types of artifacts. One of my collaborators, F. Stallmann, published the first complete wave-recognition program in 1961 {4}. It was later refined by Charles Batchlor with great improvements in reliability. The program is based on the rate of change in spatial velocity derived from the three orthogonal leads. In later years, many new wave recognition programs were developed, but they were all based on the same principles. For this reason, Rautaharju called the Stallmann program "the mother of all ECG computer programs." Since a sharp delineation of all wave forms is critical for any further analysis, the Common Market countries in Europe organized a multicenter study in order to test all available ECG programs. This should facilitate any future data exchanges between different program designers. I am proud to say that, compared to their standard, obtained through cooperation of many experienced electrocardiographers, our old program fared best {6}.

I should add here that since 1960, several other investigators developed automatic ECG analysis systems. The one with the greatest impact was probably that developed by Caceres {7} and coworkers who developed a program for analysis of the 12-lead electrocardiogram. I am sure that he will elaborate in greater detail on this system. Other early systems were developed by Cady and coworkers {8}, Pordy {9},

Smith at the Mayo Clinic {10}, and Bonner {11}. There are many more systems available now, but enumeration of all of them would go too far.

ECG Programs for Diagnostic Classification

As soon as the various wave forms are identified, one can think of diagnostic classification. As I mentioned earlier, we were convinced that, through the use of computers, ECG diagnosis could be improved considerably. This opinion was not shared by many electrocardiographers who felt that automation of present-day methods was all that the computers could accomplish. For our own project, we were fortunate to have the collaboration of many very competent biostatisticians. They taught us two things very early in our research. The first was that we needed very large record samples, which were in excess of the material we could collect from our own hospital. The second point, which they stressed, was the independence of diagnostic non-ECG information needed for development of new procedures and their testing. In brief, this meant that we could not use ECG data proper for diagnostic testing.

In order to obtain sufficiently large numbers of records, we started in 1960 a cooperative study with eight hospitals participating. For each diagnostic entity, we set up a clinical data sheet to document the pertinent findings. This allowed us to collect ECG records and clinical data from large numbers of patients. At the end of this data collection, we had more than 20,000 records on analog tape, together with the clinical information needed. In cooperation with participating cardiologists, we set up strict criteria for each diagnosis. In addition, we obtained more than 1000 records from patients who had come to autopsy.

There was a great variety of statistical classification procedures available, which we were able to test. There are probably few statistical methods we did not test in the search for improved classification. Eventually, we found that a multivariate procedure, linear discriminant function analysis, proved best for our purposes. Without going into too much detail on the many trials, I will discuss here only very briefly the procedure we ended up with. The selection of this procedure was due almost entirely to the late Jerome Cornfield, who had joined our group as consultant in 1969. For those of you who knew Cornfield, it was no surprise that he selected a Bayesian classification scheme, which proved more efficient than anything that we had tried before. A new feature in this scheme was the selection of prior probabilities based on tentative diagnoses made on admission of the patients. In Figure 2 you see an ECG request form, which is filled out for every patient. If, for

FIGURE 2
ECG request form

CARDIAC STATUS (Tentative or Final Diagnosis)

"No ECG will be taken unless this section is completed by requesting physician."

☐ 1. Normal Cardiovascular Status   ☐ 5. Pulmonary Disease

☐ 2. Coronary Artery Disease   ☐ 6. Primary Myocardial Disease

☐ 3. Hypertensive Cardiovascular   ☐ 7. Other diseases not related to
      Disease   cardiovascular system

☐ 4. Valvular or Congenital Heart
      Disease

example, a myocardial infarct is suspected on admission, the physician checks number 2, which indicates coronary artery disease. With this tentative diagnosis, the prior probability for myocardial infarct automatically becomes approximately 50%. The remaining 50% of the priors are distributed among other diagnoses that may be associated with coronary artery disease. The fine-tuning of priors is largely based on empirical grounds.

Results with this procedure are shown in Table 1. On the first line, the computer classifications are shown as percentages of the total. The second line indicates the results of physicians' interpretations. The difference between the two interpretations was almost 20%, based on 1192 records. It should be noted here that the patients were known to the interpreting physicians. They were also responsible for the selection of priors before computer analysis.

TABLE 1

| | ECG Diagnosis | | |
	Correct	Partially Correct	Incorrect
Computer analysis (3-lead ECG)	86%	5%	9%
Physician's interpretation (12-lead ECG)	68%	4%	28%

1192 records including ventricular conduction defects

Clinical Data Processing

TABLE 2

| | ECG Diagnosis | | |
	Correct	Partially Correct	Incorrect
Equalized for all diagnostic categories	66%	8%	26%
Adjusted according to number of records in each diagnostic category	69%	9%	22%
Adjusted according to clinical diagnosis	87%	5%	8%

1092 cases, ventricular conduction defects not included.

Table 2 shows the effect of the predetermined prior probabilities as compared to priors based on sample sizes. The first line indicates the diagnosis for all categories with equal prior probabilities. The second line indicates results based on sample sizes. The third line shows the results you saw in Table 1. A Bayesian method, which is usually adjusted according to sample size, achieves only a very moderate improvement of 3%. A more significant improvement can be obtained with the third method. The most drastic change is seen in the last column where the percentage of incorrect diagnoses is shown. What is most important here is the demonstration that the addition of any available information at the time of the ECG request leads to a significant improvement in classification. One can think, of course, of many other items that can be added to the information that lead up to building new sets of prior probabilities such as age, weight, and sex of the patient. They are some of the simplest that are readily available.

Evaluation of Existing ECG Computer Programs

Independent evaluation of available EGG computer programs appears most important, particularly for those program users who are not expert electrocardiographers. Most early attempts of evaluation were performed by program designers using their own program and their diagnostic criteria. The early reports were, therefore, extremely good, but such evaluations are of little or no use to the potential customer. An early and more valid test was performed by J. Bailey {12–14} who used records for this test sampled at a rate of 1000/sec. In the first experiment, only even samples, and in the second, only odd samples were used in the analysis. It was found that in a good number of records the diagnoses changed when even or odd samples were used. Typical findings were that 20% to 30% of the diagnoses changed with the test. Only when programs based on multivariate analysis were tested was the change of diagnoses less than 5%. Evaluations against independent diagnostic information represent a more stringent and more desirable test. Such independent tests have been discussed frequently, but results have not yet become available. One test is being performed by the cooperative study of the Common Market countries in Europe {15}. We have seen only some preliminary results based on a limited number of records. Best results were obtained with two programs based on multivariate analysis. It is too early, however, to draw conclusions from these preliminary results.

I was chairman of the ECG committee of the American Heart Association for 14 years. During that period, I pleaded continuously to initiate independent tests of the various available computer programs, but my pleas were not successful. I am not aware of any such testing in the U.S. at the present time.

Progress in computer analysis of electrocardiograms in the United States has been relatively rapid in the last five years. Sheffield reported in his recent review that, of approximately 60 million ECGs performed annually in the U.S., between 22 and 28 million are interpreted by computer {16}. This represents a growth rate of 12% per year in the last five years. The most commonly used programs were developed by ECG manufacturers, and detailed descriptions of these programs are mostly unavailable. The output of these programs has to be over-read by trained cardiologists or internists. The most common complaint is that the output is oversensitive and over-diagnoses in a good number of cases.

The present situation is far from satisfactory and far from the original plans to improve ECG diagnostics by computer use. In this connection, I would like to quote, again, from Thomas Sheffield's recent review in the *Journal of The American College of Cardiology*. Commenting on the various approaches to ECG computer analysis, he states:

> At the same time, academic health scientists such as Pipberger and his colleagues realized the potential that computer power gave to making a new and scientific approach to ECG interpretation. They organized the collection of a database that would correlate clinical and cardiac catheterization data with ECGs to yield interpretive results based on probability density algorithms and not on arbitrary clinical impressions. This was a landmark effort, and its full value and impact will not be realized for years to come. It was not an immediate success with its clinical users because of its unfa-

miliar diagnostic probability statements, and because it forces the user to employ clinical acumen in weighing likelihood of competing diagnostic statements presented by the computer. This program made its appearance before its time. Future physicians will be more familiar with such statements and will be better equipped to make the best use of the approach pioneered by this effort. {16}

From our experience and the comments by Thomas Sheffield, the time is not ripe for advanced ECG diagnostics, and we might have to wait another 10 to 20 years before our approach to ECG diagnosis becomes more popular.

The use of additional but readily available information for improvement in ECG diagnosis is very obvious in many instances. This has been demonstrated many times in the past and is obvious to the experienced clinician. For the final diagnosis, any additional information available to the doctor should be used for adjustment of prior probabilities.

Our computer program for ECG analysis has been made available very freely in the past. From the evaluations that have been made public so far, it appears that our program is definitely one of the best, both in terms of automatic wave recognition and of ECG diagnostics. Except for some medical schools in Europe, the use of the program has been very limited. One can only guess whether acceptance of the program will become more widespread in the future. Until then, program users will have to be satisfied with the existing commercial programs.

References

1. Simonson, E., Tuna, N., Okamoto, N., *et al.* Diagnostic accuracy of the vectorcardiogram and electrocardiogram: A cooperative study. *Am. J. Cardiol.* 17:829, 1966.

2. Frank, E. An accurate, clinically practical system for spatial vectorcardiography. *Circ.* 13:737, 1956.

3. Taback, L., Marden, E., Mason, H.L., and Pipberger, H.V. Digital recording of electrocardiographic data for analysis for digital computer. *IRE Transactions on Medical Electronics* ME-6:167, 1959.

4. Stallmann, F.W. and Pipberger, H.V. Automatic recognition of electrocardiographic waves by digital computer. *Circ. Res.* 9:1138, 1961.

5. Rautaharju, P.M. The current status of computer application in ECGJ and VCG analysis. *Computer Application on ECG and VCG Analysis*, Zywietz, C. and Schneider, B., (eds.). Amsterdam and London: North-Holland Publishing Co., 1973, p. 34.

6. Willems, J.C., Lesaffre, E., and Pardaens, J. Comparison of the classification ability of the electrocardiogram and vectorcardiogram. *Am. J. Cardiol.* 59:119, 1987.

7. Caceres, C.A., Steinberg, C.A., Abraham, S., *et al.* Computer extraction of electrocardiographic parameters. *Circ.* 25:356, 1962.

8. Cady, L.D., Woodbury, M.A., Tick, L.J., *et al.* A method for electrocardiogram wave pattern estimation. Example: Left ventricular hypertrophy. *Circ. Res.* 9:1078, 1961.

9. Pordy, L.H., Jaffe, K., Chesky, C.K., *et al.* Computer diagnosis of electrocardiograms, IV. A computer program for contour analysis with clinical results of rhythm and contour interpretation. *Comput. Biomedical* 1:408, 1968.

10. Smith, R.E. and Hyde, C.M. Computer analysis of the electrocardiogram in clinical practice. *Electrical Activity of the Heart*, Manning, G.W. and Ahuja, S.P., (eds.). Springfield, Ill.: Charles C. Thomas, 1969, p. 305.

11. Bonner, R.E. and Schwetman, H.D. Computer diagnosis of electrocardiograms, II. A computer program for EKG measurements. *Comput. Biomedical Res.* 1:366, 1968.

12. Bailey, J.J., Itscoitz, S.B., Hirshfeld, J.W., Jr., Grauer, L.E., and Horton, M.R. A method for evaluation computer programs for electrocardiographic interpretation, I. Application to the experimental IBM program of 1971. *Circ.* 50:73, 1974.

13. Bailey, J.J., Horton, M., and Itscoitz, S.B. The importance of reproducibility testing of computer programs for electrocardiographic interpretation: Application to the automatic vectorcardiographic analysis program (AVA 3.4). *Comput. Biomedical Res.* 9:307, 1976.

14. Bailey, J.J. and Horton, M.R. Reproducibility of version 2 of the IBM program with and without the serial comparison option. *Progress in Electrocardiology*, Macfarlane, P.W., (ed.). London: Pitman Medical Publishing Co., 1979, p. 259.

15. Willems, J.L., Arnaud, P., van Bemmel, J.H., *et al.* Assessment of the performance of electrocardiograph computer programs with the use of a reference database. *Circ.* 71:523, 1985.

16. Sheffield, L.T. Computer-aided electrocardiography. *JACC* 10:448, 1987.

HEALTH CARE INFORMATION SYSTEMS

This session considered the history of health care information systems from the 1960s through the early 1970s. Carlos Vallbona, MD was the discussant. He made some brief introductory remarks and closed the session with some observations.

Morris F. Collen, MD was the first presenter. He spoke of his initial assignment in medical computing in 1961. There was a need for "an integrated, continuing patient medical record," and he had an undergraduate degree in electrical engineering. The match seemed obvious to the executive director. He described his early work, his success with automated multiphasic health testing, and how—in 1973—the system was retired when the external grants were terminated. Clearly, technical success was a necessary but not a sufficient condition. Following the presentation, Dr. Collen and the attendees discussed the need to establish long-term financial commitments.

The second speaker was Charles D. Flagle, DEng, who offered a different perspective. The primary focus of his presentation was the analysis of health systems for the reduction of uncertainty in its dynamics (through organization, planning, or scheduling) and its substance (through screening and diagnostic aids). In this paper, the computer plays a role that is secondary to the analytic methods used. The objects studied are systems and not patients.

SPEAKERS

Morris F. Collen   Health Care Information Systems: A Personal Historical
              Review
Charles D. Flagle   The Perception of System and the Reduction of Uncertainty
Carlos Vallbona   Discussant

Morris F. Collen, MD is consultant, Division of Research, Kaiser-Permanente Medical Care (since 1983). He received BEE, MB, and MD degrees from the University of Minnesota in 1934, 1938, and 1939, respectively. He joined Kaiser-Permanente as chief, Medical Services, Oakland in 1942. He later served as director, Medical Methods Research (1968–1979) and director, Division of Technology Assessment (1979–1983). He is a member of the Institute of Medicine and the second president of the American College of Medical Informatics. He is the author of four books and is on the editorial board of four journals. In 1987 he became an NLM scholar-in-residence.

Charles D. Flagle, DEng is Professor Emeritus, Department of Health Policy and Management (professor, 1963–1984) and senior research associate, Health Services Research and Development Center, The Johns Hopkins University. He received the BE, MSc, and DEng degrees from The Johns Hopkins University in 1940, 1954, and 1955, respectively. His honors include the Kimball Medal of the Operations Research Society of America (1984). He is on the editorial board of *Methods of Information in Medicine* and *Health Systems Research*.

Carlos Vallbona, MD is professor and chairman of Community Medicine (since 1969), professor of Rehabilitation (since 1976), and professor of Family Medicine (since 1981), Baylor College of Medicine. He attended the Universidad de Barcelona where he received BA and BS degrees in 1944 and an MD degree in 1950. He joined the Baylor faculty in 1956 and four times has been elected to the Outstanding Faculty by a graduating class. He is on the editorial board of seven journals including *Methods of Information in Medicine* and *Informatics and Medicine*.

Health Care Information Systems: A Personal Historical Review

Morris F. Collen, MD
Kaiser-Permanente Medical Care Program, Oakland

Introduction

In 1961, a major career change occurred when I abruptly went from medical practice into medical computing. I had practiced internal medicine since 1942, when I was chief of medicine in Kaiser-Permanente's Oakland Medical Center. Later, when I was physician-in-chief of Kaiser-Permanente's San Francisco Medical Center, the founder and first executive director of Kaiser-Permanente, Dr. Sidney Garfield, decided that it was time for the organization to begin to use computers in the practice of medicine. Since he knew that I had a degree in electrical engineering before I went to medical school, he told me that he felt I should get involved in medical computing and plan how to use computers and technology to develop better methods for taking care of patients. In September 1961, Kaiser-Permanente established a department of Medical Methods Research.

Reflecting back, our primary goal was to develop a comprehensive health care information system to provide an integrated, continuing patient medical record. Kaiser-Permanente was an ideal environment for such an activity, since it provided comprehensive medical care to patients, often continuing from cradle to grave, including ambulatory and hospital care, with all the ancillary and supporting services. Furthermore, Kaiser-Permanente had multiple medical centers in the San Francisco Bay Area; and patients freely obtained care in Oakland where they lived, or in San Francisco where they worked. As a practicing physician within a group practice, the major problem was that the patient's medical record was not available for 10% to 15% of office visits, since the record would be en route somewhere from a prior visit to another physician. To have access to the patient's relevant prior medical information was of the highest priority. The essential information from every office visit, every hospitalization, every lab test and X ray, every consultation and procedure should be available always whenever any physician needed it, wherever in the system the physician was located. Another common problem was that when the record was available, it often was so thick, containing the accumulated documents over many years, that it was a time-consuming chore to browse manually through the record to find the desired, relevant past data. When the appropriate page in the chart was found, sometimes the notes were quite illegible. The traditional manual patient's chart is very inadequate as an efficient information source; and from the viewpoint of being the focal database of a patient information system, the chart is an embarrassment. It would be a great blessing to physicians to exploit the power of the computer (with its communications) for storage, search and retrieval, and for the rapid transfer of patient data to multiple physicians in all facilities. To develop such a health care information system (HCIS) became the driving goal that directed our next 20 years.

In studying our group medical practice, we found that 80% of physicians' services were for outpatient care and 20% for hospital care. Approximately one-fourth of all visits to the clinics were to the department of medicine; and more than one-third of all new patients requesting appointments with internists wanted some form of health checkup. In the hospital services, it was determined that about one-third of the daily hospital costs were for information processing (reporting test results, communicating orders, etc.). Accordingly, we concluded that we should direct computer applications to these areas.

Multiphasic Testing: A Mini-HCIS

Since the beginning of our organization, Dr. Garfield had established preventive medicine as a basic service to be included as a prepaid benefit. Accordingly, the medical department was obligated by contract to provide, within its budget, health checkups to well persons. We had to be competitive with other health plans that only provided diagnostic checkups and sick care and did not include any health checkups or well care as covered benefits. As a result, in 1951, we developed in the San Francisco and Oakland medical centers a lower cost, systematized programmed approach to providing health checkups based on the experience of Dr. Lester Breslow, who, as the San Jose Public Health Officer, modified mass screening by using a battery of low-cost screening tests, which he called multiphasic screening. The Oakland and San Francisco multiphasic screening systems solved the immediate problem of containing costs when each processed 40 to 50 patients a day.

With the initiation of the department of Medical Methods Research (MMR) in 1961, it became evident that the multiphasic screening program was an ideal system to use as a site for research and development in medical computing. First, seriously ill patients never went through the system, so all the patients tested were relatively healthy; and if we made any mistakes in the system we probably wouldn't jeopardize anyone's health. Second, the multiphasic system was actually a mini-

FIGURE 1
Floor plan of Oak-
land multiphasic cen-
ter

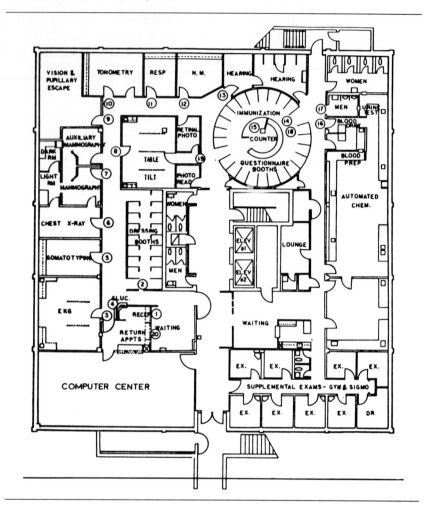

health care information system (mini-HCIS), since it included patient's identification, appointment scheduling, registration and referrals, patient's histories, physician's physical examinations, diagnoses and follow-up referrals, lab tests, X rays, ECGs, physiological measurements (blood pressure, spirometry, etc.), specialty procedures (tonometry, visual and hearing acuity), immunization records, and others. Finally, the developmental costs for such a mini-system approach appeared to be manageable and should eventually pay for itself.

In 1962, we obtained our first of a series of grants from the U.S. Public Health Service (USPHS) to automate and improve our existing manual multiphasic screening program. By 1966, our Oakland multiphasic center had been redesigned and enlarged as shown in Figure 1. The Oakland facility began to process 2000 patients each month and also provided computer processing to the San Francisco multiphasic center. To this day, the Oakland multiphasic center provides an average of 180 multiphasic checkups each day.

During the late 1970s, Oakland patients went through 20 stations in two to three hours. When a patient made an appointment for a multiphasic examination, a packet of data processing cards, onto which results from tests would be punched or mark sensed, were prepared by prepunching into the card the patient's unique medical record number. Patients registered at a rate of approximately one every three minutes. They each received a clipboard containing a medical history checklist questionnaire form and a packet of cards (prepunched for computer input with their medical record number) on which were recorded the test results at each station.

Six electrocardiogram (ECG) leads were recorded simultaneously. The ECGs were subsequently read by a cardiologist who recorded his interpretation on a "mark sense" card. A chest X ray was obtained, to be read subsequently by a radiologist who recorded his interpretations on a mark sense card. Mammography was performed on all women aged 48 and over. Mammograms also were subsequently read by a radiologist who recorded his interpretations on a mark sense card.

Weight and skinfold thickness were measured and the data keypunched into the patient's anthropometry test card. By means of an automated anthropometer, 12 height and transverse body measurements were recorded directly into the patient's punch card within three minutes. Supine pulse rate and blood pressure were measured by an automated instrument and the results directly punched into a card. Vital capacity was measured with a spirometer and recorded on a mark sense card. Visual acuity and ocular tension were measured and the readings recorded on a mark sense card. Hearing was tested with an automated audiometer and the graphed readings transferred to a mark sense card.

The self-administered checklist medical questionnaire form, which the patient received on registering, had been completed during any waiting periods between stations. The patient was then assigned to a questionnaire booth and received a letter box containing a deck of 207 prepunched cards, each having a single dichotomous question printed on the card (Figure 2). Typical "inventory by systems" questions had been selected that were judged to be medically of value in discriminating patients with specific diseases from those nondiseased. The patient responded to each question by taking the card from the top section of the divided letter box and dropping the card into the middle section if his answer to the question was "yes," or into the bottom section if her answer was "no." This procedure automatically sorted "yes" responses for direct input to the computer by means of a card-reading machine. In order to retest the "yes" responses, when the patient had completed

FIGURE 2
Sorting the pre-
punched health ques-
tionnaire cards

sorting all the questions, the nurse removed the "yes" cards from the middle section of the box, placed them back in the upper section and asked the patient to go through them once more "to be sure the answers were 'yes'." This additional step decreased the "false yes" responses by about 10%.

The patient was then sent to the laboratory where blood samples were drawn for a hemoglobin test, white blood cell count, and venereal disease research laboratories test for syphilis (VDRL). The test values were recorded on mark sense cards. From a single sample of serum, eight blood chemistry determinations (serum glucose, creatinine, albumin, total protein, cholesterol, uric acid, calcium, and transaminase) were simultaneously done within 12 minutes by the first multichannel automated chemical analyzer, made by Technicon. We interfaced a card punch machine to the chemical analyzer so test results were directly punched into cards (Figure 3).

A urine specimen was collected, and tests were done for pH, blood, glucose, and protein (paper strip tests). The results were entered on the patient's test mark sense card.

The patient returned to the questionnaire booth and then received a second box of questionnaire cards for psychological testing. The patient sorted 155 psychological questions into "true" and "false" re-

FIGURE 3
First 8-channel Auto
Analyzer interfaced
to the automated
card punch

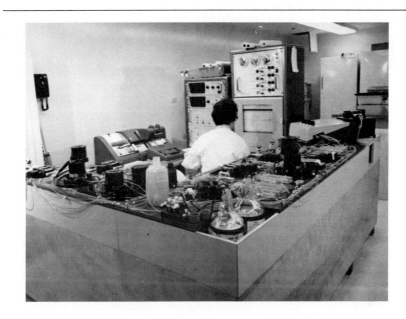

sponses, using the sort box in the same manner as with the medical questionnaire.

By the time the patient had completed the psychological questionnaire, the "on-line" computer processing had been completed, and supplemental tests and appointments, "advised" by the programmed rules of the computer, were arranged for the patient. Routinely advised were a sigmoidoscopy for all patients aged 40 or more; and, for women, a gynecologic examination with cervical smear for cancer detection.

Most of the data generated in the automated multiphasic laboratory were recorded on prepunched or mark sense cards to permit their immediate introduction into the data processing system. As an "on-line" procedure, while the patient was in the last station, the computer processed the information from the punched cards from anthropometry and chemistry; the prepunched sorted cards from the medical questionnaire box; and the reproduced mark sense cards from spirometry, hearing, vision, urine tests, hemoglobin determination, and white cell count. The punched cards were read into a data communication system, and the data transmitted via telephone line to the central computer in a separate building in Oakland.

The computer processor, using a program containing various test limits and decision rules, printed out a report constituting "advice" as to any additional procedures that should be done before the next visit, and the date and length of the follow-up appointment with the physician. For example, if the urine analysis showed proteinuria, the computer printed out instructions to the receptionist to ask the patient to return to the laboratory with a first morning specimen for retest. If a serious abnormality was detected, the computer printout advised the receptionist to arrange an early appointment with the physician; and in some instances to ask the nurse to take the patient to see a physician in the emergency room. A trained nurse supervisor was always on site to handle any questions or problems.

The efficiency and quality of the multiphasic testing process was the result of the standardization of the repetitive procedures routinely included in health checkups, in contrast to the variability necessary for sick patient examinations. At the last station, where a physician had previously manually reviewed all test results and then arranged for any indicated secondary tests, or retests of abnormalities found, the computer's automated review and advice rules now replaced this reviewing physician.

As an off-line procedure, the computer collected and stored the remaining information which arrived a few days later (mark sense cards with physicians' interpretations from the ECG and X rays, the remaining laboratory test reports, and the keypunched medical questionnaire form). When all information had been received, the computer produced a printed summary of all test results and history questions answered "yes" (Figure 4).

At the time of the patient's first office visit, the physician reviewed the summary report and directed further history review toward elaborating the questions to which the patient had answered "yes" and to the test abnormalities reported from the automated multiphasic laboratory. The physician completed a physical examination, recorded the findings and diagnoses on a preprinted form which was automatically scanned by an optical mark reader, and then arranged whatever medical care was necessary for the patient in the usual way.

Our clinical decision support program at that time consisted of two sequential processes: 1) decision rules to provide "advice" on secondary sequential testing, and 2) likelihood ratio probabilistic programs to suggest that the physician "consider" likely diagnoses. Consider rules were developed for a variety of diseases (bronchial asthma, gastrointestinal diseases, heart disease, diabetes). A neuro-mental questionnaire, the basis for developing consider rules for psychiatric diagnoses, was given to 10,000 patients in 1966 and 4% received "consider refer to psychiatry" for conditions which made up 85% of psychiatrists' diagnoses. The neuro-mental questionnaire was discontinued after one year; and its results were never published as our psychiatrists were concerned it might not be used appropriately by internists, and the referrals might overload the psychiatrists' schedules.

FIGURE 4

Example of a computer printout of a summary report

```
            PERMANENTE MEDICAL GROUP - OAKLAND
  FINAL SUMMARY REPORT - MULTIPHASIC HEALTH CHECKUP - 2/24/65

DOE, JANE                                   DR. SMITH J J
M.R.NO. 9876543    BIRTHDATE 05-27  FEMALE   OAKL

   ANTHROPOMETRY: 127.5 LB., 64.5 IN

**ECG: LT.VENT.HYPERTROPHY
**PHONOCARD: SYSTOLIC BASAL MURMUR
**SUPINE BLOOD PRESSURE: 165/80           SUPINE BRACHIAL PULSE: 76.

   VITAL CAPACITY: 2.3 L 1 SEC            3.2 L TOTAL
**CHEST XRAY: CARDIAC ENLARGEMENT HEART/CHEST RATIO =.52
   BREAST XRAY: NSA

   VISUAL ACUITY: R.E.20/40 OR BETTER      L.E.20/40 OR BETTER
   PUPILLARY ESCAPE: NO PUPILLARY ESCAPE
   OCULAR TENSION: R.E. NORMAL            L.E. NORMAL
**RETINAL PHOTO: MINIMAL DIABETIC RETINOPATHY
   HEARING: NO CLINICALLY SIGNIF.HEARING DEFECT

**URINE: PH 6    GLUCOSE MED.   PROTEIN 0   BLOOD 0      BACILLI NEG.
          CLINITEST 1+2+       ACETONE 0
   VDRL 0           BLOOD GROUP AB      LATEX AGGLUT. 0
   HEMOGLOBIN 12.3 GM (NORM.12.0-15.2)   WHITE COUNT  9,000

   SERUM:              (NORMAL)      SERUM:              (NORMAL)
**GLUCOSE (1 HR.) 215  MG (UNDER 205)  CHOLESTEROL 195   MG (140-270)
**GLUCOSE (2 HR.) 170  MG (UNDER 151)
   TOTAL PROT.      6.7 GM (5.8-7.8)   CALCIUM      9.5 MG (8.4-10.8)
   ALBUMIN          4.0 GM (3.4-5.0)   URIC ACID    3.9 MG (3.0-6.3)
   CREATININE       .90 MG (UNDER 1.3) SGOT         21  U  (UNDER 50)
 * 2 HR.BLOOD DRAWN  10 MIN.LATE

**PATIENT RECEIVED THE FOLLOWING (ADVICE RULE) DIRECTIONS:
   700-2 HR.BLOOD SUGAR              800-ROUTINE MEDICAL APPOINTMENT

 * CONSIDER REFER TO ASYMPT. DIABETES STUDY IF FOLLOW-UP CONFIRMS DIABETES.

PATIENT ANSWERED YES TO THESE QUESTIONS ON 1964 FORM:
   249-HAD BAD REACTION OR SENSITIVITY TO PENICILLIN?
IN THE PAST MONTH:
   434-THROAT BEEN SORE ALMOST EVERY DAY?
IN THE PAST 6 MONTHS:
   450-SHORTNESS OF BREATH WITH USUAL WORK OR ACTIVITY?
IN THE PAST YEAR:
   476-REPEAT PAIN,PRESSURE,TIGHT FEELING IN CHEST IN MIDDLE OF BREAST BONE?
   478-REPEAT PAIN,PRESSURE,TIGHT FEELING IN CHEST WHEN SITTING STILL?
   482-REPEATED PAIN OR PRESSURE, IN CHEST WHEN WALK FAST,LEFT ON REST?
   483-REPEATED PAIN,PRESSURE OR TIGHT FEELING IN CHEST FORCED STOP WALKING?
   484-REPEATED PAIN OR PRESSURE, IN CHEST LASTING MORE THAN 10 MINUTES?
   574-ALWAYS HAVE TO GET UP FROM SLEEP TO URINATE?



   ** CONSIDER ABNORMAL,OR POSSIBLE VARIATION FROM NORMAL
   NSA=NO SIGNIFICANT ABNORMALITY
    * NOTE
```

The statistical approach used by this "consider" program was the method published in 1950 by Neyman. The ratios of the frequency of sets of selected symptoms in the diseased patients to the frequency of the same sets of symptoms in the nondiseased were termed the likelihood ratios. The ratios were then arranged in order of increasing magnitude. The region for which a "positive" diagnosis was made (termed the "positive region") was then demarcated by selecting a specific ratio from a consideration of the sensitivity and specificity of this test. All symptom sets associated with ratio values equal to or higher than the selected ratio were included in this positive region. Those symptom sets with ratio values less than the selected value fell outside this positive region and were therefore in the region for diagnosing the non-diseased (termed the "negative region"). We preferred the likelihood ratio method to other probabilistic methods (such as Bayes's theorem) because it did not require symptoms to be mutually exclusive; we did not need to know disease prevalence in our patients, and clinicians seemed to understand it more easily.

Our experience with the multiphasic health checkup showed that computer data processing of a continuing, integrated patient record file provided to the physician in a timely manner a comprehensive profile of the patient's current and prior status. It allowed efficient handling of large volumes of medical information on greater numbers of patients over long periods of time. It permitted quality control of tests and data on-line, thereby decreasing rates of errors due to instrumental variations and personnel actions.

The productivity of physicians was greatly improved when they completed health checkups on patients who had received prior testing by automated multiphasic laboratories. Where automated multiphasic testing had been completed in advance of the physician's physical examination, 50% to 70% of patients completed their "checkup" with the one visit to the physician. With the addition of computer "advice" rules which automatically proposed necessary retesting and additional procedures, 90% of patients could be taken care of by one physician office visit.

Multiphasic health testing provided not only more information on groups of patients, but more information on each patient, thereby producing greater individualization of patient care. Broad and less appropriate population norms were not used, since the computer permitted application of specific norms to each individual patient, based on age, sex, height and weight, time of day, and hours since last food ingestion, thus improving the quality of testing. Since the boundaries between health care and sick care were primarily controlled by programmable limits for normal versus borderline versus diseased, this capability to generate specific normal values was essential to minimize the numbers of false positives and false negatives. With all patients scheduled to see their physicians following the multiphasic laboratory testing, the problems of handling false negatives and positives were then similar to those for periodic health examinations by any traditional method.

Automated multiphasic health testing rapidly diffused during the late 1960s so that in the early 1970s there were a few hundred programs in the United States and several in Europe and in Japan. There were so many visitors to our Oakland multiphasic center in the late 1960s that the USPHS gave us a contract to support a half-time physician to conduct tours. Several Japanese groups drove up in buses, took pictures of every phase of the Oakland multiphasic center, and later duplicated it in Japan. Congressman Fogarty paid a special visit to the center and was very impressed when, while he was standing there, the computer printed out to consider leukemia in a patient. The next day, he called from Washington to ask if the diagnosis was correct, and indeed it was.

Since the costs of providing health checkups to well persons was not paid for by health insurers, multiphasic programs gradually closed down in the United States, except in health maintenance organizations (HMOs) in which health checkups were included as a prepaid benefit. In Japan, in France, and in some other European countries, automated multiphasic programs still continue to operate.

Automated multiphasic testing provided a useful experience for us in developing a computer-based mini-HCIS; and demonstrated how essential stable financing was for the continuing development of a large technological system.

From the viewpoint of providing us with experience to go forward in developing an HCIS, the multiphasic system had required development of computer processing of:

1. Patient identification data, appointment scheduling, daily patient appointment lists, preparation of card packets, specimen labels, registration, operations control data, statistical reports, and quality control procedures.

2. Patient data including patient history, physicians' physical examination data, test and procedure results, physician's interpretations of ECGs and X ray diagnoses.

3. Clinical decision support including alert and warning signals for findings outside of predetermined normal limits, "advice" rules for secondary sequential testing, "consider" rules for likely diagnoses; comparison of history questions with previous histories and identify "new" symptoms reported by the patient for the first time.

4. Provide research data services for epidemiological, clinical, and health services research.

5. Provide a continuing, long-term patient computer medical record to permit comparisons of current patient data to prior data.

6. Provide a system with reliability, security, and confidentiality.

The computer file strategy which developed an integrated, continuous variable-length, variable-format record will be described in the next section.

Pilot HCIS

In 1969, we received a grant from the newly established National Center for Health Services Research and Development (NCHSR&D); the director at the time was its first, Dr. Paul Sanazaro. We were one of seven Health Services Research Centers (HSRC), and ours had its focus in medical technology and computer applications. The objective of our HSRC was to develop a computerized medical data system using our San Francisco Medical Center as a pilot hospital. Ted Van Brunt was the project chief of the San Francisco hospital computer system. Lou Davis was the manager of the computer center containing an IBM 370/155 computer (Figure 5), and he was responsible for developing the computer-stored medical record and its database management system.

By 1973, in our San Francisco Permanente Medical Group offices, patient registration data and physicians' diagnoses from 13 outpatient specialty clinics with an aggregate 2000 visits daily, were recorded on specially designed, standardized "encounter" forms. Between 90% and 95% of the diagnoses were entered by the physicians from a structured format. The remaining unstructured data were manually inscribed in free text on the form and required keypunching for input. The data from these forms were initially entered by an optical scanner, but later, because of the high error rates, the data were entered via on-line electric typewriters directly into each patient's computer record.

In the outpatient pharmacy, data from 1200 prescriptions daily (including patient and physician identification, drug name and dose, prescription refill and drug usage data) were entered by pharmacists, directly (i.e., in real time) into the appropriate patients' computer medical records, using on-line electric typewriters connected by telephone line to the central computer. Subsequently, on entering a prescription refill number, a new label was printed and the cumulative number of dispensed prescriptions automatically recorded for each patient. Container labels were produced under program control in real time, to be dispensed with the drug. Because this large on-line database existed as an integral part of the patients' computer medical record, we also received a contract from the Food and Drug Administration to use the San Francisco drug and diagnoses data to develop a drug reaction monitoring system.

A clinical laboratory computer system was developed, capable of handling data for 3000 tests a day. The automated multiphasic health testing program in San Francisco, described above, entered the data for 150 patient health checkups a day. An on-line electric typewriter in the emergency clinic could retrieve, at any time, selected or all of the above outpatient data from the patient's computer medical record. The clinical benefits of this HCIS to the emergency room staff were substantial, since it eliminated the waiting time to retrieve the manual chart from

FIGURE 5
Equipment configu-
ration for the com-
puter center in 1970

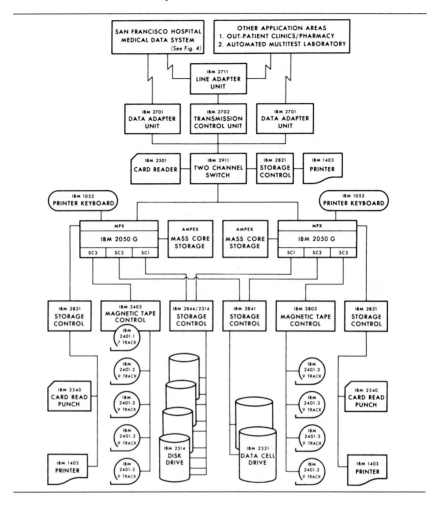

the record room, and it swiftly provided relevant legible information in a chronological or problem-oriented format.

By 1973, the pilot HCIS was being tested within our San Francisco Kaiser Hospital on the Pediatric Service and with an admission-discharge-bed census application (Figure 6). The hospital data subsystem consisted of a satellite minicomputer linked by telephone line with the central computer facility in Oakland. The satellite processor drove 24 visual display terminals, each with an associated light-pen sensor and an electronic printer enclosed in a sound-proofing box. The physicians, identified by plastic identification cards, were able to enter orders and patient's diagnoses directly into the computer by using the light pen. Nurses, using their plastic identification cards, could similarly chart administered drugs to inpatients.

FIGURE 6
San Francisco pilot
HCIS in 1972

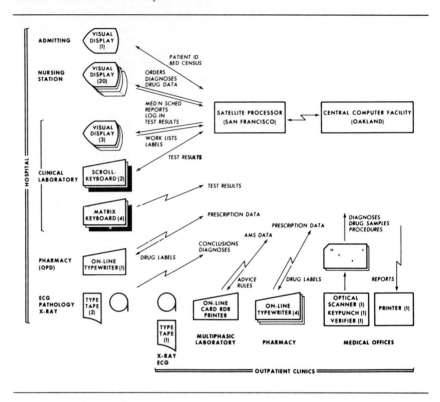

The system of terminals was evaluated by pediatric doctors and nurses for data input and output of diagnoses, physicians' orders (including orders for drugs and general nursing orders), drug administration data, medication schedules, and clinical laboratory results.

A computer-stored, continuing, integrated medical record was operational, which was so structured as to store all classes of patient-related data: identification, administrative, and medical inpatient, outpatient, and ancillary records. It was capable of being continually updated over the lifetime of the patient, of accepting the variable format of medical data input, and of responding to the need for real-time inquiry to individual patient records. All records were individually retrievable by each patient's medical record number on a direct-access basis. Each individual's record within the computer direct access storage facility was kept and moved together as a continuous string of data; it was never split or fractionated for any reason.

The primary file for the medical record database consisted of 1.2 billion bytes of on-line, direct-access disk storage. A patient computer medical record (PCMR) existed for each patient in the Health Plan. Each PCMR formed a physically contiguous record in the file. When a

PCMR was updated with new medical data, the entire PCMR was re-written on disk, with the new data inserted in its proper place. This file then contained all medical data and current essential identification and administrative data. Nonessential or obsolete identification and administrative data, which were not needed for real-time applications, were stored on magnetic tape and constituted an off-line database in a lower hierarchy than the on-line file. The database resided on 12 IBM 3330 disk drives, each of which had a storage capacity of 100 million bytes. The effective maximum capacity of this file was about 1.2 billion bytes. Of 1.5 million patient records in the database in 1972, about 1 million contained only identification and administrative data. Of the remaining 500,000 records, the average PCMR had a length of 1600 bytes and contained seven visits.

The PCMR was a logical branching tree structure in which information was represented at each branch point (node) by data elements, and in the hierarchical structure by the relationship between nodal points (Figure 7). Data were stored at the nodes in two different forms: fixed-length, fixed-format indices; and variable-length, variable-format definitions and values. Relational data between nodes were implicitly represented by the tree structure itself: Data elements within a node or subtree modified the higher level nodes from which they branch. There could be as many as 13 node levels in a PCMR. Indices, which were of fixed length and format, served primarily as pointers to specific por-

FIGURE 7
Tree structure for the computer medical record

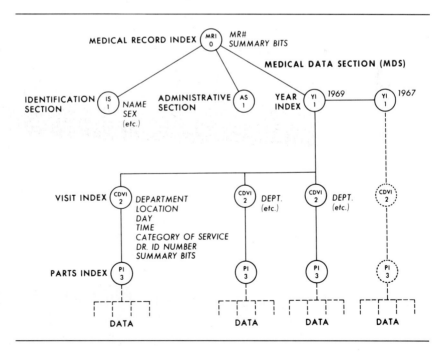

tions of the PCMR. They also contained certain types of identification and visit data. The "medical record index" at level 0 contained the patient's seven-digit medical record number, summary bits, various counters, and field lengths. The "year index" at level 1 was in the "medical data section," and contained the year of visit or visits. A computer defined "visit index" at level 2 was in the "medical data section," and contained visit parameters and dates. The parts index at level 3 specified the parts into which medical data from a visit had been stored.

"Summary bits" were a series of 56 binary flags that were "set" whenever certain data were stored. There were bits corresponding to general and specific data categories, procedures, and laboratory specimens. The principal function of summary bits was that they were easily and rapidly tested by retrieval programs to determine whether the data of interest were present in that record.

Within a PCMR, data were stored in one of three main sections: identification, administrative, or medical. The "identification section" contained all secondary identifiers and other information characteristic of the individual patient. The "administrative section" contained information on health plan coverage, Medicare, and other data of a nonclinical nature. The "medical data section" contained clinical data for each patient visit, indexed and stored in reverse chronological order. Medical data were further subdivided for storage purposes into 10 parts. Each part represented a general category of medical data. History data were stored in part 0, laboratory data in part 2, physician reports on X rays and ECGs in part 3, nurses notes in part 4, diagnoses in parts 5 and 6, prognoses in part 7, treatments in part 8, other recommendations in part 9. Within each part, data were stored in a tree structure.

The pilot HCIS described above was financially supported about half from federal research funds and about half from our organization. The research support funds were discontinued in 1973 with the termination of the Health Services Research Center grants. As a result of the large cost requirements associated with the development of the HCIS, an organizational decision was made to discontinue this program.

By the end of 1973, there had been sufficient experience with testing and operating the HCIS so that its costs were identifiable. Table 1 lists the estimated costs for staff, services, computing equipment, and database storage for the Oakland and San Francisco regional medical services computer operations at that time.

We were then reminded that John Kenneth Galbraith (*The New Industrial State*, 1967) had pointed out the extraordinary requirements of large complex technological systems which needed (a) long-term, heavy investment of capital and manpower, (b) accurate planning to inflexibly commit people and capital for long lead times, (c) specialized technology manpower, and (d) a long-term commitment from an orga-

TABLE 1
Estimated HCIS Costs in 1973

Computer Center	Annual Cost	Unit Cost
Staff and equipment	$1,000,000.00	$1.00/member/year $0.18/office visit $1.50/hospital day
Computer medical record	$250,000.00	$0.25/member/year $0.09/office visit $0.25/hospital day

Application		
Multiphasic testing	$50,000.00	$2.50/patient
Clinical laboratory	$50,000.00	$0.06/test
Pharmacy	$15,000.00	$0.05/prescription

nization competent to coordinate mixed medical, systems, and engineering specialists. We had failed to obtain long-term financial commitments.

In retrospect, this pilot HCIS probably represented the state of the art in 1973. In 1987, the concepts and objectives of this HCIS would not change significantly; however, it would benefit from some software reprogramming, and it would definitely be enhanced by hardware modifications using advances in computing and communications technology such as microprocessors, distributed databases, networking, and workstations.

Bibliography

Collen, M.F. Automated multiphasic health testing. *Information Systems for Patient Care*, Blum, B., (ed.). New York: Springer-Verlag, 1984, Chapter 28.

Collen, M.F. Computer analyses in preventive health research. *Method Inform Med* 1967;6(Jan):8–14.

Collen, M.F. Computers in preventive health services research. *Seventh IBM Medical Symposium*, Poughkeepsie, Oct. 27, 1965.

Collen, M.F. Data processing techniques for multitest screening and hospital facilities. *Hospital Information Systems*, Bekey, G. and Schwartz, M., (eds). Marcel Dekker, Inc., 1972, Chapter 6.

Collen, M.F. The functions of a HIS: An overview. *Proceedings of MEDINFO 83*, Amsterdam, August 1983.

Collen, M.F. General requirements. *Hospital Computer Systems*, Collen, M.F., (ed.). New York: John Wiley & Sons, 1974, Chapter 1.

Collen, M.F. General requirements for clinical departmental systems. *Proceedings of MEDINFO 83 Seminars*, Amsterdam, August 1983.

Collen, M.F. General requirements for a medical information system. *Comp and Biomed Res* 1970;3(Oct).

Collen, M.F. Hospital computer systems: Reasons for failures and factors making for success. *Public Health in Europe. 1. Health Planning and Organization of Medical Care*. Copenhagen: WHO, 1972.

Collen, M.F. Information processing of physical examinations for computerized medical records. *Information Processing of Medical Records*. Amsterdam and London: North-Holland, 1970.

Collen, M.F. Machine diagnosis from a multiphasic screening program. *Fifth IBM Medical Symposium*, Endicott, New York, Oct. 1963.

Collen, M.F. Multiphasic screening as a diagnostic method in preventive medicine. *Methods Inform Med* 1965;4(June);71.

Collen, M.F. The multitest laboratory in health care of the future. *Hospitals* 1967;41(May):119.

Collen, M.F. Patient data acquisition. *Med Instrumentation* 1978;12 (Aug):222–225.

Collen, M.F. Periodic health examinations using an automated multitest laboratory. *JAMA* 1966;195(Mar 7):830–833.

Collen, M.F. Planning and implementing large medical information systems. *The Management of Health Care*, Abernathy, W.J. and Prahalad, C.K. Cambridge: J. Lippincott, 1974, Chapter 9.

Collen, M.F. Preventive medicine and automated multiphasic screening. *Ninth IBM Medical Symposium*, Burlington, Vermont, Oct. 24–26, 1969.

Collen, M.F. Problems with presentation of computer data. *Information Processing of Medical Records*. Amsterdam and London: North-Holland, 1970.

Collen, M.F. and Davis, L.S. Computerized medical records in multiphasic testing. *Computer* 1973;23–27.

Collen, M.F. and Davis, L.S. The multitest laboratory in health care. *J Occup Med* 1969;2(July):7.

Collen, M.F. and Linden, C. Screening in a group practice prepaid medical care plan. *J Chronic Dis* 1955;2(Oct):400.

Collen, M.F. and Terdiman, J. Technology of multiphasic screening. *Annual Review of Biophysics & Bioengineering,* Vol 2. Palo Alto, Calif: Ann. Rev., Inc., 1973, pp. 103–114.

Collen, M.F., Davis, L.S., and Van Brunt, E.E. The computer medical record in health screening. *Methods Info Med* 1971;10(July):138–142.

Collen, M.F., Rubin, L., and Davis, L. Computers in multiphasic screening. *Computers in Biomedical Research,* Vol 1., Stacy, R.W. and Waxman, B.D., (eds.). New York: Academic Press, Inc., 1965, Chapter 14.

Collen, M.F., Rubin, L., Neyman, J., *et al.* Automated multiphasic screening and diagnosis. *Am J Public Health* 1964;54(May):741.

Collen, M.F., Van Brunt, E.E., and Davis, L.S. Problems of computerization of large computer medical record systems. *Med Informatics* 1976;1:47–53.

Collen, M.F., Davis, L., Van Brunt, E.E., and Terdiman, J. Functional goals and problems in large scale patient record management and automated screening. *FASEB Fed. Proc.* 1974;33(Dec):12.

Davis, L.S., Collen, M.F., Rubin, L., and Van Brunt, E.E. Computer-stored medical record. *Comp and Biomed Res* 1968;(May):1,5.

Gleser, M.A. and Collen, M.F. Towards automated medical decisions. *Comp and Biomed Res* 1972;5:180–189.

Kodlin, D. and Collen, M.F. Automated diagnosis in multiphasic screening. *Sixth Berkeley Symposium on Math. Stat. and Prob.,* Vol IV, Neyman, J., (ed.). Berkeley: University of California Press, 1971.

Rubin, L., Collen, M.F., and Goldman, G.E. Frequency decision approach to automated medical diagnosis. *Fifth Berkeley Symposium on Mathematical Statistics and Probability,* Vol. IV, LeCam, L., and Neyman, J., (eds.). Berkeley: University of California Press, 1967.

Van Brunt, E.E. and Collen, M.F. Nursing station subsystem. *Hospital Computer Systems,* Collen, M.F., (ed.). New York: John Wiley & Sons, 1974, Chapter 6.

Van Brunt, E.E., Davis, L., and Collen, M.F. Kaiser-Permanente Hospital computer systems. *Hospital Computer Systems,* Collen, M.F., (ed.). New York: John Wiley & Sons, 1974, Chapter 21.

Van Brunt, E.E., Collen, M.F., Davis, L.S., *et al.* A pilot data system for a medical center. *Proceedings of the IEEE* 1969;57(Nov):ll.

Participants' Discussion

Bruce Waxman	I've been wondering why multiphasic screening systems haven't been more successful. Bill Yamamoto just explained the economics of it to me. Then, a few minutes ago, I reflected on the success of the COSTAR system that Octo and I developed. For reasons that I don't really understand, we had the wit to design a billing system into COSTAR. It could be easily argued that the reason COSTAR succeeded was because it addressed economic concerns.

When I was in California installing COSTAR systems, invariably a large number of clinics adopted it because they were interested primarily in the billing system. It made money for them. Subsequently, 30% to 40% of the clinics used the medical records part of COSTAR, and in many cases successfully. So I support the observation you made that unless one addresses the economics of medical computing—unless these systems serve the prevailing economic needs—you've got a problem.

Morris Collen	Yes, we could spend a lot of time on that, but I've learned a lot of lessons from Octo—he's much wiser and more pragmatic than I. I remember my site visit to the MGH Laboratory years back when he wanted to expand. The hospital administrator said that the clinical laboratory was so efficient and saving them so much money that whether Octo got the grant or not they were going to continue it. They had cut down on repeat lab tests by 15%. So Octo had started with modules that would fly regardless of outside funding.

Well, when I started with the computer medical record system, it was very hard to justify. Octo's approach of starting from modules that pay off does ensure survivability. But you eventually reach the stage of needing to develop a computer-stored medical record system. Why doesn't COSTAR, which is an office record system, also have an inpatient record system? Technicon did a beautiful job on the hospital record, but why don't they have an outpatient record system? If you don't have total system planning, you can start with whatever module you want, but you'd better have your eye on the ultimate computer-stored record if you want to get it in the final comprehensive system. Most systems didn't do that, and they ended up with nonintegrated modules.

William Yamamoto   When I went to George Washington University in 1971, Dr. Caceres had installed a multiphasic health screening clinic for the university. The history of the clinic follows the financial problems of freestanding health clinics. Subsequently, about six multiphasic units were set up by various corporate entities in Washington, D.C., and all of them have failed. But George Washington, because it had some institutional financial backing, has managed to keep its multiphasic screening unit intact. However, we still have the same wallpaper on the wall, and in many ways we haven't modified or improved the system.

It has been an interesting experience for me as a nonclinician to see the evolution of the availability of preventive medicine services to the general public. Particularly interesting in the last year has been the provision of preventive medicine services through the open PPO mechanisms, particularly Metropolitan Life Insurance Company. I think that some of the problems that you were reflecting on as to why they didn't survive may turn around as the body politic becomes more interested in preventive medicine as an over-the-counter service. We, George Washington, survive largely by rendering services to people who must have an obligatory administrative health examination for such purposes as applying for immigration, being employed by some corporation, a public association or the government, and things of this sort. I think financially that is the only viable pattern for multiphasic screening units at present, perhaps until the third-party payment structure changes.

Morris Collen   If you are flexible on the concept, my perception of all the health fairs, health-hazard appraisals, and health-risk appraisals is that they are just a modification of health checkups, because they are parts of health evaluations. They collect all the tests and make some assessment of the patient, and then they go on to try to educate and alter behavior. But it's still essentially a multiple-screening approach.

Carlos Vallbona   To add to Dr. Yamamoto's remarks, the Health Care Financing Administration is also now reassessing the value of health screening in the elderly and planning to reimburse organizations.

Thomas Lincoln   Toffler has made the cogent remark that successful technologies have to make either a buck or a big bang, and we only have the first option in health care. Our technologies have to pay for themselves.

The Perception of System and the Reduction of Uncertainty

Charles D. Flagle, DEng
The Johns Hopkins University, Baltimore

Introduction

Inspired by the 1963 photograph of Drs. Clark and Molnar with the LINC, I recalled my own efforts along somewhat similar lines and dug from the files a picture of the QUEUIAC. While working with Paul Dunn in the Intelligence Division of the Army Operations Research Office in the early 1950s, we built a device to simulate the random flow and congestion of battlefield communications and to demonstrate the effect of changes in technologies, message handling, and decision processes {1}. The QUEUIAC, as we dubbed it facetiously, was a simple machine—banks of bidirectional stepping switches actuated by variable-speed paper tape drives. Tapes were punched at intervals to simulate message arrival patterns and service times. It displayed the erratic pattern of system states—the number of messages in process or waiting—by rows of lights and was easily manipulated to show the effects of changed speed of transmission, priorities, or network configurations.

As a means of simulating real or hypothetical situations, the QUEUIAC had some good points. There was realism in its display of congestion and delay in operating systems subject to random demands. However, it was noisy and too slow for analytical work, i.e., the estimation of distributions of state probabilities and elapsed times to information processing. Rapidly developing techniques of Monte Carlo simulation using digital computers doomed the QUEUIAC to oblivion, but not before it—and awareness of the kinds of problems it addressed—caught the attention of people in the health services, and set in motion a set of activities and relationships that continue to this day.

One outgrowth of military operations research of World War II was a sharpening recognition of the pervasiveness of random processes and their consequences in human affairs. Not only communication systems, but transportation, manufacturing operations, emergency care arrivals at hospitals—all were recognized as stochastic, or chance-dominated, processes requiring surplus capacity to accommodate uncontrollable peaks and valley of demands. While the mathematics of design of telephone systems had been worked out in the early part of the century, the formulas did not cover the range of waiting-line problems (or queu-

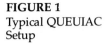

FIGURE 1
Typical QUEUIAC
Setup

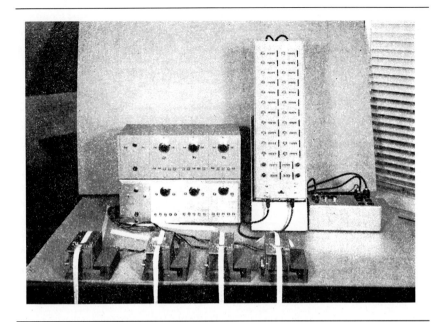

ing problems or stochastic systems) encountered in other fields. This gave rise to a number of efforts to solve particular type of problems analytically, but complications in real-life systems quickly outran the capability for mathematical solution, hence the recourse to simulation.

Paradoxically, mathematical analysis is possible when the flow of messages, people, or other things is either tightly scheduled or when it is a completely unscheduled set of chance events. There is system—in the sense of patterns—in what might seem to be pure chance. It is the ability to perceive the obscured system in the pattern of random events that paves the way for designing appropriate human organizations to deal with those events. Whoever must respond to random events as they occur lives in a world of uncertainty, an unenviable position, particularly if resources are scarce. The natural tendency is to try to get hold of processes and to control the flow of events over time; to reduce the uncertainty of what is happening, or what will happen next.

At about the time of these activities, the deans and administrators at Johns Hopkins met at the behest of the university's president, Dr. Lowell Reed, to determine ways in which the diverse schools and affiliated research agencies (which included the Army Operations Research Office) might give each other assistance. Thanks to the insightfulness of the director of the hospital, Dr. Russell Nelson; the director of the Operations Research Office, Dr. Ellis Johnson; and my mentor, Dean Robert Roy, of the School of Engineering, the potentials of operations research approaches to help the hospital were seen to be promising. The concept was given a try, beginning in 1956, with the establishment of an operations research division within the hospital, and it was my good fortune to head the group.

Early Operations Research in Hospitals— Inpatient Care

Once we were on the job, some pressing problems were given priority. Recall that we are speaking of a period not long after World War II. The nation's building and renovation of health facilities was just beginning. Some floors of the hospital were closed for lack of professional nursing staff. Substitutes in the form of nursing aides trained on the job helped to staff the open floors, but understaffing remained a problem and work stress caused high turnover. There was urgent need for a system of equitable staffing assignments. In addition to the problems on the nursing units there was a great deal of congestion in the outpatient clinics. These conditions were recognized as symptoms of deeper problems in the totality of health services of the times, but we could not wait for solutions at a national or community level. It was necessary to carry on through best use of the resources at hand.

One clue to the possibility of solutions lay in the observable fact that, while indeed there were periods of extreme congestion, there were also periods when not much was happening. In part this was predictably periodic, but in part it was sporadic and unexpected. Some work studies had noted considerable staff idleness even though there were complaints of personnel shortage. Administrators were quick to attribute this to poor supervision, and it was around this point that some of our first studies were organized. The situation looked suspiciously like the natural consequences of inherently random processes affecting the levels of illness of patients as well as the availability of nurses. We set out to determine what we labelled an "optimum" staff and facility for a nursing unit and found that the optimum was something that varied continuously but could be predicted and achieved. After painstaking hours of observation of patient care, we uncovered first some evidence of different categories of patients, measured in terms of amounts of nursing care given. Patient-dependency classification was not a new idea, but this work added knowledge about the day-to-day variation in numbers of patients in the categories or levels of dependency.

Of particular interest was the distribution of critical, or intensive care, patients, which closely approximated a Poisson distribution, evidence of the purely random process described earlier. This was not surprising, since the arrival or relapse of intensive care patients into a tertiary care hospital was indeed an independent, random process, and the length of stay was also highly variable {2}. The number of intensive care patients on the 30-bed wards varied from as few as two to as many as 15, and, because these patients received nearly five times as much attention as other patients, their number dominated the need for nurse staffing.

What made the problem tractable was that the patient classification could be made quickly on the basis of factors observable to nurses, and that the work loads estimated were reasonable predictions for the following day. This work was reported by Connor, *et al.* {3}, describing how the process of patient-dependency classification formed the basis of a management process for day-to-day computation of staffing requirements for inpatient nursing units in acute-care hospitals. The information system developed for the management process was a manual one, requiring daily patient classification by a head nurse, followed by a few calculations to arrive at predicted staff needs for the following day. It was the forerunner of computerized systems for nurse staffing {4}. Several such systems are available commercially today.

Several parallel developments took place, ultimately of significance to medical informatics—a term not even dreamed of at the time. While we at Johns Hopkins were concentrating our attention on day-to-day management of inpatient care by augmentation of staff in response to signals of predicted heavy work loads, colleagues in the U.S. Public Health Service were examining an alternative form of organization known as Progressive Patient Care {5}. As in the Johns Hopkins procedure, they recognized levels of intensity of care, but used patient classification as a basis for transfer to facilities appropriate to the level of need. Designed as a response to shortages of acute beds and special-duty nurses, the concept of progressive care spawned the reality of the intensive care unit and the dream of hospital-based, long-term care. The intensive care unit, by concentrating the number of critically ill patients, gave economic justification and operational necessity to the automation of monitoring processes, a major area of importance for medical informatics.

Another development of importance emerged from the work studies and activity analysis of inpatient care. Though everyone knew that written communication consumed much of the professional nurse's time, the measurements came as a surprise—something on the order of one-third of available nurse time was spent in transcribing and other paperwork. The Lockheed Company can be credited with bringing aerospace technology to bear on this problem. Using light pen technology to activate a hierarchy of displays on a CRT, physician orders for medications and treatments, and nursing orders for procedures could be entered, analyzed, consolidated, and recorded for retrieval. My involvement was peripheral and not in the development phase. However, in 1968, while serving as special assistant to the surgeon general for applied health technology, I participated in the economic analysis of the concept of the ward-based hospital information systems, concluding that the commercial potential was sufficiently large to justify industrial investment in its development, but that federal support of demonstration and evaluation would be an appropriate government role. Evaluation of the El Camino Hospital installation, supported by the National Center for Health Services Research, has provided quantitative information on a major product in the armamentarium of medical informatics {6}.

Another major development in research on inpatient care was related again to the notion of patient classification. Colleagues at Yale, John Thompson and Robert Fetter, examined patient classification from the point of view of overall resource requirements for an episode of hospitalization. Using data from hospital discharge abstracts, applying a computerized procedure for pattern recognition, Autogrp, they looked for clusters of patients with similar patterns of costs in terms of length of stay and use of other resources. Their groupings were strongly associated with diagnosis, hence the name Diagnosis Related Groups (DRGs) {7}. This scheme of classification, not of the patient day but of the patient episode of hospitalization, has been adopted as a basis for hospital reimbursement of federally supported inpatient care. Within DRGs, variation in length of stay is large; further refinements continue.

Studies of Outpatient Care

The problems of outpatient services, characteristic of large medical centers, were manifest in crowding and patient delays. Traditionally, if an appointment system existed, a large number of patients would be scheduled early to avoid the possibility of physicians waiting for patients. Bailey studied the problem in England, reaching the conclusion that the phenomenon of patient delay could be understood only if the ratio of computed value of physician time to patient time was nearly infinite {8}. Patients responded by disregarding appointment times or failing to appear; in a pediatric clinic studied it was not uncommon to have a missed-appointment rate near 50%. The net result was a pattern of actual patient arrivals showing a high degree of randomness. The problem was compounded by a form of sequential and separate services, e.g., registration, payment, weighing in, interview, treatment, and rescheduling of a subsequent visit. Variability in service times caused delays and congestion before each of these services. The situation lent itself to analysis by simulation, which proved to be a useful approach

{9}, for it permitted demonstration of the probable behavior of reorganized services. In the specific example of the pediatric clinic, simulation of parallel lines of patient flow relieved bottlenecks but pointed up the need for tighter scheduling of patients and clinic staff. Manual systems were devised for this at the time, paving the way for computer-based systems, still a few years away.

Both the inpatient and outpatient problems and the approaches to their solutions had common characteristics. First was the need to perceive in the behavior of a perplexing set of activities the dynamics of the demands of illness and accident on a system of health service resources. When it was seen in a quantitative sense that the dynamics of demand were largely dominated by chance, the way was paved for operational solutions. One approach was to combine operating units to take advantage of the relative reduction of chance variations as size increases. This was illustrated in a simulation of the effect of combining maternity visits {10}. Another was to develop means of predicting future demands in time to deploy resources, as in the case of the inpatient nurse staffing. A third was to regulate the flow of scheduled patients to compensate for the uncontrollable, random amounts of emergencies. All have the character of attempts to reduce uncertainty, or the consequences of uncertainty in dynamic or time-dependent processes. Another kind of uncertainty exists, one having to do not with the dynamics of a process, but with the substance—the actuality of what one is dealing with. This is the kind of uncertainty inherent in problems of screening and diagnosis, and this problem was first brought to our attention by colleagues in public health.

Studies in Screening and Diagnosis

In the midst of our studies of hospital care in the late 1950s, students from the School of Public Health began to appear in our courses in operations research. Among them was Dr. Michel Lechat,[1] a leprologist from the then Belgian Congo, bearing a large trunkful of data and a copy of von Neumann and Morgenstern's *Theory of Games and Economic Behavior* as evidence of his faith that quantitative analysis might help some of the problems of control of tropical diseases. The specific problem troubling Dr. Lechat was the overwhelming load on the ambulatory care services for leprosy—the "clinics under the trees." The development, during the 1940s, of the sulfones for treatment and control of lepromatous leprosy had made outpatient care possible, and this brought on a dramatic increase in the number of persons who pre-

---

[1] Dr. Lechat had been medical director of the Leprosarium at Cocquiatville.

sented themselves for screening and care. The traditional procedure for screening for contagious cases involved the preparation of 10 to 20 tissue smears for microscopic examination. Laboratory resources were swamped. The questions were, could fewer tissue smears detect cases with adequate sensitivity, and if so what number of slides would maximize the rate of detection of contagious cases? The answer lay, it was hoped, in the trunk, with its screening data on hundreds of contagious cases.

The answer to the second question was found with little trouble. After some painstaking search for patterns of appearance of *lepromatous bacilli* in tissues smear slides from various sites, it became apparent that one slide could detect 80% of the cases. Combining this knowledge with some work studies of laboratory preparation and examination of slides, we determined that, for fixed laboratory capacity, case-detection rate was maximized with one slide {11}, but the ethical question was raised of the adequacy of a test with 80% sensitivity, implying that 20% of the true positives would be missed. Adding slides to the screening procedures increased sensitivity, thereby detecting more cases among those examined, but losing cases among those who were excluded from examination by limited capacity of the laboratories.

We formulated the problem in decision theoretic terms, as a game against nature {12} which forced us to make some estimates of the costs associated with the missed case. It happened that the marginal contribution of a second slide was substantial, placing administrative pressure on an increase in laboratory capacity.

The experience gave us a healthy respect for the magnitude of the problem of estimating costs of missed cases. In some later efforts to find optimal screening strategies, that is to determine the choice of level of a screening measure that minimizes the total costs or regrets associated with false negatives and false positives, it became apparent that there is no single threshold of a screening measure that is universally optimal {12}. The optimal threshold is a function of both the prevalence of undetected disease in the population screened and the ratio of costs of false positives and false negatives—all ephemeral quantities, not knowable with confidence. However, the importance of these numbers diminished as the sensitivity and specificity are increased jointly. This forces better screening procedures than the traditional approach of basing decisions on the results of a single test, seeking a tradeoff between sensitivity and specificity. One approach to improvement has been to reach for patterns of several key variables, perhaps in conjunction with the screening test, which increases the accuracy of detection. To do this requires statistical analysis of a database containing a number of true positives and true negatives, itself a process requiring computational power {13, 14}. Beyond that there must be a medical record system in operation in a screening clinic to capture measures of the key variables and to recognize significant patterns related to diseases. In these early approaches to using statistical methods to improve the accuracy of screening and diagnosis and to automate the analytic processes as an integral part of records keeping, we see some of the beginnings of the domain of medical decision making in the field of medical informatics.

Conclusions

All the reminiscences mentioned so far have been culled from experiences at the clinical or administrative levels of direct health services. This is where exciting work has been done and is being done. However, the picture would be incomplete without some mention of the efforts to build information systems for decision making at community, state, and national levels. Historically, such efforts were an integral part of the Hill-Burton Program, which demanded from an applicant for hospital construction funds a community-based plan demonstrating the need for new facilities. Further, the concept of progressive patient care, as endorsed by the Public Health Service, envisioned the hospital as the center of a coordinated set of comprehensive services. The technique of patient classification had the purpose not only of assignment of patients to appropriate levels of care within the hospital but, in addition, to promote organizational ties with various forms of rehabilitation and extended care. This form of vertical integration, shaped by comprehensive health planning, it was hoped, would replace the traditional "nonsystem" of "fragmented services."

As we know, the nonsystem successfully resisted vertical integration for a long time. Only recently, under the pressures for care reimbursement—made possible by the information systems growing out of a patient classification—have we seen a trend toward hospital initiatives in comprehensive services. It is interesting to recall that the development of information systems for comprehensive community health services were part of the stream of developments in the Hill-Burton Program. Computer-based patient-flow simulation models—deterministic rather than stochastic—have been in use for years to forecast trends in health services demand and manpower needs. Somehow these activities, which influence decision making at policy levels rather than clinical and institutional levels, have become a major interest in medical informatics. However, in the long run, the knowledge gained from the research in medical informatics at the clinical level will be drawn on for refinement of decision processes at policy levels—and this will be another challenge for the evolving field of medical informatics.

Summary

Until the mid-1960s we had two separate streams of development for medical information systems. One proceeded from efforts under the Hill-Burton Program to develop management systems for hospitals and community health planning, with little stress placed initially on the interactive use of computers. The other, centered within medicine and medical decision making, was from the outset an effort to exploit the growing potential of computers in clinical matters. Creation of the National Center for Health Services Research in 1968 was a key event in the merging of these two sets of activities, with formation of a program and study section in health systems development and a common source of funding for projects with either administrative or clinical significance, or both.

The establishment of the National Center was preceded by more than a decade of health services research with the objective of improved management systems. The concepts and systems growing out of this research were forerunners of many of the activities in modern medical informatics; they were foundations for the still-developing techniques of resource allocation, staffing, scheduling, and for screening and diagnosis.

A common theme runs through the early research and development. Researchers were faced with perplexing pictures of the behavior of both patients and the people and organizations serving them. Through direct observation of the central actions in patient care and support services, it was possible to perceive some pattern, order, or system in the demands stemming from illness and accident, and these patterns were inherently variable and apparently unpredictable. Whether physician, nurse, or administrator, the provider was confronted with the need to make decisions under uncertainty.

Having gained insight from research, the task was one of finding ways to reduce uncertainty: by developing timely predictors of demands, by developing flexible administrative mechanisms to move resources to demands (or vice versa), and by reducing error in the assessment of patient condition. The early work in patient classification by level of dependency has led to management systems for nurse staffing and patient placement. Refined by the inclusion of diagnosis as a variable, patient classification led to mechanisms of resource allocation and reimbursement. Early work in outpatient services drew on techniques of computer simulation to test alternative approaches to control of congestion and delay in outpatient services through computerized appointment scheduling and record-keeping systems. Early work in applying statistical decision theory to disease screening led to awareness of the need to reduce uncertainty of testing, touching off a wave of efforts to base decision rules on multivariate analysis to increase sensitivity and specificity. The path to implementation of all these systems has led appropriately to computer-based information systems.

In retrospect one can see in the decades of research and development a process of inexorable growth of intelligence in an evolving health system, growth in precision of sensing, analysis, communication, and memory. In this perspective, the disparate research and development efforts began years ago finding meaning in the content of medical informatics, and the role of medical informatics itself can be better understood in the context of the evolving health system.

References

1. Dunn, P.F., Flagle, C.D., and Hicks, P.A. The QUEUIAC: An electromechanical analog for the simulation of waiting line problems. *Operations Research*, Vol. 4, No. 6, December 1958.

2. Flagle, C.D. The problem of organization for hospital inpatient care. *Management Sciences: Models and Techniques*, Churchman, C.W. and Verhulst, M., (eds.), Vol. 2. New York: Pergamon Press, 1960, pp. 275–287.

3. Connor, R.J., Flagle, C.D., Hsieh, R.K.C., Preston, R.A., and Singer, S. Effective used of nursing resources: A research report. *Hospitals* 35, 30–39 (1961).

4. Miller, H.E. and Pierce, F.A. The implementation of nurse scheduling using mathematical programming. *Proceedings, Forum on Nurse Staffing, National Cooperative Services Center for Hospital Management Engineering*, New York, September 8–9, 1975. Nuffield Provincial Hospitals Trust. *Studies in the Function and Design of Hospitals*. London: Oxford University Press, 1955.

5. Haldeman, J.C. and Abdellah, F.G. Concepts of progressive patient care. *Hospitals* 33: May 16 and June 1, 1959.

6. Coffey, R.M. How a Medical Information System Affects Hospital Costs: The E1 Camino Hospital Experience. NCHSR Research Summary Series, DHEW Publication No. (PHS) 80–3265, March 1980.

7. Fetter, R.B., *et al.* Case-mix definition by diagnosis-related groups. *Med. Care* 18, 1, 1980.

8. Bailey, N.T.J. A study of queues and appointment systems in hospital outpatient departments, with special reference to waiting times. *J. Roy. Stat. Soc.* 14, 185–199, (1952).

9. Gabrielson, I.W., Soriano, A., Taylor, M.M., and Flagle, C.D. Analysis of Congestion in an Outpatient Clinic. Final report on USPHS

grant W-96. Baltimore: School of Hygiene and Public Health, The Johns Hopkins University, 1962.

10.   Thompson, J.D., Fetter, R.B., McIntosh, C.S., and Pelletier, R.J. Computer simulation of the activity in a maternity suite. *Proceedings of the Third International Conference on Operational Research*, Oslo, 1963. Paris: Dunod, 1964.

11. Flagle, C.D. Statistical decision theory and the selection of diagnostic and therapeutic procedures in public health (with M. Lechat). *Actes de la 3ieme Conference Internationale de Recherche Operationnelle*, Kreweras, G. and Morlat, G., (eds.). London: English Universities Press, Ltd., 1964, pp. 194–202.

12. Flagle, C.D. Allocation of medical and associated resources to the control of leprosy (with M.F. Lechat). *Acta Hospitals 2*, June, 1962. Also published in *Management Sciences in the Emerging Countries*, Barich, N.N. and Verhulst, M., (eds.). Oxford: Pergamon Press, 1965, Chapter 9.

13. Gleser, M.A. and Collen, M.F. Towards automated medical decisions. *Comput. Biomedical Res.* 5, 180–189 (1972).

14. Lincoln, T.L. and Parker, R.D. Medical diagnosis using Bayes's theorem. *Hlth Serv. Res.* 2, 34–45 (1967).

Bibliography

Flagle, C.D. A decision theoretical comparison of three methods of screening for a single disease. *Proceedings of the Fifth Berkeley Symposium on Mathematical Statistics and Probability*, LeCam, L. and Neyman, J., (eds.)., Vol. 4. Berkeley: University of California Press, 1967, pp. 887–901.

Flagle, C.D. Communication and control in comprehensive health planning. *Ann. N.Y. Acad. Sci.* 161:714–729, 1969.

Flagle, C.D. The role of simulation in the health services. *American Journal of Public Health*, 60:2386–2394, 1970.

Participants' Discussion

Thomas Lincoln   As things have gone on, we now see a convergence between the new issues of quality assessment, risk management, and utilization review bringing together many of the considerations that have their inception in the slides you presented. I wonder if you would speak briefly to that incipient synthesis that is, in fact, not yet in place as far as I understand it.

Charles Flagle   You've touched on a matter that came up yesterday as well, and it has to do with the boundaries of medical informatics. A good bit of my life has been spent with the people in this room in the field that has developed as medical informatics. But I am aware that there is a big chunk of life that's spent in what seems to me to be outside the field of medical informatics. It is in that very area that you speak of that would include not only the problems of utilization review, quality assurance, and reimbursement mechanisms, but the whole notion of planning—of attempting to match national resources to national requirement. What comes immediately to mind is the Institute of Medicine's study on nursing education and nursing requirements for the country. The principle analytical model used there was one that was called the vector model in the Health Resources Administration. The Veterans Administration has something very similar to it—the bed sizing models in which the forecasting process relates the projection of the aging population to the kinds of medical needs that it will require.

    All of that certainly involves computers, and it involves medical information if you think of epidemiologic information as medical information. If you think of utilization statistics and resource requirements as part of the databases of informatics, then I would say that we have been reminiscing about the good old days and just haven't said much about what we've been doing in the past 10 years. That might be a part of medical informatics not yet accepted and emphasized. That, I think, needs to be thrown open to the public. It should not be just a dialogue between Tom and me.

321

PATIENT MANAGEMENT SYSTEMS

This session presented experience in the development of systems that could manage information in the support of patient care. William E. Hammond, PhD was the discussant, and he introduced the problem with some interesting slides and comments that we include here. He also prepared a paper on his early involvement with systems, which is at the end of this section.

The first speaker was Melville H. Hodge. His paper described the history of a medical information system and offered a perspective from the commercial business world. Because of the time limitation, he chose to present this history in the context of the press reaction to the El Camino Hospital system during its early development. As we all know, it was a difficult process with a happy ending. Time has healed the wounds, and the narrative is filled with humor. We include both the formal paper and major extracts from the oral presentation.

Homer Warner, MD, PhD was the second speaker. He began his narrative in the 1950s with the description of an early analog device. He continued with a discussion of the evolving challenges that he has met and the impact that others have had on his development. Because he heads the nation's first Department of Medical Informatics, there was some question about the meaning of the term. Dr. Warner concluded, "That's sort of what we are doing here. We are defining what we do." The paper is an extended transcript of his talk.

322

SPEAKERS

Melvin H. Hodge History of the TDS Medical Information System
Homer R. Warner History of Medical Informatics at Utah
William E. Hammond Patient Management Systems: The Early Years

Melville H. Hodge has a consulting practice and is a member of the board of directors of TDS Healthcare Systems Corporation. He received a BS degree from Northwestern University in 1952 and was a Sloan Fellow at the Stanford University Graduate School of Business (1960–1961). He was with the Lockheed Missiles and Space Company from 1955 to 1971. In 1971 he joined Technicon Data Systems where he later served as president and chief executive officer (1973–1977). His present consulting activities build on his experiences in early-stage, technology-oriented companies as well as his understanding of the sophisticated management techniques used by the larger corporations.

Homer R. Warner, MD, PhD is professor and department chairman, Department of Medical Informatics (formerly Medical Biophysics and Computing), and research professor of surgery, Department of Surgery, University of Utah (since 1973 and 1966). He received BA and MD degrees from the University of Utah in 1946 and 1949 and a PhD degree from the University of Minnesota in 1953. He is the editor of *Computers and Biomedical Research* and is the principal investigator for the Utah IAIMS Development Project.

William E. Hammond, PhD is professor of Community and Family Medicine, professor of Biomedical Engineering and head, Division of Medical Informatics, Duke University. He received BSEE and PhD degrees from Duke University in 1957 and 1967, respectively. He has served as the program chair for two AAMSI Congresses and is on the editorial board of *Computers and Biomedical Medicine* and *CRC Critical Reviews in Medical Informatics*.

Introduction for Patient Management Systems Session

William E. Hammond, PhD
Duke University Medical Center, Durham

I must admit to a little bit of embarrassment at being included in this group of speakers. I really view the people that have presented before me as being the barnstormers. I think that if we really want to capture the history of medical informatics we should take our tape recorders out into the hallway during lunch and the breaks and listen to the conversation. This opportunity reminds me a great deal of how life must have been sitting around listening to the barnstormers talk about their early aviation days. That was the period during which everybody thought airplanes would fly, but nobody quite knew what to do with them, or what kind of maneuvers. You are the group that really did define the concepts and the maneuvers. I view myself more as being in the next period, a transition period. I had viewed most of you as father figures, but, in view of some recent remarks, I think that I now have to change that from father/son relationships to grandfather/father relationships.

Continuing my analogy, I think I'm very much like some of the pilots in World War II. We are taking some of those concepts and maneuvers that you have discovered and invented and are applying them in real-world situations. Perhaps I could correctly say in combat situations.

It's important for us to recognize that the generation we're training now really represents—again, using aviation as a model—the kind of young pilots that are flying our aircraft today. In these high-performance aircraft, it is difficult to identify the barrier or the interface between the human and the computer. It requires the combined talents and decision making of both the human and the computer to fly the aircraft.

Duke University, where I've been for all of my career, is one of those places that has spent over the years a considerable amount of money and person power in developing patient management systems. I'd like to show you some of the contrasts. At Duke there have been a number of significant changes over the past 20 or 30 years. Figure 1 shows the construction of Duke Hospital in the 1930s. If you go there now, you can see (Figure 2) that there is a tremendous change in the

FIGURES 1 and 2

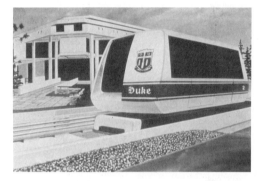

FIGURES 3 and 4

appearance of the buildings. Certainly in terms of structure it's very, very modern now.

Figure 3 shows how our patients arrived at Duke Hospital in the 1930s. If you look at what's happening at the Duke Medical Center now, you find high technological advances in transportation. Figure 4 shows a person-moving vehicle in which, at least theoretically, an operation could be performed while the vehicle is in transit. Emergency patients now can arrive by helicopter, a mode of rapid transportation that has had a significant impact on the survival rate of individuals with certain types of trauma.

If we look at the operating room from not so many years ago (Figure 5), as compared to the operating room of today (Figure 6), again we can see the significant advancement of technology.

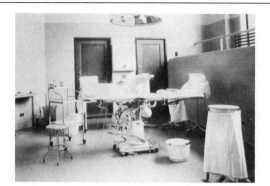
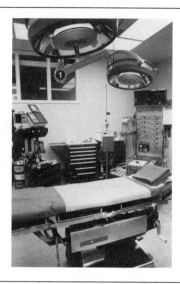

FIGURES 5 and 6

Finally I'd like to show you a slide that represents the medical record room of perhaps 20 years ago (Figure 7), and also a slide that represents the medical record room of today (Figure 8). I think that makes the point.

The two speakers for this session have traveled different pathways to arrive at the development of a patient management system.

Our first speaker, Dr. Homer Warner, represents an academic approach. He developed a system starting with subsystems that were designed to address a particular component of patient care and had the goal of providing direct impact on the delivery of health care. Over the years that he has continued to develop and produce this system; he has very wisely used the data collected at each step of the way to increase the value of the system. A major contribution from this system and from Dr. Warner has been the number of individuals that he has trained in medical informatics who are now researchers and contributors in their own right. The importance of his contributions to the field of medical informatics, as well as the patient management system, has been reflected in the lives of many of the individuals that are sitting in this room.

The approach represented by Mel Hodge was supported by the aerospace industry. He applied some of the concepts and techniques that were developed as part of that industry to what was assumed to be a very similar problem dealt with in that industry. Over the years this type of interaction has resulted in a significant and well-known

FIGURES 7 and 8

system today—the Technicon system. It's interesting to look at the contrasts as well as the similarities between the systems developed by these two speakers. One of the interesting things I have learned is that there have been at least two opportunities for these two systems to merge during the lifetime of their development.

I'd like to read a comment from the preface of Mel's 1977 book titled *Medical Information Systems*:

> I am a believer. I happen to believe that the problems of health care delivery are susceptible to well-considered, well-executed approaches and that the introduction of information systems technology is among the more powerful approaches available. I have invested more than a decade of my life in this belief.

History of the TDS Medical Information System

Melville H. Hodge
TDS Health Care Systems Corporation, Santa Clara

Introduction

The application of computer and communication technology to medicine—medical informatics—may be viewed from several perspectives. Application of this technology may range from the molecular level to the individual patient or clinical level and ultimately to the health care delivery system level. Alternatively, a motivational perspective reveals objectives ranging from academic research directed toward publication to enhancement of the investigator's practice or his institution's performance to a profit motive. Assessment of any given medical informatics undertaking must necessarily be in the context of these perspectives.

The TDS Medical Information System—known as MIS—is perhaps both the earliest and currently most comprehensive, professionally oriented hospital information system in widespread commercial use, ranging from suburban community hospitals to major tertiary teaching and research institutions. Its scope has been the hospital, or group of hospitals, and increasingly, the outpatient, or ambulatory patient population served by those hospitals. The motivation of its builders was to provide measurable economic benefits exceeding its costs, resulting in a shared net economic benefit sufficient to provide both an incentive to users to acquire MIS and a return on investment to its builders to continually attract capital for system enhancements and further installations.

Our purpose here is to describe MIS, to record its history, which generally spans the entire epoch of medical informatics, to consider its contributions to both patient care and to computer technology, and finally, to speculate briefly about the future.

MIS Description

The unwavering goals of MIS have been to reduce costs and improve patient care. Economic considerations in health care are often fuzzy; phrases such as "improved productivity," "increased efficiency," and the like abound. The unambiguous goal of MIS is to provide "cost-lowering technology" to the hospital, with the result that the total value of checks written by the hospital to employees and suppliers (including the MIS supplier) are lower *after* its installation than *prior* to its installation.

The patient care objective, unfortunately, for a system purporting to impact an entire health care delivery system such as a hospital, with patients whose ills may run the entire gamut of ailments and injuries afflicting humankind has not thus far been amenable to "outcome" studies. Instead, patient care enhancements must be measured by improvements in input variables intuitively related to improved outcomes such as error reduction, timeliness enhancement, and improved, even structured, information availability for clinical decision making.

The visitor to an MIS hospital would find CRT terminals and printers located at all hospital work sites and interfaces to specialized systems (e.g., clinical laboratory systems), all connected to a large computer located in the hospital, or alternatively, in a remote regional center serving multiple hospitals. These components appear at least superficially similar to other commercial systems in other hospitals. On closer examination, however, the unique characteristics of MIS would begin to emerge—extensive direct use of terminals by physicians, nurses, and other professionals and patient chart content consisting of up to 80% or more of MIS printer-produced documents attesting to a predominantly "on-line" patient record.

The observer at a nursing station would witness a physician using a CRT terminal with light pen menu selection providing fractional second display responses. Screen content would be entirely in standard medical terminology with no special coding or "computerese." This content might be general, organized by medical specialty, personalized in "order sets" for each physician, or, in research settings such as the NIH Clinical Center, representing extensive research protocols. Nurses would be observed charting through the same terminals and working from system-produced patient care plans. None of the traditional documents associated with the nursing station such as order sheets, Kardexes, medication slips, requisitions, or the like could be found. IV scheduling, acuity-based staffing, and numerous other supports to nursing would be evident.

The usually incessant telephone ringing at nursing stations and in ancillary departments would be absent as status information is readily available through any terminal. Physicians entering the hospital would use the first terminal they encounter to do "electronic rounds," reviewing the up-to-the-minute reported clinical status of all of their patients in the hospital and planning their rounds based on that information. Ancillary department work lists, labels, requisitions, and the like would be automatically produced on department-controlled schedules. Medical record indexing and abstracting would be automated.

Since all patient care transactions are captured at their source, data entry into hospital financial systems is automatic, feeding sophisticated multitiered insurance proration systems, cash management systems, and the like. Spanning both the clinical and the financial systems is a powerful fourth-generation, distributed relational database capability for *ad hoc* decision support, permitting hospital executives to employ advanced quantitative tools in matters such as PPO pricing, resource requirement forecasts, cost analysis, etc.

Visiting other MIS hospitals in the U.S., Canada, or the U.K., our observer would be struck by great differences in functionality and usage as all terminal displays, reports, schedules, and applications are matched to the unique needs of each hospital and are independent of underlying MIS software. Despite their diversity, MIS hospitals, at least those that have undertaken formal studies, share certain common results—reduced costs, shorter patient stays, and markedly reduced error rates.

Origin and Objectives

If a single word must be selected to characterize the men and women who collectively created present-day MIS (now the foundation of TDS Healthcare Systems Corporation's Health Care 4000 System), it is *perseverance*.

The origins of MIS may be traced to the Lockheed Missiles and Space Company in Sunnyvale, California in the early 1960s—then, as now, the nation's largest missile and satellite contractor. From a need to diversify from this enviable, but at the same time vulnerable, position came a decision to exploit then-fledgling computer communications technology by applying it to hospitals. Omniscient counsel in reaching this decision came from the late Dr. Raymond White, director of socio-economic affairs for the American Medical Association, the late Dr. Howard Aiken, founder and director of the Computation Laboratory at Harvard, and the late Dr. Clarence Lovell, director of switching systems at the Bell Telephone Laboratories.

The Lockheed Information Systems Division was born in 1964 and staffed by a small group of technically capable, but medically naive, managers, engineers, and analysts. Reflecting their aerospace backgrounds of seeing desired achievement limited only by their collective ability to solve perceived technical problems, this group faced a then-uncomprehended education in the many nontechnical factors that control progress in health care institutions. Applying aerospace systems analysis skills, the potential economic benefits of automating information flow in the hospital were quantified with Public Health Service contract support, convincing the Lockheed group that their objective was economically feasible.

In 1966 this group was invited under contract to assist the Mayo Clinic in a comprehensive assessment of computer system needs of the clinic and its two associated hospitals. Twelve Lockheed engineers worked intimately with a like number of Mayo Clinic physicians for two years in Rochester, resulting in development and experimental use of a three-terminal prototype of MIS. A proposal for development of an operational system submitted by the Mayo Clinic to the (then) Department of Health, Education, & Welfare was not funded, and finally, 12 no longer medically naive Lockheed engineers returned to Sunnyvale with a more sophisticated view of the needs of a physician-oriented medical information system.

Lockheed management, lead by Herschel Brown, its executive vice-president, and Kenneth Larkin, its Information Systems director, then decided to fund the commercial development of MIS. El Camino Hospital in Mountain View, under the leadership of R. Edwin Hawkins agreed to serve as the development site. By 1971 development neared completion (or so it was thought) and operational service contract negotiations between Lockheed and El Camino were initiated. This was a stressful period for Lockheed, however, as it encountered severe difficulties with its C-5A and L-1011 aircraft programs, necessitating curtailment of all discretionary new business programs, including MIS, resulting in a decision to seek an outside equity partner for its fledgling medical division.

Interest was expressed by Technicon Corporation, which, under the leadership of Edwin C. (Jack) Whitehead, had pioneered and then came to dominate automation of the clinical laboratory and which now saw in MIS an opportunity to extend automation from the laboratory to the entire hospital. Partnership with a struggling aerospace company seemed unattractive, however, resulting in outright acquisition of Lockheed Information Systems by Technicon, which was then renamed Technicon Medical Information Systems Corporation.

Initial Installations

The Technicon acquisition agreement and the El Camino Hospital MIS contract were signed on the same day, May 28, 1971. The El Camino contract was unique in that it provided that the Hospital would pay Technicon *only* the actual savings experienced by the hospital as measured by a joint hospital-Technicon cost bureau in which the hospital reserved the tiebreaking vote. Placing (properly) the full economic risk on Technicon, it also taught the company an important lesson, that hospital managers, not computer systems, save money. A well-designed information system can provide impressive *potential* cost benefits, but only motivated hospital managers guided by a carefully prepared benefit realization plan can achieve actual savings.

A threat far graver than economic emerged when the system became operational—massive resistance from important segments of the El Camino medical staff. Spreading quickly from the confines of the hospital to local and even national newspaper headlines, this resistance, initially justified in part by early system shortcomings, seemed intractable. It was countered, however, by the effective leadership of more visionary El Camino physicians, Bryan Shieman, Joseph Ignatius, and especially Ralph Watson, who successively chaired the medical staff MIS committee. These physicians withstood the intense criticism of their colleagues, worked patiently on correcting deficiencies, and converted their colleagues with "hands-on" assistance. Their efforts were supported by the rapidly growing enthusiasm of nurses now freed from paperwork drudgery to the point that physician-opponents alleged that they were being ostracized by nurses for their failure to use MIS!

The (now) Department of Health and Human Services' National Center for Health Services Research played an important role by sponsoring a comprehensive, independent evaluation by the Battelle Columbus Laboratories of the economic and patient care benefits of MIS at El Camino. Believed to be the most exhaustive studies of this kind ever conducted, the Battelle reports clearly supported the views of system proponents [1].

By 1974 physician acceptance and measured cost savings reached levels resulting in the hospital proposing that the old contract be torn up and replaced by a new long-term agreement providing that Technicon receive its full fee, with the hospital retaining the net savings beyond that fee. Both Technicon and the hospital had paid a high emotional tuition for a second important lesson, that introduction of technology with impact as pervasive as MIS into a health care delivery setting requires extraordinary attention to the management of change in a human organization. The universal applicability of this lesson has subsequently been demonstrated in numerous other MIS hospital installations. Yet, a present-day visitor to El Camino would find all-embracing acceptance of MIS and, indeed, would find no evidence of the slender thread by which its existence hung in the early 1970s.

Installation of MIS at the Ralph K. Davies Medical Center in San Francisco in 1972 offered validation of Technicon's regional, multi-hospital center concept, necessary to secure computer equipment economies in an era of high computer costs. This was followed in 1973 by the first hospital-operated MIS installation at the Nebraska Methodist Hospital in Omaha.

From its second regional center in Fairfield, New Jersey, Technicon next installed MIS at New Jersey's largest hospital, St. Barnabas in Livingston. This was quickly followed by the Maine Medical Center in Portland, the first tertiary hospital to employ MIS.

In 1975 Technicon undertook its most challenging installation to date at the Clinical Center of the National Institutes of Health, where patient care functions were overlaid by extensive research protocols. Initially operated from the Fairfield center, operations were transferred some years later to the NIH computer facility in Bethesda. Under the leadership of NIH's Thomas Lewis, MD, the utility of MIS in supporting extensive and sophisticated clinical research has been thoroughly demonstrated.

Current Status

In the last decade MIS installations have multiplied. Eighty-five systems have been or are being installed in the United States, Canada, and the United Kingdom. These installations include major teaching institutions from coast to coast—New York University, Temple University, Medical College of Virginia, University of Illinois, Loyola University of Chicago, Baylor University, University of California, Irvine, and others.

Some institutions acquiring MIS have, in turn, become regional centers serving their own affiliated hospitals or others. Examples include Nebraska Methodist Hospital, Omaha; Hospital Sisters of the Third Order of St. Francis, Peoria; Total Business Systems, Albuquerque; and St. Johns Hospital, St. Johns, New Brunswick.

In 1980, Revlon Corporation acquired Technicon Corporation and its subsidiary, Technicon Data Systems (renamed from Technicon Medical Information Systems). Progress slowed under a large, multiunit company whose diverse interests extended well outside health care. Revlon in turn was acquired in December 1985 by Pantry Pride, whose avowed purpose was subsequent sale of Revlon's health care-related units, providing an opportunity for a successful purchase initiative in August 1986 by John Whitehead, then TDS president and son of Edwin C. Whitehead. The present TDS (now TDS Healthcare Systems Corporation) board includes Edwin C. Whitehead, former Technicon Corporation founder/chief executive officer and founder of the Whitehead Institute for Biomedical Research at the Massachusetts Institute of Technology, John Whitehead, TDS's principal owner and chief executive officer, Joseph Orlando, former Technicon Corporation chief financial officer and now president of Whitehead Associates, and myself, who had been a TDS founder and its chief executive officer until 1977. Thus, direction of MIS has been returned to those who have both shared its vision and had a long standing commitment to the health care field.

MIS has been continually updated to state-of-the-art computer technology and is provided in a wide variety of IBM computer and operating system configurations, ranging from the IBM 9370 to the IBM 3081 under the DOS-VSE, MVS-SP1, MVS-SP2, and VM operating systems. This architecture supports the fully integrated Health Care System 4000, which combines patient care, patient administration, patient accounting, and decision support functions.

Under experienced, health care-oriented ownership, TDS has overcome the stagnation encountered in the latter period of Revlon ownership and sale. A number of significant product enhancements were introduced in 1987, and hospitals are contracting for TDS systems in accelerating numbers.

The growing, loyal group of hospitals who have adopted MIS as the foundation for automating information processing in their institutions have played an important role in furthering MIS through MISA, perhaps the most effective hospital user's group in the industry.

Impact on Health Care Delivery

The first objective of MIS, to permit hospitals to achieve an absolute reduction in costs {2}, has been achieved and independently documented in numerous hospitals. The chief executive officer of El Camino Hospital, the first MIS installation, reported in 1985,

> Ten years later, the savings have multiplied to an approximate value of $20 to $21 per patient day. These savings are above and beyond the cost of the system itself.... The hospital inpatient cost per case is 40% less than the county average for 13 similar community hospitals. {3}

The chief executive officer of the second MIS hospital, the Ralph K. Davies Medical Center, reported savings of $9 per patient day as early as 1976 {4}. Waukesha Memorial Hospital has reported achievement of originally targeted savings of $2.5 million over the initial seven-year period. Despite a reduction in census from 298 to 218 following installation of MIS, this hospital reports the lowest cost per patient day and the lowest number of full-time equivalent employees per adjusted patient day for a hospital its size in the state of Wisconsin {5}. Studies at The Medical Center of Central Georgia reported that "...extended cost benefit of the HIS (MIS) for a cumulative seven years is over $13,000,000" {6}. An independent analysis performed at the National Institutes of Health Clinical Center reported that,

FIGURE 1
Manual performance of a hospital task

**PREPARATION OF NEW CHART &
PROCESSING OF NEW MEDICAL ORDER**

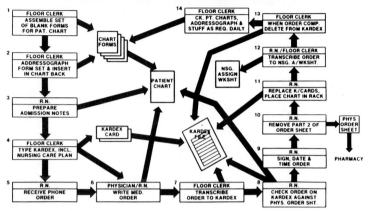

The results of the cost-benefit analysis show that MIS provides greater benefits than less automated alternatives, that the value of the benefits it provides exceeds the costs of the system, and that the net value (i.e., value minus cost) of MIS is greater than that of less automated alternatives. {7}

As noted elsewhere, achievement of impressive savings is the consequence of management action in effectively using a powerful tool, not merely the result of installing a computer system. Management engineering analysis reveals the sources of these savings.

1. Realized labor savings—In a now-classic 1966 paper, Jydstrup and Gross assessed the substantial labor investment of hospitals in information processing and estimated that 24% of the total cost of operating the hospitals they studied were attributable to such activities {8}.

   The opportunity for substantial labor displacement is suggested by Figures 1 and 2. Figure 1 charts a single hospital information processing task—preparation of a new chart and processing a telephoned medical order for the new patient—as it is typically performed manually. Figure 2 charts the same process following the installation of MIS. By estimating times for each eliminated task, multiplying by task volumes, and replicating this process for each hospital task affected by MIS, an estimate of potential savings by skill category, work site, and shift is obtained. Then, working with affected managers and supervisors, practical work-force adjustments are planned, resulting in realizable savings, typically ranging from 50% to 70% of potential savings.

FIGURE 2
Performance of
same task with MIS

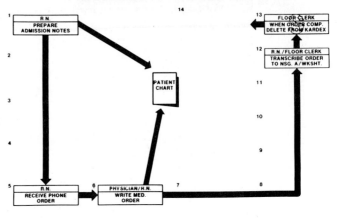

**PREPARATION OF NEW CHART &
PROCESSING OF NEW MEDICAL ORDER**

2. Reduction in length of patient stay—The Battelle study {9} documented a 10% length of stay reduction attributable to MIS, resulting primarily from substantially reduced test turnaround times. Under prospective payment, length of stay reductions have a significant impact. For example, a 5% reduction in length of stay in a 300-bed hospital with 30% fixed payment patients (e.g., DRG and HMO) will result in a $67,500 per month savings.

3. Reduction in forms usage—Elimination of manual information processing tasks as suggested by Figure 2 also eliminates associated forms. Additional preprinted, often multipart, forms are replaced with less expensive MIS-printed documents. Forms savings of $5,000 per month or more are not unusual.

4. Advance of billing date—Advancing the billing date three days in a 300-bed hospital results in a onetime revenue capture of $385,000, or $3,200 per month, assuming a 10% return on capital.

5. Reduction in wasted meals and supplies—Up-to-the-minute information on patient bed location and diet orders substantially eliminates misdirected or inappropriate meal trays. Similarly, waste of requisitioned materials, including drugs, is substantially reduced.

6. Reduction in bad debt losses—By flagging patients with poor payment histories in a long-term MIS file, one 750-bed hospital estimated a bad debt saving of $41,000 per month.

7. Reduced rework resulting from fewer errors—In addition to the patient care implications of error reduction (discussed below), a corollary result is avoiding the need to repeat a task. For example, the patient transported to radiology for an upper GI series and

then found to have eaten breakfast must be rescheduled after dieting; this kind of error is virtually nonexistent in MIS hospitals.

In addition to the more easily quantifiable economic benefits which have been reported, additional contributions to hospital economic performance may result from improved decision making resulting from more accurate, complete, and timely information, better resource allocation resulting from "real-time" visibility into needs, and more timely and comprehensive performance monitoring permitting immediate and precise corrective action.

Assessment of patient care improvements must rely on improvements in input variables plausibly related to better care as suggested earlier, admittedly a less satisfying approach than the conceptually preferable but thus far impractical use of outcomes studies. This methodological limitation does not mean that such improvements are any less real, only that they may not be directly quantified.

A comparison of pre- and post-MIS medical records at New York University Medical Center demonstrated a 22% reduction in physician medications orders omitting site, route of application, or schedule, a 6% reduction in orders that were hard to read, a 2% reduction in ambiguous pharmacy and radiology orders, and a 32% reduction in radiology orders omitting clinical indication {10}. A study at Georgetown University Hospital (not an MIS site) reported 16% of the handwritten words in physician progress notes were illegible as were 8% of physician signatures. Comprehension losses of greater than 5% were measured on 12% of the progress note found in patient charts {11}. Nursing and ancillary error reduction has also been measured. At NYU, MIS resulted in a 22% reduction in medication site and route charting omissions, a 10% reduction in radiology schedule variances, and a 16% reduction in laboratory schedule variances {12}.

Undoubtedly, the consequences of most of these measured errors are trivial; however, patient care in a high-error environment must necessarily be considered to be at some risk. The contribution to patient care of other error-reducing components of MIS such as automatic drug-drug interaction monitoring and IV administration monitoring has not thus far been measured, but does lead toward a more error-free environment.

Improved timeliness may also contribute to patient care as well as being economically important by contributing to reduced length of stay. The NYU study measured reduction in departmental ordering turnaround times {13}, as shown in Table 1.

More efficient use of physician time, while representing an economic benefit to the hospital only in the case of house staff, may have a favorable effect on care. "Electronic rounds" from any hospital MIS terminal (or increasingly, from a terminal located remotely in the

TABLE 1

Department	Hours	%
Pharmacy	4.9	71
Radiology	9.0	8
ECG	6.1	14
Hematology	4.4	22
Chemistry	2.4	9
Microbiology	4.6	4

physician's office) result in more frequent and timely monitoring of status and more efficient planning by the physician of his hospital itinerary.

Most MIS hospitals have implemented impressive care-planning systems produced by the system, integrating physician orders and nursing inputs. Nursing staffing reports result in continually adjusted staffing to meet changing patient care needs. Communication between nurses, particularly between shifts, is greatly enhanced by care-planning and status reports.

Finally, use of MIS shifts the physician from a mental process of reliance solely on memory to one of recognition from among presented alternatives. These alternatives may be general, specific to a given specialty, or even personalized by and for each physician for a variety of clinical situations. In an ever more complex medical information environment, it seems indisputable that the synergistic partnership between the enormous information storage and manipulation capabilities of the information system and the superior decision-making capabilities of the physician contribute importantly to a level of patient care unattainable in a purely manual information processing environment.

Impact on Computer Technology

Given its commercial objectives, publication concerning the technical aspects of MIS has never been encouraged. The unsettled nature of law concerning property rights in software necessitated a policy of trade secrecy rather than patents or copyrights. Hence, technology transfer from MIS has been limited; similarly, no effort has been made to trace MIS technology migration into other systems. Subject to the limitations suggested by the foregoing, it is believed that a number of important concepts were pioneered or furthered in the development of MIS. While TDS's present-day Health Care System 4000 represents the combined contributions of hundreds of dedicated men and women, the key underlying concepts predominantly reflect the genius of Paul Williams—the most outstanding system design "philosopher" with whom I have ever worked; Charles Tapella, a brilliant systems architect; and Bradner Hisey, MD, whose unusual perception of the needs of his profession was combined with outstanding computer systems insights.

The unwavering commitment to providing a system capable of direct use by medical professionals served as the stimulant for several of the most important of these concepts. It was the belief of MIS's developers that the system must meet the physician (or nurse) on his or her own terms, that is, require no special knowledge (codes, etc.), function in the natural language and vocabulary of the user (medical English), require no special skills (typing), or increase the time required by the user to perform his or her encounters with the system contrasted with that required for the corresponding tasks in a manual paper environment. While it was believed that important and attractive benefits could be provided to the professional user through application programs, the challenge was to design a terminal subsystem that professional users could be induced to use voluntarily, discarding their traditional dependence on ward clerks or other intermediaries for information processing.

To meet this challenge, the first commercial use of the CRT/light pen terminal with menu selection was developed, chosen over the typewriter keyboard terminal (special skill requirement), the template keyboard (cumbersome and inflexible), the touch screen terminal (choices limited by finger dexterity, finger shading, screen contamination), mouse/trackball (hand-eye coordination reduces speed well below the light pen, limited terminal location work surface availability), and speech recognition (then primitive, with high ambiguity and error potential). This choice has withstood more than two decades of experience without being obsoleted by a superior technique.

Professional acceptance was found to require extremely fast terminal response to light pen selections to avoid user impatience. Based on experiments conducted with Mayo Clinic physicians it was found necessary to keep response time within the "thinking time" of the physician as he contemplated successive selections; it was essential that the clinical thought processes not be intruded on by a need to wait for a system response. A response requirement of 0.4 seconds was established for peak-hour system loading (later, it was found necessary to contractually *guarantee* response times subject to penalties). This response was provided in a mainframe environment by segregating terminal handling, from applications processing, assigning highest priority to terminal handling, and performing all edits on the input message prior to transferring the input message to the applications processor. This latter step also permitted immediate return of "edit ok" messages to users, allowing them to leave their terminals without risk. This response time was believed to be unparalleled for many years, and even today is unusual in hospital information systems where terminal hand-ling and applications processing are typically intermixed.

Perhaps as important as response time is the need to absolutely assure medical professionals of data integrity. Given a world in which both equipment failures and software "bugs" are inescapable, MIS's developers created a "soft recovery" system in addition to the custom-ary transaction tape-based "hard recovery" system. The soft recovery system created a system-synchronization point at defined intervals (say, five minutes), quiesced the task queue, and wrote old records to a pre-decessor file. In the event of a failure, the predecessor file records were overwritten into the main file and the task queue was reprocessed, omitting the offending transaction (usually the consequence of a soft-ware "bug") which was output with an appropriate error message. Soft recovery times of perhaps 30 seconds contrast vividly with the conven-tional hard recovery times of several hours. It is understood that this technique has been more recently applied in other systems.

Another pioneering technique was the matching of each applica-tions display with a corresponding "Type II" hidden display or direc-tory, which contained data coding of each element on the display. This permitted creation of completely generic applications programs free of any function-specific content. This, in turn, contributed enormously to system generality. Thus, MIS represented an early (perhaps the earliest) relational database system with variable length fields.

For regional hospital operations, high-speed (56 Kb) lines were em-ployed with an MIS-developed, highly efficient, thoroughly reliable protocol. Now, in an era when computer costs continue to plummet, the efficiency of these techniques is no longer required to maintain rea-sonable system costs. The multihospital processing capabilities have, however, proven extremely useful in the presence of modern multi-hospital organizational trends.

Business Perspective

From a technical and functional performance perspective, MIS has been judged to be highly successful by most observers, a conclusion even confirmed privately by some of TDS's most vigorous competitors. It has been less successful, however, from a business perspective. This management shortcoming is attributable primarily to mismatching TDS's products to the needs of the hospital marketplace.

In 1966 the Medicare and Medicaid amendments to the Social Se-curity Act were enacted as a centerpiece of President Lyndon Johnson's Great Society. While the federal government had previously exercised some influence over the private sector hospital community through the Hill-Burton program for hospital construction funding, the 1966 land-mark Medicare legislation suddenly thrust the federal government into the role of principal third-party payer of hospital bills. It elected to exercise its newfound power through a cost-reimbursement system.

The hospital community responded by demanding systems for charge collection and patient billing from the computer services industry. Hospitals (and their computer vendors) prided themselves on their ability to charge for a single cotton ball even though little management information was available permitting control to be exercised over the nursing department payroll, representing about *half* of the total cost of operating the typical hospital! It was an era when revenue equalled costs plus. ...

A number of hospital computer services companies were created in response to this new federally created need; perhaps Shared Medical Systems and the McDonnell-Douglas Automation Company have been the most successful, attracting hundreds of shared patient billing accounts. Meanwhile, the TDS team (under its earlier Lockheed banner) was deeply engrossed in system design to reduce hospital costs absolutely and provide better patient care. Regrettably, this focus was unresponsive to the then-perceived needs of most hospitals. Given the vital dependence of hospitals on patient billing and Medicare accounting, hospital chief financial officers emerged as the dominant executives, controlling their institutions' computer system acquisitions. Physicians, nurses and other health care professionals, TDS's natural constituency, had little influence over these acquisitions. Exceptions occurred mainly in institutions headed by unusually strong chief executive officers who saw their role as one of partnership with medical professionals to bring lower costs and better care to the population they served.

The government's cost-reimbursement policies produced an enormous escalation in health care costs. Efforts were undertaken to find an alternative. In 1983 a system of prospective payment by diagnosis-related group (DRG) developed at Yale University in the early 1970s was adopted by the Health Care Finance Administration for federally funded care. As this system was adopted and its implications understood it became apparent that a sick person in the hospital, formerly an asset, was now a liability. To do as little for him (or to him) and get rid of him as soon as possible became the new strategy. Further, cost reduction, formerly seen simply as a path to revenue reduction, came to be seen as a new strategy for economic survival and even profitability.

Thus, it appears now that MIS represents a concept whose time has come. From a business standpoint it is regrettable that TDS did not attune its offerings more to the needs of the marketplace it elected to serve. Had it done so, however, it is unlikely that the resultant orientation to enter hospitals through the business office door rather than the medical staff door would have ever permitted building an organization committed to what good system design practice seemed to dictate back in the sixties, enhancing the capability of the hospital and its medical staff to carry out their primary mission—to strive in an efficient manner to make the sick well!

Outlook

It is often said that those who do not learn from history will be forced to relive it. It seems unlikely, however, that the future of medical informatics at the health care delivery system level will be merely a cyclical repetition of the past, nor even a linear extrapolation of past trends. Our lessons concerning the penalties associated with failure to accurately divine the needs of the hospital marketplace as they may exist at any point in time makes it seem imperative not to sidestep the task of considering the likely future nature and role of a system such as MIS.

First, past battles of professional acceptance and achieving important net savings will not have to be refought at the conceptual level. It is imperative, however, to never forget that introduction of MIS into a new hospital profoundly impacts a *human* organization to perhaps an unparalleled degree. If the need to manage the change process is ignored, resistance and even rebellion may be reasonably predicted. The business of doctors is *not* to make computer systems successful; success has repeatedly been demonstrated to be the consequence of each doctor, one at a time, coming to see how his performance is enhanced and his hospital practice facilitated by investing his always scarce time in learning how to use MIS efficiently. Similarly, hospital managers, not computer systems, reduce costs when they employ fewer people and order fewer goods in carrying out their missions. Since these actions are counterinstinctual to experience when the goal is a high level of performance, hospital managers must both participate in and "buy into" a carefully designed benefits realization program before they can be reasonably expected to act.

It seems likely that the future will find increasing structure in the practice of medicine. The unrelenting pressure of third-party payers led by the federal government appears to be leading toward the eventual imposition of standards of care. It would not be unexpected to see the pioneering work of Dr. Lawrence Weed on the problem-oriented medical record find rebirth, perhaps in a metamorphosed form. Physician-oriented systems such as MIS seem to be the appropriate vehicle to support such trends.

Progress in medicine appears to be leading to the same conclusion. Newer modalities of diagnosis and therapy are often sufficiently complex and require a degree of coordination among health care professionals sufficient to obsolete conventional methods of information processing and coordination.

The pressures cited above may also focus providers on clinical benefit versus cost tradeoffs. Perhaps the day will come when physician-ordering displays will present costs along with indications, counterindications, adverse interactions, side effects, and the like for consideration in formulating a diagnostic or treatment program. Cost staging may be routinely correlated with disease staging.

Performance evaluation and audit is likely to become more sophisticated with the widespread advent of the on-line medical record. Emphasis will increase on truly concurrent review to permit timely intervention.

Hospital managers will employ system-produced data in sophisticated resource-allocation processes. Hospital data and external data will be accessible to hospital executives for use in market segmentation, bidding on preferred provider contracts, service pricing, and the like.

Strategic planning by hospitals may, in fact, be necessary strategic survival. Under intense pressure from a society that is no longer tolerant of health care cost escalation outstripping national income growth, only three out of five present hospitals may exist 10 years from now. The capacity of the hospital to foresee community needs and accurately match its services to those needs in a competitive environment is likely to make comprehensive, powerful decision support systems seem indispensable.

The objectives of improved patient care at a lower cost set for MIS more than 20 years ago seem even more relevant for the 1990s. If a single lesson is drawn from the brief history of medical informatics at the health care delivery system level it is that despite errors in both judgement and execution along the way it has proven to be worth doing. Medical historians have suggested that medicine crossed the boundary from doing more harm than good to the inverse sometime around 1940. Perhaps insufficient time has elapsed to permit a similar judgement about medical informatics applied to the health care delivery system, but one might say the signs are encouraging!

References

1. Barrett, J.P., Barnum, R.A., Gordon, B.A., and Pesut, R.N. Final Report on Evaluation of the Implementation of a Medical Information System in a General Community Hospital. Battelle Columbus Laboratories, December 19, 1975.

Barrett, J.P., Hersch, P.L., and Caswell, R.J. Evaluation of the Impact of the Implementation of the Technicon Medical Information System at El Camino Hospital: Part II. Economic Trends Analysis; Final Report. Battelle Columbus Laboratories, May 14, 1979.

2. For a discussion of economic considerations differentiating cost-lowering technology from cost-increasing technology, see Hodge, M.H. *Medical Information Systems*, Aspen Systems, 1977.

3. Buchanan, N.S. and Norris, J. A businesslike hospital gets business's attention. *Health Cost Management*, Vol. 2, No. 3, May–June, 1985.

4. Private communication from George D. Monardo, president, Ralph K. Davies Medical Center to A.L. (Jack) Hahn, president, Methodist Hospital of Indiana, January 30, 1976.

5. Blask, D. and Miller, G. A computerized medical information system can be cost effective. *Healthcare Computing & Communications*, April 1984.

Blask, D., Cleary, J., and Dux, L. A computerized medical information system—Sustaining benefits previously achieved. *Healthcare Computing & Communications*, December 1985.

6. Carter, L.A. The hospital information system—A weapon for survival under DRGs. *American Hospital Association*, 1984.

7. Blackmon, P.W. Evaluation of the Medical Information System at the NIH Clinical Center. Volume 1: Summary of Findings and Recommendations. Analytic Services, Inc., January 1982.

8. Jydstrup, R.A. and Gross, M.J. Cost of information handling in hospitals. *Health Services Research*, Winter 1966.

9. Barrett, *et al., op. cit.*

10. Grams, S., Grieco, A., and Williams, R. *Physician Use of the Technicon MIS Provides Major Benefits and Savings to New York University Medical Center*. (In press.)

11. White, K.B. and Beary, J.F. *New England Journal of Medicine*, February 6, 1986.

12. Grams, *et al., op. cit.*

13. Grams, *et al., op. cit.*

Direct Use by Physicians of the TDS Medical Information System[1]

Melville H. Hodge
TDS Healthcare Systems Corporation, Santa Clara

In my written paper, "History of the TDS Medical Information System," I have attempted to present a balanced overview of the development and deployment of a major medical information system. In my remarks this afternoon, time permits me to focus on just one aspect of that history.

As many of you know, our work has been devoted for 20 years or so to building comprehensive, integrated hospital information systems, or medical information systems as we call them. Our objective has always been two-fold; first, to improve patient care, and second, to have the hospital spend substantially less money with our system than they would without it; that is, produce real cost savings. The system can be characterized by its design for direct professional use, and the most important user, in our view, is the physician. Today, I would like to share with you our experiences in getting physicians involved in using medical information systems, trading in their fountain pens for light pens! You must bear in mind that we are from the commercial business world and not the academic world. Consequently, physicians undoubtedly see us somewhat differently than if we were their colleagues in an academic institution.

The initial installation of our system was in a hospital in Mountain View, California, called El Camino Hospital. It is a 440-bed, short-term, specialist-dominated, general community hospital. It is also a public district hospital, which means that its board is elected by the voters of the hospital district, and their meetings are necessarily held in the "goldfish bowl" of public scrutiny. We signed our initial contract with them in May 1971 to implement this system which, at the time, we thought we had completely developed. We didn't realize that in some respects we had barely started! This contract was unique in that it guaranteed net cost savings to the hospital; that is, the hospital's monthly payment to us was limited to an amount equal to the cost savings as measured by them!

---

[1] This paper was prepared by Mr. Hodge from the transcript of his conference presentation.

Most of us in science and technology are used to the peer review process; i.e.,to having our work commented on and criticized in the technical literature and by peer review groups. I have to confess to you, however, I was not prepared to be pilloried in the public press for what I was doing. Consider this headline,[2]

DOCTORS LOOK WITH ILL FAVOR AT NEW COMPUTERS

which appeared in July 1972 in the *San Jose News*, one of the first reports of our work. Obviously we didn't feel very good about this. Quoting from the second paragraph, "Strongest opposition to the new system comes from the hospital's Department of Medicine, the majority of which voted to dump the system last month."

We encountered an interesting dichotomy. While many internists opposed us, for some reason most surgeons liked us. Could it be that if the internist didn't like it, the surgeons automatically liked it? We speculated about that. Some thought that internists, as "thinking doctors," were being threatened, but the surgeons, who were "gadgeteers," didn't feel endangered. But the truth was, the system really didn't work very well during that period. There were many problems that we hadn't been smart enough to foresee. We made the doctors lives reasonably miserable, and we deserved to be criticized.

The following headline appeared on July 20, 1972, in the *San Jose Mercury* under the byline of Dale Mead,

PHYSICIANS DEEPLY SPLIT OVER "DREAM COMPUTER"

The first of a number of heros emerged in this story. I quote, "Hospital director, Ed Hawkins, has indicated that if MIS is not economical or 'if it is not good for physicians we will have serious questions about it. There is no more opposition to it than originally estimated.'" That's a pretty good line. What else needed to be said? He at least temporarily preempted the issue!

I'll leap forward a year. We are now in the summer of 1973. Again, let me just give you one quote out of Mead's *San Jose News* article, which appeared under this headline,

"WORK-SAVING" COMPUTER ENSLAVES HOSPITAL STAFF, DOCTORS CLAIM

and introduced another group of heros, the hospital board: "Thursday evening almost 50 doctors appeared for a special meeting with the five member board on the matter, and many of them complained of wasted time, potentially dangerous errors and tensions rising from the project." You can imagine five helpless directors in front of 50 doctors on the attack! I recall sitting in the back of the meeting room; the hospital PA

---

[2] Slides of actual news stories illustrated Mr. Hodge's remarks; only the headlines and selected quotes are included here.

system went on and announced, "The MIS system is down!" I've tried to suppress that evening from my memory!

My next headline, just a few days later on June 6, reads;

Some Claim System a "Nightmare"
MDS AT ODDS OVER HOSPITAL MIS

We were now starting to get national attention; this article is from *Computer World*. It reported, "Dr. (name omitted), one of the leading opponents of the integrated system said, 'The system has caused deterioration of our ability to care for patients.'" You can imagine the impact that has on the hospital's lawyers! Probably the biggest individual hero of this entire experience is also quoted later in the story, "Dr. Ralph Watson, chairman of the MIS Physician Committee takes a more positive position. 'The system can do the job we want it to.'" This man worked tirelessly with the doctors in that hospital over a period of years. He had a great deal of help, but I think that he, more than any other single individual within the hospital, helped turn attitudes around.

A week later, another Dale Mead *San Jose News* headline appeared;

Independent El Camino Hospital Study Discloses
"COMPUTER DOESN'T HELP DOCTORS OR PATIENTS"

Despite the headline, there was a positive story buried here, the first report on two very important contracts and grants that had been let by some additional heros, Dick DuBois, Jerry Cohen, and Bruce Waxman of HEW's National Center for Health Services Research who had the foresight (perhaps courage was a more appropriate word back in 1971) to recognize that the El Camino MIS installation offered an opportunity for an interesting experiment. They did two things: First, they commissioned the Battelle Columbus Laboratories to do an independent evaluation; second, they gave some money to El Camino Hospital to augment its management engineering staff to perform the economic cost-benefit measurement. You will remember that what they paid us was tied to those benefits, and this allowed them to evaluate savings in a professional and thorough way.

The next Dale Mead article provided the very first hint of what was coming out of that study,

Among Most Doctors
HOSPITAL COMPUTER UNIMPRESSIVE

The subhead, "*Among Most Doctors*," suggests he was beginning to temper his comments a bit. Buried in paragraph 27 Mead reported, "Perhaps the biggest single factor in MIS's favor is the money it saves." But only the careful reader who went beyond skimming the headlines noted that.

Several weeks later in August 1973, the favorable trend became more evident. The August 1 *San Jose News* reported,

U.S. Offers More Aid
"AUTOMATED HOSPITAL" BACKED

and quoted HEW's Gerry Cohen, "This system represents a high water mark in the efforts to provide an automated hospital. ... No other system in the country is as well developed. MIS is a considerable achievement with all its faults." That the authorities in Washington were now making favorable judgements got the attention of some of the people in California.

Later in 1973, we started to extend beyond national to international attention, as the *San Jose Mercury* reported on August 29,

MEDICAL COMPUTER DRAWS A WORLDWIDE AUDIENCE

El Camino Hospital had begun getting visitors from all over the world! But we weren't out of the woods yet. In the fall of 1973, *Datamation* headlined a story,

WHAT WILL THEY ZAP AT EL CAMINO?
THE CRT OR THE TWO-YEAR-OLD MIS?

which led off, "Mention the computer to some doctors at El Camino hospital in Mountain View, California, and they become profane."

In December 1973, the AMA's *Computers and Medicine* provided a reasonably objective and balanced view of how things were going in a story headlined,

MIS-1 AFTER A FULL YEAR'S OPERATION—PROS & CONS

and on January 9, 1974 under the headline,

HOSPITAL COMPUTER'S RATING UP

the *San Jose Mercury* reported, "The final version of an independent evaluation of El Camino Hospital's futuristic computerized record keeping system declares it, 'in general acceptable to the staff.'"

On January 27, 1974, the *San Jose Mercury* shifted attention from physician acceptance to cost justification. Under the headline,

COMPUTERIZED HOSPITAL REACHES PIVOTAL YEAR

it said, "More important, however, the system must prove it can pay for itself by saving as much as the $82,000 per month bill for running it. ... The loss, however, is not being absorbed by the hospital but by Technicon Corp."

By the summer of 1974, however, victory was in sight. The *San Jose Mercury* proclaimed on July 10 that,

PAPER-WORK COMPUTER SAVES HOSPITAL MONEY

and reported, "MIS at El Camino appears to be saving as much as it would cost, administrators here announced." In fact, it was saving *more* than it cost. The hospital came to me and said, "How about tearing up that 'we'll pay you what it saves contract'; we'll just pay you your regular price, and we'll keep the difference." And I agreed!

On August 1, Dale Mead capitulated and under the headline,

DOCTORS FAVOR COMPUTERIZED SYSTEM

he reported, "As El Camino approaches the final decision on its futuristic computerized information system, a poll of doctors shows about 60% now favor it." And on August 10 he wrote his final story under the headline,

HOSPITAL OK'S COMPUTERIZED DATA SYSTEM

and said, "A computerized medical information system under development for a decade Friday was made a permanent feature of El Camino Hospital. ... The board gave its verdict: MIS is both medically practical and economically advantageous." He also spelled my name wrong!

By 1976 the second Battelle evaluation report came out. *The Wall Street Journal* summarizes this report under the headline,

Technicon's System for Hospital Data is Praised in Report
FEDERALLY BACKED STUDY URGES U.S. TO PUSH
WIDER USE OF SUCH COMPUTERIZED UNITS

Technicon stock went up from $12 to $16 that week, adding about $80 million to the value of the company! I don't recall how long this higher valuation persisted, but I felt good about it for a few days.[3]

I guess the highlight of my life was when that El Camino Hospital internist put his arm around the medical information system terminal and said, "It's just like breathing, I couldn't get along without it." Where is Dale Mead now? I suppose good news just isn't newsworthy!

In concluding my remarks today I want to share with you some of the lessons we learned from this experience with the hope that they might have some value to others who are going down similar paths. My final three slides deal with why direct physician use of medical information systems is so important, what obstacles to direct use exist and some keys to overcoming them.

The first observation in Figure 1 may seem trite. It is obvious that a hospital is a place where doctors take care of patients. I emphasize it

---

[3] The presentation then went on to catalog briefly other hospitals that, in 1973 and beyond, showed the courage to install MIS before all the evidence was in. This was followed by a video, taken in 1987 at El Camino Hospital without the knowledge of Technicon, to be used by Pacific Presbyterian Medical Center in San Francisco as an orientation and training tool for their physicians. In it, El Camino doctors, nurses, and administrators frankly discuss their feelings about the now relatively mature MIS. They describe their ability to deliver a level of care superior in quality and substantially lower in cost than other area hospitals as a direct consequence of the medical information system. We pick up the transcript following that tape. The next comment by Mr. Hodge refers to an exchange between the unseen interviewer and a physician. [Editors]

FIGURE 1

IMPORTANCE OF DIRECT PHYSICIAN USE

- ☐ A hospital is a specialized environment in which physicians can efficaciously and efficiently care for patients.
- ☐ Maximum benefits result from capturing information from its originator and delivering it to its user(s) at a time(s), at a place(s), and in a form(s) most convenient to each.
- ☐ Physicians are both the principal originators and consumers of information.
- ☐ Direct physician use ranges from desirable to essential for achievement of potential benefits.

---

because it has not proven in practice to be so obvious to hospital computer system designers. Most commercial hospital system developers have viewed the hospital from the point of view of a hotel—make reservations, admit and discharge people, and, most importantly, collect charges and bill accurately, completely, and promptly.

If you start from what I believe is the fundamental mission of the hospital, patient care, then almost all information processing transactions will be captured, and hence any requirement for information can be satisfied. There is almost no limit to what you can ultimately do. If, on the other hand, you start from the "hotel" perspective, you will find it is very difficult to "swim upstream." You can build a system that is a very efficient billing system or charge-collection system, but if it doesn't, for example, have the response time and human factors that are required by physicians and nurses, it cannot be upgraded into a complete hospital information system. You will have to throw it out and start over again.

The second observation explains why we put so much emphasis on getting physicians, nurses, and other professionals involved. If we want to get the maximum benefits out of this technology, then we must deal with the *users*, who are both the primary originators and consumers of information. Moreover, we must meet them on their terms and give them the information they need, when they need it, in the form they need it, and so forth. If we are isolated from them through data terminal operators, then we can't possibly serve them as well, and therefore we won't get the benefits out of the system even though our dollar investment may be just as high.

The third observation really ties back to the first two. The physician is both the principal originator of information and also the principal consumer. The hospital administrator is remarkably dependent on the actions of physicians. Imagine, 200 people wander into the hospital every morning, none of whom work for him or are responsible to him

FIGURE 2

OBSTACLES TO DIRECT PHYSICIAN USE

- □ Physicians have little perceived self-interest in making hospital computer systems successful.
- □ Even well-designed systems require a period of physician training/experience before perceived value outweighs effort-time investment.
- □ Most physicians' hospital activities are routine, seen by them as requiring little intellectual support.
- □ Benefits are valued principally by their contribution to physicians' time, convenience, and income.
- □ Traditional cultural roles in information processing may represent barriers.

but who collectively determine the work to be done (and the costs to be incurred) by the hospital that day. In that light it seems a bit ludicrous to hold the administrator responsible for hospital costs! And these work-instigating physicians bear no financial responsibility for the cost consequences of their actions. You can see the predicament the hospital administrator is in. By engaging the physicians through the medical information system, however, the hospital has an important tool to provide some structure to their decisions—use of generic drugs, for example, or assuring that complete information is provided—an order to hold breakfast when an upper GI series is ordered—to prevent rework.

Some benefits simply cannot be attained without the physician being involved. For example, if you want to provide drug information to influence physician ordering behavior, and you don't have the physician interacting with the system but simply have him writing medication orders on an order sheet that is later transcribed by a nurse onto a medication requisition, you are wasting your time. You also have no chance of eliminating the labor cost or error potential of that trancription step. Some benefits, of course, can be achieved without direct physician use. But since the cost of systems in terms of terminals, printers, computers, and so forth is substantially fixed, the cost-benefit relationship will be much less favorable for systems without direct professional use. In fact, I know of no hospital information system that convincingly lowers hospital costs that does not involve direct professional use.

The first observation in Figure 2 must be taken quite seriously, particularly in community hospitals and other nonteaching hospitals. Attending physicians are in the business of practicing medicine and making their living. They have their own set of values, but one of them is not making hospital computer systems successful. If you take them for granted, you are making a mistake. You have to understand that their support must be earned. If you take that point of view and work at it, you *can* earn it. But if you take them for granted and lose them, life can be very, very difficult.

Even a well designed system takes perhaps two to six hours of training and use before a physician gets to a level of proficiency where he perceives that the benefits to him exceed the effort he has to invest to use it. The key is how do you induce him to make that investment of his time—his scarcest resource?

It is also important to remember, particularly in nonteaching hospitals, that the activities of most physicians are seen by themselves as very routine; they don't see a need for very much intellectual support. Others, looking at what they do may decide they need a lot of help, but they themselves don't perceive it. Let me quote from a private communication written recently by the director of pathology of a major New York hospital, a physician:

> Most physicians do not need help most of the time to handle most situations in most of their patients. That is, the average physician sees only a limited number of different clinical situations with which he is quite familiar and which he treats in a routine manner, using a personally developed protocol which has proven successful in his hands. He generally does not need to refer to the literature for either diagnostic or therapeutic assistance. When he feels insecure, he uses several options: one, he muddles through, two, he seeks a 'sidewalk consultation' from a colleague, three, he seeks a formal consultation (frequently to document the fact that a consultation was secured for regulatory medical-legal reasons), or four, he consults the medical literature, mostly in the form of medical texts and ready references, such as the PDR. Rarely, he goes to the current medical literature.

Some of us may be uncomfortable with that as a characterization of most physicians, but I think we have to accept reality when we are trying to introduce a new technology.

Our experience has been that physicians respond in quite human terms. They value innovations that contribute to saving their time, increasing their convenience, or enhancing their income. If you think about the comments of the physicians in the video tape, they all reflect this in one way or another. They didn't say anything about saving more lives, although they did talk about improving quality in some cases. Most of their impressions of a system have to do with things that are tied to their everyday lives, their routine activities.

Another thing that we discovered, sometimes the hard way, was that you need to be sensitive to the cultural roles that are traditional in hospitals and health care. I've had doctors tell me, for example, that, "...entering orders is a nurse's or ward clerk's job, it's not my job. You

FIGURE 3

KEYS TO SECURING DIRECT PHYSICIAN USE

☐ Leadership and example within the medical staff are crucial.

☐ Effective training and assistance, preferably from within the medical staff, are vital.

☐ Benefits related to routine, not exceptional, physician activities are perceived as providing the most value.

☐ Nurses, interns, residents, and others influence medical staff attitudes.

☐ Clinically innovative systems are most likely to succeed when "piggybacked" on already accepted systems.

have a secretary; she does your typing. I have a nurse; she enters my orders."

There's also frequently a role reversal in know-how that occurs because nurses are in the hospital eight hours a day while attending physicians are typically in the hospital for only an hour or so. Consequently, nurses may become proficient in system use more rapidly than the doctors. All of a sudden, the nurses have a superior skill to the doctor, and this reversing of the traditional knowledge-skill relationship can be a problem when it forces the doctor to seek assistance from the nurse.

Figure 3 summarizes some of the ways of overcoming these obstacles to securing direct physician use of the system. Leadership and example within the medical staff are indeed crucial. You must win over the key opinion makers before you proceed. If you don't do that you are running a very, very serious risk. Most medical staffs demonstrate a pronounced "pecking order." If you are opposed by physicians who make up the leadership of the medical staff, you will find cooperation very difficult to secure. Fortunately, the converse is also true. Medical staff leaders must be an integral part of the system selection and decision process. They must come to thoroughly understand the benefits the hospital, the medical staff, and their patients can expect. Don't wait until rebellion is on you to attempt to enlist their support. Why should they bail you out?

Effective training—that two to six hours of training—is necessary. The most effective way we have found to do it is through a member of the medical staff. The hospital may hire a young doctor on a part-time basis for this task which he can devote to one-on-one training sessions for his colleagues. He doesn't have to accept the specious excuses that a non-physician might encounter from a doctor that he's attempting to train because he is one of them.

Again, benefits that are related to routine rather than exceptional circumstances are the ones physicians will perceive as most valuable—getting a list of their patients in the hospital, finding out what orders are in effect on their patients, which other physicians are taking care of their patients, and so on. Be sure that physicians receive these benefits from the start by carefully coordinating system implementation and physician training. Don't test their tolerance for delayed gratification!

Make the hospital culture work for you, not against you. In some hospitals, for example, doctors will hang out in radiology or in the laboratory as an informal practice. If the laboratory or radiology staff is hostile to the system for whatever reason it can affect the attitudes of the whole staff. Turn that around, and be *sure* the radiology and lab people are enthusiastic supporters before confronting the attending physicians with the system. Winning nurses as supporters is vital for the same reason. In teaching institutions, attitudes of interns and residents can significantly affect those of senior physicians.

Finally, as I have listened to some of the experiences that others here have described in introducing and seeking acceptance for their medical informatics projects, I have been reminded that it's difficult to win acceptance from physicians for a new computer system at the same time you are trying to introduce a clinically innovative step into their lives. We had a wise advisor in the early days, a mathematician from Mississippi who was formerly director of switching systems at the Bell Telephone Laboratories. One of the lessons he taught me was,

> ...you can use a new tool to do an old thing, or an old tool to do a new thing, but never, never try to do a new thing with a new tool!

This lesson means that one should first install a basic medical information system, secure its acceptance by doctors, nurses, and other hospital workers, and when system operation is stable, benefits have been realized, and the system enjoys broad support from its users, *then and only then* "piggyback" new, innovative changes in clinical care. One should not expect the medical staff to accept a new system while, at the same time, you are trying to get them to practice medicine differently.

In closing, let me just say that I think that if I knew then what I know now, I might have lacked the courage to even try. But I'm glad I did. It is a source of some considerable satisfaction to walk through any of a hundred hospitals or so in the U.S., U.K., or Canada and see doctors, nurses, and other professionals routinely doing their jobs with a light pen in hand. Last year, while a patient in an MIS hospital, I remember feeling that along with other patients, I could also feel more secure knowing that computer and communication technology had now been successfully harnessed to augment the vital human skills on which I was so dependent. It made it all seem very worthwhile!

Participants' Discussion

Carlos Vallbona	I believe that the nursing staff at El Camino Hospital played the major role in developing the system. I remember the days when Margo Cooper developed the care plans and saw to it, along with all the people on the nursing staff, that they were automated. I thought that made the major impact. That is my personal opinion in addition to the testimony by the physicians. My question is, in the period between 1973 and 1975, did Dale Mead develop gastric ulcer and was he admitted to El Camino Hospital?
Melville Hodge	As far as I know, Dale Mead has disappeared from the planet. I had completely forgotten about him until I went back and looked at those old clippings a few weeks ago in preparation of coming here today.
Question	I'm a family physician who works in this neighborhood. We have an office that is not yet computerized because we're waiting for superconductor technology. Is this a wise decision? As individual practitioners, should we wait for this, or will it take too long?
Melville Hodge	I think that superconductor technology will impact this only in terms of cheaper, faster computers, and that is 10 to 15 years away. From a technical judgement point of view, we've come to the conclusion in planning systems for the 1990s to forget about equipment costs. They are going to be so cheap that we won't care. This overstates it a little bit, but we are not waiting for superconductor technology. It's going to be a time before it gets here. But other apparent technological trends will lead to a further dramatic decline in equipment costs over the next few years. My advice is, don't wait.
Thomas Lincoln	My question takes up right from where you left off. To stay alive, systems have to metabolize, grow, and change. Homer had just moved his system to a new technology by reprogramming. Could you say a few words about growth into the 1990s—how you see a system of a certain age rejuvenating itself.

355

Melville Hodge   I'm sure in the 1990s we'll be talking distributed systems. I'll just give you five quick examples of what we're working on right now. One thing we want to do is expand into the integrated inpatient/outpatient environment. We're expanding the system to handle 16 million patients on line, to add outpatient episodes and encounters capacity and a comprehensive patient appointment scheduling capability, and to provide a continuous medical record capability.

A second thing is to go to a workstation philosophy for terminals. This involves a PC-based philosophy so any user could write PC programs, download information, and then upload the results back into the system. We think that's going to be important, to give the user a sense of control over his destiny.

We think we've got to find ways of reducing the cost of installation and training. While hardware has come down in cost, two things that have not come down are installation and training. So, we're automating the installation process to acquire data that's needed to install, and automatically generating the system displays and tables. We are also automating training with computer-based training. It's keyed into the system so that it automatically captures the keystrokes or light pen selections and can generate courses in no time at all to train all the different categories of users.

Finally, we are experimenting in five hospitals with so-called "point-of-care" or bedside terminals to see if we can measure additional cost or quality benefits. The idea is to put a terminal at every bed in the hospital.

History of Medical Informatics at Utah

Homer R. Warner, MD, PhD
University of Utah, Salt Lake City

This has been a very special experience for me to attend this conference, meet people that I haven't seen for a long time, and reflect on our associations over the past years.

My goal today is to "minimize your grief" in the terms used by our last speaker by trying to keep it as light as possible and at the same time convey some of the feel for the environment in which the developments that we've worked on have evolved.

In order to do that, I'm going to keep it sort of personal and hope this will be of some interest to you and not be offensive.

My background is cardiology, and I came to Latter Day Saints (LDS) Hospital, which is a 525-bed, tertiary-care, private hospital with a university affiliation in Salt Lake City, in 1954. At that time, I had learned how to do a heart catheterization. There was one surgeon at LDS Hospital who was already in this business, and I came there to set up a catheterization laboratory.

The first year we managed to get a diagnostic facility running, and, fortunately, about a year later the hospital got a sum of money from the Ford Foundation. Apparently, it was a grant given to most private hospitals across the country to use for something other than direct patient care activities which already existed.

Well, with that kind of constraint, it wasn't too hard to talk the hospital administrator into establishing a research department. So with that, we built our little cath lab, one floor up in a one-room research laboratory, and on top of that a room for some dogs, and we began doing some research.

The first project that I was interested in involved trying to understand how a pressure wave gets distorted as it travels from the aorta down to the radial artery. Well, I'd done a thesis back in Minnesota on a method for calculating stroke volume from the shape of aortic pressure wave. One of the assumptions we made in that work was that the pressure wave didn't get distorted as it traveled down the artery. We made that assumption only because we didn't know how to handle the distortion. It was an interesting question to me.

At the time I was taking a course at the university to learn something more about mathematics. I didn't know very much, and in this course the instructor introduced me to the notion of Fourier analysis—transforming information into another domain. I think that is what informatics is all about isn't it?—rearranging information to give one additional insights. I was fascinated by this, and I bought myself a long slide rule, which I still have, with trigonometric functions on it. I remember spending a whole day analyzing a single aortic pressure wave into its Fourier components. Well, the next day the instructor talked about another concept, which was the notion of a transfer function. If you know the Fourier components of the upstream pressure or the input to a system, and you also know the output in terms of its frequency components, then you can develop in terms of just ratios some notion about what's happening to each of those harmonics as it traverses the system.

Of course, I analyzed in the same heartbeat, then the downstream wave form and plotted the ratio of these—it peaked. It looked like a resonant system. Well, the instructor was talking about systems that did this kind of thing, and one of the systems that will do this is a resonant circuit, an RLC circuit. So, I thought it might be interesting to build such a circuit with variable components so that we could feed the signal from the pressure transducer measuring upstream pressure wave form into the resonant circuit and then tune the circuit by varying the values of R, L, and C until the downstream wave form matched the circuit output. So we did that. We built that kind of a circuit with big capacitor, inductor, and resistor and set it up in this little laboratory above the cath lab. With a patient on the table for some kind of diagnostic procedure and a catheter in the aorta and another one down in the radial artery, I'd let my assistant talk to the patient while I ran upstairs and started "twiddling the knobs." I would adjust the system until the downstream wave from from the artery overlapped the downstream wave form from the RLC circuit. At that point, we could read the settings for the components of the circuit that represented the electrical analogs of the resonant properties of the arterial bed between the two recording sites. This was our first analog computer and the thrill of building a model and testing its performance against a real biological system is still the motivation for much of our work in medical informatics. It got me excited about it.

We published a paper as a result of studying some 80 patients, which demonstrated that the resonant frequency of the aorta increases with age. This isn't too surprising, but for the first time we had a method for actually getting a quantitative feel of a physical phenomenon that we couldn't measure directly. In fact, I remember talking to Allen Toronto, who was the resident working with me at the time and later worked for many years with me, that maybe we shouldn't publish this quite yet, "It's so exciting that we ought to explore this tool a little bit before we tell the rest of the world about it." You've got to realize that we're living at LDS Hospital out there in Salt Lake City in a sort of isolation, and we thought that we had the world by the tail. But anyway, we went ahead and published of course. As a result, we got our first NIH grant.

That first grant was a real break for us, because now we could really justify spending some time in research. We began studying all kinds of systems using this sort of approach.

We looked at the same kind of transfer function using indicator dilution curves. By recording an upstream curve and a downstream curve and deriving a transfer function, one had a measure of the distribution of their transit times across any segment of the vascular bed. We built models of control mechanisms in the circulation using this approach. We looked at the carotid sinus for instance. We measured its transfer function using for input the carotid artery pressure and for output the frequency of action potentials recorded from a single fiber of the carotid sinus. It was an exciting period.

This was 1956. After a few years of exploring this tool, l learned that the university had acquired a digital computer. This sounded like a very interesting device, but I needed some kind of excuse to spend time learning how to use it. By that time, l was trying to support a family by running a diagnostic cardiovascular laboratory, and I couldn't just run off and play with a computer. I read an article in *Science* by Ledley and Lusted that suggested using a conditional probability approach to modeling the way a physician thinks. At the time, we had lots of patients coming through our laboratory who had congenital heart disease, and we began systematically collecting data on the incidence of history and physical findings that were obtained before catheterization revealed the ultimate diagnosis. We accumulated a data matrix by asking each physician who referred a case for study to fill out a checklist as to what the manifestations were. After we had enough data to get some statistical estimates, we compared the computer diagnosis using Bayes's theorem to what the physicians thought the diagnosis was before they sent the case in. The computer outperformed all but one of the physicians, most of whom only occasionally saw a patient with congenital heart disease.

We reported this work at the American Heart Meeting in 1961 and it was an interesting experience. Some of the senior cardiologists in the country were there. A number of them got up and expressed how upset they were about the very suggestion that a computer could do anything quite as subtle as suggesting a diagnosis to a clinician.

That was a very positive experience for me, and much of our subsequent thinking has been based on our optimism about the fact that indeed the computer does have this kind of capability if we're just clever enough to devise ways to take advantage of it.

We published that study, and again that was helpful in getting our first grant for a digital computer. So, we began to find ways to use that digital computer, and of course the first thing we applied it to was the heart catheterization lab because that was an environment that I had some control over. We interfaced the various instruments that we used—the pressure transducer, the oximeters, the ECG signal—directly to the computer. That was not a trivial job in those days. That was the early days of analog–digital converters.

I was very intrigued by some of the comments that Dr. Caceres and Dr. Pipenberger made this morning about analog signals, because we were going through the same kind of experience in learning to perform pattern recognition. We were able to get a program for the cath lab up and going, and it did have a significant impact on the efficiency of performing a diagnostic procedure in the laboratory. Before the program was in use, it required as much time to manipulate the catheter into the various locations in the patient's heart and record measurements as it did to analyze that long scroll of paper, calibrate the recorded wave forms, and generate a report. The program generated the report by the time the last measurements had been recorded.

So, we thought after doing the cardiovascular lab, "Why can't we do that in some of these other areas?" About 1968, we moved into the operating room. These were the early days of open heart surgery, and we had the responsibility of doing the monitoring during surgery on these patients. Our first systems allowed the anesthesiologist to record in the computer all his or her observations and procedures and control the sampling by physiological transducers of signals directly from the patient. We developed methods for inserting small-diameter arterial catheters the night before surgery percutaneously through a thin wall of 18-gauge needle into the radial artery, and we trained nurses to do this in order to make the procedure cost effective. The nurses learned how to put those arterial catheters in very efficiently. When the patient came up to surgery the next morning, all the anesthesiologist had to do was connect and calibrate the pressure gauge, and he was on his way. When this was working well, we moved into the intensive care ward. We wanted to provide a continuity of the patient's record and much the same kind of activities occur in the ICU, at least in the post-op ICU, that take place in the operating room. It is essential for patient care that an accurate and current record of blood, other fluids, and medications given the patient be recorded and made available as the patient is moved to the intensive care unit from the operating room.

Reed Gardner has been the man in our department primarily responsible for patient monitoring activity. Reed had the foresight to see that this activity could be spread to the rest of hospital. These same monitoring principles, where one samples information at specified intervals or on demand and provides immediate access to the information in a convenient form, could be applied to other areas of the hospital as well.

When Reed first came to our group, we were already a department of the University of Utah. The department was established 22 years ago as the Department of Biophysics and Bioengineering in the School of Engineering although we were physically off-campus at the LDS Hospital. Reed came to us with a degree in electrical engineering and earned a PhD in our department. He has taken the responsibility not only for the monitoring activities, but for many other interesting aspects of the system that I'll be describing to you.

I think our success, if we have had any, has been our ability to get and keep good, bright people that have come along. And Reed typifies these; in fact he was the first of these to join our faculty.

In patient monitoring, our focus initially was largely on collecting information and devising displays to present the data in some transformed way, either a graphics or tabular report. We tried a variety of ways to display information to physicians that would make it useful, and we finally came full cycle. We found ourselves after several years coming back to some of the original tabular methods. We pretty well explored methods for data display, and I discuss some of the ramifications of this later in this paper.

I was asked to join the computer study section, and I met Bruce Waxman. That experience had a major impact in my professional life, and I want to say a few words about him. I consider Bruce to be the "Oliver North" of the medical informatics field. I mean, he found a way to get things done. If he believed in something, he made it happen, and it didn't really matter what kind of gyrations he had to go through. We've already heard about the LINC experience. Bruce took our patient monitoring system, which was beginning to blossom in the ICU, and managed to find funds to plant copies of it at Massachusetts General Hospital and at George Washington University. It didn't survive very well in either place. Bruce put computers in doctors' offices all the way from Boston down to Washington. I remember he tried to put our Bayesian history-taking program in this system, but it was written in MUMPS, which couldn't handle all the computation required.

Bruce really is responsible for initiating what was called the Information Exchange Group. At the time, there were already one or two of these groups established in biochemistry and some other areas where NIH had established a system for exchanging information among people in a very active research area. Bruce asked me to start one of these in medical computing, and I did. The rules of the game were that anyone could belong to the group if they submitted at least one paper. Once you submitted a manuscript (and you had to submit the paper before you submitted it to any journal), NIH guaranteed that the paper would be distributed to everybody else in the group within two weeks. There was no editing done to it at all. The author sent it to me, I sent it to NIH, they'd publish it and distribute it to the people in the group. It was great. I mean we had a great communication link going, but it only lasted for a couple of years because several of the journals didn't like it, and they began saying, "If a manuscript was circulated this way, we won't publish it."

But out of this experience grew the beginnings of the journal *Computers and Biomedical Research*. Bruce asked me to negotiate with Academic Press about starting a journal, and I got together many of leaders in the field—some whom I have worked with since 1968 are in this room. We had only one meeting of the editorial board in the Chicago airport. We met there during the day and flew home that night. That's the only meeting we've had as a group, but we've had a lot of good correspondence over the years—back and forth and sharing information about specific manuscripts. It's been a wonderful experience for me, and I thank you, Bruce, for initiating all that.

Now, the next subject we tackled in our laboratory was also in the area of signal processing. A fellow by the name of Allan Pryor came into our program. Al had a background in mathematics and came with us to pursue a PhD. For his thesis, he developed a system for classifying ECG signals. He took an approach using three orthogonal leads even though this isn't the approach physicians use. He was able to generate all of the other leads synthetically for display to physicians. This ECG program was put in operation at the LDS Hospital in 1969 and has been in continual use until just this year when it was replaced by interfacing a commercially available ECG analysis program to the HELP system.

We implemented that ECG system by using a cart that could be wheeled into any patient room in the hospital. Using the phone line in the room and the modem on the cart as the input channel, the computer output was displayed on a memory oscilloscope, which had a TV camera focused on it that then would broadcast on Channel 13 to all patient rooms. I remember on one occasion, Jack Whitehead of Technicon was in the hospital following a skiing accident in Salt Lake, and he happened to tune to Channel 13 as he lay in his bed. He saw these messages about ECGs and asked the nurse what it was all about. As a result, I had the chance to go down and meet him.

Al has provided to our department not only mathematical and statistical expertise, but computer know-how. He is really the professional "computenik" in our group. Most of us had never had a course in computer science; there weren't such things in those days. But Al had some experience with NASA before coming to Utah, and that proved to be very valuable for us. Pryor has provided the system's know-how over these years that has resulted in a decision and database system that really works in a clinical environment.

This was about the time we began working to interface the clinical lab with the computer. It was apparent that if we were really going to serve the information needs in the ICU, we had to have information from other sources as well. John Morgan, one of our students, devised the first interface to the laboratory for us—not the first in the world, I'm sure, but it was a first for us. He interfaced a number of the analog laboratory instruments and developed a system that allowed the computer to sample those signals directly. We had a Control Data 3300 in those days that used to do everything. We built our own time-sharing system, and all the applications programs were written in assembly language.

That system was used to sample all the ECG monitoring beds (200 samples a second) while it was sampling the laboratory data, the pressure signals from different areas around the hospital, as well as interfacing with all the terminals. Each user had 2000 (24-bit) words of memory to work with and had to control his own overlays. It was not the most efficient system to program, but it hummed like a top. We used that computer system for 18 years.

John Morgan joined our faculty after graduating but didn't really like the academic environment. He preferred to write programs rather than manuscripts. He left the university and with his own initiative and resources developed a company called Code 3 to automate the coding of discharge diagnoses. He recently sold that company to 3M for $16 million, a nice success story. He gave a grant of $100,000 to the department to establish a fellowship.

We started developing a self-administered history—largely the result of Tony Gorry and Octo Barnett's work on sequential Bayesian decision making. We developed a sequential Bayesian history that we implemented as part of a screening program for elective surgical patients. I had been on site visits to Morris Collen and knew about his work in screening. Our implementation included ocular tension measurement, ECG measurements, spirometry on every patient that was coming in for elective surgery, this history program, and a battery of laboratory tests. The screening was designed to pick up secondary problems. The patient's primary problem was known, since he or she was being admitted for elective surgery. This program has served us well over the years. We've done over 35,000 sequential Bayesian self-administered patient histories. Patients react very well to it, and it's been a useful source of information for the surgeon. Incidentally, in 70% of patients, the primary diagnosis can be made from history alone.

One day I was down in the ICU looking at one of the displays on the computer terminal. We had, at that time, a display with a red, yellow, and green light for each patient. When the red light was on, some emergency had occurred. The nurse had to press the light (interrupt button) to see what had caused it to go on. The yellow light was used to indicate that a trend had occurred. For this patient, there was a yellow light on, and the nurse was over at the bed pumping up a blood pressure cuff and on the other arm was an arterial catheter recording the pressure. I waited until she got through and I said, "Why are you doing that?" It turned out that she was simply frustrated. We were overloading her with information, and she didn't know what to make of it. We were asking her to do something she hadn't really been trained to do. It was really this experience that moved us into thinking, "We need to do something more than just display data; we need to help the nurse with the decision making." In this case, it turned out that the patient was having a cardiac tamponade. We went through a half-hour or so of reviewing information with the resident before coming to that conclusion, and I thought, "Why don't we build a program that would allow us to preserve that logic that we've just been through so the next time this kind of situation occurs, the system will recognize it?" It was from this experience that the decision support components of the HELP system evolved.

The HELP system is built around a central patient database that interfaces to a dictionary and to a knowledge base. The knowledge frame is driven by the data as it is acquired. The dictionary has pointers from each item to the frame using that item. Execution of a frame may result in a decision that can then be fed back to various places in the system. The knowledge base is built on the assumption that we want to not only provide consultation, but we want also to provide alerts. That is, we want to provide help for people that may not know they need help. Some of the mistakes made in patient care are the result of not knowing. They are just oversights. A lot of our effort has gone toward recognizing the latter type of errors. One of the most successful is a system for alarming at the time the prescription is written on a potential adverse drug reaction.

Paul Clayton developed a clever system for ordering radiology procedures. At the time an x-ray procedure is ordered, frames representing all the possible interpretations of that procedure are processed. Each frame is associated with a certain set of clinical manifestations. For example, if a chest film is ordered, there is a 30% chance that it will be normal. But if that patient is coming from a post-op ICU ward, is running a fever, and has an elevated white blood count, the chances are much more likely that the interpretation will be pneumonia. So at the time the procedure is ordered, this "expert system" generates a requisition that has on it the five most likely interpretations based on the relevant clinical findings in the patient's database.

We developed many of these kind of applications. When the regional medical program came along, we jumped on the band wagon and over a weekend wrote a grant that got us a second computer that helped us get into a position to support clinical applications 24 hours a day in a real clinical setting. We used one machine for development and one machine for providing service.

After 18 years with the CDC 3300 computer, we began thinking how we were going to get funds to move the HELP system to another piece of equipment. We explored possible relationships with the Navy, with NIH of course, and with Health Services Research. Nobody wanted to support a reprogramming effort; that's not research. We finally went to our hospital administration. The hospital, which had already committed to each one of these applications as the research phase ended, now was asked to make a decision, "If you want these computer-based services we've been providing, are you willing to pay for a new machine and the reprogramming effort?" The medical staff and administration made that commitment, and so LDS Hospital funded reprogramming HELP on a Tandem computer. This is an example of the friendly, supportive environment in which we have worked.

Over the 22 years since our department was established as an academic unit of the University of Utah, its name has changed a number of times. After 10 years as "Biophysics and Bioengineering" in the College of Engineering, we moved to the School of Medicine as the "Department of Medical Biophysics and Computing" and three years ago changed the name to "Medical Informatics." We have 13 full-time faculty and about the same number of auxiliary appointments of people in other departments. We feel it's very important that Medical Informatics be involved with every department. We look to these departments for real problems to solve. Last year there were 54 graduate students in the program, and there seem to be plenty of opportunities for them when they graduate. Often in these years, I've wondered if informatics is just a passing phenomenon, and after we solve today's problems it will go away. I don't think so. I think we're into a discipline that is going to stand on its own feet, that we have challenging things ahead of us to solve and that medical informatics represents a major new direction for medicine.

Finally, there have been some spin-offs into industry that I think are significant. Because the Dean wanted some material to go to the legislature and prove that we are doing something for the economy of the state, Reed Gardner collected a list of some of the companies that have taken advantage of the technology spun off from our department. Reed estimated that the annual payroll from these companies amounts to approximately $90 million a year just in the state of Utah.

I have been fortunate in having bright and enthusiastic companions to work with and a supportive environment both on the local and national scene. We have all participated in the blossoming of a new discipline whose domain touches the intellectual core of medicine and at the same time provides opportunities for immediate solutions to practical problems. And I have a feeling that we have only scratched the surface of this exciting new field.

Participants' Discussion

Lindley Darden I'm very interested in your self-conscious awareness of forming a new discipline. I wonder where the term "medical informatics" came from and to what extent you really do see it now as a separate discipline.

Homer Warner Yes, I'm more positive about it now than I was even a couple of years ago. I first heard the term from Morris Collen. It's been in use in Europe for some time, and I remember we had a very lively discussion in our School of Medicine about renaming the Department of Medical Informatics. I think the name is a good one myself. You'd have laughed at the discussion we had in the executive committee of the medical school when we proposed "medical informatics" as a new name for our department. The chairman of the Department of Anatomy, who's pretty outspoken, said he spent the afternoon trying to look up "informatics" and couldn't find it in any dictionary. He was quite disturbed that we proposed something like that. I think we just have to establish it as a field. Once, Otto Schmidt was asked by someone, "What is biophysics?" and he said, "That's what biophysicists do." That's sort of what we are doing here. We are defining what we do.

Morris Collen May I give Homer the credit for being the first Department of Medical Informatics in the United States? Homer indicated that in Europe there had been Departments of Medical Informatics, especially in the Benelux countries, for several years. The term is contested as being derived from the Russian "informatika" or from the French "informatique." English dictionaries credit the term as being derived from the Russian "informatika."

The International Medical Informatics Association (IMIA) was the first to popularize the term throughout the world, and, because of IMIA, I think that in the years to come all the schools in our country will follow Homer's example.

Jochen Moehr I'm not aware of the Russian origin, but I'm certain that the French version "informatique" has influenced the word "Informatik" in Germany and "informatics" in England. While the English had some difficulties in adopting it, they are, I think, moving in that direction. In Germany the computer scientists adopted the word "Informatik" for their field in 1969, and they defined the field of what is here called computer science accordingly. So from 1969 on we had the "Gesellschaft fuer Informatik," which is the German computer society. From there stems the tendency, I think, to call the medical applications of computer science "Medizinische Informatik." This term was reflected in the choice of "MEDINFO" as the name for the first world conference on the topic in 1974. I don't know about the background of these decisions, but I think the term sprang up in this connection in the early 1970s.

Morris Collen

It is correct that in the German literature in the late 1970s the term "Informatik" does appear, but the first documentation of the term comes earlier from the Russian. John Anderson published a book with Gremy and Pages in 1974 titled *Education in Health Informatics*. Anderson documented how the "informatics" in the title of the book was derived from the French "informatique," and he anglicized it to "informatics." The word appears in the title but nowhere else in the book; so they coined the word but never defined it. Gradually through the years it was defined and began to appear in all the literature, as was pointed out.[1]

Bruce Waxman

As Homer was talking, I was reminiscing about MEDLAB. He indicated that we made several attempts to move MEDLAB around. I asked Bill Yamamoto (sitting next to me), who had the experience of living with one of the MEDLAB transplants, why it didn't work, and he gave the answer that I anticipated. There wasn't anything technically wrong with the system; it was a people problem. The people who had to run the system in another environment couldn't make it happen. It really had very little to do with the technology.

I also noticed this "people problem" with COSTAR, where we weren't dealing with one or two systems, but more like 20 or 30 that were transplanted to California. I saw a spectrum of situations where, in one environment COSTAR was enormously successful and in another environment it was a total failure. Most of the installations were in the middle—that is, they worked adequately. Whether the system worked or didn't had much more to do with the people responsible for using it than anything about the technology. It makes you wonder as you move on to other things, whether there might be some way of developing a system that is immune to most of these "people prob-

---

[1] Editors' note: For a more complete discussion of this topic see M.F. Collen, Origins of medical informatics, *Western Journal of Medicine*, 145:778–785, 1986.

lems," in the sense that using the system doesn't require someone with either a lot of inspiration or dedication.

Homer Warner   I think if I had one comment to make about what's the primary need in this field—I think it's people. We just need to find people who catch the spirit of it, get enough basic training that they can understand what some of the opportunities are, and catch that enthusiasm to move it ahead.

Patient Management Systems: The Early Years[1]

William E. Hammond, PhD

Duke University Medical Center, Durham

As I scanned through old papers and reports in preparation for these remarks, I became depressed in the "sameness" of those proposals and descriptions with what is happening today. Then I realized there are major differences—today's systems work and are affordable.

The health care delivery system is an industry whose magnitude, complexity, and pervasiveness are rarely acknowledged. In a few decades, the industry has literally changed from a cottage industry to a multibillion dollar giant with whom every individual in our society has come into contact. It is a personal industry, yet at the same time, one of our most technically sophisticated industries. It is not surprising that computers are becoming an integral part of that system. This paper discusses some of the experiences in reaching that goal.

As a beginning engineer back in the 1960s, I, with many others, felt that the development of computerized patient management systems was not only natural but mandatory. One merely needs to observe the process to realize that keeping track of what was done and charging appropriately, of sending information from one place to another, of storing data and printing it on demand, and of controlling process and flow are tasks that computers perform well. Many medical specialities already used forms for the collection of data. Most medical knowledge was already clearly identified in textbooks, including what questions to ask, what parameters to measure, what tests to order, how to diagnose, and how to treat. "A simple matter of programming" was a phrase often used and believed. It later became a standing joke. Many predicted that the use of computers for medical applications would develop into a multimillion dollar market whose potential would be quickly realized. The actual events proved to be quite different.

The development of patient management systems has been influenced by several factors. The first, and perhaps one of the most significant factors, is that of technology—hardware and software. During this development period, computers evolved from single tasking, "untouch-

---

[1] For a history of Dr. Hammond's early work, see W.E. Hammond and W.W. Stead, The evolution of GEMISH and TMR. *Implementing Health Care Information Systems*, H.F. Orthner and B.I. Blum, (eds.). New York: Springer-Verlag, 1989, pp. 33–66.

able" and "unfriendly" mainframes to highly interactive, multiuser minicomputers.

A second factor is that of the people involved—both the developers and the users. The developers had to learn first what to do and how to do it and then learn how to package and sell it to the ultimate user.

Economic factors also influenced progress. As computer costs decreased, the cost of delivering patient care increased. Computers seemed to offer one way to reduce and control these costs.

Another factor was the tremendous increase in the amount of data generated and the demand for that data by a variety of individuals. For example, both the number of laboratory tests available and the number of tests actually ordered increased exponentially during this period. Estimates on the costs of information handling vary between 25% and 39% of the total cost of health care {1}. With the influx of many research dollars from NIH, actual medical knowledge increased.

Finally, the influence of external factors such as the government and third-party payers contributed significantly to the development of patient management systems. As one observer commented,

> I think that just as the Medicare legislation forced hospitals, almost without exception, to use the computer for financial processing, patient accounting, and patient billing, the PSRO type of thing—which will get built on more and more, particularly with national health insurance likely to go in within the next year—will force computerization of the clinical side of the hospital. {2}

The digital computer became available for general use in the late 1950s. These first systems provided few user-oriented features and required considerable knowledge and skill to use. Early systems were batch oriented and supported single tasking only. These computers were large, required specially prepared spaces, and were quite expensive. In addition to machine language, followed by assembly language, only FORTRAN and COBOL were available as higher level languages. Most programs were written by computer specialists who had only limited interaction with those who would ultimately use the systems. The reliability of early systems left much to be desired. Hardware failures were the norm rather than the exception. Software crashes were commonplace. Perhaps life with these early systems was best described as "working with a machine you couldn't touch; working with a machine that didn't work; working with a machine that you couldn't afford; and working with systems that were not useful."

I shared office space with two cardiology fellows who seemed to spend most of their day making meticulous measurements of amplitudes and time durations of the various waveforms of the ECG. After recording these carefully on paper, they applied a set of rules to interpret the ECG readings. This task seemed to me to be a simple engineering problem that could be solved almost trivially by a computer. Unfortunately there were the problems of noise, wandering baselines, arrhythmias, and PVCs, variations in patterns and other factors to solve to produce the same result as the human. Researchers quickly learned that it was difficult to teach the computer to recognize patterns that were easily identified by humans {3, 4, 5}.

Gordon points out difficulties of attempting to overlay the computer's orderly, pedantic, and, indeed, binary world with the softness, variability, and "between the lines implications" of medical data under human direction—a point that is still valid {6}. He notes that the adoption of computer technology in practice must be concerned with the customs of 200,000 physicians serving independently or in 7000 hospitals and clinics. Changes from manual documentation to automated procedures are often bewildering and ineffective.

The early development of patient management systems was supported primarily by NIH grants. Since 1968, the National Center for Health Services Research has played a major role in supporting the development, application, and evaluation of patient management systems {7}. No hospital could afford a computer. Since the funding came from external sources, developers often did what they wanted to do and how they wanted to do it, rather than interfacing with users who wanted to have nothing to do with the system in the first place.

Developers were consistent in their reasons for developing patient care systems. Almost all papers or proposals started with a line, "We are currently in the midst of a health care crisis. The average cost of a hospital bed has tripled since 1957." Systems were proposed to reduce the costs of patient care, reduce length of stay, improve patient care, improve nursing care, improve communication, and improve decision making. Little evaluation was done. For the most part, we did what we knew how to do and wrote research papers to justify it.

Melville H. Hodge sets the stage for this period in the Preface of his book *Medical Information Systems* {8}. He states that, in the early 1960s, a small group of hospitals became identified with one common goal, that of a commitment to serve as a site for the development of computerized handling of patient information. Some of these early hospitals include Akron Childrens' Hospital in Ohio; El Camino in Mountain View, California; Baptist in Beaumont, Texas; St. Francis in Peoria, Illinois; Charlotte Memorial in North Carolina; Washington Veteran's Administration Hospital; Henry Ford Hospital, Detroit, Michigan; Monmouth Medical Center, Long Branch, New Jersy; Mary's Help Hospital, Daly City, California; Deaconess Hospital, Livingston, Indiana; Latter Day Saints Hospital, Salt Lake City, Utah; and Downstate Medical Center, New York City, New York. We owe a debt of gratitude to these early pioneers, and I might say suffering sites.

Most major computer companies, such as IBM, Burroughs, Control Data, Honeywell, and NCR, seeing the potential of significant sales, were active in their support. Industries experienced in using computers to manage complex systems joined in. Some of these companies include Lockheed, who supported the early development of the Technicon Hospital Information System; McDonnell-Douglas, who is still active in the field; and other companies, such as GE, who later abandoned these efforts. Most of these systems were well reported in the literature (See, for example {9, 10}).

Many groups in Europe were developing systems at the same time: the Danderyd Hospital {11} and Karolinska Hospital {12} in Sweden; London Hospital {13} and Kings Hospital {14} in England; and the Hanover Hospital {15} in Germany to mention a few.

Unfortunately, most of these early systems resulted in resounding failures. The reason primarily for these failures and for the slow progress into the 1970s was largely due to underestimating the complexity of the information requirements of patient management systems. Furthermore, users, as contrasted to developers, were not involved at an adequate level and, in fact, were not ready for computers. Hardware and software tools were inadequate. Hospitals felt that they had been oversold an unattainable product and, at the loss of millions of dollars, abandoned their efforts in computerization. As Hodge notes, optimism and enthusiasm were replaced by skepticism and then cynicism.

Fortunately others persisted. As technology advanced, driven by the space efforts of the 1960s, developers learned to appreciate the complexity of the problem and began to address smaller, more easily defined components of the overall system. A few successes appeared, although some projects failed in the transition from carefully nurtured demonstration projects into systems which interfaced with, usually, the least paid, least motivated, and least educated employees of the medical support staff.

By the early 1970s, however, some of these early systems, after years of development and many more development dollars than anyone anticipated, became commercially available {16, 17}. After a period of overpromise and underachievement, some progress could be noted {18}.

The Technicon system, begun by Lockheed in the 1960s, was installed at the El Camino Hospital in Mountain View, California and became, perhaps, the best known "successful" application. The "success" of this system in its early years at El Camino can perhaps be measured by an article in the October 1973 issue of *Datamation* {19}. El Camino was truly a guinea pig in the development of the hospital information system and suffered through the many bugs. During the first year of installation, more than 2000 changes were made to the system, many of these major changes, which affected the appearance of things such as reports. Each passing day saw improvement in the attitude of doctors and nurses. In mid-1972, 66% of the doctors opposed the system. By the beginning of 1973, the majority of doctors, except for internists, favored the system. The El Camino system is perhaps one of the most thoroughly evaluated systems of any of the early development systems {20, 21}. The results of this evaluation did encourage further development in patient management systems.

The ultimate success of the system at El Camino led to the spread of this and other systems into other hospitals. New crises were encountered, however, as reduced funding from the federal government forced hospitals to decide if computerization was worth the cost and then to find the money to do it. Some hospitals abandoned systems even though they looked promising.

Patient management systems tend to be primarily an automation of manual processes. In 1969, Feinstein noted that while computers had been applied effectively in situations where a standard mechanism already exists for dealing with the data, computers had not yet had an important impact on the more inherently clinical features of medical strategy and tactics {22}. Many of the points made in this article are still valid criticisms of patient management systems. Schwartz makes a similar point. He states that

> few systems have fully explored the possibility that the computer as an intellectual tool can reshape the present system of health care, fundamentally alter the role of the physician, and profoundly change the nature of medical manpower recruitment and medical education—in short, the possibility that the health care system by the year 2000 will be basically different from what it is today. {23}

We clearly have some distance to go.

The development of many of the components of a patient management system was driven in the late 1960s and early 1970s by interest in automated multiphasic health testing. The work of Dr. Morris Collen and his colleagues at the Kaiser-Permanente Medical Group in California {24, 25} contributed to both a high level of interest in this field and in the progress of automation of tests, data collection, and analysis. Dr. Collen stressed the need for AMHT systems to provide high quality testing, to provide good service to doctors and patients, and to be economical. In the early 1970s, only the first of these conditions had been met. The same could be said about other components of patient management systems.

Barnett, in an article in *The New England Journal of Medicine*, again argued the cause for computer applications in areas of medical care {26}. He identified seven major areas in patient management systems that had made progress in development. Caceres similarly reviewed the state of the art and stressed that the physician and patient care data must interact via the computer to realize automated patient management system goals {27}.

Patient management systems, to be effective, do need to become a part of the physician-patient interface. Early systems were designed partly by the scientist, partly by the business world, and very little by the practicing physician. Systems designed in our computer laboratories often had major flaws, which were obvious when we introduced them into the real world. Intelligent use of computers requires an understanding of the things computers do well: quantified information, well-defined vocabulary, great speed, repetition, accuracy, and versatile control. Humans, on the other hand, communicate by speech, vision, and touch, and have an unlimited vocabulary and great adaptability. It is when the computer is applied in areas of human incompetence, that previously impossible results can be achieved {28}. Too few systems take advantage of this fact. Often we fail to realize that the computer is no substitute for intelligence. It is not a magic box that can make gold from straw.

One early experience at Duke is typical of the early days. For over two years, Duke had been involved with IBM in the development of a system called CDS Systems (CDSS). Duke had sent several MDs to work with IBM to develop a system in which the doctor would sit down with a computer terminal, describe the patient's history, physical findings, and laboratory data, and the computer would return the diagnosis and recommend a treatment. A remote system was set up at Duke, and the system was to be demonstrated to the faculty and house staff. Before the grand opening, a few doctors sat down and entered data on patients with some "easy" problems, such as influenza or pneumonia. After an hour of conversation with the computer, the computer was no closer to a conclusion than it was at the beginning. It seems that the computer did not know of the more common diseases, since they were not well defined in the literature. The decision was made not to demonstrate or implement the system.

Instead, Duke then decided to develop a smaller subset of the system—the automation of the initial or screening medical history. A 19-page mark sense form was designed to be completed by the patient, processed by the computer, and presented to the doctor in narrative form. After three iterations, the form was complete, and actually did an effective job of collecting the initial medical history. Unfortunately, the logistics of processing this form on a large, remotely located mainframe computer led to its failure. The 19-page history was scanned by a mark sense reader and the results written on a 9-track magnetic tape. The patient's name, address, and free text data were keypunched onto cards; and the tape, cards, and program were submitted for delivery to the Triangle Universities Computation Center (TUCC), located some 12 miles away, for processing. Rarely did the tape, data, and program arrive at TUCC at the same time, and we spent most of our time trying to track down the components and get them together for processing. And when we managed that, the tape, created on one vendor's machine, could not be read on the other vendor's tape unit. The result was the history usually arrived in the doctor's hands a week after the patient had been seen. This problem was ultimately solved with a minicomputer directly interfaced to the scanner, which produced the histories immediately.

We tried to use what we had learned with the automated histories to develop a computerized medical record for the Division of Obstetrics at Duke. We met with a group of physicians, argued over what parameters constituted an appropriate database, and finally compromised by including any parameter any person felt they might use. The result was a 23-page, narrative printout for a new OB workup. Obviously, this computer program was neither reducing the paper work nor helping the doctor. A quick redesign with the assistance of only one physician reduced the output to an acceptable amount; in fact, the essence of the output was reduced to approximately ten lines on the first page in a starred box. We learned an important lesson—the difference between "what I might want" and "what I need."

Technology produced the minicomputer in the mid-1960s and removed some of the problems associated with the mainframes. The cost of these computers was around $30,000. The first of these was the LINC or Laboratory Instrumentation Computer, developed at MIT and distributed to a number of system developers by NIH. This move by NIH was, in my opinion, one of the most significant events in the field of medical informatics, and really led to the development of the minicomputer industry. The LINC permitted affordable, hands-on, real-time interaction with a computer. The minicomputer moved into the locations in which the projects were developed. The first minis were single user and had to be programmed in assembly language. The University of Washington in St. Louis developed a popular operating system that solved many of the system problems.

The minicomputer opened the door for many new developments in patient management including clinical laboratory systems, automated ECG systems, and ambulatory care patient record systems. Octo Barnett, at Mass General, led the way with the development of COS-TAR and the programming language MUMPS {29}.

At Duke, we learned of the power of the minicomputer on a borrowed LINC-8 and designed a system in 1967 to create on-line surface maps of cardiac body potentials—a process that had previously been performed on a mainframe at a much greater expense of time and money. A group of us then became interested in developing a computerized medical record. Our newly acquired DEC PDP-12 was a dream. It had a 4K memory of 12-bit words, a CRT screen that had to be refreshed under program control, two 135K DEC minitapes, 12 binary control switches, six A–D channels, and six potentiometers A–D inputs. Our first system was the Obstetrical Medical Record in which detailed data was retained during the pregnancy of some 1500 women who subsequently delivered at the Duke Medical Center. One tape would contain the records of approximately one month's pregnancies. Near the end of each month, someone was on call to change the tapes as the women came to Duke for delivery. The output was in uppercase only on a teletype located just outside the delivery suite. One lesson we learned was that MDs did place value on the ability of a system to deliver information reliably as it was needed.

The programs were written originally in assembly language and used the LAP-6 operating system. These assembly language programs were later converted into a programming language called GEMISCH, which we use today.

The PDP-12 gave way to a PDP-11/20 in the early 1970s. The addition of a movable head, 1.2M hard disk seemed to offer more storage than we could ever need. This minicomputer had 28K words of 16-bit memory. We wrote a multiuser operating system which supported seven simultaneous users via a round-robin swapping algorithm.

User acceptance of computers played a major role in the development of patient management systems. The success of any innovation in a medical setting depends on the attitude of the physicians involved. Surveys indicated that physicians were reluctant to touch the keyboard of a CRT {30}. They were doctors and "not typists." Systems designed and introduced by physicians were more apt to be accepted than those designed by non-MDs.

At Duke, we conducted one experiment that demonstrates this attitude. We asked a number of primary care physicians to look at a computer-generated medical history and a handwritten, human-generated history. The physicians overwhelmingly selected the handwritten form. We then reversed the process, taking the computer-generated medical history and copying it by hand, reformatting it slightly. We then took a human-generated history, typed it into the computer, and printed it on a drum printer so that it was obviously computer-generated. We showed these two histories to a number of physicians and again they overwhelmingly selected the handwritten form.

Many worried, and perhaps justly, that computers would be over-accepted, and the computer's "word" would become truth. In an editorial in *JAMA*, M. Southgate compares today's physician with the medicine man of a primitive tribe who consults his spirits for knowledge {31}. To the modern physician, the computer becomes the powerful and all-knowing spirit.

Patients had little problem in accepting the computer as part of their health care delivery team {32}. Our own experience with using the PDP-12, certainly a rather imposing creature to a unenlightened patient, for collecting headache histories suggested that patients were less intimidated by the computer than by the doctor. The adventuresome spirit of our patients was best illustrated by one incident involving a 67-year-old lady. While answering questions about her headache, she would occasionally laugh. Not thinking our displays were humorous, we finally asked her what was funny. She replied that she was just waiting until the man hidden in the "computer box" would step out and greet her.

The developers of patient management systems were committed to the task. Typical of that attitude is Mel Hodge:

> I am a believer. I happen to believe that the problems of health care delivery are susceptible to well-considered, well-executed approaches and that the introduction of information systems technology is among the more powerful approaches available. I have invested more than a decade of my life in this belief {8}.

Many of us can now say we have invested a career in this belief.

Both of our speakers in this patient management systems section have contributed significantly to the development of this field. Both have been involved from the early years. Melville Hodge headed the development team that was responsible for the Technicon Medical Information System. This system was the first successful HIS that was subsequently implemented in a number of institutions and is today still a leader in the field of patient management systems.

Homer Warner, with his colleagues at the Latter Day Saints (LDS) Hospital in Salt Lake City, Utah, developed a number of subsystems over this period, which constitute a patient management system called HELP.

The HELP system had its beginning in the late 1950s when Dr. Warner and colleagues began exploring the use of computers in the diagnosis of congenital heart disease {33}. The HELP system grew out of a group of subsystems designed to directly help the doctor or the nurse with specific data as relates to recognizing and dealing with specific events in a patient's illness {34}. These efforts included the goal of using the computer to enhance the decision making process in the medical arena {35}. Dr. Warner and colleagues dealt early with specific data collection, management {36}, and analysis in such areas as the clinical laboratory, patient monitoring {37}, and electrocardiographic interpretation by computer {38}. In the early 1970s, these areas were integrated to use a common database. Warner describes the HELP system in a recent book {39}.

The Technicon system, and the contributions of Hodge, is important because it was one of the first systems that worked and was accepted. This system primarily dealt with the service-related components of a patient management system—order entry and result reporting. Contributions were made in what was done and how it was done, even though other systems did not necessarily follow exactly the same patterns. The Technicon system represents one milestone in the development of patient management systems.

Warner and his group, through years of development, have added an important and necessary component of clinical involvement. By collecting data early on, Warner and his group were able to develop their own probabilities for diseases and their relationship to signs, symptoms, and findings. Most impressive is that the HELP system is still evolving and even now represents a state of the art approach to automated patient management.

These early years of development had to occur. I am always impressed that, as we became smart enough to recognize what we should do next, technology was always just available to enable us to do it. We are now entering a stage in which the tools seem to be adequate, the users seem to be receptive, the results justify the costs, and the applications seem to be useful. Perhaps we have now arrived at the point in which computerized patient management systems can change the way we teach physicians, the way we practice medicine, and the way we do medical research.

References

1. Jackson, G.G. Information handling costs in hospitals. *Datamation* 15:56, 1969.

2. Wide variety of computer based systems available to hospitals. *Datamation*, March 1975, pp. 115–121.

3. Caceres, C.A., *et al.* Computer extraction of electrocardiogram parameters. *Circulation* 25:356, 1962.

4. Pipberger, H.V., Stallman, F.W., and Berson, A.S. Automatic analysis of the P-QRS-T complex of the electrocardiogram by the digital computer. *Ann. Intern. Med.* 57:776, 1962.

5. Bonner, R.E. and Schwetman, H.D. Computer diagnosis of electrocardiograms. II. A computer program for EKG measurements. *Comp. Biomedical Res.* 1:366, 1968.

6. Burgess, L.G. Regularization and stylization of medical records. *JAMA* 212:1502–1507, June, 1, 1970.

7. Computer Applications in Health Care. NCHSR Research Report Series, DHHS Publication No. (PHS) 80–3251, June 1980.

8 Hodge, M.H. *Medical Information Systems: A Resource for Hospitals.* Germantown, Maryland: Aspen Systems Corp., 1977.

9. Ball, M.J. An Overview of total medical information systems. *Meth. Inf. Med.* 10:73, 1971.

10. Bekey, G.A. and Schwartz, M.D. *Hospital Information Systems.* New York: Marcel Dekker, 1972.

11. Abrahamsson, S., Bergstrom, S., Larsson, K., and Tillman, S. Danderyd hospital computer system. II. Total regional system for care. *Comp. Biomedical Res.* 3:30, 1970.

12. Hall, P., Mellner, C., and Danielsson, T. J5—A Data processing system for medical information. *Method. Inform. Med.* 6:1, 1967.

13. Barber, B. and Abbott, W. *Computing and Operational Research at the London Hospital.* London: Butterworths, 1972.

14. Anderson, J. Kings Hospital computer system (London). *Hospital Computer Systems.* New York: Wiley, 1974.

15. Reichertz, P. University of Hannover Hospital computer system (Hannover). *Hospital Computer Systems.* New York: Wiley, 1974.

16. Ferderber, C.J. A standardized solution for hospital systems. *Datamation* 21:50, 1975.

17. Ball, M.J. Computers: Prescription for hospitals. *Datamation* 21:50, 1975.

18. Spencer, W.A., Baker, R.L., and Moffet, C.L. *Hospital Computer Systems—A Review of Usage and Future Requirements After a Decade of Overpromise and Underachievement.* Baylor College of Medicine, 1972.

19. What will they zap at El Camino? The CRT, or the two-year old MIS? *Datamation,* October 1973, pp. 142–146.

20. Pesut, R.N. and Barrett, J.P. Assessment of the Impact of an Interactive Computer Based Medical Information System on the Quality of Care. Battelle Columbus Laboratories, Contract HSM 110–73–331, 1975.

21. Evaluation of a Medical Information System in a Community Hospital. HRA 76–3144, Research Digest Series, NCHSR, 1977.

22. Feinstein, A.R. A position paper—Computers in medicine: Automation vs. improvement of status quo. *Spring Joint Computer Conference,* 1969, pp. 715–716.

23. Schwartz, W.B. Medicine and the computer: The promise and problems of change. *NEJM* 283:1257, 1970

24. VanBrunt, E.E. The Kaiser-Permanente medical information system. *Comp. Biomedical Res.* 3:477, 1970.

25. Collen, M.F. Automated multiphasic health testing. *Hospital Computer Systems*. New York: Wiley, 1974.

26. Barnett, G.O. Computers in patient care. *NEJM* 279:1321, 1968.

27. Caceres, C.A., Weihrer, A.L., and Pulliam, R. *Information Science Applications in Medicine*. George Washington University Medical Center, 1971.

28. Limitations of computers in medicine. *CMA Journal* 104:234, 1971.

29. Greenes, R.A., Pappalardo, A.N., Marble, C.W., and Barnett, G.O. Design and implementation of a clinical data management system. *Comp. Biomedical Res.* 2:469, 1969.

30. O'Toole, R., Cammarn, M.R., Levy, R.P., and Rydell, L.H. Computer handling of ambulatory clinic records. II. Sociological analysis of physicians' responses. *JAMA* 197:113, August, 29, 1966.

31. Demythologizing medicine; or, how to stop worrying and love the computer. *JAMA* 232:515, 1975.

32. Slack, W.V. and VanCura, L.J. Patient reaction to computer based interviewing. *Comp. Biomedical Res.* 1:527, 1968.

33. Warner, H.R., Gardner, R.M., Pryor, T.A., and Stauffer, W.M. Computer automated heart catherization laboratory. *UCLA Forum in Medical Sciences*. Berkeley: UC Press, 1969.

34. Bishop, C.R. and Warner, H.R. A mathematical approach to medical diagnosis: Application to polycythemic states utilizing clinical findings with values continuously distributed. *Comp. Biomedical Res.* 2:486, 1969.

35. Warner, H.R., Olmsted, C.M., and Rutherford, B.D. HELP—A Program for medical decision-making. *Comp. Biomedical Res.* 5:65, 1972.

36. Warner, H.R., and Morgan, J.D. High density medical data management by computer. *Comp. Biomedical Res.* 3:464, 1970.

37. Warner, H.R. Experiences with computer-based patient monitoring. *Anesth. Analg. Current Res.* 47:453, 1968.

38. Pryor, T.A., Russell, R., Budkin, A., and Price, W.G. Electrocardiographic interpretation by computer. *Comp. Biomedical Res.* 2:537, 1969.

39. Warner, H.R. *Computer-assisted Medical Decision-making*. New York: Academic Press, 1979.

CLINICAL DECISION MAKING

The final session of the symposium was devoted to clinical decision making. The discussant was Casimir A. Kulikowski, PhD, who introduced each speaker and concluded the session with an overview that integrated the various activities up to 1977. He gave this date as the end of the first generation of AI systems; henceforth, experimentation would no longer be limited to decision prototypes for specific diseases. An expansion of his comments is the final paper in this collection.

Lee B. Lusted, MD was the first speaker of this session. Because of the limited time for a presentation, he concentrated on only two issues: a discussion of Bayesian analysis (which included a picture of Bayes's grave) and a citation analysis of the field of medical decision making through the mid-1970s. The paper includes this material plus a discussion of the history of the NIH Advisory Committee on Computers in Research (ACCR) and the events that followed. Dr. Lusted's chronology shows how the challenges of the early 1960s brought together many of the presenters whose work is included in this volume.

The last speaker was Jack D. Myers, MD. In contrast to many of the other participants, Dr. Myers came to medical computing following a long and distinguished career in internal medicine. After he retired as chairman of the Department of Medicine and was appointed to the rank of university professor, he chose to embark in research on the use of computers in medical diagnosis. His paper reviews that history and examines some of the unresolved issues. He observes that, just as he has helped mold the computer program's actions, its behavior also has had an impact on the way he practices medicine.

SPEAKERS

Lee B. Lusted   Some Roots of Clinical Decision Making
Jack D. Myers   The Background of INTERNIST-I and QMR
Casimir A. Kulikowski   Artificial Intelligence in Medicine: A Personal
                          Retrospective on its Emergence and Early Evolution

Lee B. Lusted, MD is clinical professor, Department of Radiology, University of California, San Diego and Adjunct Distinguished Member, Department of Academic Affairs and Department of Radiology, Scripps Clinic and Research Foundation (both since 1978). He received a BA degree from Cornell College in 1943 and an MD degree from Harvard Medical School in 1950. From 1969 to 1978 he was professor of Radiology and vice-chairman, Department of Radiology, The University of Chicago. A co-organizer of the Society for Medical Decision Making in 1979, he was editor-in-chief of *Medical Decision Making* from 1979 to 1985.

Jack D. Myers, MD is University Professor Emeritus (Medicine) Retired at the University of Pittsburgh (since 1985). He received the AB and MD degrees from Stanford University in 1933 and 1937. He was on the faculty at Duke University and came to the University of Pittsburgh in 1955 as professor of Medicine and chairman, Department of Medicine; in 1970 he was appointed university professor (Medicine). He is a past president of the Association of Professors of Medicine (1963–1964) and past chairman of the National Board of Medical Examiners (1971–1975). His honors include the Robert H. Williams Award, APM (1974), the Alfred Stengle Memorial award, ACP (1979), and the Distinguished Teacher Award, ACP (1981). He has been a visiting professor of Medicine at over 35 universities.

Casimir A. Kulikowski, PhD is professor and chairman, Computer Science Department, and director, Laboratory of Computer Science Research, Rutgers University. He received BE and MS degrees from Yale University in 1965 and 1966, and a PhD degree from the University of Hawaii in 1970. He has organized several workshops on "Artificial Intelligence in Medicine" and is the principal investigator of the Rutgers Research Resource on Artificial Intelligence in Medicine. He is the co-author of a book on building expert systems.

Some Roots of Clinical Decision Making

Lee B. Lusted, MD
University of California, San Diego

In early August 1960 I received a telephone call from the Division of Research Grants, National Institutes of Health (NIH). The caller informed me that Dr. James A. Shannon, the director of NIH, had decided to establish an Advisory Committee on Computers in Research and asked whether I would be interested in serving on the committee. Would I come to Bethesda, Maryland, the home of NIH, to discuss matters further? I replied that I would be glad to participate; since the early fifties I had had an interest in the medical applications of computers.

On the first of several visits to NIH before the Advisory Committee on Computers in Research (ACCR) was activated, I found that the NIH Division of Research Grants (DRG) had been receiving research grant applications requesting funds for support of computer processing of data collected in basic research and clinical research projects. The peer-review process of research grant applications was performed by members of NIH Study Sections, and there were very few scientists who felt familiar enough with data processing and computer financial charges to evaluate the grant applications that requested funds for a computer or for computing time to support a particular type of research. Study Section members were often troubled by dollar amounts requested for computer-related activities that seemed large compared with "reasonable" laboratory costs. The DRG saw a problem developing and since they were responsible for processing the bulk of the research grant applications for all the NIH, they decided to review the situation with Dr. Shannon.

Dr. Shannon, the imaginative and innovative director of NIH (1955 to 1968), presided over NIH during a period of rapid expansion and helped to build that organization into one of the strongest medical research organizations in the world. In that capacity he was a major force in the development of national policy and the mobilization of national resources for the support of biomedical research and research training. In my opinion he is responsible, in large part, for stimulating the growth of biomedical computing in the U.S., an effort which enabled

385

scientists and clinicians in the 1960s and 1970s to provide worldwide leadership in the development of biomedical computing and computing aids to medical diagnosis. A development that led to the development of medical informatics.

By 1960 Dr. Shannon had spent quite a bit of time thinking about the possible contributions that automated computational devices could make to biomedical research. He had taken a one-week intensive course on the operational capabilities of the "modern" computer at IBM Laboratories in Poughkeepsie, New York. About 1957 he suggested to the scientific directors of the NIH institutes that they pool funds to supply NIH with a modern computational facility. His suggestion was rejected, so out of the director's office account he purchased an IBM 300 computer. On the national scene Dr. Shannon, through NIH channels, made an offer to approximately 10 topnotch U.S. universities that NIH would purchase and support for five years a respectable computational facility within an adequate biology department, if courses in advanced mathematics and computational sciences would be made compulsory courses. The offer was informal, and all of the universities refused. The incident illustrates Dr. Shannon's foresight concerning the contributions to be made by computational science to the biological sciences.

These frustrations and the conviction that computers and computational science were important to biological sciences probably contributed to Dr. Shannon's decision to establish an Advisory Committee on Computers in Research. By the time DRG presented the grant application review to Dr. Shannon, he had a plan; he would establish NIH-ACCR.

On a second visit to NIH in early September 1960, Dr. Dale R. Lindsay, assistant chief and later chief of the Division of Research Grants, Dr. Fay M. Hemphill, executive secretary of NIH-ACCR (1960 to 1961) and later assistant chief, Division of Research Grants, reviewed details of an advisory committee operation and names of individuals to be invited to serve on the committee. I was asked to be Committee chairman. I agreed readily. After a visit with Dr. Shannon to get his ideas concerning the committee's responsibilities, the first meeting of NIH-ACCR was scheduled for September 20 and 21, 1960. Dr. Shannon would address the opening session of the committee.

Meantime, staff members of the DRG were in the final stages of committee organization. As a result of two earlier meetings, the staff had compiled a list of scientists who had used a computer in research projects or who were designing computers for medical applications.

The first meeting was an *ad hoc* panel of biomathematicians and biostatisticians convened by the NIH Division of General Medical Sciences at the National Institutes of Health on February 11, 1960. Dr.

Frederick L. Stone, who was then assistant chief, Division of General Medical Sciences (DGMS), welcomed the group. Dr. Stone later became chief of DGMS and played an important role with respect to NIH-ACCR activities. Stone pointed out that in the Report of the Senate Appropriations Committee in 1959 the U.S. Public Health Service, the parent organization of NIH, was requested to provide some ideas and plans relative to the establishment of various types of central research facilities to universities (including medical schools) with special mention being made of clinical research centers (multipurpose) and biomathematical centers. NIH-DGMS had been established in 1958 with the primary responsibility for providing the focus of support and interest in the basic medical sciences at NIH. The original charter of DGMS mentions preclinical and clinical disciplines (not otherwise covered by the categorical NIH institutes)—along with basic biological and health related fields. The flexibility of the DGMS charter enabled the division to provide a large amount of monies to be committed for the development and support of biomedical computer activities.

The *ad hoc* panel, chaired by Dr. John W. Fertig, Columbia University, concluded that all evidence placed medicine behind the fields of business and physical sciences the use of computers. The panel agreed that more use could be made of computers and that manpower must be developed for "computer centers," and "biometrical institutes." The development of computing centers was thought to be an appropriate multiple-agency undertaking. NIH-ACCR was later to take quite seriously the idea of "computing centers" and the committee attempted to stimulate several university hospital biomedical computing centers.

The second meeting, an *ad hoc* panel of consultants representing the National Science Foundation (NSF) and the NIH, was sponsored by the NIH Division of Research Grants and met at NIH on February 19, 1960. Dr. Richard Bolt, associate director of the NSF (on leave of absence as chairman of the board of Bolt Beranek and Newman, Inc.), chaired the meeting. Dr. Dale R. Lindsay, assistant chief and soon to be chief, DRG, opened the meeting. He suggested that the discussion of the group might be directed toward answering the following questions:

1. Have the life sciences reached the stage of sophistication that would primarily justify a costly computer center?
2. Should computer centers be established only in high-density concentrations of scientists, and should they be regional versus institutional?
3. Would the NSF program involve sufficient funds and scope to permit superposition medical and biological needs on centers they were already establishing?

The NSF provided $224,000 in 1958 and $424,000 in 1959 for computer use. An estimated $250,000 in NIH funds had been provided for computer use in 1959. Most committee members felt that requests for financial support of computer use would increase sharply in the near future.

To meet the computational needs the committee developed the idea of computational centers. According to the minutes of the meeting only brief mention was made of the small, personal, laboratory computer.

The committee recommended that the review of grant applications as well as advising NIH on ways to meet the research needs, should be by a separate but overlapping committee of NIH choosing, but incorporating NSF consultants, to ensure liaison and coordination. NIH-DRG staff now had the endorsement of an eminent group of scientists to organize a new review committee—soon to appear as NIH-ACCR.

Dr. Max A. Woodbury, mathematician from New York University, and Dr. Otto H. Schmitt, biophysicist from University of Minnesota, were active participants in the February 1960 *ad hoc* committee meetings and were subsequently helpful and influential members of NIH-ACCR.

At the first meeting of the NIH-ACCR, September 20, 1960, Dr. Shannon welcomed the committee members and outlined the committee responsibilities for

1. studying the needs of computers in medical and related biological research and advising him as to the proper role the NIH should play in the support of computer centers and of other research involving the use of computers;

2. reviewing applications for research grants involving computer adaptation or utilization and making recommendations to the NIH Advisory Councils; and

3. surveying as scientific leaders the status of research in this general field in order to point out areas in which research activities should be initiated or expanded.

Dr. Shannon encouraged the members of NIH-ACCR to plan broadly, and to look to long-range gains for medical research through the use of computers. He assumed that as individuals we would encourage and stimulate activities in the broad field he had outlined.

So the NIH-ACCR was assigned dual duties—first, as an advisory group to the director of NIH, on problems related to biomedical information processing and to "stimulate activity" in the biomedical computing field; and second, as a reviewing body, to adjudge the formal grant applications related to biomedical information processing. Ordinarily the programming or stimulation activity is separate from the evaluation of grant applications, but Dr. Shannon felt that the computer field required that both activities be assigned to a single committee.

The dual duties of the committee would cause problems later when grant applications "stimulated" by ACCR members were presented to the entire ACCR for evaluation. The dual duties however lasted throughout the three-year lifetime of NIH-ACCR. In January 1964 the committee was renamed the Computer Research Study Section, and the dual duties were dropped. The Study Section was to emphasize grant evaluation.

After the opening remarks by Dr. Shannon at the September 20, 1960 meeting, the committee members were introduced, and I was introduced as the committee chairman. I felt some uneasiness about being in this position because I did not know the majority of the committee members and this was my first experience with an NIH extramural grant review committee. NIH intramural activities were somewhat more familiar as a result of my two years (1956 to 1957) of active duty in the Public Health Service as a radiologist in the Department of Radiology, Clinical Center, National Institutes of Health. It was during this two-year assignment that I first met Dr. Shannon.

My anxieties about committee operation were considerably alleviated by Dr. Fay Hemphill, chief, Statistical Design and Analysis Section, NIH-DRG, who had agreed to be executive secretary of ACCR. Fay knew NIH procedures and personnel and was a great help to me personally and to ACCR. He was executive secretary from 1960 to 1961, and Dr. Bruce D. Waxman was executive secretary from 1961 to 1963. Bruce continued the excellent help to the committee. Later when I found myself or the committee in difficulty, two individuals were available with wise counsel and advice—Dr. Dale R. Lindsay, chief, NIH-DRG, and Dr. Frederick L. Stone, chief, NIH Division of General Medical Sciences (later the National Institute of General Medical Sciences).

The majority of ACCR members did not know each other so there was no "old buddy" feeling about the group in the early days. Members had been selected for their expertise in some aspect of biomedical or computer science, but no one person could claim to be an expert in the field of biomedical computing. The committee members decided, I think wisely, to spend some time getting acquainted and educating each other. The original ACCR members whose committee tenures were staggered according to NIH tradition were:

William R. Adey, MD (UCLA)

Paul Armer (Rand Corporation)

Mary A.B. Brazier, DSc (MIT and later UCLA)

David Garfinkel, PhD (University of Pennsylvania)

Alston S. Householder, PhD (Oak Ridge National Laboratory)

William N. Papian, MS (Lincoln Laboratory-MIT)

George A. Sacher, Jr., BS (Argonne National Laboratory)

Joseph E. Schenthal, MD (Tulane University)

Otto H. Schmitt, PhD (University of Minnesota)

Norman Z. Shapiro, PhD (NIH)

Ralph W. Stacy, PhD (University of Ohio)

Max A. Woodbury, PhD (New York University)

Lee B. Lusted, MD, chairman (University of Rochester).

Members who joined the committee later were Scott Adams, BLS; Robert C.F. Bartels, PhD; Julian Bigelow; Jerome R. Fox, Jr., DSc; Gordon K. Moe, PhD, MD; Alan Perlis, PhD; James M. Sakoda, PhD; Allen Scher, PhD; Homer R. Warner, MD, PhD; and consultant George S. Malindzak, Jr., PhD. Committee members posed for a portrait in 1962.

This group of talented individuals took seriously the original charge from the director, NIH, that its responsibility should include "stimulating activities" with a very broad view of the problems of biomedical computing.

FIGURE 1
NIH Advisory Committee on Computers in Research—1962
Seated left to right: Mary A.B. Brazier, W. Ross Adey, Otto Schmitt, Ralph W. Stacy, Joseph E. Schenthal, William N. Papian, James M. Sakoda, and Homer R. Warner.
Standing left to right: Fay M. Hemphill, George S. Malindzak, Jr., Rose S. Doying, George A. Sacher, Jr., Max A. Woodbury, Lee B. Lusted, Alston S. Householder, Bruce D. Waxman, Scott Adams, and David Garfinkel.

Committee members accompanied NIH staff members on numerous "stimulation visits" to universities, medical schools, and hospitals throughout the country to discuss local problems dealing with biomedical computing and to determine how NIH could help the investigators or institutions with their needs. In the early phases of the NIH-ACCR activity, these visits were very helpful; the suggestion to many investigators that they make use of a small "planning" grant proved particularly worth while.

Committee members felt that they needed to develop their own abilities and wisdom concerning the field of biomedical computing through the use of workshops, symposia, and consultants. Two special sessions were held for the purposes of educating committee members and planning committee activities.

The first special meeting, a "Workshop on Biomedical Computing," was organized and directed by Dr. Ralph W. Stacy. The meeting was held at Ohio State University, July 3 to 13, 1961. The workshop gave committee members an intense 10-day exposure to information about the current state of biomedical computing in the United States and provided time to consider what guidelines might be proposed to the director, NIH, for the national support of biomedical computing. The second special meeting of NIH-ACCR was held at MIT's Lincoln Laboratory, Lexington, Massachusetts, on November 15 and 16, 1961. Lincoln Laboratory was a large laboratory facility operated for the U.S. Air Force by MIT. Computer development at Lincoln Laboratory had been impressive, with computers such as average response computer ARC-1, TX-0, TX-2, and RX-1. The TX-2, with the possible exception of the IBM Stretch, was at that time the most powerful computer in operation for biological modeling and laboratory data processing. There was also a really small, inexpensive "general purpose" computer called "LINC" being developed at the Lincoln Laboratory, and the committee members wanted to see LINC in operation.

At the November 1961 meeting the committee worked on the topics of biomedical computing centers, financing of data processing equipment, medical and health services automation, and special problems related to the development of biomedical computing equipment. A "guidelines" report was prepared for the director, NIH, as a result of the meeting.

A demonstration of the LINC computer was given for Committee members by Wesley A. Clark. The demonstration of LINC was received with enthusiasm, and the committee urged further development of LINC. The first time that LINC was presented at a scientific meeting was at the "Conference on Special Aspects of Electronic and Computer-assisted Studies of Biomedical Problems," Washington, D.C., September 14 to 16, 1961. The conference was cosponsored by NIH-ACCR and chaired by Dr. Otto H. Schmitt. A number of NIH-ACCR members participated in the discussions. One of the questions pertinent to NIH-ACCR interests was: What features would characterize a widely useful electronic computer specially designed to serve the needs of research in the life sciences?

As a part of the discussion of this topic, Wesley A. Clark discussed the LINC (Laboratory INstrument Computer) which had been designed at Lincoln Laboratory. The event is noteworthy because LINC is a unique contribution to biomedical data processing. The development of LINC and the subsequent manner in which it was introduced for use among biomedical researchers is a historical landmark.

The committee supported the continued development and evaluation of LINC and appended the history of LINC development to the final report to the director, NIH, entitled *Guidelines for the National Institutes of Health Support of Biomedical Computing* by the Advisory Committee on Computers in Research, December 1963.[1]

The story of LINC is a success story, and it is said that success has many fathers. Several years ago there was a symposium at the NIH celebrating the 20th anniversary of LINC. Many persons and organizations that contributed to the success of the LINC program were recognized. In reporting the proceedings of the LINC anniversary, The NIH Record, January 3, 1984, said, "Perhaps equally important, the LINC program demonstrated that resourcefulness and imaginative federal management could influence the course of both science and industry."

It is gratifying to think that NIH-ACCR played a small role in this successful enterprise.

In the early 1960s there was evidence of increasing acceptance of the role of computers in biomedical research by this country's biomedical research scientists and evidence of what was the beginning of a major transition from traditional methods toward a truly quantitative and theoretical biology.

Congress was in a mood to increase the funds of NIH. The Eighty-Seventh Congress of the United States approved five million dollars in the fiscal year 1962 budget of the NIH Division of General Medical Sciences for the support of regional biomedical computer centers and instrumentation centers. Consideration must be given to the interest and encouragement of Senators Lister Hill and Hubert Humphrey, Representative John Fogarty, and Mrs. Mary Lasker, health care activist and philanthropist.

The committee was much concerned about the shortage of personnel in this country who were knowledgeable at the interface between bioscience and computer science. The committee urged that NIH now concentrate some attention on training programs at this interface

---

[1] Appendix B from that report, with the LINC history, is included at the end of this chapter.

through NIH training programs and fellowships. Later, in commenting on the committee report, Dr. Shannon said that he would emphasize training to a greater degree than the committee recommended.

During the September 1960 through December 31, 1963, lifetime of NIH-ACCR, the committee held 10 regularly scheduled meetings, reviewed 307 grant applications, and site-visited about 60% of these applications. A total of 178 applications were finally approved and paid, for a total first-year commitment of $17,873,263 (as of December 1963). The future years' commitments on these applications totaled $23,081,114, which gives a total for all years of $40,954,377. In 1987 this amount of money does not seem surprising, but in the early 1960s it represented a substantial commitment by NIH to the development of a national biomedical computing capability.

In closing this brief review of NIH-ACCR activities, I think it is interesting to look at the types of computers primarily engaged in life sciences research in the early 1960s. Table 1 (see p. 421) shows the installation by state and is reproduced from the NIH-ACCR *Final Report of The Director, NIH*, December 1963.

I have given the preceding time and space to tell a little of the NIH-ACCR story because the joint effort of ACCR and NIH gave great impetus to biomedical computing and indirectly to quantitative biomedical sciences. I have not seen the NIH-ACCR activities described elsewhere.

The "stimulation" activities and the grant review site visits offered unusual opportunities for the committee members to meet a large number of scientists who were working in a variety of disciplines. My long-time interdisciplinary interests in computer aids to medical diagnosis and in medical decision making were stimulated by several of the professional contacts I made during NIH-ACCR trips. Next, I recount some events and activities that influenced my work on computer aids to medical diagnosis and medical decision making.

During my college years, from 1939 to 1943, World War II was in progress, and accelerated programs were advised for men students, particularly if one were a science major and draft eligible. My majors were mathematics and physics. Scientists were in great demand during the World War II period both by the military services and the U.S. government civilian research agencies, such as the Office of Scientific Research and Development. With the help of my mathematics professor at Cornell College, who had left college teaching for a research position at Harvard University, and Leo L. Beranek, a Cornell College graduate who was an acoustics engineer at Harvard, I obtained a position as research associate at the Radio Research Laboratory (RRL), Harvard University. RRL was operated by Harvard University under a contract with Division 15, Office of Scientific Research and Development. The director of the laboratory was Dr. Frederick Terman, on leave of absence from the engineering school at Stanford University. The purpose of the laboratory was to do research and development on techniques and equipment to "jam" enemy radar; i.e., to confuse enemy radar so that the target could not be identified. I was assigned to work on electronic airborne jammers. This equipment was to be carried by bombers or fighter planes and was to confuse the enemy radar used to direct antiaircraft artillery.

I had no training in electronics or engineering principles, but with night school classes and tutoring at the work bench I quickly learned the basics of electronic engineering. My electronics experiences during the 1943 to 1946 period served as the basis for later medical electronic, biomedical engineering, and computer engineering interests. Interdepartmental seminars were held regularly at RRL, and at one of the seminars I heard a discussion of signal detection theory in the context of defining the requirements to "see" a radar signal against a noisy background. Later these discussions were to come to mind as I was developing the use of receiver operating characteristic (ROC) analysis of radiologic images in the context of medical decision making.

When World War II ended many of us who had worked as civilian engineers were undecided about what to do—get a job in industry, go to graduate school, or change career path. Most of us had been deferred from military duty and still had service requirements facing us. In addition to my physical science and engineering interests, biology and psychology had been in the back of my mind as areas ripe for application of physical science principles. Interdisciplinary programs were very rare in the mid-1940s so I decided that medical school offered the most likely path to develop my interests.

My application to Harvard Medical School was accepted in December 1945, and in the fall of 1946 I began medical school. A biophysical laboratory had been organized about this time by Dr. A.K. Solomon, and in the summer between my first and second years in medical school, I worked on instrumentation projects for Dr. Solomon. Drs. Dewitt and Marney Stetten had set up their laboratories in the Biophysical Laboratory area, and I helped Dr. Dewitt (Hans) with some instrumentation. By the time I was assigned to NIH in 1956 the Stettens had moved to NIH, and I renewed our friendship.

During the summer between the second and third medical school years I applied for a position with the U.S. Public Health Service to work on a Heart Disease Control Program in Newton, Massachusetts. The position offered a reserve commission in the U.S. Public Health Service and guaranteed that a medical student could finish medical school before being called to active duty. Since I was still eligible for military service, having been a civilian scientist during the war, I saw this as a way to assure medical school graduation. The decision was fortuitous because it resulted in my Public Health Service active duty at NIH 10 years later.

Harvard Medical School students could choose clinical assignment at the various teaching hospitals associated with Harvard. My favorite was Massachusetts General Hospital (MGH) for medicine, surgery, and radiology rotations. The experiences at MGH as a medical student were not to be forgotten in 1961 and 1962 when I worked to "stimulate" a computing center at MGH on behalf of NIH-ACCR.

Interdisciplinary programs for biomedical, physical and engineering science were not yet satisfactory in my opinion in 1951, so I decided to pursue my interests in the specialty of radiology. My advisor, Dr. Shields Warren, a pathologist who had made an extensive study of tissue damage resulting from radiation exposure, advised me to apply for a residency with Dr. Robert Stone, chairman of the Radiology Department at University of California, San Francisco.

The years 1951 to 1956 in San Francisco were spent learning radiology, pursuing some medical electronic interests, and renewing my friendship with Dr. Jerre D. Noe at Stanford Research Institute in Palo Alto, California. Jerre and I had worked together in England in 1944 and 1945 at the American British Laboratory in Great Malvern. American British Laboratory was the name given to the overseas branch of the Harvard Radio Research Laboratory. Jerre was the leader of a group of engineers assigned to a variety of projects. My projects included supervision of the installation of radar frequency receiver equipment in P-38 fighter aircraft to be flown over enemy V-1 and V-2 missile launching sites to determine whether the missiles were radio- or radar-guided (they were not so guided); and supervising the reassembly and testing of a captured enemy gun-directing radar (FuSe62). The radar contained some circuits for calculating target distance but did not have what we would call computer elements.

After the war ended Jerre Noe returned to Stanford University to obtain a PhD in electronics and in the early 1950s was the engineer in charge of a project at Stanford Research Institute to build a large computer for the Bank of America. The computer called ERMA (Electronic Record Machine Accounting) was the first large computing system made specifically for banking procedures. On weekends I would visit Jerre to watch ERMA grow, and we would talk about the possibility that a computer like ERMA could process patient's medical records in hospitals and help physicians with medical diagnosis. There was concern expressed in medical journals that a knowledge explosion was enveloping the field of medicine, and there was speculation that computers could be used to help solve some of the problems. I felt that medical data could be processed by computer and that medical information could be made more useful to physicians by repackaging it in a more usable form. I wasn't sure how this could be done, but the idea of making information more useful by making it more usable stuck with me.

The Stanford University-Palo Alto environs in the early 1950s were showing signs of an electronics boom. William R. Hewlett, president of Hewlett-Packard Corporation in Palo Alto, was national president of the Institute of Radio Engineers (IRE, now called the Institute of Electrical and Electronic Engineers) in 1954; Dr. Frederick Terman, who had directed Harvard's Radio Research Laboratory during World War II, had returned to Stanford University and was provost of the University. The first chapter of the IRE Professional Group on Medical Electronics was established in Palo Alto, and I was an active participant. (IRE Professional Groups were started as special interest groups within the IRE Society.) It was through these activities that I kept in touch with developments in the electronic and computing fields.

I had planned a career in academic radiology and intended to stay at University of California, San Francisco, until I received a letter on August 3, 1955, from the regional medical director of the U.S. Public Health Service located in San Francisco. The letter informed me that my Inactive Reserve Commission would expire shortly and asked whether I wished to be reappointed. If I dropped the commission I would be subject to the "Doctor Draft" and if I continued the Public Health Service Commission I would be required to serve two years active duty. The choice seemed obvious—select two years with Public Health Service. After several lengthy discussions with PHS Division of Personnel I was assigned to the Department of Radiology, Clinical Center, National Institutes of Health for duty, January 1956.

The Radiology Department at the NIH Clinical Center was fairly new. It had been designed by Dr. Henry Kaplan who had left to take the Radiology Chairmanship at Stanford Medical School, and the department head was Dr. Theodore Hilbish when I arrived. The department provided the commonly requested radiographic studies but emphasized cardiovascular radiology because of the strong leadership of Dr. A. Glenn Morrow, chief of the Clinic of Surgery, and Dr. Eugene Braunwald, chief of Cardiology Branch, National Heart Institute.

The daily work schedule of fluoroscopic examination reporting was fairly light, and I was left with time to explore other NIH opportunities. The NIH library provided excellent opportunities for browsing, a pastime I have always enjoyed, among a large collection of books and journals. I renewed my acquaintance with Dr. Dewitt Stetten and paid frequent visits to the laboratory of Dr. Robert L. Bowman, who was chief of the Laboratory of Technical Development in the National Heart Institute. I had met Dr. Bowman through the activities of the IRE Professional Group on Medical Electronics. On one of my visits to Dr.

Bowman's laboratory he told me he was on his way to see Dr. Shannon to discuss an instrumentation problem and that I might accompany him. And so I met Dr. Shannon. In later visits I had opportunities to tell Dr. Shannon about my interests in electronic instrumentation and electronic computers.

Early in 1956 an opportunity arose to do consulting work for Airborne Instruments Laboratory (AIL), Mineola, Long Island, New York. The president of AIL was John Dyer, an engineer who had been in charge of the research and development group I joined at Harvard Research Laboratory in 1943. AIL had organized a department of medical and biological physics, headed by Walter E. Tolles, and I was invited to act as a consultant on the general application of electronic methods to medicine. AIL had obtained a contract from the NIH National Cancer Institute to develop an instrument to be used in the mass screening of cytological smears for the detection of cervical cancer. At that time the cytological smear, when used according to the technique established by Papanicolaou, had become the most important method for the early detection of cancer of the cervix, but there were not enough people trained to screen the smears. The instrumentation problems seemed challenging, and I requested permission from the Public Health Service to act as a consultant on medical electronics. My request, to my pleasant surprise, progressed rapidly up through the administrative hierarchy to the chief, PHS Division of Personnel, and returned promptly, approved and initialed by all parties including the director, NIH.

The consulting activities at AIL had two fortuitous outcomes. The first was a series of events that led to meeting Robert S. Ledley. We subsequently collaborated on studies of mathematical and implemented aids to medical diagnosis. The second outcome came as a result of discussions about criteria to be used for performance evaluation of the cytological smear screening instrumentation. Ideas developed at that time led me later to introduce Receiver Operating Characteristic (ROC) analysis for medical image observer performance and medical decision making. I will recount the story of work with Ledley first and discuss ROC analysis later.

William J. Horvath, PhD was assistant head of the AIL medical and biological physics department, and it was his responsibility to evaluate the performance of the Cytoanalyzer, the experimental instrument designed to screen the cytological smears. On several occasions Horvath and I discussed my interests in providing computer aids for medical diagnosis. Horvath said he had heard a paper presented at a meeting of the Operations Research Society by a young dentist named Robert Ledley on the topic of logical aid to medical diagnosis, and he thought an article had been published subsequently {1}. He thought Ledley could be located at the National Bureau of Standards in Washington,

D.C., and he suggested I contact him. With several telephone calls I did locate Ledley, we had a short chat and agreed to meet in my office at the NIH Clinical Center.

We found that we had been thinking about similar problems and possible solutions. The problems were caused by the large and increasing volume of medical literature. The possible solutions involved mathematical and computational aids for the physician. Ledley had obtained a degree in dentistry and subsequently had done work in mathematics and physics, receiving a masters degree in mathematics. I can remember some brisk discussions. Ledley knew more mathematics and computer science than I did, and I knew more clinical medicine. Eventually we proposed mathematical techniques and the associated use of computers as an aid to the physician in diagnosis and treatment selection. In an article published in *Science* in 1959 with the provocative title, "Reasoning Foundations of Medical Diagnosis" {2}, we suggested that symbolic logic, probability, and value theory aid our understanding of how physicians reason.

The article was a medical "best seller" in terms of the number of reprints requested and the number of citations by other authors subsequently. Before the days of abundant copying machines one criterion of the success of an article was the number of requests for a reprint of the article received by the authors. Requests for the "Reasoning Foundations" article ran into the thousands. Exactly how many requests were received is uncertain, since both Ledley and I sent out reprints. I remember a request that came from a science teacher at the Bronx (New York) High School of Science asking for a large number of reprints to be used in mathematics and science classes. The article was promptly translated into Russian and appeared in a monograph published in Moscow in 1961.

There were outspoken critics of the article, and most of the criticisms seemed to be directed at our proposal that Bayes's theorem be used. Some commentators said, "Doctors don't think Bayes"—we never said they did. Some critics pointed out the inapplicability of Bayes's theorem to medical diagnosis because patient signs, symptoms, and laboratory tests are not independent, and the diagnoses being considered are not mutually exclusive.

The "Reasoning Foundations" article pitched me into at least three areas of controversy, some of which persist to the present day. The first involved the appropriateness and acceptability to the medical profession of computer-aided medical diagnosis; the second involved the appropriate use of Bayes's theorem in computer-aided medical diagnosis; and the third led into the struggle between two schools of thought about statistical inference: the Bayesian school and the classical school. I was thoroughly unprepared for the third controversy. The Bayesian position appealed to me, and I worked hard to understand what the controversy was about.

Bayes's theorem is an uncontroversial consequence of the definition of conditional probability and the fact that probabilities sum to 1. If probabilities describe orderly opinions, Bayes's theorem describes how such opinions should be revised in the light of new information.

In the early 1960s physician-investigators who wished to use Bayes's theorem were often discouraged by a consultant who was often a classical statistician. Ward Edwards, an early-on and still-active Bayesian, influenced my thinking greatly by his writings and helped me in various ways to develop the field of medical decision making. He commented recently,

> When the Bayesian point of view became visible in the 1960s, most Bayesians were convinced that in time classical null hypothesis testing would die out. The Bayesians of the 1960s clearly underestimated the power of human inertia. More important, perhaps, they underestimated the difficulty of making a transition from one form of statistical inference to another. {3}

Despite the difficulties, interest in the use of Bayes's theorem was evident in the early 1960s and continues to the present time. Very few clinical investigators were able to test the applicability of Bayes's theorem to computer-aided diagnosis because they didn't have good data in readily usable form. Two investigators who did were Dr. Homer R. Warner and Dr. Gwilym S. Lodwick.

I met Dr. Warner at a meeting of the NIH National Heart Institute Training Grant Directors at Dearborn Inn, Dearborn, Michigan, June 3 to 4, 1960. I gave a talk on biomedical computing and discussed the use of Bayes's theorem. Dr. Warner said he had access to a Burroughs 205 digital computer and had good data on the signs, symptoms, and electrocardiographic findings in a group of patients with congenital heart disease. He would try Bayes's theorem. He reported his results on the diagnosis of congenital heart disease from clinical data with a digital computer at the American Heart Association Meeting, St. Louis, Missouri, October 21 to 23, 1960, and subsequently published what I believe to be the first article that used a set of clinical data to demonstrate the applicability of Bayes's theorem {4}. Warner and colleagues at Latter-day Saints Hospital, Salt Lake City, Utah, expanded and improved the early computer activity to attain a hospital information system that provides decision-support programs for clinicians {5}.

Dr. Lodwick, chairman, Department of Radiology, University of Missouri, had collected data on a large series of primary bone tumors and showed that he could predict the histologic diagnosis of each case from examination of the roentgenogram. His average rate of accuracy in predicting the correct histologic diagnosis was 80%. I heard about

Dr. Lodwick's data on a trip about 1959 to the University of Missouri to work with Dr. Theodore E. Keats on the *Atlas of Roentgenographic Measurements*. I was always on the lookout for good clinical data to test the use of Bayes's theorem. Dr. Lodwick readily agreed to develop a research program for a probabilistic approach to the diagnosis of bone tumors. Lodwick submitted a grant application that was processed by NIH-ACCR—I believe it was the first research grant from a radiologist that the committee recommended for approval. The grant CA-06263, "Computer Analysis of Tumor Roentgenograms" was active for 17 years, an excellent record.

An early publication by Lodwick and colleagues {6} reported that the computer program using Bayes's theorem and Lodwick's roentgenographic criteria could predict the correct histologic diagnosis in 77.9% of the cases. Predictive accuracy improved with more experience. Lodwick's work did a great deal to stimulate interest in computer-aided analysis of radiographic images, and I think helped raise the level of awareness about possible uses of computers in medical care. During my visits to the University of Missouri I met Dr. Donald A.B. Lindberg, a member of the Department of Pathology. We discussed possible uses of computers in pathology, and I told him about Dr. Baldwin Lamson, a pathologist at UCLA Medical Center, and his interests. Dr. Lindberg subsequently became director of the University of Missouri Medical Center Computer Program and made significant contributions to computer usage in pathology and to the development of the general field of medical informatics.

Drs. Warner, Lodwick, and Lindberg are members of a very small group of individuals who have made significant contribution to the biomedical computational field from the early 1960s for a period of 25 years or more. Many individuals have made shorter and less prolonged contributions, very few have stuck to the subject for a significant length of time.

Meanwhile, whatever happened to Bayes's theorem and the problems of conditional nonindependence of medical data? Ledley and I investigated the problems caused by nonindependence of patient attributes (signs, symptoms, laboratory data, etc.) during the 1959 to 1963 period with a grant from NIH (RG-7844, Mathematical and Implemental Aids to Medical Diagnosis) using data from patients with proven lung cancer. We found that clusters of attributes could be formed, and those could be treated as a new conditionally independent attribute even though the attributes within the clusters were not independent. I don't think we published on the subject. Warner was careful not to include in the list of symptoms any two symptoms that invariably occurred together in a patient with congenital heart disease, and he grouped certain mutually exclusive symptoms that required special handling.

Several investigators continued to investigate the limitations of mutually exclusive diagnostic outcomes and attribute dependency. One who pursued the subject was Dennis G. Fryback at the University of Michigan. I met Fryback in the early 1960s at a Bayesian Research Conference organize by Ward Edwards at the University of Michigan. The Bayesian Research Conferences started in 1962—the 25th Anniversary Conference was in 1987—were a focus for medical decision making discussions and provided important undergirding for the formation of the Society for Medical Decision Making. Fryback's work {7} demonstrated that the greater the numbers of variables used in the Bayesian calculation, the more the degradation of the model's performance when the data violate conditional independence.

The Bayesian computer-assisted medical decision-making systems of Dr. F.T. de Dombal and associates deserve special attention. Some time in the late 1960s or early 1970s I met de Dombal at an international meeting—probably in London. He had read about Bayes's theorem and was interested in developing a computer system to aid in the diagnosis of abdominal pain. De Dombal is a surgeon at St. James's Hospital in Leeds, England, and abdominal pain is a common problem seen in hospital emergency room patients. De Dombal did develop a Bayesian computer-aided diagnostic system that was more accurate than the physicians' diagnosis of abdominal pain. If the computer diagnostic recommendations had been followed, fewer "unnecessary" appendectomies would have been performed and fewer patients with actual appendicitis would have been delayed in receiving appropriate surgery {8}. De Dombal was also concerned about whether the computer-aided diagnostic system would be transferable to a variety of clinical and geographic settings. Through a series of experiments he has shown that system is transferable {9}. The Bayesian system for the diagnosis of acute abdominal pain runs on microcomputers and is being used extensively in British emergency departments. The United States Naval Submarine Force has adapted de Dombal's Bayesian diagnostic programs for use by medical corpsmen aboard submarines to help in the evaluation of abdominal pain, chest pain, and psychiatric disturbances {10}. Preliminary discussions with U.S. National Aeronautics and Space Administration (NASA) have been started to explore the applicability of the computer-assisted diagnostic systems for orbiting space stations.

If "doctors don't think Bayes's theorem," what do they think about in doing patient diagnoses and management? Many attempts have been made to answer this question and studies of physicians' clinical reasoning have provided important roots for the field of clinical decision making. Although medical educators and clinicians have given attention to diagnostic reasoning, I wish to emphasize the work of cognitive psychologists who have focused on the information processing approach to cognition. This approach aims to characterize the underlying thought processes by recording and analyzing the verbalizations of persons as they attempt to solve problems. The focus is on explaining human thinking in terms of basic psychological elements and principles {11}.

Elstein and other investigators have suggested that physicians' diagnostic reasoning is a hypothetico-deductive inference process in which the physician is involved in a sequential hypothesize-and-test process. The physician conceptually constructs a "model" of the patient. It is interesting to note that the psychological studies of problem solving by medical experts have been influential in current medical AI research {12}.

My interests in Bayesian and information-processing approaches to medical diagnosis were combined in a project I undertook for the American College of Radiology in 1971. There had been allegations that for some types of x-ray examinations between 10% and 30% of the examinations were "wasted"; i.e., they did not contribute useful information for diagnosis or treatment of a patient. The American College of Radiology (ACR) decided to study the problem. An ACR Committee on Efficacy Studies was appointed which I chaired. We undertook a study of the use of x-ray examinations in hospital emergency rooms.

The ACR Committee on Efficacy Studies had to develop definitions of efficacy and to determine how to measure the efficacy of diagnostic procedures. It was decided, and I think the idea was proposed by Ward Edwards, that a hierarchical approach to efficacy be defined. This was the first time that levels of diagnostic test efficacy had been defined and tested. The efficacy levels would be called efficacy-1, efficacy-2, and efficacy-3. They were defined as follows.

Efficacy-3 can be thought of as an ultimate outcome efficacy to the patient. *Ex post*, an x-ray procedure is efficacious-3 for an individual patient to the extent that the patient is better off as a result of the performance of the procedure than he would have been if the procedure had not been performed.

Efficacy-2, which can be called patient management efficacy, is less long range in outlook. It concentrates on the use of diagnostic information. *Ex post*, a procedure has efficacy-2 to the extent that physicians are led to treatment outcomes as a result of the procedure that differ from the actions that would have been taken in the absence of the diagnostic procedure.

Efficacy-1 refers to the information content of the procedure, regardless of whether or not the information content had an effect on subsequent management. In this sense, a diagnostic procedure is efficacious-1 to the extent that physicians are led to change their thinking about the nature of patients' conditions by the information provided by the procedure.

During 1972 and 1973 Drs. Ward Edwards, Dennis Fryback, and radiologist Dr. John Thornbury conducted a pretest of procedures for the measurement of efficacy including data collection forms at the University of Michigan. As a consequence of physician response problems that were found in the pretest, the ACR Efficacy Study decided to concentrate on efficacy-1.

The operational definition of efficacy-1 comes directly from Bayes's theorem that may be expressed in a particularly simple form: final odds equals initial odds times likelihood ratio or $FO = IO \times LR$, where LR stands for "likelihood ratio." The likelihood ratio for a diagnosis given certain diagnostic information is defined as the ratio of two conditional probabilities, the probability of the diagnostic information given the truth of the diagnosis and the probability of the diagnostic information given the falsity of the diagnosis.

The likelihood ratio LR is the precise assessment of how the diagnostic information from an x-ray procedure (or laboratory test) transforms the initial odds IO to final odds FO. We adopted the likelihood ratio as the efficacy-1 measure for x-ray procedures. An undiagnostic or inefficacious x-ray procedure would have a likelihood ratio of 1. The more the likelihood ratio deviates from 1 the more efficacious the procedure is in terms of efficacy-1.

Emergency room physicians, after some training in the use of probability and odds, were asked to judge initial odds or probabilities of a diagnosis before an x-ray examination was obtained and corresponding final odds or probabilities after the x-ray examination had been completed and the physician knew the result. We calculated the likelihood ratio to obtain the efficacy-1 of the examination.

A total of 381 emergency room physicians and 52 radiologists provided approximately 14 judgments of initial and final odds or probabilities each; the study included 8658 protocols. The seven x-ray procedures studied (skull, cervical spine, chest, abdomen, lumbar spine, extremities, and intravenous pyelogram) together account for approximately 90% of all radiographs taken in emergency rooms.

We found that physicians were able to judge odds or probabilities with a high degree of consistency and a reasonable degree of calibration. Physicians tended to over estimate probabilities attached to abnormal diagnoses.

For the seven x-ray procedures we found a total of 4% inefficacious procedures as defined by efficacy-1 and found that about 6% of the procedures were requested primarily for medical-legal reasons. The project ended with recommendations for future studies of efficacy-2 {13}.

In an interesting extension of the American College of Radiology Efficacy Study, Dr. Eugene L. Saenger and colleagues demonstrated efficacy-1 and efficacy-2 for nuclear medicine lung scans in patients suspected of having a pulmonary embolism. The study and analyses, which were sponsored by the Society of Nuclear Medicine Committee on Public Health and Efficacy, compared two methods to evaluate efficacy, namely, logistic regression and entropy minimax pattern detection. The study showed that lung scan findings had a significant influence on the physician's diagnostic thinking and that no combination of patient signs and symptoms was found that would predict reliably, *a priori*, which patients had pulmonary emboli {14}.

Efficacy studies of diagnostic tests including laboratory tests and imaging procedures and the efficacy assessment of new medical technologies continue to be high-priority areas of research.

Before proceeding I want to recount stories of two NIH-ACCR "stimulation" activities in which I was involved. Both have had favorable long-term outcomes.

The first incident occurred at a "stimulation" talk I gave on biomedical computing for the San Francisco County Medical Society on January 18, 1962. I mentioned that NIH was interested in receiving grant applications requesting funds for biomedical computation projects. After the meeting Dr. Morris F. Collen introduced himself and said that he had been developing a multiphasic screening and diagnosis program for California Kaiser-Permanente in the San Francisco Bay Area. He said the multiphasic screening data could use computer processing, and he would like to know more about NIH grant funding. I put him in touch with Dr. Homer Warner, a member of NIH-ACCR, to work out a grant application. Dr. Collen has been a pioneer and a major medical information systems builder {15}. Lindberg has published an interesting account of the Kaiser-Permanente medical information system in his book *The Growth of Medical Information Systems in the United States* {16}, and Dr. Collen has described his experiences elsewhere in this volume.

The second activity involved a series of events whose purpose was to stimulate the development of a computation center at Massachusetts General Hospital (MGH). Earlier in this article I wrote that during my medical school experience I had several clinical clerkships at MGH. I have also noted that as a member of the NIH-ACCR I took seriously the challenge to develop biomedical computation centers in universities and hospitals. I decided that MGH would be an excellent site for a computation center, and I set out to see what could be done. I visited Dr. John Knowles, the Central Director of MGH, in late 1961 or early 1962. Dr. Knowles was interested in developing a computer system for patient information management that would include clinical data, medical record data, and financial data but he pointed out that he did not have knowledgeable persons on his staff. How could we get started? I knew from conversations with my friend, Leo L. Beranek, president, Bolt Beranek and Newman, Inc. (BBN, a consulting firm in Cambridge, Massachusetts), that BBN had computer scientists and computers available. Perhaps BBN could help MGH. Beranek found that a member of the BBN staff, Jordan J. Baruch, was eager to work with MGH. Dr. Knowles assigned members of his staff to work with Baruch and discussions continued from 1962 into 1963 when I think Baruch submitted an application to NIH for funds to develop a computational facility for MGH. I think all of us who were involved in the planning, and that very much included Dr. Knowles, recognized that MGH should develop "in-house" computer equipment and staff competence as quickly as possible.

Fortunately, the individual to lead the MGH development appeared in the person of Dr. G. Octo Barnett. I have heard that Octo was recruited for the position by Dr. Robert Ebert, who was then Dean of Harvard Medical School and had been chief of medicine at MGH. Dr. Barnett has been the first and, to 1987, the only director of the MGH Laboratory of Computer Science. Dr. Barnett and his group have been very productive in a variety of medical computational and decision-making areas {17}.

I return now to some recollections of the introduction of Receiver Operating Characteristic (ROC) analysis to medical decision making and events associated with writing the book, *Introduction To Medical Decision Making* {18}.

In the summer of 1962, I left the Department of Radiology at the University of Rochester for a position that combined radiology at University of Oregon and a directorship of the automatic data processing program and computation facility at the Oregon Regional Primate Research Center. The computational facility included a Scientific Data Systems model 920 computer with 8192 words (24 binary bits/word) of random access memory. The machine could do 60,000 additions per second and was probably the first such computer to be used solely for experiments in biomedical record keeping and biomathematical modeling. Max Palevsky, president, Scientific Data Systems, came to visit us several times to see the applications of the SDS 920 computer.

The position provided me with a respite from an active clinical radiology schedule, and it was during this time, 1962 to 1968, that I worked out the application of ROC analysis to medicine and wrote a book on medical decision making. By March 1965, we had a computer-based medical record system in full operation at the Oregon Regional Primate Center. Robert Coffin and I recounted experiences with the system in the book *PRIME* (Primate Information Management Experiment) {19}. Walter Stahl and I had studied several conceptual models of medical diagnosis and had experimented with Turing Programming on the SDS 920 computer as a promising method for stimulating the mixed logical processes and algorithms that occur in a medical diagnosis problem {20}.

Receiver operating characteristic analysis is now generally recognized as the most appropriate methodology for evaluating the diagnostic performance of medical imaging procedures, and ROC curves are used to compare the performance of laboratory tests. ROC analysis is derived from the theory of signal detection based on the theory of simple dichotomy. The research and applications of signal detectability had been in the fields of engineering and psychophysics since the days of World War II, but the importance of these developments had not filtered into medicine by the late 1950s and early 1960s.

Through an interesting set of circumstances, which I have recounted in a recent editorial, I was able to introduce the concepts of ROC analysis to medicine {21}. Briefly, the significant events were: hearing about signal detection theory at Harvard Radio Research Laboratory in 1944 or 1945 in the context of an observer seeing a radar signal against a noisy background; participating in a study of "observer variation" for the detection of pulmonary tuberculosis by chest x-ray examination (1945); preparing a performance curve from the data of the tuberculosis study to try to explain observer variation (see Figure 2) with the substantial help of William Horvath at Airborne Instruments Laboratory, 1957 {22}; reading in 1965 a book on signal detection edited by Swets {23} and reading a book in 1966 by Green and Swets {24} and observing that the observer performance curve from the tuberculosis chest film study was an operating characteristic curve that closely matched ROC curves shown in the two books on signal detection theory.

After observing that the performance curve for the tuberculosis chest film study had a similar shape to an ROC curve that might result from an auditory or visual signal detection experiment in psychophysics, the questions in my mind were: Could disease process such as tuberculosis result in a "signal" as seen on a chest X ray film? In signal detection theory terms, could a normal population of persons be compared to a "noise distribution" and an abnormal population containing the disease to be detected be compared to a "signal plus noise distribution?" If "yes" was the answer to the questions, then medical science and clinical medicine would have statistical decision theory and ROC methodology to tackle a host of problems such as observer variation and observer performance, evaluation of diagnostic test and imaging procedures, and comparison of the performance of diagnostic proce-

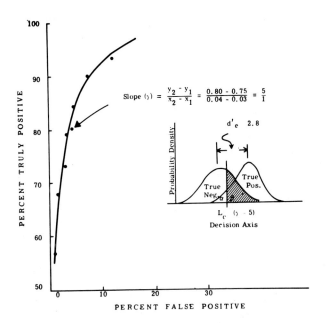

FIGURE 2
Operating characteristic curve for the interpretation of chest photofluorograms for the presence of pulmonary tuberculosis. From L.B. Lusted, *Introduction to Medical Decision Making*, 1968. Courtesy of Charles C. Thomas, Publisher, Springfield, Illinois.

dures including cost-benefit analysis comparison. I concluded that the answer was "yes" to both questions, and I said so in a 1967 lecture {25}. However, it was not until 1971 that work with colleagues Charles Metz and David Goodenough at the University of Chicago provided the experimental studies to demonstrate the great generality of medicine of the ideas concerning signal detection and ROC analysis with which signal detectability theorists had been working {26}.

I do not wish to pursue the basics of ROC analysis. An excellent primer has been provided by Metz {27}, and more recently Metz has reviewed the status of ROC methodology and summarized ROC analysis in diagnostic radiology and radionuclide imaging {28}.

By the fall of 1967 I had finished a draft of the book, *Introduction to Medical Decision Making*. ROC analysis was included as an important procedure to be used in medical decision making studies, and with the substantial help of Ward Edwards a translation of signal detectability theory into more general Bayesian language was provided {29}. I believe this was the first published material that provided a table of equivalent terms for Bayes's formulae and signal detectability formulae. We demonstrated an isomorphism between Bayesian decision theory and the signal detection psychophysics approach. Particular attention was given to the use of the likelihood ratio L because of the difference in emphasis placed on L by the two schools of thought.

In Bayesian terms the decision maker does not base his decision on a critical likelihood ratio L_c, where L_c is the critical likelihood ratio just adequate to transform initial odds into final odds; $FO = L_c IO$. He bases his decision on his final opinion, which is controlled both by his initial opinion and by the observations he has made. It is the final opinion that controls the decision after all observations have been completed.

The reader will remember that we adopted this strategy in the American College Radiology Efficacy Study. We asked the physician to judge the initial odds IO and the final odds FO. We calculated the likelihood ratio LR_c.

Signal detection theorists were particularly interested in giving an account of the process of observing as separated from the decision process to which the observations are an input. Therefore, they preferred to partition the decision problem in a way that emphasizes the critical likelihood ratio, L_c.

An ROC graph does emphasize the likelihood ratio since the curve is generated by a series of points each of which is a likelihood ratio. The curve represents all of the possible combinations of true positive fractions (TPF on y-axis) and false positive fractions (FPF on x-axis), which describe the inherent detection performance of an observer or the detection characteristic of a diagnostic test.

The likelihood ratio is $L = TPF/FPF$. L_c, the critical likelihood ratio, is calculated from the costs and benefits associated with the true and false decision outcomes. We have now reached the chronological point to recognize the emergence of decision analysis and to note the significant effect that it had on clinical decision analysis and medical decision making. The period from 1963 to 1971 was clearly the time when decision analysis emerged as a viable activity. I have borrowed extensively from the interesting account of decision analysis history by von Winterfeldt and Edwards {30}. Decision analysis seems to have occurred at Harvard, Stanford, and University of Michigan as a result of groups led by Howard Raiffa, Ronald A. Howard, and Ward Edwards. In 1968, Raiffa published a fairly small paperback book called *Decision Analysis*, which contained relatively implementable treatments of decision strategies including cost-benefit and cost-effectiveness strategies. Though Raiffa did not coin the term "decision analysis" (R.A. Howard did that), Raiffa's 1968 book gave the topic much visibility and academic interest. A large number of medical articles and the book *Clinical Decision Analysis* {31} testify to Raiffa's influence.

Although I had read some of the articles by Howard and had heard of decision analysis, I did not mention the term in my book, *Introduction to Medical Decision Making*, which appeared in 1968, the same year as Raiffa's book. By the mid-1970s the number of medical journal articles and scientific papers presented at meetings indicated that a few individuals appreciated the potential medical contributions of decision sciences supported by computer information processing. My friend and colleague, Dr. Eugene L. Saenger at the University of Cincinnati, reminded me that the time was ripe to focus the diverse medical decision-making interests by organizing a society and that we should do so promptly. I was still involved with the American College of Radiology Efficacy Study, and I was not very enthusiastic about organizing a society. Saenger persisted, and I am glad that he did. A one-day meeting entitled "Decision Making in Diagnostic Medicine" was sponsored by The Society of Nuclear Medicine and held in Atlanta, Georgia, January 25, 1967. The chair was Barbara J. McNeil, MD, PhD, Harvard Medical School. A panel discussion on "Problems in Translating These Concepts (of decision making) into Medical Practice," chaired by Henry N. Wagner, Jr., MD, The Johns Hopkins Medical Institution, plus informal conversations convinced me that Saenger's timing was right and that we should make plans for a Society for Medical Decision Making. I thought the Society should have a journal and that the Society and the journal should be started simultaneously. Saenger took on the responsibility for the Society, and I worked on the journal. The Society For Medical Decision Making was officially chartered under the laws of the State of Ohio and the first annual meeting, largely organized by Saenger, was held at the University of Cincinnati in September 1979.

Starting the journal *Medical Decision Making* took a bit longer. Volume I appeared in 1981. I was editor-in-chief for the first five volumes of the journal during the period 1981 to 1985. Many individuals contributed to the early success of the society and the journal. The help of Harvey V. Fineberg, MD, PhD, Harvard School of Public Health, and Stephen G. Pauker, MD, Tufts-New England Medical Center, deserves special recognition.

Several years ago Dr. J. Robert Beck, Dartmouth-Hitchcock Medical Center, suggested to me that it would be interesting to do a study of the literature of medical decision making using the techniques of citation analysis. The study was motivated by a desire to identify the most highly influential early references in two research fronts of medical decision making; computer-assisted diagnosis and clinical decision analysis. The objective of the study was to compile a core reference list for teaching. The technique of citation analysis was chosen to develop a manageable historiography of these research fields.

The study appealed to me, particularly because Beck and Kathryn I. Pyle, AMLS, a medical librarian at Dartmouth would do most of the work. The study produced results, which are presented as an evolutionary tree of the field of medical decision making, 1959 to 1982, and as such, seems appropriate to conclude this article {32}.

Citation indexing was developed by Garfield as an aid to the compilation of bibliographies. Before the publication of the "Science Citation Index" (SCI), one could only perform bibliographic studies backward in time. With the advent of citation indexing, forward literature searching became possible. Each annual volume of SCI is organized by cited article and contains a list of publications that have cited the specific early work in that year.

A concept derived from citation indexing is cocitation frequency. In cocitation analysis, pairs of articles are studied for the links between them. Cocitation strength is a metric of the relative importance and linkage of two primary documents. As such, it is suitable for various multivariate analyses. We used multivariate procedures that included a hierarchical cluster analysis. The output of the procedures was a set of graphs each depicting the 2-space representation of the relationship among a set of articles over a time interval. The placement of the articles on the plot reflected their global cocitations; clustered articles were circled together.

The final analysis of the study was the development of the historical tree of the fields of computer-aided diagnosis and clinical decision making. To build this tree a simple rule was devised; each document was connected to the most recent core article it cited.

The literature of medical decision making, beginning with Ledley and Lusted's 1959 article in *Science*, was studied. From five experts in the fields of computer-aided diagnosis and clinical decision analysis and from a review of *Index Medicus* subject headings, a list of 56 articles and five books was compiled and analyzed. These core documents are shown at the end of this section. Three time periods were selected for analysis; 1961–1970, 1971–1975, and 1976–1980. Cocitation maps for 1961–1970 and 1976–1980 are shown in Figures 3 and 4.

The letter–number combination on the cocitation map refers to an article on the core document list. For example, in Figure 3, L59 identifies the Ledley-Lusted 1959 article in *Science*, W61 identifies Warner and colleagues' 1961 article in *JAMA*. These two articles are the oldest documents in the core list. Cluster analysis also identified Warner and colleagues' 1964 paper on Bayesian analysis of congenital heart disease (W64), and Boyle and associates' 1966 paper from the *Quarterly Journal*

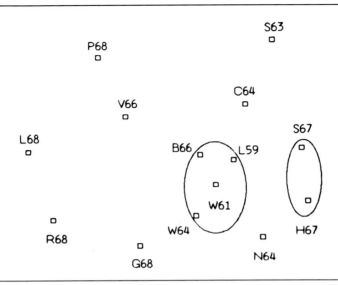

FIGURE 3

Cocitation map, 1961–1970. In Figures 3,4, and 5, documents are identified by the first author initial and year of publication (e.g., L59 = Ledley 59). The documents are listed in Figure 6, following the references. The cluster of four articles in the center of the figure (Ledley 59, Warner 61, Warner 64, Boyle 66) represent early review articles and papers in computer-aided diagnosis. Note that distances on this graph represent strength of association, but because of scaling can only be treated as approximate. Reprinted with permission from J.R. Beck, *et al.*, A citation analysis of the field of medical decision making, 1959–1982. *Medical Decision Making* 4:449–468, 1984.

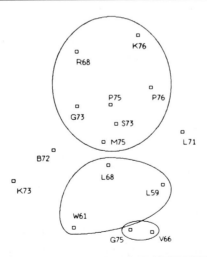

FIGURE 4

High-frequency cocitation map 1976–1980. Only the top 15 articles, in terms of cocitation between 1976 and 1980 are graphed. The large upper cluster represents the early general work in clinical decision analysis. Reprinted with permission from J.R. Beck, *et al.*, A citation analysis of the field of medical decision making, 1959–1982. *Medical Decision Making* 4:449–468, 1984.

of Medicine on computer-aided diagnosis of goiter (B66) as bibliographically related to the two early papers. Two articles from *The Lancet* in 1967, from Hall (H67) and Scadding (S67), were also cited together frequently up to 1970.

In the period from 1976 to 1980, 61 articles and books were analyzed. Figure 4 shows the relationships among the 15 most frequently cocited (minimum 10 between two documents) articles and books from the core list over the final five-year period. The two early articles, Ledley 59 and Warner 61, are once more clustered, with cocitation of Lusted's 1968 monograph (L68). Galen and Gambino's book (G75), *Beyond Normality,* is recognized as bibliographically related to Vecchio's 1966 article on predictive value (V66). There is a large cluster of leading articles on clinical decision making, with the greatest cocitation frequency over the 1976–1980 period being between Schwartz 73 (S73) and McNeil's 75 "Primer" (M75). Other articles in this cluster include Gorry and associates' companion piece in the *American Journal of Medicine* 1973 (G73), Raiffa's 1968 textbook on decision analysis (R68), two articles by Pauker in 1975 to 1976 (P75, P76), and Kassirer's 1976 (K76), "The Principals of CDM. An Introduction to Decision Analysis," from the *Yale Journal of Biology and Medicine*. As time passes, the principal effect of the cocitation analysis is to show a merging of clustered articles.

An evolutionary tree of the field of medical decision making from 1959 to 1978 is shown in Figure 5. By means of a tree diagram linking documents by citations, the central evolution including roots, trunk and tree branches of the fields computer-assisted diagnosis and clinical decision analysis is portrayed. Pre-1971 articles that did not cite other documents in the list (i.e., articles in the original set of 36 documents that graduated in the final list) are included, connected to future documents that cited them. Documents are connected by a simple rule, the most recent publication on the core list cited. For example, Feinstein 1973 (F73) cites no articles after Scheff's 1963 (S63) article on decision rules in *Behavioral Science*.

Figure 5 shows four general areas of scholarship, among which there is some overlap. In the left center is the early work in computer-assisted diagnosis and Bayesian reasoning, flowing from Warner 1961 (W61). Hall 1967 (H67) quotes Vecchio 1966 (V66), a paper that had no citation to early core documents, but achieved a progressively wider exposure over time.

Above and further to the left, de Dombal 1972 (D72) cites Ledley and Lusted 1959 (L59) and continues the computer-aided diagnosis stream of scholarship. In this latter section of computer-assisted diagnosis papers, several come from the field of laboratory medicine.

The right central section begins with Lusted 1971 (L71), which borrows from Collens's 1970 article (C70) on cost-effectiveness of multi-

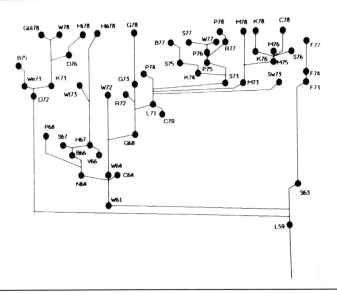

FIGURE 5

Evolutionary tree of the field of medical decision making, 1959–1978. Only journal articles are shown in this tree. Solid lines represent direct citation in later works of earlier papers in the tree. Reprinted with permission from J.R. Beck, *et al.*, A citation analysis of the field of medical decision making, 1959–1982. *Medical Decision Making* 4:449–468, 1984.

phasic screening and quotes Gorry 1968 (G68). The Lusted 1971 (L71) article appeared in *The New England Journal of Medicine* and spawned the field of clinical decision analysis as shown above and to the right of L71 in Figure 5. I attribute the influence of this article in large part to the fact that it was published in *The New England Journal of Medicine,* a journal widely recognized for the influential role it plays. *The New England Journal of Medicine* gave the medical decision-making field a tremendous boost when the editor, Dr. Franz J. Ingelfinger, devoted the entire issue on July 31, 1975, to decision making in medicine; the first time *The New England Journal* had ever devoted an entire issue to a single topic. Barbara McNeil's "Primer" (M75) appeared in that *New England Journal* issue and the branches from M75 would be numerous if we had structured the tree beyond 1978.

At the far right of Figure 5 is Feinstein's work (F73, 74, 77), three articles in the 1970s connected to the early literature (S63 and L59).

We have reached a favorable stopping point in the exploration of the tree of computer-aided diagnosis, clinical decision analysis and medical decision making, It remains for me to thank the many individuals who have participated in this exploration and contributed to its success.

Appendix: Computer-Aided Diagnosis and Clinical Decision Analysis. Core Document List, 1959–78

Authors	Title	Journal	Year
Ledley RS Lusted LB	Reasoning foundations of medical diagnosis	Science	1959
Warner HR Toronto AF Veasey LG Stephenson R	A mathematical approach to medical diagnosis	JAMA	1961
Scheff TJ	Decision rules, types of error and their consequence in medical diagnosis	Behav Sci	1963
Collen MF Rubin L Neyman J Dantzig GB Baer RM Siegelaub AB	Automated multiphasic screening and diagnosis	Am J Public Health	1964
Nugent CA Warner HR Dunn JT Tyler FH	Probability theory in the diagnosis of Cushing's syndrome	J Clin Endocrinol Metab	1964
Warner HR Toronto AF Veasey LG	Experience with Bayes' theorem for computer diagnosis of congenital heart disease	Ann NY Acad Sci	1964
Boyle JA Greig WR Franklin DA Harden RMcG Buchanan WW McGin EM	Construction of a model for computer-assisted diagnosis. Application to the problem of non-toxic goitre	Q J Med	1966
Vecchio TJ	Predictive value of a single diagnostic test in unselected populations	N Engl J Med	1966
Hall GH	The clinical application of Bayes' theorem	Lancet	1967
Scadding JG	Diagnosis. The clinician and the computer	Lancet	1967

Gorry GA Barnett GO	Sequential diagnosis by computer	JAMA	1968
Lusted LB	Introduction to Medical Decision Making. Springfield, Illinois: Charles C. Thomas		1968
Pipberber HV Klingeman JD Cosma J	Computer evaluation of statistical properties of clinical information in the differential diagnosis of chest pain	Methods Inf Med	1968
Raiffa H	Decision Analysis. Introductory Lectures on Choices Under Uncertainty. Reading, Massachusetts: Addison-Wesley		1968
Cornfield J	The Bayesian outlook and its application	Biometrics	1969
Collen MF Feldman R Siegelaub AB Crawford D	Dollar cost per positive test for automated multiphasic screening	N Engl J Med	1970
Lusted LB	Decision-making studies in patient management	N Engl J Med	1971
Barnoon S Wolfe H	Measuring the Effectiveness of Medical Decisions. An Operational Research Approach. Springfield, Illinois: Charles C. Thomas		1972
De Dombal FT Leaper DJ Staniland JR McCann AP Horrocks JC	Computer-aided diagnosis of acute abdominal pain	Br Med J	1972
Reece RL Hobbie RK	Computer evaluation of chemistry values. A reporting and diagnostic aid	Am J Clin Pathol	1972
Warner HR Olmsted CM Rutherford BD	HELP. A program for medical decision-making	Comput Biomed Res	1972
Feinstein AR	An analysis of diagnostic reasoning. I. The domains and disorders of clinical macrobiology	Yale J Biol Med	1973

Gorry GA Kassirer JP Essig A Schwartz WB	Decision analysis as the basis for computer-aided management of acute renal failure	Am J Med	1973
Knill-Jones RP Stern RB Girmes DH Maxwell JD Thompson RP Williams R	Use of sequential Bayesian model in diagnosis of jaundice by computer	Br Med J	1973
Metz CE Goodenough DJ Rossman K	Evaluation of receiver operating characteristic curve data in terms of information theory, with applications in radiography	Radiology	1973
Schwartz WB Gorry GA Kassirer JP Essig A	Decision analysis and clinical judgment	Am J Med	1973
Swets JA	The relative operating characteristic in psychology	Science	1973
Werner M Brooks SH Wette R	Strategy for cost-effective laboratory testing	Hum Pathol	1973
Winkel P	Patterns and clusters. Multivariate approach for interpreting clinical chemistry results	Clin Chem	1973
Feinstein AR	An analysis of diagnostic reasoning. III. The construction of clinical algorithms	Yale J Biol Med	1974
Katz MA	A probability graph describing the predictive value of a highly sensitive diagnostic test	N Engl J Med	1974
Patrick EA Stelmack FP Shen LYL	Review of pattern-recognition in medical diagnosis and consulting relative to a new system model	IEEE Syst Man Cybern	1974
Blomberg DJ Kimber WD Burke MD	Creatine kinase isoenzymes. Predictive value in the early diagnosis of acute myocardial infarction	Am J Med	1975
Galen RS Gambino SR	Beyond Normality. The Predictive Value and Efficiency of Medical Diagnoses. New York: Wiley		1975

McNeil BJ Keeler E Adelstein SJ	Primer on certain elements of medical decision making	N Engl J Med	1975
McNeil BJ Varady PD Burrows BA Adelstein SJ	Measures of clinical efficacy. Cost-effectiveness calculations in the diagnosis and treatment of hypertensive renovascular disease	N Engl J Med	1975
Pauker SG Kassirer JP	Therapeutic decision making. A cost-benefit analysis	N Engl J Med	1975
Sunderman FW	Current concepts of "normal values," "reference values," and "discrimination values" in clinical chemistry	Clin Chem	1975
Dawid AP	Properties of diagnostic data distributions	Biometrics	1976
Kassirer JP	The principles of clinical decision making. An introduction to decision analysis	Yale J Biol Med	1976
McNeil BJ Adelstein SJ	Determining the value of diagnostic and screening tests	J Nucl Med	1976
Pauker SG	Coronary artery surgery. The use of decision analysis	Ann Intern Med	1976
Sisson JC Schoomaker EB Ross JC	Clinical decision analysis. The hazard of using additional data	JAMA	1976
Büttner J	Die Beurteilung des diagnostischen Wertes klinisch-chemischer Untersuchungen	J Clin Chem Clin Biochem	1977
Feinstein AR	Clinical biostatistics XXXIX. The haze of Bayes, the aerial palaces of decision analysis, the the computerized Ouija board	Clin Pharmacol	1977
Rifkin RD Hood WB Jr	Bayesian analysis of electro-cardiographic exercise stress testing	N Engl J Med	1977
Safran C Desforges JF Tsichlis PN Bluming AZ	Diagnostic planning using computer assisted decision-making for patients with Hodgkin's disease	Cancer	1977
Tompkins RK Burnes DC Cable WE	An analysis of the cost-effectiveness of pharyngitis management and acute rheumatic fever prevention	Ann Intern Med	1977

Weinstein MC Stason WB	Foundations of cost-effectiveness analysis for health and medical practices	N Engl J Med	1978
Casscells W Schoenberger A Grayboys TB	Interpretation by physicians of clinical laboratory results	N Engl J Med	1978
Elstein AS Shulman LS Sprafka SA	Medical Problem Solving. An Analysis of Clinical Reasoning. Cambridge, Massachusetts: Harvard University Press		1978
Fryback DG	Bayes' theorem and conditional nonindependence of data in medical diagnosis	Comput Biomed Res	1978
Goldberg DM Ellis G	Mathematical and computer-assisted procedures in the diagnosis of liver and biliary tract disorders	Adv Clin Chem	1978
Gorry GA Pauker SG Schwartz WB	The diagnostic importance of the normal finding	N Engl J Med	1978
Habbema JD Hilden J Bjerregaard B	The measurement of performance in probabilistic diagnosis. I. The problem, descriptive tools, and measures based on classification matrices	Methods Inf Med	1978
Hilden J Habbema JD Bjerregaard B	The measurement of performance in probabilistic diagnosis. III. Methods based on continuous functions of the diagnostic probabilities	Methods Inf Med	1978
Kassirer JP Pauker SG	Should diagnostic testing be regulated?	N Engl J Med	1978
Metz CE	Basic principles of ROC analysis	Semin Nucl Med	1978
Patton DD	Introduction to clinical decision-making	Semin Nucl Med	1978
Wardle A Wardle L	Computer aided diagnosis. A review of research	Methods Inf Med	1978

Acknowledgments

This work was presented, in preliminary form, at the Fifth Annual Meeting of the Society for Medical Decision Making, Toronto, October 3–5, 1983.

Our thanks to Eugene Garfield, Ph.D., for his helpful introduction to the field and comments, and to Jay J.J. Christensen-Szalanski, Ph.D., and Barbara J. McNeil, M.D., Ph.D., for their careful review of this manuscript.

References

1. Garfield E: Citation Indexing — Its Theory and Application in Science, Technology, and Humanities. Philadelphia: ISI Press, 1983, pp 62–147
2. Clark KE: The APA study of psychologists. Am Psychol 9:117–120, 1954
3. Pearson RE: Drug information services activity, 1961–1979. A citation analysis. Drug Intell Clin Pharm 15:272–277, 1981
4. Price DJD: Networks of scientific papers. Science 149:510–515, 1967
5. Wade N: Citation analysis: A new tool for science administrators. Science 188:429–432, 1975
6. Keller MM: Bibliographic coupling between scientific papers. Am Documen. 14:10–25, 1963
7. Small HG: Co-citation in the scientific literature. A new measure of the relationship between two documents. J Am Soc Inform Sci 24:265–269, 1973
8. Small HG, Griffith BC: The structure of scientific literature. I: Identifying and graphing specialties. Sci Stud 4:17–40, 1974
9. ISI Atlas of Science. Biochemistry and Molecular Biology 1978–80. Philadelphia: ISI Press, 1981
10. Ward JH: Hierarchical grouping to optimise an objective function. J Am Stat Assoc 58:236–244, 1963
11. McGee VE: The multidimensional scaling of elastic distances. Br J Math Stat Psychol 19:181–186, 1966
12. Yerushalmy J: Statistical problems in assessing methods of medical diagnosis, with special reference to X-ray techniques. Public Health Rep 62:1432–1449, 1947

FIGURE 7

APPENDIX B

The history of the LINC (Laboratory Instrument Computer) development goes back to 1957 when Mr. Wesley A. Clark designed the Average Response Computer (ARC-1) at Lincoln Laboratory-MIT. The ARC-1 was used in studies of electroencephalograms and was found to be a useful research instrument. About this same time another Lincoln Laboratory Computer, the TX-0, was being used to analyze EEG patterns. From this computer-aided EEG research experience Mr. Clark concluded that it would be helpful for biological researchers to have a stored program type of computer which would be somewhere between an ARC-1 and TX-0 in size. The design for a stored program type of machine, subsequently called LINC, was worked out by Clark and L. Charles E. Molnar, AFCRL. They stated that "In designing the LINC, the principal underlying objective has been to maximize the degree of control over the instrument by the individual researcher. Only in this way, it is felt, can the power of the computer be usefully employed without compromising scientific objectives.

In 1960, Clark and Molnar (working in the group directed by Mr. William N. Papian at Lincoln Laboratory-MIT) began the actual design and construction of a laboratory type, general purpose digital computer, the goal being a machine which would

(1) be small enough in scale so that the individual research worker or small laboratory group could assume complete responsibility for all aspects of administration, operation, programming and maintenance;

(2) provide direct, simple, effective means whereby the experimenter could control the machine from its console, with immediate displays of data and results for viewing or photographing;

(3) be fast enough for simple data processing "on line" while the experiment is in progress, and logically powerful enough to permit later, more complex calculations if required;

(4) be flexible enough in physical arrangement and electrical characteristics to permit convenient interconnection with a variety of other laboratory apparatus, both analog and digital, such as amplifiers, timers, transducers, plotters, special digital equipment, etc. while minimizing the need for complex intermediating devices;

(5) include features of design which facilitate the training of persons unfamiliar with the use of digital computers.

The name LINC was coined sometime during 1961 and it was used to describe the laboratory-type, general purpose digital computer at both the ACCR "Workshop on Biomedical Computing" in July, 1961, and at the NSF-Sponsored "Research Training Conference in Computer Techniques for Biological Scientists" at MIT in the summer of 1961.

During late 1961 and early 1962 word about LINC spread rapidly in the scientific community. Interest among researchers was so favorable that in the latter part of 1962 discussions were held with representatives of NIH and NASA* and, as a result, NIH Contract PH43-63-540 was drawn up to support a LINC Evaluation Program. The contract required the selection of scientific advisory committee to be charged with (1)choosing participants for the LINC Evaluation Program, (2) monitoring the progress of the program and (3) making a final evaluation of the program. The evaluation would ascertain how well the LINC meets the five design objectives listed above, and determine its mechanical and electronic reliability in prolonged laboratory usage. More generally, the evaluation program hopes to determine whether the use of digital computers in the biomedical laboratory significantly advances the acquisition of knowledge.

The LINC Evaluation Board accepted the proposal that the most efficient procedure for providing appropriate background training would be to have each biological scientist participating in the Evaluation Program assemble his own LINC from prefabricated components. During each of two "assembly" phases, July 1-25 (6 participants) and August 5-30, 1963 (6 participants), the participants were given lectures on programming, operation and maintenance of LINC. How the LINC development group finally managed to assemble the needed components by July, 1963, and how the class teaching was organized is another interesting story. However, the fact remains that all 12 LINCs were assembled and each participating scientist did learn how to program and maintain his LINC. These LINCs, plus 9 others, are now in operation in as many different biomedical research laboratories distributed around the country.

The LINC Evaluation Program continues through 1964 and 1965 but one important point has already been proven by the LINC training program. The summer program in 1963 demonstrated that it is possible, with proper planning and execution, for biologists to learn a great deal of computer technology in a very short time.

TABLE I

COMPUTER INSTALLATIONS PRIMARILY ENGAGED IN LIFE SCIENCES RESEARCH, 1964

State and Institution	Type of Computer
ALABAMA	
Alabama, University of	IBM 1620
CALIFORNIA	
Camarillo State Hospital	IBM 1440
California, University of, Davis	IBM 7040* - IBM 1710*
California, University of, Los Angeles	IBM 7094 - IBM 1410 - CDC 160A
California, University of, San Francisco	IBM 1410
Pacific State Hospital	G-15
Southern California, University of	IBM 1710
Stanford University	LINC (2)

COLORADO
   Colorado, University of, Medical Center   CDC 160A

DISTRICT OF COLUMBIA (Washington)
   Georgetown University   IBM 1620*

FLORIDA
   Miami, University of   IBM 1401
   Communication Research Institute of
      St. Thomas   LINC

GEORGIA
   Emory University   IBM 1620

ILLINOIS
   Chicago, University of   IBM 7090* – IBM 1401
   Northwestern University   LINC – IBM 1710+

INDIANA
   Indiana University   IBM 1410

KANSAS
   Kansas, University of   IBM 7040*
LOUISIANA
   Tulane University   IBM 1410 – IBM 1401

MARYLAND
   Johns Hopkins University   IBM 1401 – LINC (2)
   Maryland, University of, Medical School   IBM 1620

MASSACHUSETTS
   Massachusetts General Hospital   PDP 4+
   Harvard University   IBM 1710 – PDP 4 – IBM 1620+
   Massachusetts Institute of Technology   LINC (3)
   Clark University   IBM 1620

MINNESOTA
   Mayo Association   IBM 1620

MISSOURI
   Missouri, University of   IBM 1410+
   Psychiatric Research Foundation of
      Missouri   IBM 1710+
   Central Institute for the Deaf   LINC
   Washington University   LINC
NEW JERSEY
   Seton Hall University   IBM 1620

NEW MEXICO
   New Mexico Highland University   IBM 1620

NEW YORK
   New York, State University of,
      Downstate Medical Center   IBM 1620+
   New York, University of, Buffalo   IBM 7044* – IBM 1620
   Health Research, Inc. – Roswell Park Div.   IBM 1620
   Memorial Hospital for Cancer and Allied
      Diseases   CDC 160A
   New York University Medical Center   CDC 1604* – CDC 160A
   Yeshiva University   CDC 160A
   New York, State University of, Upstate
      Medical Center   IBM 1620+

NORTH CAROLINA
North Carolina, University of   IBM 1410* – LINC – IBM 1620
Duke University   LINC – IBM 7072*
Bowman Gray School of Medicine,
  Wake Forest College   LINC – IBM 1620*

OHIO
Cincinnati, University of, College of
  Medicine   IBM 7040
Western Reserve University   GE 225+ – IBM 1620
Fels Research Institute   IBM 1620

OKLAHOMA
Oklahoma, University of   IBM 1620 – IBM 1401

OREGON
Medical Research Foundation of Oregon
  Inc. (Oregon Regional Primate Research
  Center)   SDS–920+
Oregon, University of, Medical School   IBM 1410

PENNSYLVANIA
Pennsylvania, University of   CDC 160A
Presbyterian Hospital in Philadelphia   LINC

RHODE ISLAND
Brown University   LINC

TENNESSEE
Tennessee, University of   IBM 1620

TEXAS
Texas, University of, Galveston   IBM 1410* – IBM 1620
Texas, University of, Houston   IBM 1710
Baylor University   IBM 1410+

UTAH
Utah, University of   CDC 3200

VIRGINIA
Medical College of Virginia   RPC 4000

WASHINGTON
Washington, University of   PB 440 – LINC

WISCONSIN
Wisconsin, University of   LINC

References

1. Ledley, R.S. Logical aid to symptomatic medical diagnosis. *Operations Research*, Vol. 3, August, 1955.

2. *Science* 130:9–21, July 3, 1959.

3. Von Winterfeldt, D. and Edwards, W. *Decision Analysis and Behavioral Research*. Cambridge: Cambridge University Press, 1986, p. 161.

4. Warner, H. A mathematical approach to medical diagnosis. Application to congenital heart disease. *JAMA* 177:177–183, July 22, 1961.

5. Warner, H. The HELP system. *J Med Syst* 7:87–102, 1983.

6. Lodwick, G.S., *et al*. Computer diagnosis of primary bone tumors. A preliminary report. *Radiology* 80:273–275, 1963.

7. Fryback, F.G. Bayes's theorem and conditional nonindependence of data in medical diagnosis. *Comp and Biomed Res* 11:423, 1976.

8. de Dombal, F.T. Computer-aided diagnosis of acute abdominal pain. *Br Med J* 2:9–13, 1972.

9. Zoltie, N., Horrocks, J., and de Dombal, F.T. Computer assisted diagnosis of dyspepsia—Report of transferability of a system, with emphasis on early diagnosis of gastric cancer. *Meth Inform Med* 16:89–92, 1977.

10. Ryack, B.L. A Computer Based Diagnostic/Information Patient Management System for Isolated Environment. MEDIC Ten Years Later. U.S. Naval Submarine Medical Research Laboratory. Report No. 1089, 4 February 1987.

11. Elstein, A.S., *et al*. *Medical Problem Solving. An Analysis of Clinical Reasoning*. Cambridge: Harvard University Press, 1978.

12. Shortliffe, E.H. Computer programs to support clinical decision making. *JAMA* 258:61–66, 1987.

13. Lusted, L.B. A Study of the Efficacy of Diagnostic Radiologic Procedures. Final Report on diagnostic efficacy to Dr. Gerald Rosenthal, Director, National Center For Health Services Research, Health Resources Administration, DHEW, 31 May 1977. See also Winterfeldt and Edwards, *Decision Analysis and Behavioral Research*. Cambridge: Cambridge University Press, 1986, Chapter 5, pp. 448–452.

14. Saenger, E.L., Buncher, C.R., Specker, B.L., and McDevitt, R. Determination of clinical efficacy: Nuclear medicine as applied to lung scanning. *J Nucl Med* 26:793–806, 1985. Gift, D.A., Schonbein, W.R., Saenger, E.L., and Potchen, E.J. Application of an information-theoretic method of efficacy assessment. *J Nucl Med* 26:807–811, 1985.

15. Collen, M.F., *et al*. Automated multiphasic screening and diagnosis. *Am J Publ Hlth* 54:741, 1964.

16. Lindberg, D.A.B. *The Growth of Medical Information Systems in the United States*. Lexington: Lexington Books, 1979, pp. 62–63; 70–71.

17. Barnett, G.O., *et al.* DXplain. An evolving diagnostic decision-support system. *JAMA* 258:67–74, 1987. See also {16}, pp. 40–42.

18. Lusted, L.B. *Introduction to Medical Decision Making*. Springfield, Illinois: Charles C. Thomas, 1968.

19. Lusted, L.B., Coffin, R.W. *PRIME. An Automated Information System for Hospitals and Biomedical Research Laboratories*. Chicago: Year Book Medical Publishers, 1967.

20. Lusted, L.B. and Stahl, W.R. Conceptual models of diagnosis. *The Diagnostic Process. Proc of a Conference at the University of Michigan, May 9–11, 1963*. Jacquez, J.A., (ed.). April, 1964. pp. 157–180.

21. Lusted, L.B. ROC recollected. *Med Decis Making* 4:131–135, 1984.

22. Lusted, L.B. Logical analysis in roentgen diagnosis. *Radiology* 74:178–193, 1960.)

23. Swets, J.A., (ed.). *Signal Detection and Recognition by Human Observers*. New York: Wiley, 1964.

24. Green, D.M. and Swets, J.A. *Signal Detection Theory and Psychophysics*. New York: Wiley, 1966.

25. Lusted, L.B. Introduction to medical decision making. *Digest of the Seventh International Conference on Medical and Biological Engineering*. Stockholm, 1967. p 297.

26. Lusted, L.B. Decision making studies in patient management. *N Eng J Med* 284:416–424, 1971.

27. Metz, C.E. Basic principles of ROC analysis. *Sem Nucl Med* 8:283–298, 1978.

28. Metz, C.E. ROC methodology in radiologic imaging. *Invest Radiol* 21:720–733, 1986.

29. Lusted, L.B. *Introduction to Medical Decision Making*. Springfield, Illinois: Charles C. Thomas, 1968, pp. 128–132.

30. Von Winterfeldt, D., and Edwards, W. *Decision Analysis and Behavioral Research*. Cambridge: Cambridge University Press, 1986.

31. Weinstein, M.C. and Fineberg, H.V. *Clinical Decision Analysis*. Philadelphia: W B Saunders, 1980.

32. Beck, J.R., Pyle, K.I., and Lusted, L.B. A citation analysis of the field of medical decision making, 1959–1982. Computer-aided diagnosis and clinical decision analysis. *Med Decis Making* 4:449–468, 1984.

Participants' Discussion

Jack Smith   Would you speculate on the value of the use of "predictive value terminology" versus the more traditional Bayesian probability terminology
(that is, *a posteriori, a priori,* conditional probability) in terms of popular-
izing these ideas? Did the restatement of the Bayesian concepts and
terminology in predictive value terms as in Galen and Gambino's book
Beyond Normality affect the popularization of this idea? It always
seemed to me that dropping the more Bayesian-oriented terminology
was a significant step in the wider acceptance of the Bayesian concepts
in the medical community.

Lee Lusted   My impression is that probability terminology and definition of terms
such as "predictive value" have appeared in medical journal articles
frequently enough during the past few years that probability terminology is better understood. Both the terminology and greater literature
exposure have helped to popularize the use of probability in the medical field.

The Background of INTERNIST-I and QMR

Jack D. Myers, MD
University of Pittsburgh, Pittsburgh

During my tenure as chairman of the Department of Medicine at the University of Pittsburgh, 1955 to 1970, two points became clear in regard to diagnosis in internal medicine. The first was that the knowledge base in that field had become vastly too large for any single person to encompass it. The second point was that the busy practitioner, even though he knew the items of information pertinent to his patients correct diagnosis, often did not consider the right answer, particularly if the diagnosis was an unusual disease.

I resigned the position of chairman in 1970 intending to resume my position as professor of Medicine. However, the University saw fit to offer me the appointment as University Professor (Medicine). The University of Pittsburgh follows the practice of Harvard University, established by President James Bryant Conant in the late 1930s, in which a University Professor is a professor at large who reports only to the president of the university. He has no department or school and is not under administrative supervision by a dean or vice-president. Thus the position allows maximal academic freedom.

In this new position I felt strongly that I should conduct worthwhile research. It was almost 15 years since I had worked in my chosen field of clinical investigation, namely splanchnic blood flow and metabolism, and I felt that research in that area had passed me by. Remembering the two points mentioned earlier—the excessive knowledge base of internal medicine and the problem of considering the correct diagnosis—I asked myself what could be done to correct these problems. It seemed that the computer with its huge memory could correct the first, and I wondered if it could not help with the second as well.

At that point I knew no more about computers than the average layperson, so I sought advice. Dr. Gerhard Werner, our chairman of Pharmacology, was working with computers in an attempt to map all of the neurological centers of the human brain stem with particular reference to their interconnections and functions. He was particularly concerned about the actions of pharmacological agents on this complex system. Working with him on this problem was Dr. Harry Pople, a computer scientist with special interest in artificial intelligence. The

427

problem chosen was so complex and difficult that Werner and Pople were making little progress.

Gerhard listened patiently to my ideas and promptly stated that he thought the projects were feasible utilizing the computer. In regard to the diagnostic component of my ambition he strongly advised that artificial intelligence be used. Pople was brought into the discussion and was greatly interested, I believe because of the feasibility of the project and the recognition of its practical application to the practice of medicine.

The upshot was that Pople joined me in my project, and Werner and Pople abandoned the work on the brain stem. Pople knew nothing about medicine, and I knew nothing about computer science. Thus the first step in our collaboration was my analysis for Pople of the diagnostic process. I chose a goodly number of actual cases from clinical pathological conferences (CPCs) because they contained ample clinical data and because the correct diagnoses were known. At each small step of the way through the diagnostic process I was required to explain what the clinical information meant in context and my reasons for considering certain diagnoses. This provided to Pople insight into the diagnostic process. After analyzing dozens of such cases I felt as though I had undergone a sort of psychoanalysis.

From this experience Pople wrote the first computer diagnostic programs seeking to emulate my diagnostic process. This has led certain "wags" to nickname our project "Jack in the box." For this initial attempt Pople used the LISP computer language. We were granted access to the PROPHET PDP-10, a time-sharing mainframe maintained in Boston by the National Institutes of Health (NIH) but devoted particularly to pharmacological research. Thus we were interlopers.

The first name we applied to our project was DIALOG, for diagnostic logic, but this had to be dropped because the name was in conflict with a computer program already on the market and copyrighted. The next name chosen was INTERNIST for obvious reasons. However, the American Society for Internal Medicine publishes a journal entitled *The Internist*, and they objected to our use of INTERNIST, although there seems to be little relationship or conflict between a printed journal and a computer software program. Rather than fight the issue we simply added the roman numeral one to our title, and it then became INTERNIST-I, which continues to this day.

Pople's initial effort was unsuccessful, however. He diligently had incorporated details regarding anatomy and much basic pathophysiology, I believe because in my initial CPC analyses I had brought into consideration such items of information so that Pople could understand how I got from A to B, etc. The diagnostician in internal medicine knows, of course, much anatomy and pathophysiology, but these are brought into consideration in only a minority of diagnostic problems.

He knows, for example, that the liver is in the right upper quadrant and just beneath the right leaf of the diaphragm. In most diagnostic instances this information is "subconscious."

Our first computer diagnostic program included too many such details and as a result was very slow and frequently got into analytical "loops" from which it could not extricate itself. We decided that we had to simplify the program but by that juncture much of 1971 had passed on.

The new program was INTERNIST-I, and even today most of the basic structure devised in 1972 remains intact. INTERNIST-I is written in INTERLISP and has operated on the PDP-10 and the DEC 2060. It has also been adapted to the VAX 780. Certain younger people have contributed significantly to the program, particularly Dr. Zachary Moraitis and Dr. Randolph Miller. The latter interrupted his regular medical school education to spend the year 1974 to 1975 as a fellow in our laboratory and since finishing his formal medical education in 1979 has been active as a full-time faculty member of the team. Several PhD candidates in computer science have also made significant contributions as have dozens of medical students during electives on the project.

INTERNIST-I is really quite a simple system as far as its operating system or inference engine is concerned. Three basic numbers are concerned in and manipulated in the ranking of elicited disease hypotheses. The first of these is the importance (IMPORT) of each of the more than 4100 manifestations of disease that are contained in the knowledge base. IMPORTs are a global representation of the clinical importance of a given finding graded from 1 to 5, the latter being maximal, focusing on how necessary it is to explain the manifestation regardless of the final diagnosis. Thus massive splenomagaly has an IMPORT of 5 whereas anorexia has an IMPORT of 1. Mathematical weights are assigned to IMPORT numbers on a nonlinear scale.

The second basic number is the evoking strength (EVOKS), the numbers ranging from 0 to 5. The number answers the question that given a particular *manifestation of disease*, how strongly does one consider disease A versus all other diagnostic possibilities in a clinical situation? A zero indicates that a particular clinical manifestation is nonspecific, i.e., so widely spread among diseases that the above question cannot be answered usefully. Again, anorexia is a good example of a nonspecific manifestation. The EVOKS number 5, on the other hand, indicates that a manifestation is essentially pathognomonic for a particular disease.

The third basic number is the frequency (FREQ), which answers the question that given a particular *disease*, what is the frequency or incidence of occurrence of a particular clinical finding? FREQ numbers range from 1 to 5, with 1 indicating that the finding is rare or unusual in the disease and 5 indicating that the finding is present in essentially all instances of the disease.

Each diagnosis that is evoked is ranked mathematically on the basis of support for it, both positive and negative. Like the import number, the values for EVOKS and FREQ numbers increase in a non-linear fashion. The establishment or conclusion of a diagnosis is not based on any absolute score, as in Bayesian systems, but on how much better the support of diagnosis A is, as compared to its nearest competitor. This difference is anchored to the value of an EVOKS of 5, a pathognomonic finding.

When the list of evoked diagnoses is ranked mathematically on the basis of EVOKS, FREQ, and IMPORT, the list is partitioned based on the similarity of support for individual diagnoses. Thus a heart disease is compared with other heart diseases and not brain diseases, since the patient may have a heart disorder and a brain disease concomitantly. Thus apples are compared with apples and not oranges.

When a diagnosis is concluded, the computer consults a list of interrelationships among diseases (LINKS) and bonuses are awarded, again in a nonlinear fashion for numbers ranging from 1 to 5. A 1 indicates a weak interrelationship and 5 a universal interrelationship. Thus multiple, interrelated diagnoses are preferred over independent ones, provided the support for the second and other diagnoses is adequate. Good clinicians use this same rule of thumb. LINKS are of various types: PCED is used when disease A precedes disease B, e.g., acute rheumatic fever precedes early rheumatic valvular disease; PDIS—disease A predisposes to disease B; e.g., AIDS predisposes to pneumocystis pneumonia; CAUS—disease A causes disease B, e.g., thrombophlebitis of the lower extremities may cause pulmonary embolism; and COIN—there is a statistical interrelationship between disease A and disease B but scientific medical information is not explicit on the relationship, e.g., Hashimoto's thyroiditis coincides with pernicious anemia, both are so-called autoimmune diseases. The maximal number of correct diagnoses made in a single case analysis is, to my recollection, 11.

In working with INTERNIST-I during the remainder of the 1970s several important points about the system were learned or appreciated. The first and foremost of these is the importance of a complete and accurate knowledge base. Omissions from a disease profile can be particularly troublesome. If a manifestation of disease is not listed on a disease profile the computer can only conclude that that manifestation does not occur in the disease, and if a patient demonstrates the particular manifestation it counts against that diagnosis. Fortunately, repeated exercise of the diagnostic system brings to attention many inadvertent omissions. It is important to establish the EVOKS and FREQ numbers as accurately as possible. Continual updating of the knowledge base, including newly described diseases and new information about diseases previously profiled, is critical. Dr. Edward Feigenbaum recognized the importance of the accuracy and completeness of knowledge bases as the prime requisite of expert systems of any sort. He emphasized this point in his keynote address to MEDINFO-86 {1}.

Standardized, clear, and explicit nomenclature is required in expressing disease names and particularly in naming the thousands of individual manifestations of disease. Such rigidity can make the use of INTERNIST-I difficult for the uninitiated user. Therefore, in QMR more latitude and guidance is provided the user. For example, the user of INTERNIST-I must enter "ABDOMEN PAIN RIGHT UPPER QUADRANT" exactly whereas in QMR the user may enter "PAI ABD RUQ," and the system recognizes the terms as above.

The importance of "properties" attached to the great majority of clinical manifestations was solidly evident. Properties express such conditions that if A is true then B is automatically false (or true as the case may be). The properties also allow credit to be awarded for or against B as the case may be. Properties also provide order to the asking of questions in the interrogative mode. They also state prerequisites and unrequisites for various procedures. As examples, one generally does not perform a superficial lymph node biopsy unless lymph nodes are enlarged (prerequisite). Similarly, a percutaneous liver biopsy is inadvisable if the blood platelets are less than 50,000 (unrequisite).

It became clear quite early in the utilization of INTERNIST-I that systemic or multisystem diseases had an advantage over localized disorders in diagnosis. This is because systemic diseases have very long and more inclusive manifestation lists. It became necessary, therefore, to subdivide systemic diseases into various components when appropriate. Systemic lupus erythematosus provides a good example. Lupus nephritis must be compared in our system with other renal diseases, and such comparison is allowed by our partitioning algorithm. Likewise, cerebral lupus must be differentiated from other central nervous system disorders. Furthermore, either renal lupus or cerebral lupus can occur at times without significant clinical evidence of other systemic involvement. In order to reassemble the components of a systemic disease we devised the systemic LINK (SYST) which expresses the interrelationship of each subcomponent to the parent system disease.

It became apparent quite early that expert systems like INTERNIST do not deal with the time axis of a disease well at all, and this seems to be generally true of expert systems in AI. Certain parameters dealing with time can be expressed by devising particular manifestations, e.g., a blood transfusion preceding the development of acute hepatitis B by two to six months. But time remains a problem that is yet to be solved satisfactorily including QMR.

It has been clearly apparent over the years that both the knowledge base and the diagnostic consultant programs of both INTERNIST-

I and QMR have considerable educational value. The disease profiles, the list of diseases in which a given clinical manifestation occurs (ordered by EVOKS and FREQ), and the interconnections among diseases (LINKS) provide a quick and ready means of acquiring at least orienting clinical information. Such has proved useful not only to medical students and residents but to clinical practitioners as well. In the interrogative mode of the diagnostic systems the student will frequently ask, "Why was that question asked?" Either an instructor can provide insight or ready consultation of the knowledge base by the student will provide a simple semiquantitative reason for the question.

Lastly, let me state that working with INTERNIST-I and QMR over the years seems to have had real influence on my own diagnostic approaches and habits. Thus my original clinical psychoanalysis when working with Pople has been reinforced.

References

1. Feigenbaum, E.A. Autoknowledge: From file servers to knowledge servers. *MEDINFO-86*, Solamon, R., Blum, B., Jorgensen, M., (eds.). Elsevier Science Publishers B.V. (North Holland), pp. XLIII–XLVI, 1986.

2. Miller, R.A., Pople, H.E. Jr., Myers, J.D. INTERNIST-I: An experimental computer-based diagnostic consultant for general internal medicine. *N Engl J Med.* 307:468–476, 1982.

3. Masarie, F.E. Jr., Miller, R.A., and Meyers, J.D. INTERNIST-I PROPERTIES: Representing common sense and good medical practice in a computerized medical knowledge base. *Comp Bio Res.* 18:458–479, 1985.

4. Miller, R.A., McNeil, M.A., Challinor, S., Masarie, F.E. Jr., and Myers, J.D. Status report: The INTERNIST-I/Quick Medical Reference project. *West J Med.* 145:816–822, 1986.

Additional Comments by Myers[1]

We still find most medical schools teaching mainly by the technique of information transfer and lectures. How successful is a faculty going to be in transferring a million-and-a-half facts, individual items of information, to its medical students? I think the answer is obvious, and I

---

[1] The following extract contains the conclusion of Dr. Myers's talk. It has been included because it augments his written paper.

certainly think that it's necessary to change our mode of education from information transfer to problem-solving techniques as many have expounded. Computer programs like ours and others can form a valuable aid in that change.

Earlier I spoke about the analysis of cases for Dr. Pople so that he would have some insight into how to compose AI programs for our case-analysis program. There's another side to that coin. Having worked with this expert system for a number of years, I'd say that I feel that I've undergone some change in working with the system. I think more like a computer now than I used to. I find that my teaching at the bedside is somewhat different than it used to be. I feel that this is all for the good. I don't regret it, but I do want to mention that I think the influence goes both ways. I certainly influenced the character of the program in an entirely proper and orthodox fashion by analyzing cases for Pople, but then I think on the other side of the coin the program has influenced me as I see it work and look intelligent.

Participants' Discussion

Morris Collen	Dr. Myers, you have used the terms "expert systems" and "artificial intelligence" more or less interchangeably throughout your talk. After all these years, and being one of the leading experts in the field, do you have any personal preference between these two terms to describe INTERNIST-I?
Jack Myers	In the first place not all expert systems necessarily are in artificial intelligence. Ours happens to be. I personally don't like the term "artificial intelligence" and therefore I would prefer to use "expert system." I see Dr. Lusted agrees with me.
Question	What makes a knowledge base an expert system? What makes a collection of facts an expert system?
Jack Myers	My point was that any expert system must have an underlying, accurate knowledge base. Persons like myself and Ted Shortliffe call these knowledge bases rather than databases, because they involve properties and rules in addition to data. It's not just a simple listing of manifestations of disease. The system knows the interrelationships among these, and all kinds of directions, and that's the reason we use the term knowledge base. But a knowledge base without a good inference engine cannot be a diagnostic advisory system. So, it takes both components.
Jochen Moehr	I was intrigued by your statement of the numbers of items that make up medicine—these one-and-a-half million pieces of information. Could you expand on what you call a piece of information? For instance, blood pressure. Is that one item, even though blood pressure can take on an infinite number of values in a certain range? On the other hand what about sputum? Sputum can be productive or nonproductive in the morning, in the evening and so on, so it's more of an ordinal or nominal type of item. What do you call an item?

Jack Myers   That's a good question. Take the blood pressure first. The blood pressure is usually low in Addison's disease. That's an item of information, so it's the blood pressure in a specific context. The blood pressure is usually high in acute glomerulonephritis, so that's a second item of information, and so on across the board. Now, sputum can be blood-streaked in certain diseases, and foul and purulent in others. Those are the things I'm calling items of information. In other words, I'm thinking of the total spectrum of diseases, and the average is somewhere under 125 or so items of information for each disease.

Artificial Intelligence in Medicine: A Personal Retrospective on its Emergence and Early Evolution

Casimir A. Kulikowski, PhD
Rutgers University, New Brunswick

Abstract

Methods of artificial intelligence were gradually introduced into clinical decision-making research from 1970 to 1974. Evolving from pattern recognition and general AI problem-solving ideas, such methods helped researchers crystallize the notions of knowledge-based systems by the mid-1970s. In 1978 the early systems gave way to either second-generation frameworks for general consultative reasoning or to new, more sophisticated knowledge representations. This paper traces some of the major events in the early evolution of AIM (Artificial Intelligence in Medicine) systems, with emphasis on the developments at the Rutgers Resource, in which I participated.

Prelude: The State-of-the-Art in Computer-assisted Clinical Decision Making in 1970

The first proposals to apply artificial intelligence (AI) to clinical decision-making evolved at Rutgers University in 1970 during the preparation of a grant proposal to the NIH Biotechnology Resources Program. They followed a decade of rapid advances in statistical methods for computer-aided diagnosis, initiated by the pioneering efforts of Lipkin, Hardy, and Engle at the New York Cornell Medical School [1], who first explored logical and probabilistic approaches to the diagnosis of hematological disorders. The applicability of Bayesian inference, utility theory, and Boolean logic to diagnostic problems was made widely known within the biomedical research community through Ledley's and Lusted's article in *Science* [2] in 1959. Warner subsequently popularized the use of Bayes's rule to calculate posterior probabilities of diseases [3] while discriminant analysis methods are applied to thyroid disease diagnosis [4] and to multidisease screening through the Cornell Index [5]. Classical hypothesis-testing methods for disease classification were used by Collen and his colleagues at Kaiser-Permanente based on the wealth of data collect in their multiphasic screening center [6]. Signal analysis and pattern recognition methods were applied in ECG interpretation {7}, while a decision-tree approach characterized Howard Bleich's well-known program on acid-base balance disorders {8}. This meant that by 1970 all traditional formalizations of reasoning had been applied to computer-assisted decision-making problems. Yet, despite this progress there appeared to be little enthusiasm in the medical community at large for computer-based methods.

Some of the difficulties in acceptability could then, as now, be blamed on the awareness of the complexities of human diagnostic reasoning that were not captured by methods of formal logic or probabilistic inference. Many of these problems were discussed as early as 1963 during a conference held at the University of Michigan on "The Diagnostic Process." From the proceedings, edited by Jacques {9} it is striking to see a clear identification of topics that still preoccupy researchers: multi-disease discrimination, temporal courses of diseases, causal relationships between disease entities, and the contrast between describing an individual patient's problems versus the statistical characterization of diseases. In 1965, Ledley published a book on the *Uses of Computers in Biology and Medicine* {10}. It not only summarized some of his early work in the field of logical diagnosis, but also gave many practical examples of the application of clustering methods and utility theory in medical diagnosis. It is again interesting to see that Ledley anticipated many of the concerns that have now become routine in the application of decision analysis and other formal methods in clinical decision-making (as evidenced by the many articles in the *Journal of Medical Decision-Making*). In 1968 Lusted summarized his experiences with Bayesian and likelihood methods for diagnosis in the book, *Introduction to Medical Decision-Making* {11}, which became for many years the only widely available monograph on the subject.

It was in this same year that I first became involved with clinical decision-making problems. My doctoral advisor at the University of Hawaii, Professor Michael S. Watanabe, suggested that I contact Dr. Robert Nordyke of the Straub Clinic to investigate the possible application of pattern-recognition methods in medical diagnosis. Nordyke had accumulated a large database of thyroid disease records and wished to have them analyzed. He also wanted to see if it would be practical to develop a computer program to help him screen the large number of nonthyroid conditions that were referred to his specialty clinic. Over the previous five years, Watanabe had developed several pattern-recognition approaches that selected only the most discriminating combinations of features for a decision. He suggested that I investigate the application of the CLAFIC (class-featuring information compression) method in particular to the medical diagnostic problem. In working with Nordyke, I rapidly found that one of the major problems in developing a computer-based screening and consultation system did indeed consist of selecting the most discriminating sets of manifestations. Over the next couple of years, I developed a group of programs for carrying out sequential diagnosis based on sets of symptoms, signs, and laboratory tests for thyroid disease {12, 13}. These were placed into operation at Straub within Nordyke's thyroid clinic, helping automate the production of reports and provide a statistical analysis of the thyroid data. However, even while completing this work in 1970, we saw that there would be problems of acceptability with the system. In observing the reaction of other physicians to the use of Nordyke's programs, it was clear that while trusting his data and his interpretations, they were very suspicious of the probabilities and discrimination scores produced by my programs based on the same data. It was somewhat disheartening to see that the work I had just completed was unlikely to be widely used unless the "black box" nature of the mathematical processing was somehow *explained*.

It was at this juncture, during job interviews, that I met Professor Saul Amarel (Figure 1), who was proposing to build a research group at Rutgers University devoted to the application of advanced computer science methods (particularly artificial intelligence) to problems of biomedical research and medical practice. Having become acquainted with some of the AI programs for game playing and planning of the time, I was skeptical that they could help in dealing with practical and "noisy" problem solving such as occurs in clinical diagnosis. Amarel brought to my attention the possibilities of more general representational frameworks, which could be used in characterizing real, complex interpretation problems. In particular, he pointed to the DENDRAL project at Stanford as a case where detailed knowledge of plausible chemical structures could be used to guide the search for an interpretation of a mass spectrogram, rather than applying pattern-recognition methods directly. It was in the following year that I began to think about the notion of finding a more detailed description of disease processes that could help provide a structure for diagnostic reasoning that went beyond a purely phenomenological association of symptoms with diseases. Only in that way, by "reasoning like a physician," would our computer-based methods become acceptable to physicians. I did not realize at the time that this represented a decisive change in my thinking, moving from a purely engineering approach towards a deeper consideration of the "cognitive model" that the human diagnostician uses.

As the result of the meetings with Amarel, I went to Rutgers and joined with him and other faculty from the newly formed Department of Computer Science, as well as faculty from the biological sciences, psychology, ecology, and the medical school, in writing a proposal to the National Institutes of Health to establish a Research Resource on Computers in Biomedicine at Rutgers. This was done with the encouragement of Dr. William Raub, who headed the Biotechnology Resources Program of the NIH at that time. Raub had been a student of

FIGURE 1
Saul Amarel, first P.I.
of the Rutgers Re-
source, trying out a
program on the PDP-
10 computer.

Dr. William Yamamoto at the University of Pennsylvania, and was very
interested in the application of a wider set of biomathematical modeling and simulation techniques in biomedical research and practice. It
was also at about this time that Dr. William Schwartz at Tufts-New
England Medical Center, working in collaboration with Dr. C.A. Gorry
at MIT, published an influential article entitled "Medicine and the
Computer: The Promise and Problems of Change" in the *New England
Journal of Medicine*. In it, he eloquently proposed that the more routine
tasks of the physician would be good candidates for computerization
{14}. Gorry had been a pioneer in developing sequential statistical
methods for test selection in diagnosis {15} and was at this time also
confronting the problems of computerized clinical decision-making by
studying the cognitive processes of human diagnosticians {16}. As
chance would have it, I had interviewed with Schwartz in 1970, in the
course of which he described to me his hope of establishing a department of medical computer science within the medical school. As things
turned out it was the Tufts-MIT collaborations that he encouraged and
participated in that became important catalysts in the development of
AIM ideas {17}.

The NIH approved our Rutgers Resource in 1971, making it the first focus of research in the application of AI to problems of biomedical inquiry. Saul Amarel was the principal investigator, and I was placed in charge of the clinical decision-making area. As I have described above, the time was ripe for the development of alternative schemes for cognitive representation and inferencing in dealing with diagnostic problems. During the next four years these seeds planted at Rutgers, Stanford, Tufts-MIT, and the University of Pittsburgh all germinated and produced the first generation of knowledge-based artificial intelligence systems for clinical decision making.

Early Developments of Artificial Intelligence in Medicine: 1970–1974

When I joined Rutgers in 1970 my first research priority was to extend the pattern-recognition methods that I had developed to a broader class of problems, continuing the research with Professor Watanabe. However, as soon as the Rutgers Research Resource on Computers in Biomedicine was funded, I started working on ways for formulating alternative formalizations of the diagnostic process. At first, one alternative that presented itself was to try syntactic methods of pattern recognition, which might enable one to describe a disease in terms of grammatical rules. During the fall of 1971, I was joined by Dr. Lyon Hyams of Rutgers Medical School, and together we tried to develop grammatical rules for thyroid disease, hematologic disorders, and other problems that we were acquainted with. Hyams was an MD-biostatistician who felt very strongly that physicians would need to learn how to think in Bayesian terms while we also endeavored to make computers "think" more like human specialists. We explored the application of Bayesian methods in medical education and did very well in this. However, Hyams's untimely death in 1971 brought an end to these investigations.

In the last months of working together Hyams had introduced me to Dr. Aran Safir, an ophthalmologist at the Mt. Sinai School of Medicine, who became very interested in the possibility of using computer models to represent those aspects of medical reasoning that involve encyclopedic retrieval of knowledge, thereby leaving the physician free to pursue the more fruitful nuances of the problem-solving process itself. In the fall of 1971, we were joined by Sholom Weiss as a research assistant pursuing his doctoral studies. Together, we experimented with grammatical representations for ophthalmological diseases but rapidly found them wanting. It was at this point that a key conceptual breakthrough took place. In our discussions with Safir it became clear that to "speak the language of the clinician," one needed to represent the cause-and-effect relationships that explain the pathogenesis of a disease. This led us to examine the nature of causes and effects. At first we considered developing a model of the normal physiology that could be subject to perturbations describing pathological conditions. Due to the myriad patterns of normal values of physiological parameters we soon abandoned this approach. We then struck on the crucial idea that one ought to look at *qualitative descriptions of pathophysiological states*, such as "elevated intraocular pressure," rather than specific numerical values of physiological parameters. The notion of a pathophysiological state as an abstract summary of observable events followed shortly afterwards. Sholom Weiss helped formulate a working computer model of these ideas, and produced a causal network (CASNET) model for glaucoma. Safir had suggested that we concentrate on this disease because of its significance as a major cause of blindness. In addition, because it had fairly well-understood mechanisms that influenced the selection of therapy, the chances of succeeding in the causal modeling were good. Yet at the same time the disease could be resistant to treatment, making consultation with a specialist important. The possibility of capturing the knowledge and expertise of the specialist in a computer program would help make it more widely available.

A first version of CASNET was run retrospectively on glaucoma data from the Mt. Sinai School of Medicine in the fall of 1972. We gave the first scientific presentation of this work at the December 1972 IEEE Conference on Decision and Control in a session chaired by Professor K.S. Fu entitled "Modern Pattern Recognition" {18}. Our paper stressed how one could apply different strategies of data acquisition using the same causal network as the underlying model of knowledge. During early 1973 we continued to develop the glaucoma model and realized that it could be viewed as a three-layered representation of knowledge. At the lowest level we placed the actual data or manifestations of the patient, at the second level the pathophysiological states summarizing the data, and at a third level the diagnostic hypotheses that describe more broadly the mechanisms of disease. For instance, tension readings on the eye within a certain high range at the first level can map into the concept of an abnormally elevated intraocular pressure, which is inferred as a pathophysiological state. Likewise, a measurement of very small angle grades in the anterior segment of the eye by gonioscopy can be mapped into an abstracted pathophysiological state of "angle closure," and certain patterns of visual field loss measured on the tangent screen are described by human experts as representing a "nasal step," or an "enlargement of the blind spot," both patterns of field loss associated with glaucoma.

It was Safir's suggestion that states such as these be linked causally to describe the mechanisms of glaucoma. Sholom Weiss and I proposed that, while one linked pathway of states could be used to define one variant of glaucoma (such as angle-closure glaucoma), another pathway could define open-angle glaucoma, and yet another a secondary glaucoma due to a mass in the anterior segment of the eye, and so on. We also suggested that in order to take into account statistical variability among patients that the mapping between observations and pathophysiological states would have to involve some probability-like measures of uncertainty, whereas the mapping from pathways of states to diseases might be purely definitional and deterministic. Furthermore, because of the inherent variability of biological processes the causal links themselves would have to be weighted: There could be no Aristotelian fixed and unique relations between states. What emerged was a probabilistic network of causes and effects.

As we put more and more glaucoma knowledge into this representation it also became clear that a diagnostic program alone would be much less exciting to physicians than a program that gave advice on the latest treatments, particularly if they referred to controversial topics. Safir deliberately selected a number of situations where surgical versus medical treatment was a matter of argument, and we were able to extend the representation to a fourth level, which contained the treatments or actions that would be triggered from a diagnosis. It was at this time that I suggested that we consider Feinstein's idea that there must be an "environmental" component to treatment that customizes a standard therapeutic regime to the peculiarities of a patient and his environment {19}. This meant that rather than having a fixed set of treatments keyed off diagnostic outcomes, the nuances of therapy are adjusted to take into account the specific set of patient manifestations that make an individual patient's situation unique. For instance, someone who has a history of being resistant to a certain kind of medication may be chosen for a nonstandard alternative, or someone who has a history of poor compliance may be recommended for more frequent checkups and treatment that relies less on his own administration of the medications.

Our progress with the glaucoma consultation program was sufficiently rapid that Safir suggested taking a prototype to demonstrate at the annual meeting of the Association for Research and Ophthalmology. It was at this meeting in April 1973 that we were able to enlist the help of several distinguished clinical researchers in glaucoma, including Dr. Bernard Becker, original coauthor of the major textbook on the diagnosis and treatment of the glaucomas {20}. He was initially joined by his colleague, Dr. Steven Podos of Washington University and by Dr. Irvin Pollack of The Johns Hopkins University. It was very reassuring for us to see that specialists in glaucoma felt that our causal models of disease did indeed correspond to many of their own paths of reasoning. At the same time, they made us aware of the limitations of the first prototype and suggested many improvements.

It was around this time that I first met Ted Shortliffe, who was working on his doctoral dissertation at Stanford University. Shortliffe was already committed to the development of a consultant program in infectious diseases, and when he visited the Rutgers Resource we discussed the problems of reasoning under uncertainty and the need to develop consultation systems that would be understandable to the clinician. At that point Shortliffe was experimenting with reasoning strategies motivated by theorem-proving techniques. He felt that PLANNER-type consequent theorems provided a good mechanism for goal directed problem solving, and his initial control structure for MYCIN was designed to "avoid the shotgun approach of a diagnostic system based solely on mechanisms analogous to antecedent theorems." Shortliffe was also strongly influenced toward a modular representation in the form of rules by Waterman's use of production systems based on situation-action rules, and by the heuristic DENDRAL project experience at Stanford. There is no question but that even during these early stages of research in 1973 there was a strong contrast between the emphasis of Shortliffe's work on the modular and judgmental components of clinical decision making as opposed to the causal "architectural approach," taken by our group at Rutgers. Meanwhile, we also became aware of work being carried out by Harry Pople on problems of abduction in biomedical theory formation. After initiating a collaboration with Dr. Jack Myers on consultation in internal medicine, he applied many of the ideas of abductive reasoning to diagnosis. In fact, the first version of their consultation program was called DIALOG (for diagnostic logic) {21} and stressed the hierarchical nature of the organization of medical knowledge. Qualitative levels of uncertainty were used to link manifestations to the disease entities. While the research emphasis of the Pittsburgh group may have seemed quite different from ours and from that of the Stanford and Tufts-MIT groups {22}, in retrospect we all shared the same concerns of introducing heuristic uncertainty measures, modularizing knowledge, and providing more flexible strategies of consultation that would be acceptable to human experts.

Steps Towards Consolidation of AIM: 1974–1978

The year 1974 saw the completion of the first two theses in AI in medicine. Sholom Weiss completed his work at Rutgers on the causal model approach to medical decision making {23}, while Ted Shortliffe at Stanford completed his rule-based approach for therapy advice in infectious diseases {24}.

It was also in 1974 that a second research resource sponsored by the NIH's Division of Research Resources was established at Stanford.

SUMEX-AIM made explicit in its title what was only implicit in the Rutgers Resource—the advancement of artificial intelligence in medicine {25}. This resource also provided time-shared computing facilities (initially on a PDP-10, later on a DEC-20) that helped many of the fledgling research groups get started with more sophisticated programs. At the same time, with the strong support of Dr. William Baker at the Biotechnology Research Resources Program of NIH, SUMEX fostered the idea of shared intellectual and physical computing resources through the development of an AIM community. At Stanford, Shortliffe's research continued to be the major focus of investigations into clinical decision making. Together with his advisor, Bruce Buchanan, he developed a model of inexact reasoning based on non-probabilistic confidence factors {26}. This served as an important component of the inference mechanism of MYCIN {27}.

The work on artificial intelligence in medicine became more widely known when a regular series of AIM workshops sponsored by the Rutgers Resource were begun in 1975. The first workshop was small and brought together the AIM researchers themselves. It was most valuable in informally exchanging tips on interdisciplinary collaboration problems and in clarifying some of the assumptions behind each group's research approach. The workshop in 1976 was larger, and included presentations by many researchers taking alternative approaches to medical decision making and modeling. These meetings helped disseminate artificial intelligence ideas and set the stage for the introduction of knowledge-based methods in a number of other research areas (geology, chemistry, and engineering).

Within the Rutgers Resource during 1974 to 1976 we were able to broaden the scope of our collaborations in ophthalmology. Thanks to Safir's efforts, an ophthalmological network of glaucoma specialists (ONET) was formed to systematically enter their knowledge and expertise in glaucoma diagnosis and therapy into our program. Sholom Weiss joined the Mt. Sinai School of Medicine as a researcher who became one of the first "knowledge engineers" before the term had been coined. He traveled tirelessly around the country working with our collaborators at various medical centers: Washington University, The Johns Hopkins University, the University of Miami, and the University of Illinois, as well as Mt. Sinai. By 1976, the glaucoma consultation program had been expanded to handle a large variety of secondary glaucoma conditions, as well as being much more sophisticated in the primary glaucomas. It was at this point that we proposed to test the system by having it challenged publicly at the meeting of the American Academy of Ophthalmology that was held in Las Vegas in October 1976. A symposium on glaucoma, sponsored by the National Society for the Prevention of Blindness, included five specialists and a moderator (Dr. Anderson), with our computer program as the sixth "panelist."

We also demonstrated our program at the Academy's scientific exhibit and gathered cases from experts who wished to challenge the system. During the symposium on glaucoma, the computer was able to respond to all the cases presented to it. It provided a summary of the diagnostic and treatment recommendations that could be compared to the comments of the specialists. The resulting exchanges of the panelists and the commentary on the computer output were transcribed in the book *Discussions on Glaucoma*, edited by Drs. Lichter and Anderson {28}. The program did very well in matching the diagnostic conclusions of the specialists. There were some discrepancies in the treatment recommendations, but these involved no more variation than that found among the specialists themselves. Our most anxious moment took place just before the panel was about to start its discussions. Someone tripped over and unplugged the phone line that connected our display terminal in the immense labyrinth of the Las Vegas Hilton Hotel conference rooms. It reminded us most vividly of the fragility of the technology. Luckily, the connection was reestablished one minute before start time. With the success of this demonstration, the consultation system proved that the expertise of specialists from around the country could be pooled and then, through computer networking, disseminated to a large number of nonspecialists. The CASNET system was the first example of a high-performance prototype covering detailed diagnosis and treatment knowledge in a specialty that could actually give advice at the level of an expert consultant {29, 30}. Kevin Kern helped with support programming. Peter Politakis joined in subsequent knowledge-base refinement research, which led to the collaboration with Drs. Lindberg, Sharp, and Kingsland on the AI/Rheum System {31}.

Also during 1976 Shortliffe published his thesis on MYCIN {32}, and the group at Stanford continued the development of the MYCIN program, leading subsequently to an evaluation of the system by a group of specialists in infectious diseases {33}. These results showed that a rule-based system could be brought to a high level of performance. The work at Stanford was widely disseminated by Drs. Feigenbaum and Lederberg, who were able to convince many skeptical biomedical scientists and computer scientists of the importance of domain knowledge as the basis of practical problem solving systems. It was Edward Feigenbaum who popularized the phrase "knowledge-based systems" {34}. An early example of such a system in clinical decision making, besides CASNET, DIALOG, and MYCIN, was the Digitalis Advisory System developed by the Tufts-MIT group {35}. It showed that a mathematical compartmental model of digitalis release could be used in conjunction with qualitative reasoning to capture clinical expertise in the administration of digitalis. An important article by Pauker, Gorry, Kassirer, and Schwartz in the *American Journal of Medicine* in 1976 {36} gave a first outline of how Minsky's frame-based struc-

tures {37} for describing and recalling information about a present illness could be used in a consultation program. The article gave a number of examples of how general symptoms could trigger a set of related
diagnostic entities into short-term memory where they would be subject to hypothesis testing. The Present Illness Program (PIP) was critical
in showing that the process of gathering medical information, generating hypotheses, testing them, and selecting new information together
represented a complex cycle of inferencing that did not easily fit into a
traditional formal framework. At this time, the work on INTERNIST
was being extended by Pople to involve reasoning about multiple diseases and associations of a causal nature {38}. The CADEUCEUS program that is still evolving shows the degree to which complex
representations of knowledge are needed for these tasks. These practical experiences with programming experiments were supported by
psychological research into problems of clinical judgment and practice
carried out by Elstein and his colleagues {39, 40}.

Conclusion: 1978 as the End of the First AIM Cycle

In looking back on the early evolution of artificial intelligence methods
in clinical decision making, it is easy to mark 1978 as the end of the first
cycle of development. It was in that year that an excellent review of the
first generation systems was published by Szolovits and Pauker {41},

who stressed the need for *both* categorical and probabilistic reasoning as well as complex knowledge structures for diagnostic reasoning. Also at this time, Schoolman and Bernstein gave broad dissemination to some of the early AIM work in an article in *Science* {42}. The previous year, 1977, had seen the first Symposium on Computer Applications in Medical Care (SCAMC) highlight the AIM systems in its session of clinical decision making. The following year marked the emergence of general model-building "shells" based on AIM work: EMYCIN {43} at Stanford and EXPERT {44} at Rutgers. These served as vehicles for developing consultation expert systems in many different medical and nonmedical domains, thereby demonstrating the generality of the knowledge-based approach. The first generation, which was bound to experimentation with decision prototypes for specific diseases, had come to an end.

References

1. Lipkin, M. and Hardy, J.D. Mechanical correlation of data in differential diagnosis of hematological diseases. *J. Amer. Med. Ass.* 166:113–125, 1958.

2. Ledley, R.S. and Lusted, L.B. Reasoning foundation of medical diagnosis: Symbolic logic, probability and value theory aid our understanding of how physicians reason. *Science* 130:9–21, 1959.

3. Warner, H.R., Toronto, A.F., and Veasey, L.G. Experience with Bayes's theorem for computer diagnosis of congenital heart disease. *Ann. N.Y. Acad. Sci.* 115:558–567, 1964.

4. Overall, J.E. and Williams, C.M. Models for medical diagnosis. *Behavioral Sci.* 6:2:134–141, 1961.

5. Brodman, K. and van Woerkom, A.J. Computer-aided diagnostic screening for 100 common diseases. *J. Amer. Med. Ass.* 197:11:179–183, 1966.

6. Collen, M.F., *et al.* Automated multiphasic screening and diagnosis. *Amer. J. Pub. Health* 54:741–750, 1964.

7. Caceres, C.A., *et al.* Computer aids in electrocardiography. *Ann. N.Y. Acad. Sci.* 118:85–102, 1964.

8. Bleich, H.L. Computer evaluation of acid-base disorders. *J. Clin. Invest.* 48:1689–1696, 1969.

9. Jacquez, J.A., (ed.). The diagnostic process. *Proc. Biomedical Data Processing Training Program.* University of Michigan, Michigan, 1964.

10. Ledley, R.S. *Use of Computers in Biology and Medicine.* New York: McGraw-Hill, 1965.

11. Lusted, L. *Introduction to Medical Decision-Making*. Springfield, Illinois: Thomas, 1968.

12. Kulikowski, C.A. Pattern recognition approach to medical diagnosis. *IEEE Trans. Syst. Sci. Cybern.*, vol. SSC-6, pp. 83–89, 1970.

13. Nordyke, R.A., Kulikowski, C.A., and Kulikowski, C.W. A comparison of methods for the automated diagnosis of thyroid dysfunction. *Comp. Biomedical Res.* 4:374–389, 1971.

14. Schoolman, H.M. and Bernstein, L.M. Computer use in diagnosis, prognosis, and therapy. *Science* 200:926–931, 1978.

15. Gorry, G.A. and Barnett, G.O. Experience with a model of sequential diagnosis. *Comp. Biomedical Res.* 1:490–507, 1968.

16. Gorry, G.A. Computer-assisted clinical decision-making. *Methods Inform. Med.* 12:45–51, 1973.

17. Schwartz, W.B. Medicine and the computer: The promise and problems of change. *New England J. Med.* 283:1257–1264, 1970.

18. Kulikowski, C.A. and Weiss, S.A. Strategies of data base utilization in sequential pattern recognition. *Proc. 1972 IEEE Conference on Decision and Control*, 1972, pp. 103–105.

19. Feinstein, A.R. *Clinical Judgment*. Baltimore: Williams & Wilkens, 1967.

20. Kolker, A.E. and Hetherington, Jr., J. *Becker-Shaffer's Diagnosis and Therapy of the Glaucomas*. St. Louis: Mosby, 1970.

21. Pople, H., Myers, J., and Miller, R. DIALOG: A model of diagnostic logic for internal medicine. *Proc. Fourth Int. Joint Conf Artificial Intell.*, Tbilisi. San Mateo: Morgan Kaufmann, 1975, pp. 848–855.

22. Pauker, S.G., Gorry, G.A., Kassirer, J.P., and Schwartz, W.B. Towards the simulation of clinical cognition: Taking a present illness by computer. *Amer. J. Med.* 60:981–996, 1976.

23. Weiss, S., Kulikowski, C., Amarel, S., and Safir, A. A model-based method for computer-aided medical decision-making. *Artificial Intell.* 11:145–172, 1978.

24. Shortliffe, E.H., *et al.* An artificial intelligence program to advise physicians regarding antimicrobial therapy. *Comput. Biomedical Res.* 6: 544, 1973.

25. Freiherr, G. The Seeds of Artificial Intelligence: SUMEX-AIM. Div. Res. Resources, NIH Pub. 80–2071, Dec. 1979.

26. Shortliffe, E.H. and Buchanan, B.G. A model of inexact reasoning in medicine. *Math. Biosci.* 23:351–389, 1975.

27. Shortliffe, E.H. *Computer-based Medical Consultations: MYCIN*. New York: Elsevier, 1976.

28. Lichter, P. and Anderson, D. *Discussions on Glaucoma*. New York: Grune and Stratton, 1977.

29. Weiss, S., Kulikowski, C., Amarel, S., and Safir, A. A model-based method for computer-aided medical decision-making. *Artificial Intell.* 11:145–172, 1978.

30. Weiss, S., Kulikowski, C.A., and Safir, A. Glaucoma consultation by computer. *Comput. Biol. Med.* 8:24–40, 1978.

31. Lindberg, D.A.B., Sharp, G.C., Kay, D.R., Kingsland, L.C., Roeseler, G., Kulikowski, C.A., and Weiss, S.M. The expert consultant as teacher. *MOBIUS* 3:2, 1983.

32. Shortliffe, E.H. *Computer-based Medical Consultations: MYCIN*. New York: Elsevier, 1976.

33. Yu, V.L., *et al.* An evaluation of the performance of a computer-based consultant. *Comput. Programs Biomedical* 9:95–102, 1979.

34. Feigenbaum, E.A. The art of artificial intelligence: Themes and case studies of knowledge engineering. *Proc. Nat. Comput. Conf.* New York: AFIPS, 1978, p. 221.

35. Gorry, G.A., Silverman, H., and Pauker, S.G. Capturing clinical expertise: A computer program that considers clinical responses to digitalis. *Amer. J. Med.* 64:452–460, 1978.

36. Pauker, S.G., Gorry, G.A., Kassirer, J.P., and Schwartz, W.B. Towards the simulation of clinical cognition: Taking a present illness by computer. *Amer. J. Med.* 60:981–996, 1976.

37. Minsky, M. A framework for representing knowledge. *The Psychology of Computer Vision*, Winston, P. (ed.). New York: McGraw-Hill, 1975.

38. Pople, H. Artificial intelligence approaches to computer-based medical consultation. *Proc. IEEE Intercon.*, 31:3, 1975.

39. Elstein, A.S. Clinical judgment: Psychological research and medical practice. *Science* 194:696, Nov. 1976.

40. Elstein, A.S., Schulman, L.S., and Sprafka, S.A. *Medical Problem Solving: An Analysis of Clinical Reasoning*. Cambridge: Harvard Univ. Press, 1978.

41. Szolovits, P. and Pauker, S.C. Categorical and probabilistic reasoning in medical diagnosis. *Artificial Intell.* 11:115–144, 1978.

42. Schoolman, H.M. and Bernstein, L.M. Computer use in diagnosis, prognosis, and therapy. *Science* 200:926–931, 1978.

43. van Melle, W., A domain-independent priduction rule system for consultation programs, *Proceedings of the Sixth International Joint Conference on Artificial Intelligence*, Tokyo, Japan, pp. 923–025, 1979.

44. Weiss, S. and Kulikowski, C. EXPERT: A system for developing consultation models. *Proc Sixth Int. Joint Conf Artificial Intell.*, Tokyo. San Mateo: Morgan Kaufmann, 1979, pp. 942–950.

45. Davis, R. Interactive transfer of expertise: Acquisition of new inference rules. *Artificial Intell.* 12:121–158, 1979.

46. Pople, H. The formation of composite hypotheses in diagnostic problem solving. *Proc. Fifth Int. Joint Conf. Artificial Intell.*, Boston, Mass. San Mateo: Morgan Kaufmann, 1977, pp. 1030–1037.

47. Schwartz, W.B., Gorry, G.A., Kassirer, J.P., and Essig, A. Decision analysis and clinical judgment. *Amer. J. Med.* 5:459–472, 1973.

48. Van Melle, W. A domain independent production-rule system for consultation programs. *Proc. Sixth Int. Joint Conf Artificial Intell.*, Tokyo. San Mateo: Morgan Kaufmann, 1979, pp. 923–925.

49. Weiss, S.M. *A System for Model-based Computer-aided Diagnosis and Therapy.* PhD Dissertation, Rutgers University, 1974.

Index